PENGUIN BOOKS

BEYOND THE BLUE HORIZON

Alexander Frater was born in the South Pacific island group of Vanuatu, the son of a Scottish medical missionary. Educated in Vanuatu, Fiji, Australia, Britain and Italy, he has broadcast widely and contributed to many publications including *Punch* and the *New Yorker*. His last book, *Stopping-Train Britain*, was a national bestseller. He is at present Chief Travel Correspondent of the *Observer* and lives in London with his wife and two children.

BEYOND THE BLUE HORIZON

On the Track of Imperial Airways

ALEXANDER FRATER

PENGUIN BOOKS

Penguin Books Ltd, Harmondsworth, Middlesex, England
Viking Penguin Inc., 40 West 23rd Street, New York, New York 10010, U.S.A.
Penguin Books Australia Ltd, Ringwood, Victoria, Australia
Penguin Books Canada Ltd, 2801 John Street, Markham, Ontario, Canada L3R 1B4
Penguin Books (N.Z.) Ltd, 182–190 Wairau Road, Auckland 10, New Zealand

First published by William Heinemann Ltd 1986
Published in Penguin Books 1987

Made and printed in Great Britain by
Hazell, Watson & Viney Limited
Member of the BPCC Group,
Aylesbury, Bucks.
Typeset in Sabon (Linotron 202)

CONTENTS

ACKNOWLEDGEMENTS

My thanks are due to Michael Meade and John Askham of Statesman-Aldwych Travel, who plotted, booked and ticketed a complicated journey impeccably, and to Ron Wilson of British Airways Archives who generously entrusted me with much of his Imperial material. To readers wanting more information on Imperial's Croydon operations I recommend *Croydon Airport – The Great Days 1928–1939* by Douglas Cluett, Joanna Nash and Bob Learmonth, published by the Borough of Sutton Libraries and Arts Services. I drew a measure of inspiration – and a good deal of material – from their meticulous research and entertaining anecdotes.

Two *Observer* colleagues in particular – Helen Simpson, my erstwhile secretary, and Trevor Grove, editor of the Colour Magazine – gave me a measure of support and encouragement for which I shall always be grateful. My gratitude is also due to Captain Alan Haywood, who flew 747s for BA and now flies them for Virgin Atlantic, and who took time off from a busy schedule to read the proofs. Thanks are due too to my family, who endured this two-year enterprise with endless tolerance and good humour, and to David Godwin, my editor at Heinemann, without whose good offices the book would never have got off the ground.

For Marlis

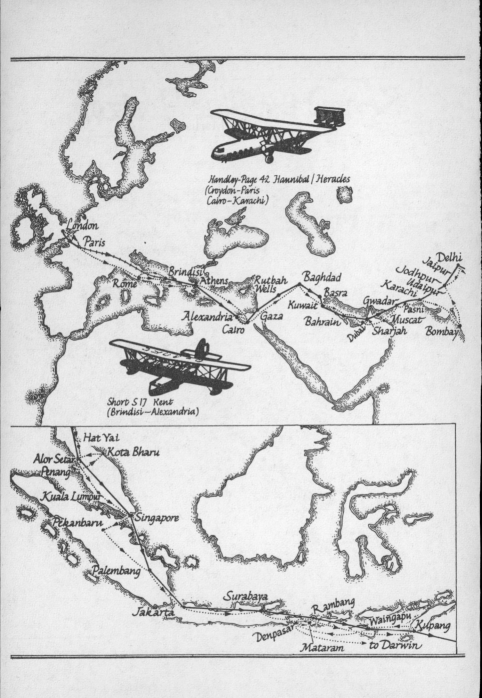

Handley-Page 42 Hannibal / Heracles
(Croydon–Paris
Cairo–Karachi)

London
Paris

Brindisi
Rome
Athens
Rutbah
Wells
Baghdad
Basra
Kuwait
Alexandria
Cairo
Gaza
Bahrain
Dubai
Sharjah
Muscat
Gwadar
Pasni
Karachi
Jodhpur
Udaipur
Jaipur
Delhi
Bombay

Short S 17 Kent
(Brindisi–Alexandria)

Hat Yai
Kota Bharu
Alor Setar
Penang
Kuala Lumpur
Pekanbaru
Singapore
Palembang
Jakarta
Surabaya
Rambang
Denpasar
Mataram
Waingapu
Kupang
to Darwin

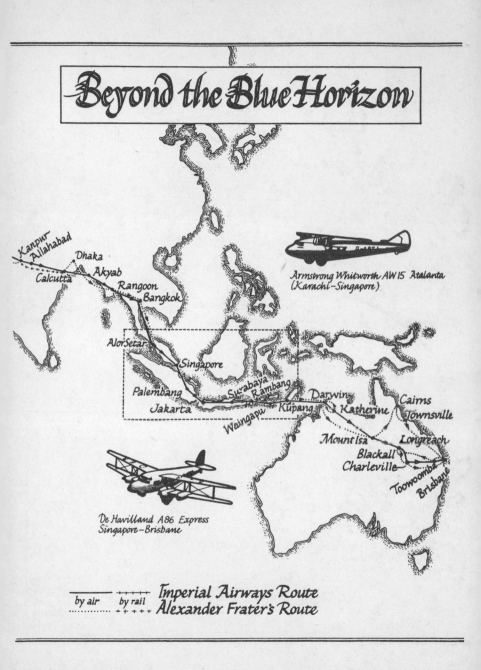

Beyond the Blue Horizon

Kanpur
Allahabad
Dhaka
Calcutta
Akyab
Rangoon
Bangkok

Armstrong Whitworth AW 15 Atalanta
(Karachi–Singapore)

Alor Setar

Singapore

Palembang
Jakarta
Surabaya
Rambang
Waingapu
Kupang
Darwin
Katherine
Cairns
Townsville
Mount Isa
Longreach
Blackall
Charleville
Toowoomba
Brisbane

De Havilland A86 Express
Singapore–Brisbane

by air   by rail   Imperial Airways Route
Alexander Frater's Route

PROLOGUE

My first love affair began early on the morning of 31 December 1946, a few days before my ninth birthday. It was with an aeroplane – one that has now entered the realms of legend – and was of such intensity that even today, like some incorrigible *boulevardier* giving the eye to every passing woman, I cannot resist looking up whenever I hear the clamour of engines overhead.

The plane was one of the old Empire flying boats and it took me and my family from Rose Bay, Sydney, to the Fiji Islands, where a new job awaited my father; after the rigours and separations of the war this was to be a fresh beginning. Shortly before dawn a motor launch carried us across the dark, calm water to our aircraft, riding at a buoy with its portholes lit. There were lights burning in the cockpit too, high on the upper deck where the captain, a grizzled, white-haired man, sat drinking tea with his officers.

As the launch driver cut the engine I noted the name *Coriolanus* painted on the Empire's massive tugboat nose and, further back, the words 'Qantas Empire Airways'; towards the tail were the registration letters VH-ABG. My mother, keeping her voice low, told us that Coriolanus, the subject of one of Shakespeare's minor plays, had been a famous Roman warrior exiled for haughtiness. We drifted beneath a high, broad wing that hid the paling sky and fading stars. Our wash sucked lazily at the flared keel and giant portside float, secured to the wingtip by a cat's cradle of wires and struts. Clambering through a low doorway with a curved lintel I sniffed a faint, heady tramp steamer aroma of coffee, grease, paraffin and candlenut which I took to be the smell of the sky itself.

The fuselage was divided, like a ship, into cabins, the one next to ours occupied by a tall, stooped Englishman in a tweed suit, so thin his body seemed to be made from wire; he was taken there by a crew member who called him Sir Brian and treated him with much deference. My father said the Englishman was the Governor of Fiji, returning from a private visit to Sydney, and the chap making the fuss was the ship's clerk. The steward brought us barley sugar and, guessing accurately that we hadn't flown before, said we should suck it during take-off to stop our ears popping.

Then, one by one, the four big supercharged Pegasus engines were started and the clerk hurried forward to the nose mooring hatch and hauled in the line. The Empire began to move, slowly and erratically, turning this way and that, the port float rising a few inches above the water as the wings tilted to starboard then, as they tilted back, splashing down again and cutting a huge creamy furrow in the surface. My father, who had spent the war near a US Navy base in the South Pacific and had daily seen PBY Catalina flying boats manoeuvring in front of his hospital, explained that the sea was too flat to get airborne. The pilot first had to roughen it artificially with his own wake, using the temporary disturbance to break the suction and prise the hull off the water and into the air.

Now, having created a respectable swell, the captain swung towards it and pushed his throttles open. We raced thunderously forward and a high foaming bow wave covered the lower deck portholes, filling the Empire's interior with an eerie green light. Then the nose began to lift and the water level dropped down the windows like a venting tank. I watched the float throwing up a terrific curtain of spray which slowly subsided and ceased altogether as, with a scraping, gravelly sound, the Empire finally rose clear and lumbered into a pink morning sky. I looked down amazed at the toy city, full of shadows and growing tinier by the minute, and marvelled at the fact that it contained millions of sleeping people no larger than sand grains. That extraordinary moment changed a number of my perceptions and made me think that God was perhaps not the good shepherd after all but, rather, a kind of entymologist, the manager and trainer of a giant flea circus.

We tracked up the broad, surf-edged beaches to Brisbane, landed there for fuel, then headed out over the Pacific to the French colony of New Caledonia where we spent the night and celebrated the new year in the French manner. (So did the crew who, next morning, turned up very late for the final leg to Fiji.) The flight may have been long and slow but I was never bored. My sister and I went to the galley after meals to help with the washing up, and on the second day ascended an oily metal ladder in the bows to meet the pilots. The flight deck, an airy glass pavilion, offered spectacular forward views that seemed bounded by the edge of the world itself. The pilots turned out to be stern, monosyllabic men, remote as windjammer captains. Then they impressed me deeply with their gruffness and the heavy responsibilities it implied, but now I realise they were probably just suffering from stupendous hangovers.

So it was not the pilots, but the Governor of Fiji who first told me about the provenance of the *Coriolanus*. He had taken me for a late afternoon swim at New Caledonia, looking thinner and more extraordinary than ever in his baggy woollen costume. I was already interested in Sir Brian because he had spent much of the flight knitting a maroon kettle holder and addressed both my father and me as 'Frater'; my father was a doctor who had just been awarded an MBE by the King, and hearing him spoken to like a schoolboy was a novelty. We went to a beach close to where the Empire was moored and, while I scavenged in the shallows for bits of coral, he floated around on his back, pale and skinny as an ironing board, with his spectacles on and his long white feet sticking up in the air like matching marble tombstones.

Despite his age and great eminence I found him easy to chat to. He told me the *Coriolanus* had been built beside the River Medway in England, for Imperial Airways. He supposed the Australians had got their hands on it during the war. They couldn't give it back because Imperial – which I vaguely took to be a department of the Royal Household – was, alas, no more. Our flight was the kind of thing one had to endure with RAF Transport Command, no frills, jolly spartan; and wistfully he harked back to the days when Imperial flew from London to Australia, the longest airline journey in the world, taking a couple of weeks and stopping at dozens of places en route. He spoke of great shiny biplanes, their interiors furnished in silks and satins, commanded by men who carried silver whistles for blowing at the ground staff, and who came back to take lunch at their own tables in the main cabin. Distinguished passengers like Mr Winston Churchill and Mr Noël Coward were invited to join them. At night the planes landed and everyone had dinner ashore before retiring. In the Middle East they even stopped at lonely desert forts guarded against marauding bedouin by armed Arab irregulars. Every flight was an adventure. Sir Brian said there had been nothing like the Imperial Eastbound service before and there never would be again, and he seemed very sorry about it.

Several years later, at boarding school in Australia, I came across a history of civil aviation in the school library and, idly leafing through it, found a map of Sir Brian's London to Brisbane air route. Recalling his disembodied voice coming from the sea, I counted the stops, 35, and tested some of the names on my tongue: Brindisi, Alexandria, Baghdad and – the desert forts he had spoken of – Rutbah Wells and Sharjah. There was Gwadar in Baluchistan, Jodphur, Kanpur, Akyab and Rangoon, Alor Star in Malaya, the Indonesian towns of Batavia and Surabaya, and islands like Lombok, Sumba and Timor (the last-named famed for its dense sandalwood forests). To me this seemed not so much a commercial airline service as an extraordinarily discursive ramble of discovery.

My family continued to live in Fiji, where my father taught basic medicine, surgery and obstetrics to native students from all over the South Pacific (he conceived the idea of barefoot doctors long before Mao Tse-Tung did), and I always went home for the long summer vacation by plane. It was one of aviation's Blue Riband runs, Sydney to Los Angeles via Fiji and Honolulu, operated by the very latest aircraft. Though I got off at the first stop I was privileged to ride in them all and, back at school, would drive my friends barmy reciting dimension and performance data like the rate of climb, service ceiling, payload, range and maximum ramp weight of a Douglas DC6-B. I knew all that stuff and dreamed of the day when I could use it to save lives, sitting perhaps in the passenger cabin of a Convair 440 Metropolitan as the distraught pilot burst in crying, 'My mind has gone blank and we are in dire peril! Quick, somebody what is the stalling speed, with flaps up, of this particular make?'

My favourite planes then were the Lockheed Super Constellations operated by Qantas and the Boeing Stratocruisers of Pan American World Airways. The Super Connies had triple-finned tails and bodies lean as a greyhound's, but were so noisy that conversing passengers often had to lip-read. Once I sat next to an American singer returning from an Australian tour who, yelling in my ear, said that her first performance, three days after arriving in

Sydney, had been an unqualified disaster because, still deafened by the racket of the four 2,200 h.p. conventional Wright radials, she could barely hear the band.

The Stratocruiser, on the other hand, was quiet and unusually commodious, with a cosy little lounge at the foot of the staircase in its bulbous nose. It was in a Stratocruiser that I smoked my first cigar, first tasted hard liquor – a large bourbon bought by an amused, worldly woman from Washington DC who knew President Eisenhower – and first witnessed an adult committing a crime. Late one night, swinging open a toilet door left carelessly unlocked, I caught a much-decorated English brigadier red-handed in the act of stealing the soap, stuffing handfuls of miniature Lux cakes into his tunic pockets and telling me, puce-faced, to bugger off. One way or another these hours in the sky played a significant role in my growth and development.

Moving on to higher education I joined my university squadron and, as a reserve Pilot Officer in the RAAF, was poised to become Australia's answer to Neville Duke, the legendary English test pilot whose many exploits included being the first Pom through the sound barrier. But, amazingly, instead of launching me at the stars they taught me sword drill and speed reading. Speed reading! When the crunch came, I protested, was I expected to give the advancing Ivans a thousand words a minute of *War and Peace* through a loud hailer? Well, I could certainly have a go, they said, but meanwhile the role they envisaged for me was in admin, not combat.

Later I did get some flying lessons but found myself constantly erring on the side of caution. This is a virtue in a pilot, of course, but not when his pre-flight instrument checks take so long that the instructor starts doing crosswords. Seated in a cockpit I saw a world filled with hazard. That seemingly innocent clump of cu-nim drifting in from the west might be harbouring a storm cell while a lone sparrow swooping by presaged the grim possibility of bird strikes. Seized, in short, by a deep-seated reluctance to leave the ground I decided that, in future, I would let less imaginative people do the flying while my role remained that of an observer.

I arrived in England – cheaply, by returning immigrant ship – married an air stewardess, set up house beneath the Heathrow glide path and went into journalism, a profession offering almost unrivalled opportunities for boarding aeroplanes at someone else's expense. In the course of my career I've scrounged rides on everything from Concorde (on one of its first commercial flights) to an antique Sri Lankan De Havilland Rapide with such a leaky roof that, during the monsoon rains, passengers had to sit beneath raised umbrellas.

My most frightening flight was in an ancient, ill-maintained Ilyushin of CAAC, the Chinese airline, soon after the end of the Cultural Revolution. We flew from Shanghai to White Cloud Airport, Canton, through a nocturnal storm of such ferocity that the co-pilot, a heavy-set, gap-toothed woman wearing dirty tennis shoes, suffered a kind of breakdown. As the plane bucked across a black sky exploding with lightning and riven by wild, gusting winds we saw her weeping with her hands pressed to her eyes and heard the loud, harsh voices of her exasperated male colleagues urging her to settle down and pull her weight. My most exhilarating flight, on the other hand, was aboard a Phantom of the Royal Navy's 892 Squadron, taking part in a mock dogfight over the North Sea. For the ninety minutes I was up the world simply stopped making sense, and the familiar points of reference – sea, sun, sky – became a whirling kaleidoscope of pale colours and spinning lights. We concluded the exercise by sinking down to 200 feet and idling along at 250 knots while the pilot, an affable young lieutenant known to his colleagues as Nutty, explained that his Phantom, lacking guns, was vulnerable when all its missiles had been fired. 'In that situation,' he had said, 'there is only one thing we can do.'

'And what's that?' I asked.

'We go up.'

There was a roar as he ignited the afterburners, and a bang in the back like an elephant's kick. The noise, vibration and power were almost indescribable; rammed into my seat it seemed that, if we did not slow down soon, we were going to burst clean out of the atmosphere. The altimeter was spinning like a top when, 18 seconds later, we levelled off at 25,000 feet, leaving me with the kind of wild, whooping high you probably get on the Cresta Run.

In terms of civil flying my preference is for small planes, powered by propellers. They go low enough to let you see the passing landscape and, like country trains, place their passengers in a position of social intimacy. There can be a curious intensity about these brief relationships, especially in bad weather, a sense of shared lives and destinies: the stranger in the neighbouring seat, knowing he will never see you again, may tell you things about himself that, in the normal course of events, would be reserved for the confessional. I take great pleasure in travelling like this and, one warm summer afternoon a while back, accidentally stumbled on an idea that enabled me to pursue it in a wholly unexpected way.

Passing the unattended desk of a colleague at the *Observer* I noticed a volume, the size of a large telephone directory, called the *ABC World Airways Guide*. I picked it up and found it contained timetables for every scheduled flight on earth. Leafing slowly through it I noted the departure details of the Rocky Mountain Airways services out of Steamboat Springs (SBS), Colorado, and the flight times of Air Ecosse Twin Otters operating from Carlisle (CAX) to Aberdeen (ABZ). There was information about getting to Galapagos ·Island (GPS) − you catch a Transportes Aereos Nacionales Ecuatoriana 727 from Guayaquil (GYE) − and Pickle Lake, Ontario (YPL), reached by direct flight from Thunder Bay (YQT). I learned of a Grumman Mallard amphibious seaplane going from Nassau (NAS) to Palm Beach (PBI) belonging to an airline called Chalks, and a daily Antonov AN24 propjet of Aeroflot connecting Samarkand (SKD) with Tashkent (TAS). Then my eye fell on the entry for Surabaya (SUB) from where, early each morning, a Hawker Siddeley 748 flew to Kupang (KOE). Those names, I recalled, had been on the Indonesian sector of the old Imperial Airways route, and I began wondering which of the other original stops still had operational airfields. I racked my brains to remember the map I had pored over in the school library. Paris had been on it and so had Brindisi. Could you fly to Brindisi today? I looked it up. There were two daily Aero Transporti Italiani DC9 services from Rome, departing at 1710 and 2135.

The name Sharjah swam into my head. Was there still an airfield there? There was. But what had been the stop after Sharjah? I got out an atlas and tracked east to Gwadar on the Baluchistan coast. Gwadar rang a bell, but it seemed unlikely that such a remote, desolate spot would still have a working aerodrome. I thumbed through the *ABC Guide* and, with mounting excitement, found that

Gwadar (GWD) offered regular Fokker Friendship services to Jiwani, Muscat, Panjgur, Pasni, Turbat and Karachi. The Imperial route had gone from Gwadar to Karachi and, half a century later, the sector was still intact! An idea had begun to take root.

I rang a friendly contact at the press office of British Airways, Imperial's direct heirs and successors. Please, could he possibly lay his hands on the route map of Imperial's original service out to Australia?

'In those days,' he said, 'they probably just scratched runes in the dust with a twig. But let me talk to Ron Wilson in Archives. I'll call you back.'

When he did so his voice was suddenly full of interest. 'I've got a book here,' he said, 'with your map in it. Extraordinary! The flight took two weeks! They stopped all down the line, and at some very rum places. I'll send it over by messenger, but Ron says to guard it with your life. It's long out of print and very valuable.'

Two hours later the book arrived. I found the map, opened the *ABC Guide* and started checking the original stops against existing operational airfields. I found, to my astonishment, that of the 35 old waypoints only two, Gaza and Rutbah Wells, had closed, together with a handful of Australian bush strips used for emergency refuelling.

I went to see my editor and reminded him I had sabbatical leave due in a few months.

'What are you going to do?' he asked. 'Paint the house?'

I told him what I had in mind then, aware that these dozens of interconnecting flights strung halfway round the world would need a schedule as intricately plotted as a mathematical equation, called a travel agent acquaintance who liked to boast he could never resist a genuine challenge. When I explained what I wanted there was a long silence.

'You must be joking,' he said.

I promised I wasn't, and invited him to come and talk about it over a bottle or two of the very best champagne.

1
OUTWARD BOUND

From London to Athens

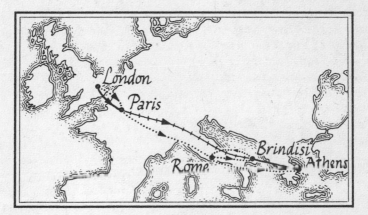

I

Appropriately, it was an aeroplane that woke me. It went thundering down the Heathrow glide path several hours before dawn, probably some vintage 707 freighter built back in the days before jet engines began to outrage the fashionable sensibilities of everyone within earshot. It woke a thrush as well which, out in the dark garden, began to sing. Rain pattered on the windows. A fitful February wind stirred the trees, stripping off the last of the old year's leaves. I lay listening to the untroubled voice of the thrush and thought again about my journey, trying once more to visualize the route I was about to travel. But all I could see was the sky itself, and the way it would grow steadily hotter and paler the further east we went, filled – I didn't doubt – with all kinds of weather; at this time of year, down beyond the intertropical front, there were likely to be cloud formations unimaginable in Europe, their vast, turbulent interiors rocked by forces able to break the backs of eagles. I imagined getting caught in one, booming with thunder and full of gaudy fire, aboard some small, ageing aeroplane buckling from metal fatigue and flown by a pilot with a severe personality disorder. Then it occurred to me that the first Brisbane-bound passengers, also waking early on the day of departure, may have felt a similar kind of pessimism as they pondered a string of distant landfalls with names so obscure they probably couldn't even pronounce them. To them, as to me now, Australia must never have seemed so far away.

The world I had elected to travel through was much changed. New borders – even new countries – had appeared, old borders had been tightened or redefined. At most, foreign journalists were banned or restricted; it had taken three months to get my visas and even now I still awaited decisions from Kuwait, Dubai and Burma. (Oman had already refused me outright, so I would have to slip in there without one.) Anybody using local air services to get down the

Imperial route today would find himself, periodically, obliged to deviate from the original track.

Like the Imperial passengers, I planned to travel during the day and put up in hotels at night. But they set off knowing they were flying the flag that held sovereignty over much of the territory through which they would pass. That, I thought, must have been immensely reassuring. All I had were a lot of last-minute worries, a closely typed seven-page itinerary and a booklet of tickets which, my exhausted travel agent said, was probably the largest ever issued on British Airways coupons. It was as thick as a paperback and he planned to write to the *Guinness Book of Records* about it.

The alarm clock said 4.30. My first flight, BA 304 to Paris, left Heathrow in three hours precisely. Wondering what sort of shape I would be in when I next slept in my own bed I got up, went to the kitchen and put the kettle on. Raindrops still spilled down the window, falling from a heavy, bruise-coloured overcast that seemed locked in just above the rooftops. A lone car, tyres whining on the wet road, accelerated away up Richmond Hill. The thrush abruptly ceased its lovely solo prelude to the day and stuck its head back under its wing.

I took my wife some tea. 'How do you feel?' she asked.

'A bit edgy.'

She listened to the wind. 'Tonight you'll be sleeping beside the Adriatic, tomorrow the Nile. Imagine being away from all this.'

Her words, intended to offer comfort, merely served to remind me that on the night after that I would be sleeping in Baghdad where, according to unconfirmed reports, the Iranians were launching rocket strikes. Feeling decidedly gloomy I went to make coffee for my son. He sipped it sleepily and we chatted. In six weeks – just a few hours after my plane was due home again from Brisbane – he was to be confirmed at St Paul's Cathedral. My schedule didn't allow for much margin of error. He told me not to worry; it was no big deal. I promised to do everything possible to be there then went to get ready. As I shaved the first of the day's 747s came over, the pathfinder for the incoming long-haul wave that regularly rattles the breakfast crockery along a broad corridor running between Heathrow and the river, their engines as much a south-west London morning sound as the clink of milk bottles on the doorstep. I drank a last cup of coffee in the living room, staring at the objects in it with the intensity of a prospective purchaser. They were part of the familiar, reassuring furniture of my life, and I memorised precisely the way everything looked before going out and closing the door behind me.

It was time to go. My wife would drive me to Heathrow. My son said goodbye with far more grace and dignity than I could muster. There was little traffic at that hour. On the M4 we passed a hearse with two laughing men in it and, parked on the hard shoulder, a broken-down brewery lorry. In the east the sky was assuming the colour of rare beef, suffusing the low, swirling cloud with a flushed, feverish pink. A Qantas 747 swung by on finals, its 18 wheels hanging from metal stanchions the length of lamp posts, bulbous snout cleaving through the murk like a ship's bow. I stared at it, trying to come to terms with the fact that it had probably crossed the Australian coast only 23 hours before; by the time I reached that same point, homeward-bound, the garden would be awash with daffodils. We turned off the motorway on to the airport sliproad. Two weeks earlier I had come out of hospital after minor surgery. It had left me little time to get fit and I envied the single-minded way Sir Samuel Hoare, Secretary of State for Air in 1926, prepared to become the first man to fly to India as a passenger, embarking on his friend 'Sir Philip Sassoon's court at Trent upon a training of intensive tennis'.

We entered the Heathrow tunnel, passing beneath a giant poster of Concorde, and drew up at Terminal One. During the drive we chatted about domestic matters. Our conversation had been ordinary and comforting. Now my wife simply told me to take care of myself and not worry about anything. She would meet me at Terminal Three on my return. Then she smiled, kissed me and drove off. She had made it a normal airport delivery, the prosaic start to any old journey, and I was grateful to her. I went indoors and presented my half-inch-thick book of tickets at a check-in desk. The clerk frowned at them. She had green eyes flecked with yellow. 'Are you a group?' she asked.

'No.'

'You'll get your boarding pass at the gate.'

I thanked her and headed for Immigration. There was no reason to hang about in the main concourse, a cavernous clearing house from which the designers had rigorously suppressed all traces of the country to which it was a major gateway. I had, to all intents and purposes, left England already. At the Security counter my bag was X-rayed and a tall, bony man subjected me to a meticulous body search, his hands flickering steadily down my person, finally clasping my ankles to see if I had pistols stuck in my socks. Then he straightened and thanked me with a warmth that suggested he had derived a measure of inspiration from our meeting. He wore a chocolate-brown bandsman's uniform and had smudges of shaving soap in his ears.

An electronic flight indicator board showed that BA 406 to Amsterdam was boarding, together with the early morning services to Rome and Frankfurt. Then a crimson arrow began to flash beside BA 304 Paris and up came the legend 'Check In At Gate 38', instantly confirmed by the bland, enamelled voice of the terminal's lady announcer. Reached along a moving rubber walkway springy as turf underfoot, Gate 38 was a large embarkation lounge with a desk at the entrance manned by two chattering girls, one of whom was named Sophie. Sophie frowned at my tickets.

'Are you a group?'

'No,' I said.

Her friend said, 'Where you going, then?'

'Brisbane. But I'm stopping off at a few places on the way.'

'Just about every street corner, by the look of it,' Sophie remarked.

'Cheaper to do it by hang-glider,' said her friend, and laughed.

I claimed my boarding pass and walked into the lounge where perhaps a hundred people were perched upon the blue, green and brown seating. The silence was absolute. There was a bar, buffet and duty-free shop – 'Save £8.05!' advised a sign proclaiming a sale of Ivoire Eau de Toilette and Glen Grant Malt Whisky – but no business was being done and the attendant sat in a trancelike state, eyes closed and head bowed. A Tristar with the letters KH on its nose pulled up to the windows and halted only a few feet from where I sat, the whine of its engines muffled by the sound-proofed glass. Then the engines were switched off and the Tristar fell silent too, an interesting addition to the room's fixtures and fittings. The two pilots completed their checklist, slipped on their jackets and left the illuminated flight deck.

The Imperial Airways passengers bound for Australia had gone not from Heathrow but from Croydon, the world's first custom-built airport and Imperial's home base, 300 acres of gently sloping grassland set beside Purley Way deep in the suburbs of south London. In summer it was carpeted with yellow buttercups, on moonlit autumn nights the staff would sneak out and pick mushrooms. Passengers for Australia, attended by a uniformed page boy, were brought here in a charabanc from the airline's new terminal at Victoria. There everyone had been asked to mount the scales (the 100-kilo, or 221-pound, personal allowance included a customer's own body weight) before receiving a route map, a set of headed inflight notepaper and envelopes, and a comprehensively illustrated introductory booklet to air travel. At Croydon they were met by the station superintendent resplendent in white gloves and a blue uniform who conducted them into the glass-domed art deco booking hall.

While waiting for the first flight of their 13,000 mile odyssey – the legendary Silver Wing service to Paris, departing punctually at 12.30 – they could examine a veneered pillar set with ticking clocks giving the time at each of Imperial's overseas destinations, or the giant North East Europe weather map, updated every hour by staff from the Met Office. The hall was lined by the polished counters of Imperial and the aerodrome's other regular users – Air France, SABENA, Swiss Air, Deutsche Luft Hansa (whose manager always farewelled his aircraft with an extravagant Nazi salute) and Koninklijke Luchtvaart Maatschappij, or KLM. On the counters stood exquisite scale models of the aircraft each line flew: Farman Goliaths, Wibaults, Fokkers, Junkers, Savoia Marchettis, Douglas DC2s, Fiats and, most alluring of all, the great silver Handley Page 42 Heracles class biplanes, one of which our passengers would shortly be boarding. First, though, they could wander to the windows and look out over the grassy acres of the aerodrome itself. The Pyrotechnic Store, Croydon's sunshine recorder mounted on its roof, stood padlocked at a safe remove, filled with rockets fired by the Duty Officer on foggy nights. Nearby was the Compass Swinging Base, a heavy wooden turntable pushed

by twenty men and, away to the right, the site of the famous Plough
Lane level crossing where, in the early days, a one-armed official
bearing a red flag – the missing arm had been amputated by a
whirling mahogany propeller – halted the traffic to allow the
bellowing old biplanes of Imperial's predecessors, Instone, Handley
Page and Daimler, to taxi through. (It was Daimler who appointed
the world's first flight attendants, 14-year-old lads chosen for their
smallness and known as cabin boys. They had been specially trained
at the Savoy and wore page boy uniforms – tight trousers and
monkey-jackets studded with gilt buttons – but remained seated
during the flights.)

Now, back at the Gate 38 embarkation lounge, we were called.
Sophie and her friend stationed themselves at the head of the
covered boarding jetty, still conversing animatedly as they collected
our passes. They remembered me. 'For hang-gliding you always
have to find a hill and jump off the top,' said Sophie, and giggled.
'Into the wind,' added her friend. 'Prevailing,' said Sophie. I gave
them a frosty smile and stepped into the Tristar's cabin. It was large,
airy and cheerful, decorated with a giant Emmett cartoon of an
aviator, scarfed and goggled, at the controls of a preposterous flying
machine fashioned from bits of discarded plumbing.

I had arranged to visit the flight deck and, after I had claimed my
seat, a blonde stewardess with a nice contralto voice offered to take
me there. On the way she told me that Theyre Lee-Elliott, the artist
who designed Imperial's legendary Speedbird logo, later inherited
by BOAC and afterwards going supersonic on Concorde's nose,
lived in a flat above her. 'The original Speedbird drawing is now in
the Victoria and Albert Museum,' she said. 'Mr Lee-Elliott's an old
man now, but still as active as ever. Did you know he once played
table tennis for England?' I did not. Her name was Miss Crowe.

She opened the flight deck door and ushered me in. Captain Peter
Strange was a youthful-looking man with thick fair hair. He shook
hands and introduced me to Michael Ahmed, his co-pilot, and Peter
Wells, the flight engineer. They were as affable as if I had come to
lunch. Captain Strange, who wore a short-sleeved white shirt and a
£10 digital watch possibly borrowed from his son, invited me to
squeeze into the jump seat located directly behind him. Mr Wells,
with a grizzled grey beard, gold-rimmed spectacles and the manner

of the senior common room, helped me into a harness secured about the waist, chest and shoulders. The cabin was as cramped as a diving bell.

'Coffee?' enquired Captain Strange.

I said yes, lovely, and Miss Crowe hurried off to fetch it.

A harassed Ramp Controller in a crimson cap popped his head in and announced that the Tristar was ready for departure. Captain Strange, who had been telling me that the Paris run was boring but mercifully brief, nodded and thanked him. 'We do Paris and back again tomorrow, but then we're off to Athens for a night stop, a rather more interesting job of work. Start up number two, please.'

As Mr Wells and Mr Ahmed, a young, dark-featured man in a pale grey sweater, got the engine going, Miss Crowe brought my coffee. All around us other aircraft were also preparing to leave. Captain Strange, frowning, noted the time and wondered aloud where the hell our tractor was. He picked up the telephone, punched the button for the public address system and told the passengers there would be a slight delay. When he had finished I reminded him that, from a spot nearby – Hounslow – the world's first daily international air service had been launched on 25 August 1919. It was bound for Paris too, a converted De Havilland bomber flown by Bill Lawford, a burly, amiable man who loved Wagner, and carried a passenger named George Stevenson-Reece, together with a cargo of newspapers, leather, grouse and several tubs of Devonshire cream. Mr Stevenson-Reece returned with Mr Lawford and, on landing at Hounslow, was sick into his hat.

Captain Strange nodded abstractedly. The historic nature of the Paris run did not alter the fact that he still had no tractor. It began to rain. I drank my coffee and thought of Imperial's Australia-bound passengers boarding their Handley Page 42 at Croydon. The four Bristol Jupiter air-cooled radial engines were being started as they emerged from the terminal and stepped through a canvas tunnel, known as the crocodile, into the aft saloon of the most sumptuously appointed airliner ever built. Only eight were made, at a cost of £20,000 each, three for the Indian service – the long-range Eastern, or Hannibal class, which our passengers would travel on from Cairo to Karachi – and five of the 38-seat short-range Western, or Heracles class intended to exploit the destination where the real profits lay: Paris. Despite its tortoise-like progress through the sky (rivals jeered at its built-in headwinds and its inability to exceed much more than 100 knots; in adverse weather the flight to Le Bourget could take over three and a half hours, and trains going the same way passed the HP 42 with ease), the flying public was bewitched. Long accustomed to regarding each trip as an endurance test from which they emerged deafened, ill and oil-smeared, they were now offered an aircraft that invoked the idea of a winged Cunarder and majestically emphasized Britain's own somewhat immodest perception of itself.

The prototype made its first public appearance at the 1931 Parliamentary Garden Party, held on a balmy summer's afternoon at the Hanworth Flying Club. The rapturous reception accorded it by an anonymous MP seems to have been pretty characteristic. 'Walking out of the Clubhouse on to the terrace,' he wrote, 'I saw a sight which made me rub my eyes. There, out on the Aerodrome, towering over the other aircraft which had assembled for the Parliamentary Garden Party, stood Hannibal, the world's largest airliner.' He hastened aboard. 'The two cabins have large windows, curtained with choice silks, set in tastefully panelled walls. There are soft shaded lights, big chintz-covered armchairs into which one sinks luxuriously, soft carpets on the floors, and flowers on tables in front of every seat – truly a veritable revolution in aircraft interiors.'

The aspect of the revolution he liked best, however, he saved till last. 'And the bar!' he exalted. 'I suppose it was owing to our licensing laws that it was locked, but from what I saw of the bottles behind the grill, to say nothing of the cups and saucers, plates and knives, the steward in attendance will be able to give a very efficient service.'

I had been lucky enough to meet the last of the HP 42 commanders. Patrick Tweedie, a former Senior Captain and Master Pilot of Imperial Airways, still lived in the house overlooking the site of the old Croydon aerodrome that he had occupied since joining the company in the early 1930s. Here he raised his son and his daughter Jill, the distinguished writer who, as a little girl, used to hang on the garden gate and wave to her father as he went roaring overhead on his way to Le Bourget and the City of Light. Captain Tweedie, a tall, handsome, straight-backed old Scotsman with a razor-sharp memory, regularly flew the Silver Wing, and, unlike

Captain Strange, who was expected to report an hour prior to departure, he rolled up a mere 45 minutes beforehand, went to the Captains' Room (sparsely furnished with a map table, a few battered armchairs and a row of steel lockers), glanced through the latest 'Notices to Airmen' then took his flight case from his locker. It contained a set of European route maps, a CDC – course and distance calculator – a Douglas protractor, a notebook, pencils and a pair of Zeiss sunglasses, bought specially for the Cairo to Karachi run on which, periodically, he was rostered.

After visits to the Met Office and the Air Traffic Control people, with whom he filed his flight plan, he walked out to his aircraft and climbed the steps to the flight deck. The engineer already had the Jupiters (two mounted on the lower mainplanes, two on the upper) fired up and running and, as Captain Tweedie entered, he would be standing behind the pilots' seats, scanning the instruments. On the port side of the cabin sat the wireless operator, holder of a special Post Office licence, headphones on and the valves of his Marconi equipment glowing as he exchanged test signals with the Tower. The pilots sat side-by-side 21 feet above the ground, the four engine throttles mounted on a pedestal between them. Also located on the pedestal was a big pneumatic lever able to brake the two non-retractable undercarriage wheels simultaneously or separately; the 'cheese-cutter' for adjusting fore and aft trim lay to hand nearby.

'The flight controls,' Captain Tweedie recalled, 'consisted of the control column with a rotatable 20-inch diameter wheel fixed to it, and a pair of huge rudder pedals; the designers must have thought we pilots had feet like elephants. None of the controls were power-operated as they are today. The elevator and rudder surfaces were about 90 feet from the cockpit, the aileron surfaces in the top wings about 110 feet apart – she had a wingspan of 130 feet – and all connected to the cockpit controls by an extraordinarily complicated system of wires, chains, cranks and pulleys. Flying the aircraft in severe turbulence was gruelling manual work. You wore gloves, took off your tunic and loosened your shirt and tie; when you'd come through it you felt as though you'd just rowed the Boat Race course. But despite that, and having wings that flexed a distance of eight feet at the tips in bad weather, it was a beautifully stable aircraft to fly, as strong and safe as houses. No passenger was ever hurt in an HP 42, and I managed to fly 400,000 miles in them without even scratching the paint!'

After the traffic clerk had brought the ship's papers for signature Captain Tweedie opened the hatch in the flight deck roof, stood and popped his head out for a look around. From a mast behind fluttered the Civil Air Ensign and Royal Mail pennant. When the Tower's big station clock said 12.30 precisely he blew two long blasts on his silver command whistle. The station superintendent standing to attention on the apron far below threw him a formal departure salute while uniformed ground staff hauled away the chocks, oak slabs the size of execution blocks. Captain Tweedie resumed his seat and pushed open the throttles. As the giant plane trundled away over the grass the First Officer scrambled out through the hatch to lower, retrieve and fold the flags. (Occasionally pilots would forget and, when airborne, receive frantic messages from the Tower warning that their streaming banners were about to foul the huge four-bladed propellers.) Then the First Officer snapped the hatch shut and prepared to assist his commander with the take-off, both men watching the Tower for the green Aldis lamp which, fitted with a telescopic sight, was trained directly at their windscreen. When it flashed they were cleared to roll.

On the flight deck of the Tristar, meanwhile, our own departure was still being delayed by the lack of a tractor. Captain Strange, growing fretful at the delay, abruptly straightened up and pointed. I looked and saw a huge, squat Hunzlitt tug approaching, puffing clouds of blue smoke. But was it coming for us? The crew watched anxiously, as though willing a passing taxi to respond to their cries on a wet day. They suddenly relaxed. It swung in underneath, locked on to our nosewheel and pushed us clear of the ramp before racing off to attend to someone else. For a few moments we just sat there, starting up the remaining engines and running down the items on the checklist, the brief questions and responses bouncing back and forth like echoes. London Ground Control told Mr Ahmed we could taxi. Captain Strange took hold of the half-moon steering wheel and gently eased the three throttles forward. With a brief roar we began to move, trundling slowly out towards Runway 28 Right. The rain had stopped but the surface was slick and shiny, the light opaque as buttermilk.

We joined the morning rush hour traffic queuing at the threshold of 28 Right. Mr Ahmed tested the rudder pedals and pushed and pulled the control column while Mr Wells checked the alarm systems. The tiny cabin reverberated to the clamour of warning hooters as Captain Strange told me that his father, also a pilot, had flown for BOAC. 'He was based at Heathrow in the post-war days when the terminal was just a few army-surplus tents and a couple of red telephone boxes beside a muddy field. Imperial became BOAC back in 1940 so he was too young to have flown those wonderful old Handley Page biplanes.' He broke off to resume his checklist, inquiring about the status of the flaps and flight instruments.

The instruments were okay, the flaps set at 40 degrees.

We had arrived at the runway threshold. The plane ahead, a little Air France Fokker jet, was in position and ready to go. Hot vapour boiled from its engines. Its nose dipped in a brief curtsy then away it thundered, laying down plumes of smoke and spray to confound the next in line. Captain Strange followed him on to the runway, confirmed that the radar and transponder were functioning, finished his coffee and said, 'We shall perform take-off, gentlemen.'

Mr Ahmed carried out final visual checks of the battery of dials and instruments as Mr Wells leant forward and prepared to grasp the throttles. Captain Strange was making last-minute adjustments to his seat which momentarily jammed. Unexpectedly, he reprimanded it in the high, crazed voice of Little Minnie Bannister from the Goon Show – the one who was always falling down wells – and, for a moment, there was merriment on the flight deck. Then he pushed the throttles forward and, with Mr Wells holding them in place, the Tristar began to move. Mr Ahmed punched his stopwatch and watched the airspeed needle. 'Eighty knots,' he said as we bellowed along the runway. Then he said, 'V1, rotate,' and Captain Strange drew the control column back. We soared into the air, climbing away over an arid landscape of roundabouts, gunmetal ponds and industrial estates as the after take-off checklist was called and answered.

'Speedbird 304, climb to 6,000 feet, no speed restrictions,' said the Controller on the Heathrow Departure Frequency.

'Roger, Speedbird 304 is cleared to climb to 6,000 feet,' Mr Ahmed acknowledged.

Staines, Datchet and Windsor passed beneath us unseen. We

were now bumping up to our cruising height through thick oatmeal cloud which Captain Strange identified as alto-stratus. 'It might even be hiding a bit of alto-cumulus,' he added judiciously. Then he dipped into the Ship's Library beside his seat and extracted a slim volume entitled *Aerodrome Booklet – Charles de Gaulle.* 'We approach Paris over Merue and then Creil,' he said, 'where he'll give us a steer and get us into a nice orderly queue for landing.'

As he began boning up on the runways, taxiways and procedures awaiting him at the other end, I contrasted the manner in which Captain Strange and Captain Tweedie went about their tasks. The Tristar skipper remained unseen by his passengers, his only manifestation a cheery, disembodied voice issuing periodically from the speakers. The Imperial commander, however, was expected to show a very high profile. After he had satisfied himself his aircraft was shipshape and safely on course Captain Tweedie climbed from his seat. 'I would tell my FO I was going aft for lunch and some socialising, and ask him to let me know when we were approaching Paris. Then I squared myself up and opened the door into the front passenger saloon. The accommodation was the most elegant I have ever seen. Passengers sat in truly luxurious armchairs, four to a table, while our two stewards, in starched white jackets, served them a piping-hot four-course meal. On each table there was spotless napery, sterling silver cutlery and a silver cruet, the blue and white company china, crystal wine glasses, a pretty red-shaded lamp and a silver vase containing fresh flowers. My rounds always took me through the front saloon and midships corridor into the aft saloon and on into the vestibule by the entrance door. On the way I would check for any irregularities – thick oil streaks on the engine cowlings, the setting of the fuel distribution cocks, unusual sounds or vibrations. In the vestibule I zipped open a panel and looked into the extreme tail end of the aircraft, at the flying control cables to the rudder and elevator.'

Then he went to talk to his passengers, starting in the aft saloon which was carpeted and curtained in pink, with pink-toned ceiling lights. Tables and chairs were a silvery blue, the latter upholstered in flowered yellow chintz; there were flower inlays in the polished blue laminate bulkheads. The forward saloon had sky blue carpets and curtains, and wood laminate bulkheads inlaid with classical designs. At the front of each cabin, beside the clock and altimeter, was a brass plate inscribed with the commander's name, so Captain Tweedie's leisurely progress back through the saloons took on the aura of a royal progress as he was greeted on all sides, his hand shaken, his autograph requested, his opinion sought on this and that. The Imperial pilots were public figures, notables in their own right, with loyal bands of fans and followers. H. G. Wells was such a fan of Captain Tweedie's that, when booking his seat, he always asked for him by name. Once, as they lunched together in the rear saloon (Captain Tweedie always stuck to smoked salmon with brown bread and butter, and a glass of Spa water) the novelist explained why: 'I would rather choose the same surgeon to operate on me again if he had successfully operated on me in the past!'

Among Captain Tweedie's other luncheon companions were Mr Winston Churchill, Mr Anthony Eden, Mrs Barbara Hutton, Mr Gordon Selfridge and Princess Marina of Kent (the Duke was also at the table, but fast asleep) who, they discovered, had attended the same small English school in Athens as Captain Tweedie's wife. The Imperial Silver Wing was, quite simply, the most celebrated and glamorous air service in the world. It was also the slowest, but nobody seemed to mind. Freeman Wills Croft wrote a best-seller about it – *The 12.30 From Croydon* – while Agatha Christie in *Death in the Clouds* contrived to have her victim murdered on the return flight. Its regulars included the Mountbattens, Charlie Chaplin, Douglas Fairbanks, Fred Astaire, Marie Lloyd, King Faisal, the King and Queen of the Belgians and, thrice weekly, a handful of passengers booked all the way through to Brisbane.

Aboard the Tristar we were approaching Worthing, climbing through 15,000 feet over a thick cover of woolly grey cloud. I mentally said goodbye to England as Captain Strange picked up his telephone once again and told the passengers we were about to cross the coast and head out over the Channel. Then he gave them the Paris weather. 'There was a bit of drizzle earlier,' he said, 'but they report that it's cleared up now, though it's still overcast. And it's slightly warmer than London, 41 degrees as opposed to 39 back at Heathrow. Because of our delay there we should land at 10.40 local time, about ten minutes adrift.' He reminded them that Paris was one hour ahead of London, said he hoped they were enjoying breakfast and replaced the phone.

I decided I'd better go and have my own, while it was still available. I returned to my seat and Miss Crowe brought me a continental breakfast on a tray. 'Just yell if you want more hot rolls,' she said, before bustling off with her pots of tea and coffee. 'We've got yonks in the oven.'

It wasn't bad, as airline breakfasts go, but not a patch on the one available on the 08.30 HP 42 to Paris – fresh grapefruit, shredded wheat or grape nuts, cold galantine of veal, sausages and tomatoes or a full mixed grill. In the early days of Imperial, when Paris was still served by thundering three-engined Argosies with open cockpits, the stewards were expected to buy the provisions themselves. First thing each morning they went shopping in Croydon market for eggs, fruit, bread and salad. Then they caught a bus back to the aerodrome where, at a small stove and sink in the Accounts Section, they prepared the salads, hardboiled the eggs and filled Thermos flasks with coffee and tea. But not everyone appreciated their efforts. The Armenian millionaire Nubar Gulbenkian, a Paris regular, always brought his own supplies and primus stove, and a valet who was dispatched to the ship's galley to prepare a light lunch of consommé and creamed chicken.

After Miss Crowe had removed my tray – the crew, she said, would have their breakfast in a cafeteria at Charles de Gaulle – I smoked a cigarette, recalling that I wouldn't have been allowed to do so aboard an HP 42. Imperial took their slogan, 'Safety First', very seriously and were at great pains to minimize all fire risks; any passenger caught ignoring the smoking ban faced a fine of £200 and six months in prison. But the only person ever prosecuted, a male who gave his address as White's Club, St James's Street, and who, despite repeated remonstrations by the captain (the stewards were even snatching burning cigarettes from his mouth) smoked his way doggedly right across the Channel, was fined a mere £10 with three guineas costs at Croydon Police Court. Now, not knowing where we were, I returned to the flight deck to find out. 'We crossed the French coast at Dieppe about three minutes ago,' said Captain Strange. 'Should be starting down any time now.'

He asked about my journey. I showed him the original Imperial route map, which he studied for some time. 'I think that's the way I'd like to have done it,' he said, reflectively. 'Working every day, stopping at night for dinner, a few drinks and a good sleep, really getting to know your passengers. For a pilot it must have been a marvellous life. And the flying would have been a hell of a lot more fun than it is these days.'

A brisk, bossy woman speaking barely comprehensible English told us to commence our descent.

'Here we go,' said Captain Strange, taking us sedately down through cloud with the colour and consistency of woodsmoke. Then France appeared, a prospect of grassy fields, little copses and country roads swimming in a thin, watery light. 'We've got a river,' announced Captain Strange, peering ahead, 'but what I'm actually looking for is a large spire.' He glanced at the letdown chart lying open in his lap. 'An . . . *edifice*.'

The bossy lady ordered us down another 3,000 feet. We continued closing on Paris, passing over a ploughed field, the earth dark as bitter chocolate, being worked by a lone red tractor. A big elm stood in a corner and a flight of white birds whirled beneath us and settled on its bare branches. We seemed to be trailing a small occluded front behind us; aft of the wing I saw it sweeping across the tractor and the tree, obscuring them in dense rain. The lady in the Tower was now talking to a Pakistani. He couldn't understand her, nor she him; their incomprehension was mutual and profound. 'Say again! Say again!' they entreated each other. Captain Strange, flying manually, eye on his glide slope indicator, said, 'We're lined up with the runway. It should appear dead ahead any minute now. Gear down.'

'Gear down,' said Mr Wells. There was a muffled thump below.

'Coming up to the marker,' Mr Ahmed warned.

We were on finals. The pre-landing checklist had been called, the coffee cups stowed away. We burst through a flapping, gauzy curtain of cloud and there, directly ahead, was Runway 27, its high-intensity white centreline lights running almost to the horizon, straight as a Roman road. We sank towards it at 160 knots. 'Flaps thirty-three,' said Captain Strange.

'Thirty-three flaps.' Mr Ahmed pushed a lever.

Then, abruptly, Captain Strange straightened. 'I don't believe it!'

he exclaimed, voice filled with astonishment. 'Go round, please, go round! Gear up!' He banged the throttles forward; the engines, murmuring away at the back, grew thunderous and the nose swung past the horizon as we began a hard climb. 'Flaps to ten, please. There's an aircraft sitting there, just where we're supposed to be touching down.'

I saw it only briefly, a toy plane dwarfed by the expanse of runway along which, in a markedly leisurely manner, it was starting to move. Then it was lost to me as Captain Strange hauled the Tristar into a steep right turn. We scrambled up into the shadowy pavilion of raincloud we had brought with us and a new controller took charge, speaking urgently in precise, accurate English. 'Stay on this frequency, Speedbird 304. We'll start your finals again as soon as we've dealt with the Russian.'

'Want to do a bit of flying?' Captain Strange asked, talking, alas, to Mr Ahmed, not me. 'I'd better explain to the passengers. Okay? You have control.'

Picking up the phone he reported that an aircraft was having problems down on the runway, thus obliging us to make an unscheduled circuit of field. He spoke casually, as though emergency overshoots were run-of-the-mill. There had, however, been perceptible tension on the flight deck, and I sensed that mine had not been the only pulse to quicken. When he had taken back the controls I asked how often it happened. 'Once in a blue moon.' He smiled. 'Still, we've managed to get your trip off to an interesting start.'

Our new controller got us into position for a fresh attempt. 'You may descend now to join the glide slope,' he said.

'Roger,' said Captain Strange, giving the runway threshold a good hard look. But it was deserted; the rogue aircraft had left and could be seen climbing away to the east, threading plumes of dark smoke through the clouds like clumsy stitches in a rumpled pile of pillows. 'Flaps to twenty-two.' As we began to sink earthwards the disquiet was still palpable. 'Flaps to thirty-three, please.'

'Flaps to thirty-three,' said Mr Ahmed. An emergency hooter sounded and was promptly stifled by Mr Wells. We drifted in towards the bright red and white lights of the touchdown zone. The rain had eased. 'One hundred feet,' Mr Ahmed reported and then,

with scarcely a bump, we were down. Mr Wells hauled at the
throttles to engage reverse thrust and we coasted, bellowing and
shuddering, to a halt. Three crows rose from the grass as we
approached the low, surreal space age terminal, and flapped away
towards a parked Air France Concorde; one settled on its roof. We
lumbered over a motorway signposted PARIS LILLE and drew up
beside a man in worn blue dungarees standing with his arms full of
old railway sleepers.

'Are those the chocks?' I asked.

Captain Strange said, 'Unless he's flogging firewood,' and
switched off the engines. One of the local British Airways ground
staff hurried on to the flight deck. 'My goodness!' he exclaimed.

'The bloody idiot!' said Captain Strange. 'Was it Aeroflot? We
had to *overshoot*.'

'Yes, Aeroflot. An Ilyushin.'

'The Tower gave him a real roasting,' said Mr Ahmed, with a
grin. 'His language got extremely fruity.'

It was time to go ashore. I thanked them and they wished me luck.
The passenger cabins were empty. Miss Crowe, someone's discarded *Guardian* tucked beneath her arm, stood chatting to a
colleague who sat knitting a yellow shawl.

'They've all gone,' said Miss Crowe. 'Isn't the silence wonderful?'

Walking through the covered jetty I thought of Captain Tweedie
approaching Le Bourget aboard the HP 42, summoned back to the
flight deck by his Wireless Operator when the Eiffel Tower hove
into sight, signing a few more menus as he made his way forward
to take the landing. Le Bourget, the premier airport of France,
was a stretch of greensward like Croydon. Sometimes there was a
bit of horseplay during the turnaround. Once Captain Tweedie
found, hanging in the aircraft's braced box tail, a swinging perch
with a toy cockatoo on it, put there by German pilots from Luft
Hansa.

'Rome, s'il vous plaît,' I said to the man on the gate.

'Alitalia?'

'Oui.'

'Satellite Six.'

'Excusez moi?'

'*Satellite Six*.'

He pointed, throwing out an arm like a cop directing rush hour traffic and, pondering this inter-galactic directive, I set off to catch my next flight.

II

A small blonde girl, painfully thin, issued my boarding pass and admitted me to the Satellite Six departure lounge. It was dirty and unswept, but I had it to myself and I looked out over the plateau on which the airport stood, 7,670 acres of empty farmland between the Seine and the Marne near the agricultural hamlet of Roissy-en-France. A distant wood lined the horizon like a fringe of stubble. Out there the sky was dark and menacing, but overhead it was clear enough to flood the airfield with a luminous, honey-coloured light that could almost be stirred with a spoon. There were no aircraft visible. Nothing moved anywhere.

A woman entered and seated herself nearby. She had white hair and a white angora cardigan and, twinkling at me through blue-rimmed bifocals, said she was heading for Rome to flee the Wisconsin winter. She had been spending $95 a month on heating bills. Then, a couple of days ago, she had paid out a small fortune for a snow blower to clear the three-foot drifts in her yard. But, while using it for the first time, there had been a bang and a lot of black smoke, and it had suddenly stopped blowing snow. The dealer, when he finally showed up, accused her of blowing rocks instead and bad-temperedly took it away in his pick-up for repairs. Early next morning her roof fell in. She found a blizzard raging in her lounge and, retrieving a bottle of bourbon from the liquor cabinet, fixed herself a drink and went back to bed in a part of the house that was still intact. At daylight she called her brother in Rome and told him she was coming over. Her granddaughter drove her to O'Hare Airport in Chicago but, on a freeway just outside the city, they were caught in a multiple pile-up caused by black ice. By jumping on the bumpers she managed to free the car, though it was not in good shape. At the airport the ticket clerk said her passport was out of date, and her granddaughter began to cry. At the Passport Office in town she was obliged to shout some at the officials, who were reluctant to issue the document in a hurry. Returning to the airport her granddaughter had to be urged, despite the treacherous conditions, to ignore the speed restrictions. By now the girl was showing definite signs of hysteria. She missed the Rome plane – just – but caught the Paris one instead. It was a good flight, with a nice chicken dinner and everything but, halfway through the movie, the 747 was struck by lightning.

I stared at her.

'Dustin Hoffman was in it,' she said.

'The plane?'

She chuckled. 'No, honey, the *movie*.'

There was a sudden, explosive roar outside and a Washington-bound Concorde in the ghostly all-white livery of Air France hurtled by on its take-off run. The angled droop-snout was horizontal to the ground, the fuselage pointed steeply into the sky and, as we watched, it was launched and climbing like a projectile. We saw its lanky, ponderous undercarriage snap into the slender underbelly and then, curving away to the west, it vanished into the haze, taking its harsh, reverberating sonic footprint with it.

My friend was awed. She had never seen Concorde before. 'My, oh my,' she murmured and, leaving her gazing after it, I went to ask the undernourished girl at the check-in desk in what direction Le Bourget lay. She pointed to the southwest. 'That way,' she said. 'About 10 or 11 kilometres, I think. But Le Bourget is nothing now.'

Today it is used by executive aircraft, army trooping flights and small third-level airlines. The last time I had called there was aboard a tiny, buzzing Beechcraft of Air Champagne en route to Rheims (where, when the engines were switched off, I heard nightingales singing in the vineyards). On my first visit a dozen years earlier Le Bourget had still been a recognized international airport, though its ornate public rooms looked sad and shabby, like a grand hotel in a dying resort. I had caught an Air Lanka 707 to Colombo, flown by a young Frenchman with oily, shoulder-length hair and dark glasses worn at midnight against – he claimed – the brightness of the moon.

Before it was downgraded Le Bourget had been a place of

unimaginable excitement and glamour. It was from here that many of the great pioneering services to Africa and the Orient had departed, and it was here too that the exhausted Lindbergh, his Atlantic ordeal behind him, had been mobbed on touchdown by 300,000 rapturous people on the night of 21 May 1927. But an Imperial Airways publicity item, issued five years later, was decidedly offhand. 'It presents the usual bustle of a French airport,' the author reported. 'More colour, more varied uniforms than its counterpart at Croydon.' Then he cunningly emphasized its tiresome foreign aspects by assuring Imperial passengers that they wouldn't be troubled by them. 'You have no tipping to do; no gesticulating French porters to contend with; no effort to remember the French for "You are charging me too much" or "I have nothing to declare"; Imperial Airways has English staff at all its stations and it is their duty to make your path smooth.'

The company was perhaps pained by the fact that, in many respects, Le Bourget was more progressive than Croydon. Gone were the days when passengers scrambled ashore on duckboards laid across the viscous winter mud. Now, in the 1930s, it had one of the most sophisticated lighting systems in existence – as well as the usual boundary lights, beacons and illuminated wind direction indicators, it boasted a unique 13,000-foot sodium-lit approach track – and the largest terminal in the world, an imposing 200-metre-long structure with a protruding central section that looked like the bridge of a multi-winged flying boat. But the first Australia-bound passengers landing at the field found themselves grounded by Mussolini, who had temporarily withdrawn overflying rights to foreigners. Obliged to travel to southern Italy by train, they rode a Pullman bus to the Hotel Ambassadors where a senior Imperial executive welcomed them, having hurried across from Airways Terminus, the company's elegant, marble-columned office on the Rue des Italiens (Telegrams: Flying Paris). Then, after dinner, he returned to cry, 'All aboard for the Empire Routes!' and deliver them to the Gare de Lyon and their sleeping compartments on the Paris-Brindisi *wagon-lits*. After a restful night they ate a breakfast of rolls, black cherry jam and grapes while trundling along the shores of Lake Geneva, paused briefly for a crew change beside the Lago Maggiore – baskets of fresh peaches were available on the platform for a lira – and rolled on to Milan for lunch. This was taken at a hotel, which also provided them with hot baths. They returned to the train, now designated the Valigia delle Indie, and embarked for Brindisi, reached at 8 o'clock the following morning. Passengers had breakfast at the Grande Albergo Internazionale (where I planned to spend the night) before boarding the Imperial pinnace which sped them, one later wrote, 'through the water past some Italian battleships and a number of Italian naval seaplanes to the Imperial Airways station, where our various documents were passed in a few seconds and we set out for the flying boat itself'.

Satellite Six was starting to fill with Rome travellers. Out on the runway there was the sudden bellow of reverse thrust being applied to some very big turbofans, and moments later an Airbus A300 with the red, white and forest-green isosceles triangles of Alitalia on its tail lumbered towards us, dipping as the pilot touched the brakes and brought it to a halt beside the departure lounge. The name *Botticelli* was inscribed on its nose. Fifty or sixty passengers streamed ashore, followed by the captain, a real matinée idol in a beautifully cut dark uniform. He strolled among us, stretching his legs, his aftershave scenting the air with a bouquet of rare spices. My Wisconsin friend caught his eye and was favoured with a faint smile. He got a pleased beam back.

The London-bound Tristar taxied past on its way back to the runway and I stifled a pang of homesickness. The crew were returning to their families, friends and gardens, to the National Health Service, good Sunday papers and pure, potable water. I turned my attention to the parked Airbus. Designed and built by a seven-nation committee of Europeans, it was a sturdy, handsome aeroplane, with a stylishly Old World look to it, the two giant underwing engine pods slung as rakishly low as the chassis of a vintage Bentley (though a PIA Airbus skipper was later to tell me, over lunch in Karachi, that they were a bloody nuisance down there, sucking up every foreign body on the runway like a pair of Hoovers).

As I stood contemplating its British advanced technology wings with their West German spoilers and French airbrakes, the Tristar raced by and lifted off. Wistfully I watched it bank away to the right as Captain Strange and Mr Ahmed set course for Dieppe and home, and then the *Botticelli*'s commander sauntered back to his ship and we were asked to go aboard too.

I passed through the Spanish door and was shown to my seat by an amiable young steward with long curly hair and a tangled black beard. My neighbour, already installed and strapped in, was tall and skinny, with greying temples and a face like a rabbit. The engines started and, as we lumbered across the Paris to Brussels autoroute and out towards the runway, the PA system clicked on and a breezy male voice welcomed us aboard AZ 335, the Airbus service to Rome under the command of Mr Da Lucca. Our flight time would be one hour and 35 minutes. Lunch would be served. We swung on to Runway 27 and halted. Then Mr Da Lucca opened his throttles and released the Messier-Hispano-Bugatti-Liebherr-Dowty disc brakes and away we went, surging down only a third of the length of 27 before soaring skywards with a minimum of noise and fuss. Down below were the massive blowers of the Turboclair fog dispersal system, set along the threshold like underground gun emplacements and able, in two minutes flat, to drill an 800-metre-long operational corridor into the most intractable overcast.

As we climbed through the North Europe cloud cover, humming electric motors screwjacked the giant flaps back into the wings for our high speed cruise to Italy. Of the earth there was no sign. All we saw was the sun-dappled topside of the alto-stratus which almost certainly had a lowering underside that was raining on France. A stewardess approached with the drinks trolley. My neighbour, who had endured the take-off with closed eyes and hands clasped tightly in his lap, asked for gin. She handed him a Gilbeys miniature and he held up two fingers.

'Due,' he said.

Waving away the ice, he emptied both bottles into the glass, leaving room for only a splash of tonic. He downed it like water, sighed and, suddenly turning to me like someone ignored too long at a dinner party, said he felt about flying the way most people feel about incoming nuclear rocketry; the gin eased the terror; talking helped too. A Roman in the wine trade, he had been travelling on business, buying the French '83s, a good year, perhaps a remarkable one thanks to the miraculous summer. The clarets, despite August storms in the Bordeaux region, would be excellent, and so would the Burgundies. 'But the best, I think, will be the Alsace. That will be a great wine, perhaps as good as the 1976, the year the vines got the noble rot. What a complaint! It withers the grapes, the sugar is heavy as honey, the wine has such *body*!'

As we raced along the Loire valley – 'Down there the '83 Sancerre will have finesse, a touch of acidity, it will be excellent!' – closing fast on Lyon, the steward with the long hair and uncombed beard, now wearing a smart, mustard-coloured jacket, distributed lunch in Dayglo orange boxes. 'It is maybe a little difficult to open,' he said. We soon saw what he meant. The boxes appeared to be made from heavy-duty industrial plastic and sealed by Alitalia's Security Division. My neighbour pondered his like a safe-cracker and then with a small grunt, applied pressure with his thumbs and snapped up the lid. Then he said 'Permesso', reached over and opened mine as well. We examined our respective meals without enthusiasm. Each box contained a couple of slices of cold meat, two olives, a peeled egg, a quarter bottle of unlabelled red wine, a container of Vittel mineral water, a small cake, a roll, wrapped biscuits labelled Cracker Doriano and a segment of Bel Paese cheese. He unscrewed the bottle and sniffed.

'Chianti,' he said. 'It will not thrill you.'

During coffee Mont Blanc came up fast on the starboard quarter. On its bright midwinter flank a tiny skier left tracks like a needle drawn across icing. My friend told me that his son, aged 16, was displaying a worrying interest in Marxism; visions of the neighbourhood chapter of the Red Brigade turning up at the apartment for coffee and cakes were starting to haunt his wife. Then the gin began to wear off and he fell silent again. I looked, without success, for the railway line that would have taken our Brindisi-bound travellers south, then settled down to work on my notes.

Soon the cloud began to disperse. It became gauzily transparent and then broke into small, milky clumps, all floating at a uniform level, like puffs of smoke from an ack-ack battery. I reckoned we must be somewhere south of Pisa when, out to the right, there was a sustained rippling flash and the western horizon suddenly filled with the glitter of the Mediterranean, flat and glassy under a hot afternoon sun. The steward distributed forms for the Declaration of Currency, Securities and Negotiable Instruments (to be completed by travellers importing more than a million lire) which said 'Welcome to Italy!' on the top in five languages.

A quarter of an hour later Mr Da Lucca snapped up his airbrakes and we began a steep, juddering descent over rounded hills, each standing beside its sickle-shaped pool of shadow. He brought us in along the beach, the breaking surf beneath one wing, stands of gnarled grey trees under the other, and then banked gently inland, sinking fast over farms, fields, empty tree-lined roads, a deserted canal with reeds growing by its banks. The *Botticelli* whistled across the threshold of 34 Right at Leonardo da Vinci Airport and, soon afterwards, we were boarding a rickety green bus that took us to an echoing hall where solemn, silent queues inched patiently forward, like penitents lining up for confession. The Immigration Officer glanced at my passport, snapped it shut, tossed it back and waved me through. He was heavy and morose, with chins like a bloodhound, and he gave off a faint but discernible smell of smoked hams.

The internal flights left from a ground-level concourse not unlike the premises of a large bus station. Having checked in and claimed my boarding pass for the 1710 service to Brindisi, I went looking for somewhere to cash a traveller's cheque. Eventually, beside the Arrivals Gates, I found a tiny branch of the Banco di Spirito Santo, a windowed cubicle containing a single clerk. There was a short queue, which I joined. Two young Arabs fell in behind me. Each wore a stained brown jellaba and shiny lace-up shoes without socks. They were bony and unshaven, and displayed a strong family resemblance; both had their eyes set close together, giving them an appearance of great cunning. When I reached the front of the queue the clerk announced, 'You are the last. After you I will go home.' He frowned at the Arabs. 'Closed,' he said.

The Arabs gave him their sly, foxy look.

'Closed! Fermé! Geschlossen!' snapped the clerk, but the Arabs stood their ground and examined him calmly.

'Are you brothers?' I asked them, to break the impasse.

They briefly turned their attention to me, but did not reply.

'I think they are brothers,' I said to the clerk.

He sighed, took my cheque and began counting out gaudy lire

notes. 'This is my last lira so now I will knock off,' he confided. 'I do not feel too well. I must work very, very much and my health is not good. You know? I don't sleep, I don't eat, there is no energy.'

I could see that all this work had taken its toll, and told him so. He brightened perceptibly but just then one of the Arabs reached past, placed a $100 bill on the counter and tapped it with a sinewy brown fingers. 'Lira,' he said.

The clerk abruptly stopped counting my money. He stared at the note and then at the brothers. His pallor was replaced by a bright mottled pink which reached right up to his receding hairline. 'Closed!' he shouted, throwing up his hands. The chair on which he sat ran on well-oiled castors, and the abruptness of his gesture caused it to shoot forward and fetch his knees up against the counter with a crack like a rifle shot. He cried out but managed to steady himself, sitting bowed and clutching his kneecaps. 'You must just wait a minute,' he gasped.

'Are you all right?'

'I have very, very much pain.'

Behind me there were some small, unobtrusive noises, like the creaking of hinges and, turning, I found the brothers registering amusement. One tapped the $100 bill again. 'Lira!' he said.

Slowly the clerk straightened up. There were beads of sweat on his forehead. 'I do not think I have broken the bones.' He stood cautiously and tested his legs. 'They are okay,' he announced. He picked up my money, counted it again and handed it over. Then he glanced at the $100 bill, crooked his finger and beckoned the Arabs towards him. 'I cannot change that,' he said, slowly, 'because *I have not enough lire.*'

'Lira!' said the first Arab.

'Lira! Lira!' said his brother.

'*No lire,*' said the clerk. 'Lire finished. Finito. Fertig.' He yanked open a drawer and, with a flourish, revealed his day's trawl of currencies. 'You want Swiss francs? D-marks? Escudos? You want yen?' He gave them a terrible glare. 'You want *Zambian kwachas?*'

The brothers gave up. They retrieved their note and wandered away, looking disconsolate, while I went and got a beer – 'Una bira! Una bira!' sang the barman, sliding a can of Heineken towards me and gesturing operatically towards a small, mean-looking colleague at the cash desk, 'pay your money over herea!' – and took it off to my departure gate. Only yards away a DC9 sporting the broad blue fuselage stripe of Aero Trasporti Italiani, the Naples-based internal airline, sat humming like a kettle. A dozen people were boarding, including a very old man in a beret and worn black suit who angrily shook off the hand of a ground hostess helping him up the stairs. The engines howled and the DC9 went bowling away across the tarmac, the rudder swinging from side to side as the pilots tested it against their checklist. A notice by the gate said it was going to Palermo.

There was dirty weather coming in from the sea, dark cumulonimbus skyscrapers bursting with rain and licked by wicked little tongues of lightning. The first Brindisi-bound passengers trooped in, men with shiny briefcases and coats draped elegantly across their shoulders. More arrived, and the atmosphere became increasingly clubby; greetings were called, hands shaken and drinks fetched; the departures hall began to ring with talk and laughter as the Brindisi men exchanged tales of their Roman adventures.

Outside it was growing dark. There was a rumble of thunder and, seconds later, a monsoonal downpour began drumming on the tarmac, falling so hard that it vaporized on impact and formed a mist which lay, opaque as marsh gas, several inches above the ground; an approaching DC9 taxied towards us as though coming through a car wash. Indoors the party was now in full swing and, when the flight was called, people were slow to respond. A pair of ground hostesses entered and began working their charges like sheep dogs, breaking up the groups, cutting out the ringleaders, herding everyone towards the door. They led the passengers, still talking, on to a bus, then sent it off across the tarmac at very high speed.

Far out on the perimeter of Leonardo da Vinci we halted by the stern of a lone ATI DC9 standing with its ground support system going and its windows lit. The passengers, briefcases held over their heads, sheltered beneath the T-shaped tailplane before forming into single file and pelting up the built-in airstairs. At the foot of the steps a tiny Fiat Topolino painted in Alitalia livery was parked, its wipers going, its sole occupant a strikingly beautiful girl with long auburn hair and an orange walkie-talkie. Two of the men waiting beneath the tail bowed low in her direction. She laughed and flashed her headlights. The men blew kisses then scrambled aboard too.

A pair of stewards built like nightclub bouncers got everyone into their seats, directing some, manhandling others. The talking went on. I found myself in the very last row and, all the way up the plane, could see hands gesturing and fluttering to emphasize this point or that. My neighbour was a fair-haired, monosyllabic Ulsterman who drank from a can of Carlsberg; when he had finished it he placed it in his bag and took out another.

A steward blew into the public address system then announced a 15-minute delay 'for air traffic control reasons'. None of the passengers paid any attention but, peering out the window, I saw that Leonardo da Vinci was flooded. A Caravelle from a Swiss charter firm taxied by and left a wash like a flying boat, while the courses of vehicles moving around the apron could be charted from their long wakes. Eventually the two Pratt & Whitney turbofans, set in pods only a foot or two aft of our seats, erupted into life. The steward closed the door sealing off the stairwell with a bang and the clamour dropped to a purposeful hum. We began to move. At the threshold of 34 Right we held briefly while an old 707, trailing plumes of dark smoke, gurgled in through the rain and splashed down like a duck on a pond.

The setting sun broke through the overcast and Fiumicino's 3,500 acres seemed, momentarily, to be awash with molten metal. Then we were off, racing down that glittering runway and climbing over a dark, boisterous sea as the hydraulically driven Menasco undercarriage came up with a series of muffled thumps. The DC9 lurched and yawed through ragged cloud, but the passengers, oblivious to the wild ride, talked on, their hands still weaving and fluttering right up the plane. The stewards sat down, picked up copies of *Corriere della Sera* and began reading. There would clearly be no food, drink or service available during our 65 minutes aloft.

But then a voice said, 'Do you fancy a lager?' and I turned to find my neighbour holding out a can of Carlsberg. I thanked him and took it. With a final violent manoeuvre we broke free of the cloud and rose into a delicate pink evening sky. Low on the western horizon, far beyond Sardinia, the sun was an iridescent smudge. We cruised serenely through the calm, cold air as the Ulsterman, his manner formal, told me that his name was Mr Pilbeam and that he was a driver of heavy duty goods vehicles. We toasted Italy, the fine evening and his new job at a petro-chemical works near Brindisi. 'There are lots of Brits there,' he said, 'and the money's very good. I haven't worked in Belfast since 1977, when I had a job at Harland & Wolff, like my dad and grandad before me. My grandad even worked on the *Titanic*.' He was proud of that fact and talked about the doomed liner with a kind of quiet intensity, listing for me some of the extravagant accoutrements of Edwardian privilege that old Mr Pilbeam had helped pack into its massive hull – the Aubusson tapestries, marble drinking fountains, lacquered brass telephones, gold fruit tymbals, even a solid silver duck press.

'They launched it down pitchpine slipways,' he said, 'lubricated with tallow and train oil and the prayers of the whole community.'

We were now high over the Apennines, an occasional snowy ridge visible in the failing light, heading for the eastern seaboard along which the train carrying the Australia-bound passengers would have approached Brindisi, halting first at Bari and Monopoli. In the crypt of a Bari church, only a kilometre from the station but unseen by them, was a silver casket containing the bones of St Nicholas of Myra – better known as Father Christmas – stolen from a tomb in Asia Minor by Bari sailors delivering a shipment of wheat to Antioch in 1087. I glanced at my watch; 20 minutes to go. The DC9 bucked occasionally as plumes of wind sheared off the mountains then began descending through a moonless night, passing across docks where container ships were unloading, turning over the sea, lining up with the main runway of Papola Casale field and, eventually, coming to rest beside a small, square terminal, brightly floodlit. On the tarmac Mr Pilbeam suddenly paused and said, 'Hang on, I promised to get a shot of the plane for the kids.' He produced an Instamatic and the flashlight flared. A blue-uniformed *carabiniero* shouted 'Che cosa?' and sprang from the shadow of the wing, attempting to wrestle the camera from him. Mr Pilbeam, badly shaken, apologized and was allowed, after an angry warning, to keep it. I found a rattling Fiat taxi driven by an elderly, bow-legged man with a gaudy postcard of the Madonna glued beside the meter. He told me there had been bad storms in Brindisi. I said there was a big storm in Rome just two hours earlier. He shrugged; what went on in Rome was of no interest to him.

Trees flickered in the headlights as we approached the city where the Appian Way ended, and where the poet Virgil, arriving from Greece in the year 19 BC, aged 51, fell ill and, despite the best efforts of the Brindisi physicians, slipped into a coma and died. The route to the Internazionale lay along slippery, rain-slicked cobbled streets which led, eventually, to the Via Regina Margherita. As I climbed out of the Fiat I sniffed the tang of salt and heard the soft splash of the tide against the sea wall. Before me, touched faintly with starlight, was the dark expanse of the Seno di Levante, the bay from which the Crusaders sailed for the Holy Land – the fountain where they watered their horses before embarkation is flowing still – and from which, heading in the same general direction, the flying boats had taken off.

The Internazionale occupied a prime waterfront position but inside there were shadows and a stale, musty smell. The lobby was baronial, its ceiling high and vaulted, the walls cluttered with prints and paintings, the floor with a plantation of potted trees and shrubs.

The reception clerk said he remembered the Imperial passengers. They had embarked from a point just acrosss the road – a familiar sight during his childhood. 'The little blue bus of Imperial Airways picked them up at the main station on the Piazzale Crispi, and brought them here for a full continental breakfast. Then they travelled by launch across to the Customs House Quay and, when they had completed the formalities, out to their plane.'

I went to the empty dining room, reflecting that often the passengers were personally welcomed at the Internazionale by the pilot himself. 'We were received by the captain of our flying boat, whose name is Bailey,' wrote Mr W. D. H. McCullough, 'who has got a little red short beard, and who wears his cap on one side and is known throughout the service as Captain Kettle. He showed us where to leave our luggage, where to wash, and explained that breakfast was waiting for us.'

I ate a solitary dinner of pasta and mussels, then lamb roasted in herbs; with the lamb I had a strong red zagarese wine. The waiter was white-haired and devout, and knew nothing about the flying boats. He told me, though, that the relics of St Nicholas at Bari floated in a manna which was discharged, miraculously, from the bones themselves; until a century ago the monks had ladled it into silver buckets and offered it to the pilgrims to drink. Then he brought me a dish of figs and almonds, and a glass of smoky cold malmsey wine from the vineyards of Gallipoli, a township lying on the far side of the Salentine Plain.

Later I went to the bar. On the walls there were sepia prints of old steamers with sharp stems and tall funnels tied up by the city. Four noisy, assertive Americans were playing poker. A wizened Italian in a smart tweed suit told me it was hard to avoid Americans in Brindisi. 'They are in oil, construction, the military. They have a big intelligence base, top secret, for listening to Soviet and Eastern Europe radio traffic, also the Middle East.'

He smiled when I told him what I was doing in Brindisi. 'As a small boy I would gather with my friends to watch the passengers embark on the launch. For us they seemed so exotic – off to India, off to the ends of the earth. The men had their sun helmets for the tropics, the women wore hats and white gloves and cotton dresses, just as if they were going to the races. Once an Indian prince gave me a sovereign for running back to the dining room here to fetch a cigarette case he had left on the table; it was made of tortoiseshell and gold. He was a small man in a suit and a cloth cap, like a plumber, but his servant wore a turban and a beautiful jacket of green silk, and at first I thought *he* was the maharajah.'

I bought my friend a chilled white wine and soda. He said, 'One of the Imperial Scipios was set on fire and sank here in the harbour. Did you know that? The man who did it worked for the railways as a ticket collector. He was a dedicated Fascist, a bit crazy, and some English passengers on his train had been making jokes about Mussolini.'

Later I went to my room and got out my bound volumes of the Imperial Airways *Gazette*, seeking an account of a Brindisi departure written by Major the Hon. R. F. Carnegie in 1932. When the launch had tied up beside the Scipio – the world's first four-engined passenger aircraft – the travellers scrambled up a small ladder into the ship. 'Here I give the information from a polished brass plate in the saloon. "Four-engined boat sea-plane

Sylvanus built by Short Brothers, launched April 1931." The cruising speed is 105 miles per hour and she develops over 2,000 HP. The saloon is very roomy, with comfortable armchairs for sixteen passengers and instrument dials giving such information as time, speed and height. "All aboard!" cries the steward, the door is shut and we start to taxi. Presently we get into a grand rush, the hull ploughs deeper into the green wave, a wall of water surges up over the windows and one realizes the immense horse power which will soon lift fourteen tons high in the air.' Major Carnegie waxed lyrical about the views from 1,000 feet, but neglected to mention that the steward's first duty, once aloft, was to uncork the clarets so that they could breathe unhurriedly before lunch.

I noted that, in 1932, the Imperial manager for Italy caught the train up to Rome for an audience with the Pope – 'the first occasion,' bragged the *Gazette*, 'on which a representative of a foreign air transport company had been received by His Holiness.' He presented the Pontiff with a photograph album bound in white pergamint paper and stamped with the Papal arms containing pictures of 'the Company's aircraft and places of interest on the Empire routes', and was much gratified by 'the Pope's great pleasure in the Photographs and interest in the work being done by Imperial Airways'. I cleaned my teeth and got into bed. Rain pattered on the window, just as it had done when I had awoken that morning in London. I rolled over like a stricken ship and, thinking of home, was asleep within seconds.

III

There were no scheduled air services from Brindisi to Athens, the next Imperial port of call, so I had to return to Rome. The taxi back to the airport was ordered for 5.30 a.m. The Internazionale did not provide breakfast at that hour, not even coffee, but an American engineer also up early for the Rome plane had stayed at the hotel for several weeks and knew how to work the espresso machine.

'They keep it in the bar, and using it can get you excommunicated,' he said, 'so we'll need to go in under very deep cover.' We drank several cupfuls while he told me, in a low voice, that he had been working on a new petro-chemical plant, and was now returning to Philadelphia with his family and his dog. 'Are you sorry to be leaving Brindisi?' I asked. He shrugged. 'As you see, I am dry-eyed and in good spirits.' But his departure was an emotional one nevertheless, the sleepy reception clerk leading an ebullient young bull mastiff out to the taxi, embracing the engineer, kissing his wife and children. Then he saw me off too, pausing to look over the dark harbour and sniff the sharp air. 'It will be a nice day,' he announced, and shook my hand warmly. 'Goodbye, Signore Imperiale.'

The terminal at Papola Casale field was thronged with young navy pilots drinking coffee at the bar; they wore dark blue flying suits studded with zips and pockets, and had the self-absorbed looks of athletes about to come under starter's orders. One of them cried 'Andiamo!' and, with a brisk rattle of crockery, they put down their cups and trooped out into the grey dawn.

As we walked across the tarmac to our DC9 I heard the high, anguished yelping of a dog. The Philadelphia engineer and his son, a good-looking, bespectacled boy of about 14, had urged their bull mastiff into a lightweight plastic cage and were now hoisting it into the aircraft's hold. The boy seemed close to tears and his father, leading him away, slipped an arm across his shoulders to comfort him. I went aboard and found myself seated next to a thin, sparrowlike American with rimless glasses and a bony nose who responded to my greeting with a curt nod. The terminal flood-lighting was switched off as we began taxiing towards an opaque, foggy horizon. A steward warned us on the PA that photography was strictly prohibited, and I soon saw why. Parked discreetly behind clumps of windblown trees were a dozen military jets painted in dun camouflage. As we trundled by the young pilots were clambering into the two-man cockpits and pulling on their visored helmets. I asked my neighbour if he knew what kind of planes they were. He looked up from his *Newsweek* and said, 'That information is supposed to be classified.' A moment later a steward came around, distributing the Rome morning papers, so I asked him instead. 'Aermacchi trainers,' he said cheerily. 'Also used as ground attack fighters. Very fast, very good. The Argentine Navy flies them. So does my cousin.' He moved on, unaware that my neighbour was staring venomously at his back. The Aermacchi pilots were starting up their Rolls-Royce Viper engines and waiting for us to vacate the air space so that they could get aloft and play with the various fixtures and fittings – Zuni rockets, Matra Magic missiles, anti-runway bombs and so on – that they carted about on their underwing hardpoints.

The DC9 rose through a dense sea mist that left trails of water droplets streaming across the windows. By the time the seatbelt sign was switched off we were riding high above a sea of white cloud through which the occasional snow-capped peak protruded, pink in the early sun. But something funny was going on above southern Italy that lovely morning; the seatbelt sign came on again as mysterious, conflicting currents began spilling across the sky, making the plane lurch and skid with such abandon that my neighbour eventually muttered 'Jesus!' and put his magazine down. When he glanced across to see how I was taking the punishment I asked if he worked in Brindisi.

He said, 'Could be.'

'With the military?'

'Why do you ask?'

'Just curiosity.'

'People who ask too many questions can land themselves in trouble.'

'What kind of trouble?'

'They can get arrested.'

I stared at him. '*Arrested*?'

'No problem. We have security guys at da Vinci. It just needs a word.'

'Blimey,' I said.

The jet began skipping like a flat stone on water, creaking each time it bounced. I hung on to my armrests, imagining myself making mailbags in Rome's piously named Queen of Heaven prison or, more likely, weaving straw bottle wrappings for the Italian chianti industry. Then some hidden force caught us under the tail and rushed us forward in a nose-down mode; adjustments were made

on the flight deck and we continued our headlong progress in a
nose-up mode instead. My neighbour's complexion, I noted, had
grown waxen.

'Goddam fucking aeroplanes,' he said, suddenly.

We now seemed to be following a trajectory like that described by
a motorcycle stunt rider leaping a row of buses. It ended with a
thump and a kind of sideways skid.

'I think I'm going to be sick,' he announced.

His forehead was beaded with perspiration and he began
swallowing convulsively.

'Arrest the pilot,' I said.

He went 'Uuurggh!' and, making a surprisingly loud noise for
someone with such a small ribcage, evacuated his breakfast into a
paper bag. The stench began to make me feel queasy too, while a
couple of middle-aged women across the aisle pulled faces and
passed each other an eau-de-cologne bottle, quickly and surreptitiously, like a hip flask.

Then, all at once, we were in calm air again, flying straight and
level. A steward, summoned by a peal of bells from the rear smoking
section, took the bag away while my neighbour lay back in his seat,
eyes closed, looking corpsed. I became aware of the bull mastiff
barking wildly down in the hold. Then the cloud thinned and
scattered and I gazed down at a prospect of stony hills etched with a
tracery of weathered tracks. Away to the right mist lay in the
hollows of the frozen mountains like pools of milk, to the left a high
solitary tower teetered on the lip of a precipice; no track led to the
tower, not even a bridle path for mules.

The wing-mounted speed brakes came up as we passed high
over a small, secret lake, round as a coin, the colour of jade. A
larger lake lay beyond, to which the woman across the aisle drew
her friend's attention; on its northern shore stood Castel Gondolfo,
where the Pope went to escape the heat of the Roman summer.
We descended over desolate, colourless country which gradually
softened, giving way to a sprawling new suburb and then, winding
away towards the sea, a corrugated green landscape of ancient
riverbeds, the grassy banks and bluffs turfed and planted with
orchards. These, I reckoned, were ghostly manifestations of the
Tiber, long ago sealed up by silt and now given over to the cultivation

of fruit. With Ostia and the Lido di Roma behind us we slid in over a large filling station and landed on a runway still puddled from yesterday's storm.

The target-type thrust reversers roared and we slowed near an abandoned farmhouse which stood, isolated and unremarked, in the middle of the airport. Its mullioned windows were smashed, but the tiles on the steeply pitched roof remained intact and a copse of quince trees still shaded the kitchen door. The DC9 taxied slowly by and parked in the vineyard or, perhaps, the acre where the dispossessed family had once harvested their olives. I said goodbye to my neighbour, still pale and angry with himself, and, down on the tarmac, watched the Philadelphia engineer and his son run to the hold and retrieve their bull mastiff. The boy released it and clipped a lead to its collar, ignoring the agitation of the baggage handlers who were afraid it would break loose and start chasing aeroplanes up and down the runways. The dog, barking joyously, peed against the DC9's nosewheel then sprang into the old green bus that had rattled up to fetch us back to the terminal.

I had three hours to kill before the 1115 departure of my TWA Boeing 727 to Athens. A notice on the unmanned check-in counter said 'Chiuso – Closed' and the clerk at a neighbouring desk knew nothing of any flight to Greece. Then I was joined by three solemn, patchouli-scented Turkish women in baggy trousers and shawls who carried brown paper parcels. Their presence was reassuring. By forming a queue we had somehow got our desk onstream; someone, eventually, would have to come and attend to us. I yawned and wished I was out among the cool green hills beside Lago Bracciano where, early in 1937, after Mussolini had countermanded his overflying ban, Imperial's C class Empire flying boats began calling on their way to Africa and Australia. A *Vogue* writer, travelling with all her expectations and priorities intact, had passed 'over the forests and the rich Campagna to Lake Bracciano where your machine comes to rest. You will spend the night in Rome, twenty miles away, and it is just as well to have an uncrushable lace dinner frock at hand, in case a party materializes.'

Before the lake was opened for traffic, water-based aircraft had operated from a spot neat Ostia, where the Tiber meets the sea, not too far from where we were now queuing. The present airport

sprawls over land reclaimed by the river after the Emperors
Claudius and Trajan had built an ambitious new port at its mouth;
interred somewhere below us were the venerable granite docks and
warehouses of Porto Claudio, the outer harbour, and Porto
Traiano, the hexagonal inner one, both steadily filled with riverine
silt until, eventually, they lay buried beneath a great flat plain – ideal
terrain for a major airfield. Work on the Aeroporto Roma-
Fiumicino (Leonardo da Vinci) commenced in 1951, after the
capital's original field, the Aeroporto Giovanni Battista Pastine, an
old airship station with a single perforated steel plate runway, was
no longer deemed a suitable gateway to the Eternal City.

Ninety minutes before our scheduled departure a plump Turk in
a purple cardigan came and took the women away. 'Dis ladeez go
Ankara,' he said accusingly when I told him we were waiting at the
Athens desk. The women gave me reproachful looks. Then a girl
with beautiful green eyes arrived and issued my boarding pass.

In the departure lounge a tall, skinny African in a cream robe and
skullcap stood with his face pressed to the window, gazing out at
the apron, his breath frosting the glass. As my flight was called a
massive shadow crept across me and I looked around to see the
gleaming white nose of a Japan Air Lines 747 slide up and halt a few
feet from my chair. The African grinned up at the pilots and clapped
his hands together. I left him, still applauding, and made my way to
Gate 34.

IV

Only seven of us assembled in the Gate 34 departure lounge, ready
to board the TWA 727 which had taxied up moments earlier,
rocking gently on its oleo-pneumatic shock-absorbers, painted and
polished like a new car. I remarked to the earnest young man at the
desk that he seemed to be having a slack day. He told me that the
TWA 747 from New York which normally connected with the 727
and invariably filled it (the 727 terminated at Tel Aviv) was running
late – so late, indeed, that the company's local Station Manager had

decided not to wait. 'You will have room to scratch your legs,' he added.

'You mean stretch.'

He nodded. 'Ah, yes, stretch not scratch which is for the itch,' he said.

Another 727 was approaching the ramp. It had a canary yellow tail with the word SUDAN painted on it and, as it disembarked a seemingly endless flood of white-robed passengers, the young man announced our flight in the ringing tones of a court usher. We straggled aboard, two giggling Greek couples travelling together, a bearded man with a guitar slung across his back like a rifle, and a tall, elegant girl wearing an ankle-length coat and a flat black Mexican riding hat.

We were welcomed at the 727's door by the two oldest flight attendants I have ever clapped eyes on. The stewardess was homely, comfortably plump and silver-haired, while her wrinkled male companion had the contented, easeful air of a senior citizen temporarily called away from his grandchildren and bowling green. 'Hi!' he beamed. 'This way, honey!' called the stewardess, who should have been carrying a purring tortoiseshell cat in her arms. I shared the rear smoking section with the girl in the Mexican hat; everyone else sat well forward, beside the blue and silver partition walling off the empty First Class section.

The trio of rear-mounted Pratt & Whitney turbofans started up. They had the discreet hum of engines fitted with full sound attenuation, and were barely audible as the steward cleared his throat and spoke over the passenger address system. 'Ahem, folks, we'd like you to pay attention to the lady demonstrating the life jacket up front here.' Everyone watched a smiling Grandma Moses slip the yellow vest over her head and fasten it adroitly, as though tying the strings of her apron before settling down to season the Thanksgiving turkey. We moved off past an Air India Super DC8 freighter discharging bundles of carpets and cages filled with tiny, brilliant birds and, out by the runway, the mournful little farmhouse with its shady trees and broken windows.

At the threshold of 34 Right, its high-intensity green lights barely visible in the thin, bright sun, the steward said, 'Ladies and gentlemen, we have been cleared for take-off at this time. Flight attendants please be seated.' The 727 soared out across a glaucous

grey sea as the hydraulics drove the retractable wing furniture back
into place (a firm called National Water Lift had helped manufacture the actuators) and, climbing hard, turned south and raced
through a bright sky towards Naples, Capri and Sorrento. The
western seaboard of Italy was scalloped and fringed with foam that,
from several miles up, looked like a layer of cream being stirred
sluggishly by the incoming waves.

The water seemed benign today, and I thought of Sir Samuel
Hoare, Secretary of State for Air, who had set out from Croydon in
1927 with his wife, the indomitable Lady Maud, to become the first
passengers to fly direct to India. They were sped on their way by a
telegram of good wishes from the King and a light-hearted reminder
from Stanley Baldwin, the Prime Minister, that the only other
Minister to have taken part in the opening of a new form of
transport had been 'Huskisson, the President of the Board of Trade,
who had been killed on the first journey of the Liverpool and
Manchester Railway'. But for an emotional moment passing over
his brother-in-law's villa at Cannes – 'the family came out to wave
their good wishes with their handkerchiefs' – the trip had been
uneventful. Then they set out across a dark and angry Mediterranean in their flimsy Imperial Airways Hercules with its wooden
spars and three radial air-cooled Bristol Jupiter engines, carrying
emergency flotation devices like 'Major Evans's patent rubber
boots and waistcoats to escape death by drowning', anxiously
seeking the chain of Royal Navy destroyers dispatched by their
chum the First Lord of the Admiralty to keep an eye on them. Sir
Samuel found the ships on station, steaming hard to maintain their
headings in a heavy sea. 'As we passed over them we exchanged
messages of greeting, and I thanked them for the care with which
they were looking after us. One of them replied, "You may think
that it is bumpy up there, but it is nothing to what it is down here,"
and, as I saw the Destroyer jumping about like a pea on a drum, I
fully agreed with the Captain's observation.'

I sat back, loosened my seat belt and lit a Sumatran cheroot. The
girl in the Mexican hat, seated across the cabin, glanced over and
caught my eye. Then she rose and came towards me. 'Please, have
you a match?' she asked.

'Of course,' I said.

She fumbled in her leather handbag and produced a small, filigreed silver box from which she extracted a plump cigarette with a twist at either end. She placed it in her mouth while I held a flame to it. What I was lighting, I realized, was a joint. She inhaled deeply, closed her eyes for a moment then opened them again. 'Can I sit with you for a bit?'

The flight attendants, I noted, were all forward, safely removed from the dense and sweetish clouds that billowed around our heads. I turned the air blowers on full. 'If you like.'

'It's because of your cigar,' she told me, disarmingly. 'Your smoke is strong enough to cover the smell. My name is Elena,' she added, transferring the joint to her left hand and holding out the right. She had a paratrooper's grip but the serene, sculpted features of a Lippi angel. 'You are staying in Athens?'

'Tonight I'm staying in Cairo,' I said.

She looked momentarily nonplussed. 'Oh, *merde*, am I on the wrong plane again?'

'No,' I stared at her. 'What do you mean, again?'

'Last summer in Calcutta there was a mix-up. Two planes were boarding at the same time, in the lounge there was pandemonium, I could not understand the announcements, and I found myself on the flight for Chittagong instead of Katmandu. At Chittagong I had a cup of tea and talked to a Swedish missionary, who told me there was a civil war going on. He said there was shooting in the streets. Then I flew back to Calcutta and had to wait another day until I could catch the next Katmandu plane. At my own expense. The Indians are *hopeless*.'

The elderly steward was making his way down the aisle, his demeanour stern. Elena popped her joint into the ashtray and closed the lid as he halted by our seats. 'Pardon me,' he said, 'but we have a rule about cigars? They're not permitted in the cabin.'

'It's only a very small cigar,' I pointed out.

He stared at me, sniffing the air and looking puzzled. He looked hard at the cigar, and then at me and Elena. But all he said was, 'Sir, I'm sorry but, uh, you're gonna have to put that cigar out again.'

I asked for a Bloody Mary. He went forward to fetch it, still frowning. Elena did not want a drink. Agitatedly she said, 'Did he guess? Could he tell them at Athens?'

I said the steward probably thought she was smoking a Turkish cigarette.

'If there is trouble I would call my father,' she mused, 'but I think just now he is with my uncle, shooting ducks near Salonika.'

The incident had unnerved her, and she decided to lie low in her own seat; before leaving me she carefully retrieved the remains of the joint from the ashtray and popped it back into her little silver casket.

The Bloody Mary was delicious, properly mixed and flavoured – economy passengers on most airlines must make do with a vodka miniature summarily tipped into a ration of tomato juice – and, as I sipped it, I glanced through *Ambassador*, the TWA inflight magazine, a slick publication containing so little of interest that I was driven to pick up the air sick bag instead. 'For Motion Discomfort' it announced. There was a gin rummy card printed on one side and, on the other, a message from the Family Film Service, an enterprise with addresses in New York, Chicago, Atlanta, Kansas City and San Franscico. 'Mail your film in this bag and SAVE ON COLOUR PRINTS!' it urged. Then a second, younger stewardess brought lunch, a tray containing a selection of cold meats, salad, cake and coffee. Wine was neither served nor offered.

Midway through the meal we turned east over Catanzaro near the toe of Italy, on a direct course for Athens. A range of snowy mountains drifted by below and, close to the coast and the warm waters of the Adriatic, a small glacier, the grey ice ridged and faintly mottled, like spruce bark. The younger stewardess fetched my tray and, after filling out my Greek Arrival Card, I went back to the aft galley to talk to her. She had short brown hair and an open smile, and she told me that this was TWA's only international 727 service. (It was also the one which, 18 months later, would seize the world's attention when it was highjacked between Athens and Rome by particularly brutal Palestinian terrorists.) 'For the 727 flight deck crews it's their one chance of working abroad,' she said. 'We flight attendants get assigned to the whole fleet, including the 747s, so we get plenty of foreign travel, but for the pilots who spend their time flying short-haul around America, this posting is really something. A month based in Tel Aviv! They work hard, four days a week with four take-offs and landings a day – we do the round trip

Tel Aviv-Athens-Rome- Athens-Tel Aviv – but nobody's complaining and, back home, pilots are queuing up for it. My husband flies 727s for the company out of San Francisco, and he'd give his pension rights for a month on this run.'

Grandma Moses came padding down the aisle. 'The chicken's in the oven for Tel Aviv?' she demanded.

'Sure,' said her companion.

I asked the older woman how she was enjoying the flight.

'Well,' she said reflectively, 'this is actually my first time on a 727 in 16 years. All that time I've been on the wide-bodies. Working on this aeroplane is really going back to basics but the funny thing is, you don't have to think. Your hands just go out automatically, and everything is right there, exactly where it always used to be.'

Midway across the Straits of Otranto the earth became obscured by a layer of cloud the colour and texture of gunsmoke. We were passing close to Corfu where, in August 1932, the Prince of Wales and Prince George had rejoined the Mediterranean fleet aboard the Imperial flying boat *Satyrus* out of Brindisi, arriving, the *Gazette* announced, 'just after the moon had risen, so that before alighting the Royal travellers had a magnificent moonlit view of the Fleet lying at anchor'. Now, using dead-reckoning, I judged that we crossed the Greek coast just south of the Albanian border, began our descent near the Pass of Thermopylae and put our spoilers out over Parnassus. Then, clipping the eastern end of the Gulf of Corinth, we headed into Athens and a very interesting storm. The ancient Greeks believed that eight classic winds ventilated their country and now we seemed to be passing through the confluence of several, boisterous as mountain streams, which made the Boeing creak like an old wooden ship. As it began bounding across the sky I thought wistfully of the summer breeze called the Meltemi which, says Herodotus, blows from 'the Rising of the Dog Star' until autumn and, on many balmy evenings, had cooled my family and I as we sat and gossiped over glasses of Demestica during our Greek island holidays.

Grandma Moses, hurrying aft, found herself made momentarily weightless as the 727 fell down a mineshaft. Suspended several inches above the floor she began rotating slowly on her axis, arms extended, until the plane rose to meet her with a force that made her tumble into the seat beside me, looking grim. 'Could you spare me a cigarette?' she asked through clenched teeth. 'I guess I'm not used to this kind of crappiola any more.'

'All I've got are some little cigars,' I said.

'They'll do just fine.'

I handed her one and lit it. She inhaled deeply, gave a single barking cough and closed her eyes. The 727 was now steeple-chasing, each leap so violent that the G-forces made our limbs seem as heavy as marble. Dropping, we hit an unyielding shoulder of wind with a bang that made the glasses in the galley chime wildly and, glancing across at Elena, who sat with her hat tipped over her eyes, I recalled Mr W. D. H. McCullough's account of his Athens leg in 1933, aboard a Scipio with Captain Kettle in command. 'The flight from Brindisi to Athens was most romantic,' he wrote. 'We flew at 2,500 feet over an exquisitely blue sea and down the coast of Italy to Corfu, and then over to Greece and along the Gulf of Corinth to Piraeus, which is the harbour for Athens. The islands and coast are wild and rocky. Part of the time we flew at over 5,000 feet to avoid the bumps due to the hot air rising from the mountains, and even from this height some of the inland peaks towered far above us. We made a magnificent landing at Piraeus. Apart from the sound of the swish of the water on the boat, it was impossible to tell that we had touched the surface of the sea.' (The Scipios actually came down a couple of miles east of Piraeus, opposite the racecourse at Phaleron Bay where Imperial shared the seaplane station – built on the gently shelving beach from which Theseus had sailed for Crete – with the Societa Aero-Espresso Italiana, who called there on their twice-weekly service between Brindisi and Istanbul.)

Flaps sprouted along the 727's wings and the undercarriage rumbled down. On a clear day the Athens approach is a memorable one, the plane passing over the bays and townships of Vouliagmeni and Glifadha towards an airport set on a narrow strip of land between the sea and the high, stony Hymettos hills, famous for their marble and honey (made, since classical times, from juniper, thyme, sage, mint, lavender and terebinth), but we descended blindly through rushing black cloud, bouncing like a cannonball rolling down a stairway. Then, with the Pratt & Whitneys shrieking, the earth suddenly swam back into focus. We banked low over a peaceful suburban street, glimpsed a man washing a red car and skimmed in past the lights of the Visual Approach Slope Indicator to land, despite the blustery conditions, as cleanly as a gull. Grandma Moses's sigh was audible even above the roar of reverse thrust. 'My God,' she said. 'Wasn't that something?'

We taxied towards the apron. Her younger colleague, seated behind us, said, 'Well, he really held it steady back there.' It had seemed distinctly unsteady back there to me, and I said so, but she contradicted me with the spirit of a pilot's wife who knew what the guys up front had to contend with. As we prepared to disembark the steward said, 'Hang on to your hats, folks. It's kinda blowy out here.'

A baby armoured car sat by the entrance of the elegant East Terminal, designed by Eero Saarinen for the use of the foreign airlines. (Olympic, Greece's national carrier, was based at the decrepit West Terminal by the coast road.) Through the vehicle's tiny slit window I saw a match flare and smoke drift up from the open turret. I caught a taxi into Athens and the Hotel Grande Bretagne where the Imperial passengers had spent the night on route from Italy to Egypt. The driver, listening intently to a radio phone-in, sped through jerry-built suburbs which incorporated the birthplace of Thucydides – called by Macaulay 'the greatest historian that ever lived' – and, further on, the coastal pumping station which supplies salt water for the Athens Fire Brigade.

The Grande Bretagne stands in Constitution Square, planted with orange trees and set beneath the pale rock of the Acropolis from which a huge blue and white Greek flag streamed in one of the eight ancient winds. I entered a hangar-sized lobby, walled and floored in polished marble and hung with a giant tapestry. A water-filled bowl on the reception desk had five prize pink roses floating in it. I asked to speak to the press officer and was told she was still at lunch. Would I care to wait? There were groups of antique tables and brocade-covered chairs in the lobby, so I sat down and had a pot of tea and a plate of sweet baklava honey cake. I asked the elderly waiter if the cake was made from Hymettos honey. He looked surprised. 'But of course,' he said.

Mrs Rena Tobler turned out to be a warm, funny, vivacious lady who, though I had turned up without any prior notice or warning, still welcomed me and whisked me upstairs to her office. 'You look tired,' she announced, examining me with her head cocked to one side. 'For you I am prescribing a large brandy.'

It did the trick, all right, lifting my spirits perceptibly as Mrs Tobler told me the hotel had been founded by a chef named Eustace Lampsa. 'Lampsa gained such fame and fortune while working in Paris – he once cooked a pilaf which moved the visiting Shah of Persia to tears – that, in 1872, he was able to come home and buy a great house in the centre of Athens. He turned the house into this hotel (though it has since been rebuilt and modernised) and handed it on to his son-in-law, Theodore Petracopoulos. Petracopoulos was a journalist and lawyer of such brilliance and influence that, when he died in 1963, the Prime Minister *and* the Leader of the Opposition walked side-by-side behind his cortège. And that, let me tell you, was a thing unique in our history.'

The Grande Bretagne has always had its share of guests with household names and unlisted telephone numbers. 'The Rockefellers, the Kennedys and the Krupps have all stayed here,' said Mrs Tobler. 'Archbishop Makarios made speeches to the people of Athens from his balcony on the second floor. The Grand Duchess Helena of Russia lived and died at the hotel. When Mary Pickford stayed she had an extra room just for her shoes. In my time Tito, Indira Gandhi and Yasser Arafat have stayed – Arafat was escorted everywhere by men who held a bullet-proof curtain around him, very disconcerting for other guests who met him in the lift. During the war the Germans set up their headquarters in the hotel. We had Goering, Himmler and Rommel – even Hitler, who turned up on a flying visit. Then the British made it *their* headquarters and we saw people like Harold Macmillan and Anthony Eden. Churchill was expected during our Communist troubles but, just before his arrival, a ton of dynamite was discovered in the sewers under the hotel. The Marxists were planning to blow him – and us – sky-high. So we didn't see him until peace was restored, when he called in for tea with Aristotle Onassis.'

I asked about the Imperial passengers. 'We still get letters, often written in beautiful copperplate, from old English travellers who say they stayed here while flying to India in the 1930s. Until recently we had some airline crews, but now we get just the occasional chief pilot who sneaks away from the Hilton or Astir Palace to come and spend the night with us.'

Mr McCullough, disembarking from his Scorpio, had been much taken by the Grande Bretagne. 'We stayed in the most luxurious hotel in the city,' he wrote, 'and I had a magnificent apartment, complete with private bathroom, and all in white tiles. Most interesting of all, I had a mosquito net. One feels like a piece of cheese in a meat safe. On a hot night it is not particularly comfortable. I should say that, on the whole, the net caused rather more discomfort to me than to the mosquitoes.'

It was time to return to the airport. Mrs Tobler asked where I was staying in Cairo. 'Shepheard's,' I said. She beamed. 'Our Food and Beverages Manager once worked there. You must come and meet him.' She steered me into a neighbouring office where a plump old man sat smiling over a large desk. 'I will send them a telex, asking them to keep a special eye on you,' he promised. 'A nice room overlooking the Nile. They know me there. It will be done.'

I thanked him. We shook hands and, as Mrs Tobler took me to the lift, she said, 'He began his career working as a kitchen boy for King Farouk. Some of the finest chefs and *maîtres d'hôtel* in the world started off that way. Farouk was fanatical about his food, demanding the very highest standards, headhunting anyone of talent or promise he heard about – even kitchen boys. Today the old Farouk men are an elite in the hotel trade. I suppose they would be his only legacy.'

2

FLYING THE
FURROW

From Athens to Muscat

I

The ramshackle West Terminal beside the coast road, home base of Olympic Airways, was suffused with a heavy late afternoon somnolence. A bored woman wordlessly handed me a boarding pass and I went through to the departure lounge, a sprawling, airless annexe with an unswept floor and scuffed, dirty seats, like the outpatients' waiting room of a run-down provincial hospital. But for a couple of hundred Egyptians sitting huddled together in the vicinity of Gate 1, it was doing little business. I looked at them and knew instinctively it was with this mob that my immediate destiny lay. They were mostly men, in rumpled jellabas, or cheap shirts and trousers and, though they had the sleepy, introspective looks of people mentally somewhere else, a miasma of anxiety hung over their heads.

I took a seat near one of the women. She was spectacularly beautiful, slim and graceful with flawless coppery skin and eyes the colour of ferns. A rag was knotted about her lovely head, but on her it looked as elegant as a lace mantilla. Her husband lounged nearby, unshaven, with bony features; noting the way I was gazing at his wife, he suddenly leered at me, baring an incomplete set of mottled brown teeth. Then he pulled up a dusty foot and absently began breaking off his horny yellow toenails, cracking them like nuts. The air of somnolence deepened. I glanced at my watch. Eighty minutes to take-off. I yawned. Outside, a KLM 747 landed, chased in by a little Olympic 737 that gave a high, exuberant bounce as it touched down.

I was falling into the torpor common to people waiting for aeroplanes, pulse running slow but the senses alert for information, when the public address system crackled into life and delivered a brief, incomprehensible message. I thought it mentioned my name, but instantly dismissed the idea as ridiculous. Only one word came through clearly – Cairo – and it produced an instant and violent response. There was a panicky gabble of voices as the Egyptians grabbed their belongings, sprang to their feet and, heaving furiously, formed themselves into a noisy, writhing queue. I stared at them. There were no planes on the tarmac and no officials at the gate, but their certainty that none of this mattered was so feverishly contagious that, after a moment, I got up too and sheepishly joined the back of the line.

We all stood expectantly, craning forward, squashed together and gazing intently at an empty apron. Then, all at once, the queue began to disintegrate from the front. People were breaking ranks and scurrying back to their seats, and I spotted a burly, tough-looking Greek Orthodox priest moving up the line, speaking rapidly in Arabic as he came. 'It was a false alarm,' he said to me in English. 'The flight is not yet. There was confusion. The woman was asking for someone. That is all.'

I thanked him. He, presumably, was bound for Cairo also? He nodded his heavy, bearded head and said yes, but only in transit. His eventual destination was to be Santa Katerina, the ancient Sinai monastery nestling directly beneath the towering rocky pinnacle from which Moses had descended with his tablets of stone. 'At Cairo in the morning I catch a Fokker Friendship of Air Sinai,' he said. 'There is a little airport in the mountains for the pilgrims, the Mount Sinai airfield, so dangerous they say the pilot and the pilgrims pray together before the Fokker goes to land.'

I returned to my seat. The beautiful woman lazily fanned herself with an Egyptian passport while her husband stolidly resumed the demolition of his toenails. Then, moments later, there was a further announcement on the public address system, understandable this time, asking for Mizzda Frehta, passenger on flight OA 325 to Cairo; I was asked to report to the desk at Gate Number 6.

A dark-haired girl in a red velvet dress pointed to a door and said it led to the First Class Lounge. Would I care to enter and help myself to a drink? I was through in a flash, recalling gratefully that, back in London, I had called the Olympic office and asked to visit the flight deck of their A300 during the Cairo leg; this unexpected bonus seemed to indicate that my request had been approved.

The lounge was furnished with deep leather armchairs. There were carpets on the marble floor and, on the wall, a photograph of the late Aristotle Onassis, the founder of Olympic, beaming in a heavy silver frame. Two elegant, white-haired American businessmen, perhaps bankers, were drinking bourbon in the corner. Near my chair a giant black man sat smoking in a pool of shadow. A pack of Marlboros lay on the table before him, his massive hands fiddled restlessly with an expensive gold lighter and, from time to time, he tapped his cigarette into a brass ashtray fashioned like a ship's porthole. Then, suddenly, he stood and said, 'Pardon me, but are you goin' to Heraklion, by any chance? On de, ah, Olympic Airwez?'

I stared at him. The voice, a rumbling basso profundo, seemed familiar, and so, vaguely, did the face; if he was the person I thought he was, though, it was now padded and misshapen with fat, the bright, restless eyes looking out mournfully from a wasteland of bulging flesh. He wore a pricey leather coat, shiny as a new shoe, and a ring set with a diamond the size of a lima bean.

'No,' I said, 'Cairo.'

He grunted, stood and walked out. The two Americans abruptly sat up straight. 'Wasn't that Idi Amin?' one of them asked.

'I'm not sure,' I said, going to the door and looking after him. He was plodding away through the departure lounge looking, in his gleaming coat, like a wet hippo.

'Do you know the name of that man?' I asked the dark-haired girl.

'I have no name,' she said.

I went back inside. 'Could be him,' I said to the Americans.

'Well, I'll be damned,' said one. 'I heard the son of a bitch was in Libya.'

'I heard Morocco,' said his friend. 'Or maybe it was the Saudis who took him in.'

I worked on my notes until the girl from the desk bundled us into a minibus. The Cairo Airbus was boarding. We hurried up the front steps, my companions turning left into the shadowy tranquillity of First Class while I was directed into the Economy cabin where 300 shouting, laughing Egyptians were having a party. The anxiety so evident ashore had now vanished. Their mood was one of happiness and elation. They had broken out their duty-free bottles and were wandering around, offering each other drinks and proposing toasts. Two were smoking. As I made my way aft I was hailed and greeted and clapped on the back. The only people not having a terrific time were the cabin crew. They rushed about distractedly, ordering the cigarettes to be extinguished, the liquor put away, begging everyone to sit down. A stewardess with a silk shawl about her shoulders complained, 'Already I am exhausted and the plane has moved not one centimetre.' She showed me to my seat, putting me by the emergency exit and a red sign on the bulkhead saying OPEN ANOIKTH. The man across the aisle reached over and patted my hand. 'Good boy!' he cried.

The engines started. Everyone sat. We took off. As the undercarriage thumped back into place everyone stood up again. Cigarettes were lit, flashbulbs popped and the bottles retrieved as we climbed steeply away out of Athens with the Fasten Seat Belts No Smoking signs brightly illuminated. The steward slumped in the jump seat opposite me said grimly, 'You just cannot communicate with these people. They are crazy.'

'Is the flight always this full?' I asked.

'Always,' he said. 'For us it is a punishment.'

The signs were switched off and he departed, gloomily, to see about dinner. The man across the aisle offered me a swig of *crème-de-menthe*. By pooling our knowledge of each other's languages we came up with a vocabulary sufficient to establish that he had been working for a builder near Corinth, and that Greek women were more obliging than Egyptian women, but much uglier.

The flight attendants distributed trays containing cold meat, potato salad, cake and a paper slip printed with the legend 'This meal does not contain pork' in English, French, German and Arabic. I found it spectacularly unappetising, but my friend tucked in with gusto, smacking his lips and washing it down with copious draughts of *crème-de-menthe*. The engines were making odd surging noises, like turbines being tripped. I thought of Mr McCullough who had earnestly noted, at about this stage in his journey, that 'There is something quite uncanny about flying over the Isles of Greece. Some day I suppose people will be quite blasé about it, but to anyone with any imagination the idea of flying over the very cradle of the history of the human race at 100 miles an hour is simply staggering.'

According to my calculations we were now closing fast on Crete where, if they had been compromised by headwinds, the flying boat skippers could stop for extra fuel at Mirabella Bay, notorious in aviation circles for its treacherously clear water. Incoming pilots tended to see it only seconds before the instant of impact and, after several dangerously heavy landings, Imperial's engineers were asked urgently to devise equipment that would give a true indication of altitude. What they came up with were net containers secured to each wingtip and filled with pingpong balls. At the appropriate moment the nets were released and the balls bouncing across the limpid surface gave the pilot his crucial visual reference. Once down, the boats taxied up the MV *Imperia*, a Company yacht moored in the bay to fuel and service the aircraft. A trim, well-found little vessel, she was commanded by Captain Francis Grant Pool, whose duties included issuing weather reports to passing pilots on his radio, and welcoming arriving passengers aboard for lunch. Shortly before the German invasion the authorities moved his ship to Port Said, but, fluent in the Cretan dialect, he elected to stay on. After the defeat of the Commonwealth forces, disguised as a peasant, he set about locating stranded troops and smuggling them off the island under the noses of the enemy. He saved so many lives that, at the end of the war, he was given the DSO and the DSC, together with the post of British Consul in the town of Volas where, contentedly, he lived out the rest of his days. (As for the *Imperia*, after seeing service off Akaba and Djerba she was sold to two British officers in 1946 and then, in one of the small, uncelebrated mysteries of the sea, found drifting in the Mediterranean with no one aboard.)

Faintly, above the roar of the party, I heard a voice on the passenger address system asking me to report to the flight deck. I made my way forward, knocked and went in. Captain Alexander Demakos was a thickset man with a grey beard and a gruff, master-mariner's voice. 'You are Alexander?' he said, shaking hands. 'Me also. That name makes you half Greek. Sit down. You will stay with us for the landing, I hope.'

I said I would like that very much. He nodded, lit a Winston and puffed at it expansively. The co-pilot, who was handsome and very young, said, 'Excuse me, Mr Alexander, but have you left a bag back there?'

'Yes,' I said.

The two pilots glanced at each other. 'To be on the safe side,' the co-pilot said slowly, 'I think. . .'

'Our passengers tonight . . . ' murmured Captain Demakos.

I went aft and fetched my bag. My neighbour noted what I was doing, winked and saluted me with his bottle. Back on the flight deck I was strapping on my safety harness when Captain Demakos suddenly pointed forward. 'Cairo!' he said. I peered through the darkness and saw a faint iridescent smudge far away, barely distinguishable from the constellation of stars strung across the horizon. It was marvellously quiet. We rode serenely over the desert, listening to the faint whisper of air hissing past the nose, cosy in the glow of the instruments, the crew exchanging the occasional word but keeping their voices low, as though reluctant to break the spell.

The winking navigation beacon of a 747 passed below us and slid away to the west, its two decks awash with light, gaudy as a boulevard. On the radio a harassed Egyptian controller ordered a drawling Indian to maintain his heading and descend to 8,000 feet. I asked Captain Demakos what Cairo ATC was like and he shrugged. 'Not so wonderful. Sometimes their radio goes. We hear nothing, we get no instructions, and we have to circle the city watching out for other aircraft until they come back on the air again. And I can tell you, Alexander, that is no joke.'

The city drew closer, a sprawling, radiant carpet that soon filled the windscreen. We seemed suspended above it, barely moving, as the young co-pilot pointed out the runway far ahead and the line of high intensity lights running through the suburbs that told us we were on course. He was going to make the landing. He had been lounging with his right foot propped comfortably on a ledge but now, as we began tracking along the lights, he drove his electrically powered chair forward and prepared to take charge.

Cairo, however, had mislaid us. An agitated voice said, 'Olympic 325, are you outbound or inbound?'

Captain Demakos sighed. 'Inbound, Cairo.'

'You are number 2,' said Cairo. 'In the landing pattern Number 2, 325.'

'Number 2, Cairo.'

The co-pilot, sitting bolt upright, made some small movements of the control column, getting the feel of it, while his companions pressed switches and muffled the bleeps of the alarm systems. Captain Demakos attended to the flap settings and, by sliding down a tiny lever with a fingertip, lowered the massive hydraulically retractable landing gear.

We whistled in sedately, the crimson threshold lights rising to meet us, the engines murmuring contentedly away behind. But the Airbus struck Egyptian soil with such violence that it seemed to buckle at the knees. Back in the First Class galley the glass and china made a noise like crates of milk bottles being dropped. The co-pilot swore softly. Captain Demakos, his face stony, said nothing. The engineer applied reverse thrust as the co-pilot, looking pale and anguished, applied his pneumatic disc brakes. Out on the wings the lift-dumpers rose like sails. We slowed quickly.

'Olympic 325, go left,' said Cairo.

'Left?' said Captain Demakos, who had grabbed the steering bar. 'Left where?' He gazed around him like a bewildered motorist.

The co-pilot produced his Cairo taxi-chart. 'Left just here,' he said. We followed a line of blue lights, passing a parked Egyptair 747 and a Lufthansa Airbus, both dark and closed down for the night, then halted and switched off the engines. The air of embarrassment on the flight deck was palpable. The co-pilot turned to me, his handsome young face set and stern with mortification. 'There was a slight ground mist,' he said. 'Cairo didn't tell me. This mist affected my judgement. It, uh, caught me on the hop.'

He glanced at Captain Demakos for support, but Captain Demakos said not a word. Instead, he picked up his checklist and cleared his throat. He and the engineer began running through the post-shutdown sequence; the co-pilot, for whom I felt very sorry, joined wanly in the chant, like a chorister with a bad cold.

I murmured my farewells and slipped away. The exhausted flight attendants were sitting slumped in the empty First Class cabin. One advised me to start running as soon as the bus reached the terminal. 'If you are not near the front of the queue for Immigration you will be here all night.'

I heeded her advice but, once off the bus, was effortlessly overtaken by the two grey-haired American bankers from the Athens Olympic lounge, going like the wind. I saw them halt briefly at a cage marked Banque Misr, shove dollar bills through and scoop up the bundles of Egyptian pounds they got in return before sprinting on to the Immigration desk. Their passports stamped, the Old Cairo Hands had passed Customs and vanished into the cool desert night before I even arrived at the barrier. The official told me to go and change some money. 'Then I will let you in,' he promised.

I took my traveller's cheques to the three youths at the Banque Misr and said I wished to change $100. They smelled of violets and said it wasn't enough. The law specified that I must change at least $150. I pointed out that I was only staying one night; what would I want with so much local currency?

The first said, 'I could spend so much before morning.'

His companions laughed. 'Easy,' they confirmed.

I changed $150. The Passport Officer smiled and said 'Welcome!' as he waved me into Egypt. I boarded a veteran, rust-pitted Mercedes taxi but, before it moved off, a policeman clasping a Kalashnikov submachine gun yanked open the driver's door and interrogated him in a high, hectoring voice. Then he walked around the car and stuck his head through my window. 'Where are you going?' he asked.

'Shepheard's.'

He passed me a tattered exercise book. 'Sign, please. Name, passport number, destination. It is for your protection. If you don't arrive there we will start with this man.'

At the taxi rank exit there was a guardpost manned by another armed cop who, when we paused, reached down with a smile of great sweetness and handed the driver some cardamon seeds. As we rattled off he cracked them between his teeth, filling the cab with the smell of liquorice. We travelled at high speed, reaching the Main Station after 30 minutes and then, with the tombs of Caliphs away to the left, arriving moments later at Shepheard's on the Kornish El

Nil. Outside the hotel a gang of weary, sweating men were digging up the road. 'How much?' I asked the driver.

'You decide.'

'Four pounds?'

He gave a small, emphatic shake of the head.

'Five?'

He sighed and shook his head again. '*You decide.*'

I decided on seven. He drove away slowly, busted exhaust booming like a tractor, as I clambered over broken paving stones and entered a dimly lit lobby. I was welcomed by a portly, peak-capped concierge who looked like an engine driver. Two haughty men in gorgeous peacock blue robes took me to my room in a rickety lift. They drew the curtains and beckoned me over to observe the Nile. Three feluccas were beached beneath my window. A line of coloured lights on the far bank glittered in the dark water, its surface etched with countless small whorls and broken, here and there, by driftwood, the detritus of the world's longest river, carried perhaps all the way from Nubia.

I went downstairs for a drink. As I closed my door the heavy brass room number fell off. I handed it to the receptionist, who seemed unsurprised. 'Ah, yes,' he said. I walked past a souvenir stall called Big Shop and into the bar where another man in a blue robe gave me an unlabelled bottle of Stella Export beer and a dish of plump pink peanuts covered with giant salt crystals that glittered in the lamplight. Two Dutchmen sat yawning at a nearby table. Beyond them, through a kind of trellis, a pretty girl was singing 'Fever' to an audience of several dozen smartly turned out young Egyptians.

This was not the real Shepheard's, and it showed. Though it had been accorded De Luxe Five Star status by the government (which owned it) it was a solemn, seedy place with an air of mournfulness so pervasive that it seemed to seep out of the masonry. The original hotel, once the palace of Alfi Bey in Ezbekieh Gardens, was burnt down on 26 January 1952 by a mob protesting against the corruption of the Farouk regime. They incinerated much of European Cairo that day, starting after breakfast, working their way methodically downtown and reaching Shepheard's during the post-luncheon siesta. A dozen men stormed up the front steps to the famous terrace, erected a pyre of wicker furniture, doused it with petrol and tossed in a match. The old place, bone dry after decades of roasting under the Egyptian sun, went up like an oil well. Farouk, giving a banquet at the Abdin Palace, watched the blaze from a balcony then strolled back inside to eat his pudding; he did nothing to halt the anarchy and neither did the Prime Minister, who was visiting his manicurist. Six months later Farouk abdicated and Gamal Abdel Nasser assumed control of the country.

To the Egyptians the burning of Shepheard's was symbolic. It had long been the glittering epicentre of British social life in Cairo, and stood for everything they most detested about the arrogant Anglo-Saxons who had effectively ruled and plundered their country since 1882. But to the Imperial passengers it was just another jolly nightstop. In August 1934 Mrs Joy Packer, an Imperial passenger, writing in the *Cape Argus*, described a night stop at Shepheard's. 'The wise retired for a few hours' rest as we were to leave the aerodrome at 2 a.m. I was not wise, but enjoyed myself at the Kit Kat cabaret instead and saw dusky smooth-faced Egyptians rocking with laughter at the buffooneries of a French clown. Afterwards one danced. The professional partners were platinum blondes, who sipped synthetic champagne.'

Mindful of my own early departure I said goodnight to the barman, who was murmuring into the ear of a plump male customer wearing blusher and eye-liner, and took the rickety lift back to my room. After looking at the Nile and noting that its aroma here was a confection of petrol fumes, stale air and the breath and proximity of 12 to 15 million Cairenes – no one has the precise population figures – I got into bed and fell asleep. Later I was awakened by a series of gunshots from outside my door. I swung it open and almost received a hammer blow in the middle of my forehead. A blue-robed man was nailing back my room number. He beamed at me. 'Hullo, mister!' he said. 'So sorry to disturb.' He banged three more times, like Black Rod at the door of the House of Commons, then padded slowly away. Out on the river I thought I could hear bullfrogs croaking.

II

Imperial had gone from Athens to Alexandria, a sector not appearing in today's airline schedules. They dictate that Alexandria can only be reached from Cairo and, at 6 a.m., I joined the dozen passengers congregrated sleepily in an annexe off the main airport concourse. It was Friday, the Muslim Sabbath, and we were mostly foreigners. A small, birdlike man cried 'Alex!' and directed us to a counter where a couple of laughing wisecracking security officers delved into our bags like boisterous kids at a lucky dip. Then we were led out to a gleaming little Fokker Friendship with the words Air Sinai painted on the fuselage. I thought of the priest flying to his desert monastery this same morning, and asked the small official whether the Fokker would be working the Santa Katarina pilgrim run after its return from Alexandria. He said, 'If God wills it.' We stooped to board the Dutch-built Friendship as, impatiently, the pilot started up his two Rolls-Royce Dart turbo-props with their high ascending whine; he took us past a parked Dakota of Pyramid Airlines and along a taxiway with blown sand heaped along its verges. The first Imperial planes had used the old airport at Heliopolis, the British base from which RAF pilots began operating the legendary Desert Air Mail Route to Baghdad in 1921; now a desirable garden suburb on the road into town, it was said to be the site of the Holy Family's resting place during their flight into Egypt. The present airport, built by the United States government during the Second World War (they called it Payne Field), was handed over to the Egyptians in 1946 and renamed – briefly – Farouk Airport. Since then it has been extensively modernised and enlarged and now occupies 3,000 acres of undulating desert terrain; as we hummed out to Runway 23 Left we passed dunes high enough to obscure the view of its lofty, mosquelike control tower.

After take-off the steward, a grave young man who had made impeccable flight announcements in three languages, served tepid orange squash in plastic cups. We rose over neat green fields that reminded me of Shropshire, rich agricultural land made fertile by the Nile which was now gleaming dully beneath us. The early sun filled the sky with a wonderful limpid, lemony light. Across the aisle the steward sat gazing out the window and singing to himself in a soft, deep voice.

The river began to twist and loop, splitting into strands like frayed rope and then coming together again. Boats drifted on the water like leaves. On the bends there were sandbanks, pale grey and smooth as soapstone. And all along its length ditches and channels had been dug to irrigate the grain, cotton and vegetables that thrive in the rich delta mud. Fingers of shadow indicated the presence of windbreaks, rows of trees planted to keep the sand at bay. The desert commenced abruptly on the western bank, stretching away towards the Libyan border and a glassy blue horizon. Here and there, in the stony wilderness, there were vivid green squares of cabbages, sorghum and lettuces, looking like grass tennis courts. Sometimes the desert was mysteriously pitted with indentations which had the luminous, scalloped appearance of inverted oyster shells.

Ten minutes from touchdown we saw prosperous little settlements built from pale mudbrick and I thought of Sir Samuel Hoare passing hereabouts 'first over a brown desert speckled with the darker patches upon which the Moslem tribes grow rain-fed barley for British brewers, and then proceeding steadily to the great city of Alexandria that lies in a crescent between the sea and a chain of lakes . . . The aerodrome at Aboukir looked like Epsom Downs on Derby Day. There were rows of motors, crowds of spectators, amongst them my sister and nephew, and a general aspect of excitement and curiosity.'

Our own arrival was celebrated only by a brief ripple of lights coming from the vegetable gardens below. The steward shrugged. 'Down in the fields they are flashing mirrors at us. They are mischievous small boys who are trying to dazzle Mr Ibrahim, the pilot.'

Mr Ibrahim, unconcerned, made a perfect landing at El Nouzha airport, a sleepy little tree-ringed field which, apart from a brief seasonal surge of Haj pilgrim traffic to Jeddah, handled only two scheduled flights a day: the morning and evening Friendship services from Cairo. We disembarked and wandered through the small domed terminal. It was fashioned from reddish stone and there were rushes growing beyond the windows. A minibus with lace curtains took us through handsome, leafy suburbs into the town proper, a graceless perspective of narrow streets and grimy tenement buildings which bore no resemblence whatsoever to the magical, decadent place evoked by Lawrence Durrell in *The Alexandria Quartet*, his unforgettable celebration of the city and its people.

The minibus stopped outside the Egyptair office in Saad Zaghoul Square; empty of customers on a Sabbath morning, the office was having its floor mopped by two weary old women with plastic pails who grumbled gently as they worked. I asked the minibus driver to direct me to the Cecil Hotel. He gestured across the deserted square; the Cecil, he said, raising his voice as an ancient double-decker tram clattered by, lay at its western end, near the railway station. Pausing at a café that was open early I had a cup of thick Turkish coffee and a freshly baked croissant that had been dipped, miraculously, in dark chocolate. The cash desk was attended by a smiling, green-eyed girl who dropped a couple of pink sugared almonds into my hand as I left.

I passed Ramleh Station – 'Yellow pools of phosphorous light,' Durrell wrote, 'and corridors of darkness like tears in the dull brick façade of a stage set. Policemen in the shadows' – and came, moments later, to the Cecil. The entrance was nondescript, near a money-changer's shop and hardly more notable, and the lobby spartan, its worn, plain furnishings contrasting oddly with the decorative art nouveau flourishes left by its forgotten architects: heavy lotus-shaped lamps suspended from chains, friezes of gilded nymphs girding the tops of the walls and columns. Several very bad nineteenth-century oil paintings were hanging in the vestibule, and one – a Highland landscape – had a fist-shaped hole through it.

Four lanky black Nubians in jeans and checked shirts sat drinking beer and murmuring together, smiling gravely and flapping their long hands like fly swats. I found a chair nearby and ordered coffee from a surly young woman wearing a tailored blue uniform, similar to the severe, post-war kind worn by air stewardesses in the 1950s. As I drank it I got out my Durrell and found a passage describing the beautiful, tormented Justine 'in the vestibule of the Cecil Hotel among the dusty palms, dressed in a sheath of silver drops, holding her magnificent fur at her back as a peasant holds his coat – her long forefinger hooked through the tag. Nessim has stopped at the door of the ballroom which is flooded with light and music. He has missed her. Under the palms, in a deep alcove, sit a couple of old men playing chess.'

Well, the dusty palms had gone and, where the ballroom had been, there was now a closed door leading to the Disco La Rotonde bearing a poster of a plump, perspiring belly dancer with heavily rouged cheeks and breasts like Spanish melons. I closed my eyes and tried to imagine them all gathered here, Justine, Nessim, Pombal, Pursewarden, Melissa, Clea, Balthazar and, of course, old Scobie, the toothless gay Bimbashi from the Vice Squad, who lived in a cockroach-infested room behind Tatwig Street – but they had vanished entirely, leaving not the faintest shadow of a ghost behind them. Nasser's revolution had seen to that, driving out the British, the King, the insidious foreign influences, the bad old foreign ways. For the first time since the Persian Conquest of 525 BC Egypt had been reclaimed by its own, and I wondered whether anyone would be able to tell me where the flying boats had landed.

The clerk at Reception knew. A small, bright-eyed man in morning dress, he looked at me with sudden interest. 'I will show you,' he said, coming out from behind his desk and leading me past the Disco La Rotonde to Monty's Bar (Alamein is only a taxi ride away). He unlocked a heavy metal gate and ushered me into a long, dimly lit room reeking of stale beer. 'Over there,' he said, pointing through a window, 'is where the planes docked. Beside the Yacht Club. They took off and landed in the East Harbour, right in front of us, protected by the breakwater. The arriving passengers boarded a bus and were brought here to the Cecil. They had tea, then walked across to the station to catch the afternoon train to Cairo. They spent the night at Shepheard's then flew on next morning, in another aeroplane, to Baghdad. It was the passengers arriving on the Cairo train, catching the flying boat to Italy, who spent the night here.'

I looked out over the East Harbour, its bright water ruffled by a chill spring wind. The city was biscuit-coloured, a frieze of minarets, towers and tenements spread around the bay. Beyond the Yacht Club stood the Ras-el-Tin Palace where, on 26 July 1952, King Farouk signed his abdication document with a shaking hand. (He misspelled the Arabic version of his name, never having bothered to master the language.) Then he boarded his yacht *Mahroussa* with 200 pieces of luggage and, at 6 p.m., sailed off to exile and death in Italy, leaving behind him the world's greatest collections of clocks and pornography.

As we returned to the lobby the clerk said, 'Perhaps later Mr Naguib will come in. He likes to call at the Cecil for a drink. He is an old man now, but he knew the English people and he remembers those days. He will be able to tell you things.' He glanced at his watch. 'I must return to my duties. But if you would like to see our bedrooms I will send a servant.'

The servant, his scalp shorn, wearing baggy khaki trousers and shirt, looked like an army conscript. We ascended from the lobby in an ancient cage lift with a gate of extravagantly wrought iron and a gleaming brass indicator board so worn by years of furious polishing that the floor numbers were barely discernible. Up on the first floor the corridors had ornate Cunarder-style ceilings but the bedrooms, though large, were now simply furnished. The servant showed me several, unlocking the doors with a bunch of keys and throwing them open. Behind one a stout, pale-skinned couple were making love on a bed in the missionary position, heaving like wrestlers. The servant snapped the door shut again, his face impassive, but not before I noted that the man had screaming eagles tattooed on his arms and wore white tennis socks.

The Imperial passengers seemed quite accustomed to the staff barging in on them. Sir Montague de P. Webb, CIE, CBE noted in the *Karachi Daily Gazette* that 'a telephone bell at my bedside awakened me at 3.30 a.m. A knock on my door at 3.40 made sure that I had not fallen asleep again. A barber to shave me appeared at 3.50 (I was in the midst of a warm bath in my adjoining marble bathroom); whilst at 4 a.m. a tray with a cup of hot coffee, a little toast and butter, a poached egg and a slice of ham appeared. My luggage was removed at 4.15; and, a few minutes later, I (and the others) were transported by car to the Flying Boat Harbour where Customs officials examined our passports and inquired, "Had we any gold in our luggage?"'

I went for a walk along the front. Durrell's glittering Corniche was now crumbling and down-at-heel, the stone parapets chipped, the unswept pavements heaped with sand. The revolution had caught up with the old names; too, the Corniche was now Army Avenue and 26 July Avenue. Two plump young men fell into step beside me and, gleefully slapping their thighs at my pronunciation, endeavoured to teach me Arabic: *mishmish* for apricot, *mooz* for banana, *limoon* for lemon, *ruzz* for rice, *shy* for tea, *alb* for heart, *sama* for heaven and *bukra fil mishmish* for 'tomorrow when the apricots bloom', which is what you say to a creditor who wants to know when he's getting his money back.

The Cecil's dining room, where I took lunch, had starched tablecloths, heavy silver cutlery and the still, somnolent air of Eastbourne out of season. Only one other table was occupied. An old man in a black tie and dinner suit brought me the menu. On it was written:

Spaghettis Napolitaine
Tournedos Hawai
Pommes Vapeur

'Have you any Egyptian food?' I asked, thinking of roasted pigeon or perhaps a dish of lamb kufta.

He gave a small, apologetic bob of the head. 'Today, sir, just the spaghettis and stek. But I will bring salad also, very swit, very good.'

The salad was sensational, huge, juicy Delta tomatoes sliced and served up with olive oil, mint and black pepper. The old man followed that with a plate of fresh figs and I remarked that the hotel seemed quiet. 'More life in the evening,' he assured me, frowning with concentration as he spooned sugar into my coffee. 'In disco there is first class belly dancer, very nice, very popular with tourists and also Egyptian mans and ladies.'

He moved off to attend to his other customer and I thought of the *Vogue* writer making her flying boat trip in 1937 and landing (after tea in the air) at Alexandria. 'Egypt, with her smells and noises and fezzes, assails you, but Imperial's travellers are spared the beggars. This is a night-stop and you may, if you please, spend the evening in one of the amusing cabarets, where between the *risqué* cabaret turns you can dance to hot "swing" music.' Then she offers practical advice. 'Wear a light cotton frock next day and a double felt hat – it need not be particularly large nor colonial looking, but it is an essential part of your outfit; if the underpart is olive green it is especially kind to your eyes.'

Durrell's Alexandria was precisely the kind of city which the goatish, profligate, debauched Farouk – who always summered at the Ras-el-Tin Palace – might have created in his own image. So many of Imperial's male passengers patronized the more notorious clubs that the company was obliged to alter the route of its early morning bus service to include a pick-up point in the red-light district. The company issued currency coupons in 2s.6d. and 5s. units which, at any port of call, could be traded for local money. But in Alexandria they were frequently used to obtain certain essential services, and the Imperial staff grew accustomed to the madame of a popular whorehouse calling at the office with bundles of coupons which she wanted cashed for piastres.

Mr Naguib arrived at the Cecil shortly after 4 p.m., a cheery, cask-shaped old man with a gardenia in his buttonhole and, in his tie, a small ruby. He accepted a cognac and told me that he had once lived in Finchley, where his uncle had a haberdasher's shop, and he remembered the flying boats very well indeed. 'Several times I travelled on them. They were noisy and often bumpy and the passengers, frankly, they were a very snobby lot. To them, of course, I was just a Gyppo, a wog, and even the stewards patronized me. But flying was still a marvellous experience, though just a month before I was due to make my first trip, something happened here which made me put it off and cancel my ticket. It was the evening of 31 December 1935 when the city, as you can imagine, was in a festival mood, everyone getting ready for New Year's parties. I had gone to the flying boat dock with some friends, all of us very merry, to watch the Brindisi plane come in; in those days it was a popular thing to do. At about 9 o'clock we saw its lights in the sky, one of the old Calcuttas, coming from the north. The flare path was lit in the harbour and, as the lights continued coming towards us and we were wondering who might be aboard – if there was a pretty girl, of course, we would ask her to our party – suddenly the lights seemed to drop very quickly. Then they vanished. For a time there was great confusion. The Imperial launch had no radio and was not big enough to leave the harbour. Finally a British destroyer was contacted and sent to the spot. They found just one survivor – the pilot. And he told them that, within sight of the flarepath, he had run out of fuel. His engines stopped and the plane fell, striking the sea with such force that it split open. Everyone else was drowned. Early the next morning they brought the bodies in. Many people cried. It was the saddest New Year I have ever known.'

In the lace-curtained minibus on the way back to El Nouzha airport I reflected on the extraordinary goings-on, three years after the tragedy, when Alexandria became the hub of the Empire Mail Scheme. Conceived by S. A. Dismore, Secretary of Imperial Airways, and approved by the Cabinet and the House of Commons on 20 December 1934, the Scheme is considered by philatelic historians as being almost as significant as the introduction of the Penny Post. It meant, in essence, that a letter sent to any part of the British Empire could go by air at no extra cost. The stamp fixed to a letter bound from Rickmansworth to Sydenham would, if desired, take it all the way to Singapore or Sydney. The £750,000-a-year contract went to Imperial who, estimating they would have to shift 2,000 tons of mail annually, ordered from Shorts, sight unseen and straight off the drawing board, 28 giant Empire flying boats.

Two clearing dumps were established – the first at London's new Airways Terminal, with direct access to Platform 17 at Victoria Station, the other at Alexandria, junction of the African and Australian services. The Scheme reached its climax during December 1938 with such an avalanche of Christmas mail that the Empires, with their three-ton cargo capacity, couldn't cope. Emergency measures had to be adopted, and any old crate that could make it across the sea to Alex with a few sacks of letters in the back was put under charter. For a few heady weeks the skies between England and Egypt were filled with armadas of freelances, cowboy pilots suddenly entitled to hoist, after landing, the exclusive Royal Air

Mail pennant – a yellow crown over a posthorn on a deep blue field, personally approved by George V.

A riotous assembly was taking place in the little domed terminal among the reeds. A throng of people, all dressed in their Sabbath best, ebbed and flowed across the circular floor, gossiping, joking and touching hands as their children played hide-and-seek among the soaring ochre columns. Near the entrance a small shop sold coffee, 7-Up, Spathis lemonade, sweets and sunglasses. A couple of resident cats watched a swallow which had gained entry through an open window and now planed around the graceful ascending galleries. Four soldiers stood in the shadows, clasping their black Kalashnikovs and idly watching it too. My boarding pass was issued by a young Egyptair official with sensitive, scholarly features who sat blowing on his hands, muffled against the evening chill in an overcoat, a woollen scarf knotted loosely about his neck.

The security officer, also wearing an overcoat and scarf, called us into the departure hall. But for a solitary Puma helicopter parked away beyond the reeds the apron was empty. The sky had assumed the velvety plum colour of dusk; clumps of cirrus drifted up from the west, shaped like stooks of wheat and suffused with a mysterious inner tawny light. At the door there was a stirring and in waddled someone looking like a sumo wrestler gone to seed on a diet of beer and dripping. His mammoth shoulders sagged over a torso the size of a freezer unit. The stupendous stomach hanging over his belt seemed to indicate that rocks had been stuffed down his shirtfront while his buttocks, in profile, were the shape of goldfish bowls. He wore tartan trousers and, on his tiny feet, white buckskin shoes which creaked in the silence that had suddenly fallen over the room. His head was small too, with gentle brown eyes that still reflected the shock of having witnessed the violent Khomeini-like revolution that had ravaged the rest of him.

He arrived at the security desk and offered two bulky brown paper parcels for inspection. Each had been tied with enough string to suggest the fastening had been done on a loom.

The officer told him to open them up.

The man pleaded in a high, breathless voice but the order was crisply repeated. Groaning, he complied, slipping off the string, easing back the paper, miserably aware that he now had the undivided attention of everyone in the departure hall. The first parcel contained a length of gaudy floral material, possibly a bedspread, the second several dozen plastic orchids and a small rhinoceros horn. The security man picked up the horn and stared at it. He called the Egyptair official who grinned but grew serious when his colleague pointed out its potential as an offensive weapon. Could it be used to intimidate a pilot or hijack an aircraft? They conferred, weighing the thing in their hands, running their fingers over its polished tip. Then they shrugged and returned it to its owner.

He painstakingly repacked his parcels and joined us, forehead beaded with sweat, eyes lowered, wearing this latest humiliation with dignity. A middle-aged German, whose only hand baggage seemed to be a paperback volume of Schiller's poems, winked at him. 'Oh là là,' he said, indicating that he knew what powdered rhino horn was supposed to be good for. Moments later the Friendship landed and came whining up through the gloaming. It was dark when we were asked to board. The fat man, moving with surprising speed, got there first, making the plane dip as he squeezed his bulk through the door. The steward asked everyone to stand back while he resolved the problem of accommodating his giant passenger who, lowering himself cautiously into a seat, was thwarted by the armrests, his enormous tartan bum suspended a good six inches above the cushion. The steward raised the central armrest and the Egyptian sat with an audible sigh, occupying two-thirds of the available space; a tiny sparrowlike Italian wearing tinted spectacles was nominated to join him, and did so without complaint. The steward, hauling and tugging at their respective lap straps, managed to tie them both in. Panting, he examined his handiwork with hands on hips. 'Okay,' he said, and waved the rest of us to our places.

The lights of Alexandria flared briefly as we climbed away over the city. It was fringed by a sea so luminous that the Corniche seemed to lie submerged under a freak tide with its street lamps still on. We banked and turned south, the dipping wing briefly obscuring a hazy crescent moon. The steward brought cartons of apple juice, each with a short plastic straw gummed to the side which had to be detached then inserted through an aperture in the top. The obese Egyptian seemed baffled by the arrangement, plucking feebly at his straw with salami-sized fingers. His little Italian neighbour took it from him, placed the straw deftly in the aperture and handed it back. The Egyptian thanked him, blushing with gratitude.

Our trajectory that evening was a simple parabola, a slow ascent to 7,000 feet followed by a leisurely slide back down into Cairo. I sat with the German, who wondered whether our travelling companion was related to King Farouk. 'Farouk was grotesque,' he said, 'and any son surviving him would probably look like that. What Farouk ate at a single meal could have supported a family of peasants for a week. He ate, drank and fucked himself to death, you know, living only for his senses. In Alex yesterday a man told me that, just before they threw him out, he bought himself a Catalina flying boat. You understand what I mean by this?'

'Also known as the PBY,' I said. 'It had retractable wingtip floats and big Plexiglass blisters in the fuselage.'

'That is correct. Well, according to this man, Farouk sent his Catalina to England to be rebuilt according to his own specifications. He wanted it to be a fantastic yacht that flew. It was to be the ultimate in luxury. And you know what he told them to cover the walls with?'

'No.'

'*Fur!*' he said.

I laughed.

'From the polar bear,' he added severely. 'Hunters were supposed to go north and shoot the bears for Farouk's aeroplane. By the time they were finished those polar bears would have been a seriously endangered species.'

Frowning, he picked up Schiller's *Gedichte* again while I looked out of the window, noting that we were following a virtually unbroken line of light. That morning I had seen crops but few signs of habitation; now it was clear that the terrain below, watered by the Nile, brimmed with life, the farms, settlements and villages providing our pilot with a shimmering flarepath that would lead him all the way to the capital. The Imperial passengers making the same inter-city trip – by rail – had found it moderately diverting. 'The train was quite a good train,' noted Major the Hon. R. F. Carnegie, 'but what a flat, flat country – not a hill, only the delta of the Nile. Mile after mile of close cultivation, with quaint mud villages dotted about, a most peaceful scene.' He displayed a lively breeder's interest in the livestock, noting that the cattle looked 'a little like Jerseys in colour, rather leggy and high at the withers'.

Perusing my notes I was reminded that Sir Samuel Hoare had bypassed Cairo, electing to fly direct from Alexandria to Gaza equipped with 'letters from the London School of Oriental Languages, written in the languages of the tribes over which we were to pass. A translation of these diverting documents, perhaps amongst the most curious that have ever issued from Whitehall, I have set out in an appendix.' It read as follows.

The bearer of this letter is Lieutenant-Colonel the Rt. Hon. Sir SAMUEL JOHN GURNEY HOARE, Baronet, Companion of the most distinguished Order of St Michael and St George, Member of Parliament, a Principal Secretary of State and one of the chief ministers of His Most Excellent Majesty George the Fifth, by the Grace of God King of the United Kingdom of Great Britain and Ireland and of the British Dominions beyond the Seas, Emperor of India. He, with his wife, staff and servants, is proceeding by air on an urgent and important British mission. The safety of this exalted personage and his companions is a matter of closest concern to the King of England, who will amply reward persons who may give them any assistance they may need on their historic journey.

> The Seal of the Air Council has been affixed in the presence of
> SIR WALTER FREDERIC
> NICHOLSON, KGB,
> Secretary of the Air Council.

We were dropping towards Cairo. After a wild, turbulent approach, we whizzed in over the shacks beside the airport perimeter and, still yawing and lurching only feet from the ground, landed judderingly on the starboard set of Dunlop twin-wheels, the port set coming down with a bang some time afterwards. We disembarked and boarded a bus. The captain, who was young and handsome as a movie star, with tie loosened and tousled yellow hair swept back over the nape of his neck, swung aboard last and took command of the bus as well, issuing instructions which the driver, grinning fiercely, proceeded to ignore. We halted in the darkness beside the little domestic terminal we had left that morning and, picking up my bag, I went to check in for my next leg, the notorious night flight to Baghdad.

III

At the Banque Misr the same three young men were working the night shift. They remembered me. 'Hello!' said the first. 'You spend the money okay?'

'All gone now?' said the second.

'You come for more?' said the third.

They all laughed together.

When I told them I wanted my remaining pounds and piastres changed into dollars they pantomimed gloom and distress, accepting the notes – for which they gave me a disgraceful exchange rate – but rejecting a pocketful of pretty silver coins engraved with the Sphinx and the Salah-ed-Din Eagle. 'These you must keep as souvenir of happy time in Egypt,' they said, shoving them back again.

I went to join the queues at Immigration. There were two, each containing perhaps 100 *felayeen*, peasants flying to Baghdad to take labouring jobs. Every man was being interrogated by a small committee of uniformed officials who painstakingly scrutinized his documents and took down particulars, hampered by the fact that most of the travellers were illiterate, able to identify themselves only with thumbprints and scrawled crosses. It took two weary, boring hours to reach the front and, as their confrontation with the officials drew closer, my neighbours began to sweat and fidget. They were young and strongly built with fine eyes and rotting teeth, and they gave off the rank, gamy smell of unwashed bodies. A handful of old men stood in the queues as well, looking dazed and dejected. One grew faint; water was fetched and he continued inching forward supported by two youthful companions, perhaps his sons, who were clearly frightened that the officials might declare him unfit to travel.

The officials, when I finally reached them, were courteous. They examined my passport and Embarkation Card. 'A journalist!' murmured one. 'With a visa for Iraq? That is most unusual. Perhaps you are going to see the fighting.'

'I honestly don't know what I'm going to see,' I said.

I went through *Gumruk* (Customs), where the peasants were feverishly tearing open their cloth-tied bundles – one contained clothing, a bottle of pink medicine and a small tin frog that was wound up and made to hop for the inspector – and found myself in the echoing, barnlike Departure Hall. It contained a snack bar with tables and chairs, and a duty-free shop. I asked the man at the shop whether the importing of liquor into Baghdad was permitted. 'Oh, yes,' he said. 'Some of the people there are jolly big boozers.' I bought a bottle of Cutty Sark and went to the snack bar for a coffee. A tall, fastidious-looking man wearing a beautifully cut black robe and a chequered Hashemite headdress shared my table. '*Assalam alaikoom*' (Greetings, Peace be with you), he said, sitting down and sipping a Coke.

'Are you going to Baghdad?' I asked.

'No. God willing, I am going to Riyadh,' he said.

Two scrawny cats were fighting beyond the next table, mewing and spitting, lurching back and forth across the floor, ignored by the patrons of the snack bar.

'Have you ever been to Baghdad?' I asked.

He nodded, and gave a slight shudder. 'Yes.'

'Is it a good place?'

'I think it is not such a good place,' he said, slowly, but he chose not to elaborate and, a moment later, his flight was called. He left me with a small bow and I turned my attention to Gate 3, where my fellow-passengers were massing to board the plane, spilling over into the Gate 4 waiting area and giving off a hum like swarming bees. Rows of yellow plastic chairs formed alleyways to the gates, and seated in one, mostly obscured by the Egyptians eddying restlessly around her, was a pretty European woman with cropped blonde hair. The fighting cats came skidding past me; one had blood oozing from a gash in the cheek. Two beefy Spanish-speaking men sat a neighbouring table and one, casually, reached out a booted foot and kicked them hard; they reeled away, screeching, towards the duty-free shop.

I finished my coffee and found a vacant chair near the entrance to the Gate 3 area. Moments later there was an announcement advising that the buses for the Baghdad plane would be boarding at Gate 5 instead. With a roar my fellow-passengers rose as one, wheeled and came stampeding towards me. I saw them approaching as in a slow motion, their faces contorted, the men to the fore shouting as they were heaved onwards by the 300 behind, and they caught me when I was halfway to my feet, hitting me with the force of a truck. Staggering, I jumped on to a chair, intending to scramble over the back to safety, but a succession of triphammer blows from passing shoulders and elbows did it for me, sending me cartwheeling into the neighbouring waiting area. I lay there, unable to move or breathe, suffering severe shooting pains, wondering whether I had sustained any grave internal injuries. Then a voice said in English, 'Are you all right?'

I discerned, dimly, the blonde woman leaning over me.

'No,' I said.

'Should I get a doctor?'

Things were slowly swimming back into focus. Soon I could see her plainly and the pain was starting to recede. I got up slowly and we followed the brawling tail-enders to Gate 5, where a major civil disturbance was taking place. An Egyptair official grabbed our arms. 'Please follow!' he commanded, guiding us around the perimeters of the combat zone and putting us on the bus ahead of the others. I expressed surprise at this preferential treatment, but was promptly hushed by the lady. 'Aboard the plane they will put us in First Class,' she said crisply. 'Not because we are Europeans, but because it is policy to separate the non-peasants from the peasants. It is the middle-class Egyptians who have always insisted on it. When we get into the air you will see why.'

We were ushered aboard the Egyptair Airbus and, sure enough, directed into the de luxe forward cabin by a burly, preoccupied steward who looked past us with a gladiatorial light in his eye. As he bunched his fists and plunged aft into the mêlée the blonde told me that her name was Kristin. She added that she was Danish, an engineer working on a construction project in Baghdad. Looking at me with amused blue eyes she unzipped her flight bag and produced a litre of duty-free Gilbeys. 'Survival rations,' she said. 'We will need this. Do you mind drinking neat gin? And warm? Such things as ice and tonic are often not available.'

A man wandered back from the flight deck. He was thin, sallow and slightly stooped, wearing a maroon pullover and a woollen scarf, and he stood beside us with his hands in his pockets, gazing into the economy section where the noise was reminiscent of Saturday night at a Glasgow prize fight.

'That is the captain,' murmured Kristin.

He glanced down at us and smiled a slow, sad smile.

'Have you got any glasses, please?' she asked. 'We would like to have a drink.'

'Glasses?' he frowned. 'Of course. There will be glasses in the galley. If you come with me we will look.'

I followed him forward and, with pursed lips, he began his search, opening drawers and peering into cupboards. 'Success!' he said, handing me a couple of plastic cups and strolling back to his flight deck. Lacking tonic but having access to water, Kristin and I decided to drink my scotch instead. She took a big swallow and told me that she had worked in Baghdad for five years as an electrical engineer with a foreign consortium. 'We do housing projects, she said. 'Baghdad is full of new ones and they are *beautiful*, imaginatively designed by the best architects, very well built, the best materials, the latest techniques, no expense spared; in Copenhagen even the rich would be fighting for such houses. In Baghdad, they are for everyone. The trouble comes after the builders finish and the tenants move in. There is no upkeep, no maintenance, no repainting, nothing and, within a little while these fabulous houses begin to look like slums.'

During our first drink the cabin gradually filled with the overflow from economy. The men sat clutching their documents, staring around them with wide eyes, pondering the mechanisms that fastened their belts and made their seats tilt back. Information regarding this latter novelty was exchanged in low voices and soon all the seatbacks were going up and down like rocking chairs. During our second drink we took off, soaring into a brilliant star-spangled sky so quickly that within a minute or so, as I craned to look, the lights of Cairo were reduced to a glowing pile of embers on the horizon. Some of the Imperial services now made for Gaza, where the airfield was no longer operational, others carried on to Iraq. Kristin talked about life in Baghdad, about the British Embassy library, the gym at the Sheraton Hotel, the difficulty of obtaining fresh vegetables, and the skin conditions that affected one during the terrible summer heat, but I listened with only half an ear, reflecting that, within the hour, we would be out of Egypt and Flying the Furrow.

At the March 1921 Cairo Conference it was formally moved that Palestine and Íraq, both mandated to Britain by the 1919 Peace Treaty, should be linked by a regular air service. Security in the two territories was already the responsibility of the RAF, who were to operate the new service between Aman and Ramadi, a settlement on the Euphrates 65 miles west of Baghdad. But senior officers pointed out that their 100 mph machines, powered by cranky old water-cooled engines, were notoriously unreliable. They were not equipped with radio and, more serious, the pilots would face severe disorientation problems negotiating a desert landscape with few landmarks. The Cairo Conference debated the matter and eventually decided that what pilots needed was something to follow. It decreed that a continous furrow should be ploughed across the desert from Aman to Ramadi, a distance of 470 miles. The delegates were mostly members of the English landed gentry who, as keen supporters of Britain's rural train services, well understood the logic of a pilot seeking guidance from a railway line. If none was available in the desert, however, you gave him the next best thing: a good no-nonsense Lincolnshire-style ditch. Flying by Bradshaw had come to the Middle East.

Three months later two motorized convoys set out from either end with orders to meet in the middle. Each had armoured cars mounted with Lewis guns at the front and, at the rear, a Fordson tractor pulling a weighted plough. Every 25 miles they were to stop and prepare an emergency landing field, its approach signalled by arrows cut beside the furrow, its identity by a letter or number engraved in the ground; the western party prepared fields A to R (to be administered by Cairo) while the eastern party were responsible for fields I to XI, marked in Roman numerals and administered from Baghdad. At many of the strips emergency fuel dumps were established. The parties used the stars for navigation and set their chronometers each night by tuning their radios towards France and picking up the time signal from the Eiffel Tower. It was hard, painstaking work, but there were occasional compensations. One of the men later recalled 'the pleasure of swimming in the pools, some hot and some ice cold, in the Azrak marsh, the joy of sitting round a camp fire varying the normal bully and biscuit diet for a stew of gazelle meat, the pleasure of being able to draw unlimited water from the wells of El Jid and to remove the caked dust and grime from the long days spent in the desert'.

For five and a half years the RAF operated a fortnightly service up and down the Furrow, going to Ramadi one week (the trip took two days) and coming back the next. The aircraft flew in pairs, a necessary precaution in view of the high incidence of forced landings and occasional musket volleys loosed off by the bedouin, and they carried mail, for which a surcharge of a shilling an ounce was levied. The British public displayed little enthusiasm for the venture. The first mail service carried just one letter, all the others were mere duplicates. The senders insisted that the originals went by surface transport which, though slow – it took a month from London to Baghdad – was at least reliable.

Then the RAF began to have second thoughts about the Furrow. It was making the pilots lazy. Their skills were starting to atrophy. No longer obliged to navigate, they were losing all their old instincts and cunning. Send them across some trackless waste to inflict damage on an enemy and you were faced with the unnerving prospect of them getting lost and bombing the wrong chaps. The Service's senior officers began to regard the Furrow with the gravest misgivings.

So did some of the pilots. One of the Furrow Flyers even put his reservations into verse:

The ashes of a fire – lit all in vain –
A thing that breathed and lived but yesterday,
The charred and blackened wreckage of a 'plane,
Are all that mark the Man Who Lost His Way.
An error of a minute; a side-slip in a cloud;
He failed to see the Track he thought he knew,
The endless days of waiting – by fear and hunger cowed –
Ere the jackals took the meat that was their due!

The man who finally got the RAF off the hook was Sir Samuel Hoare – not because he was concerned about their declining standards, but because he felt the route was not being properly exploited. He wanted it commercialized and, in 1926, he got his way. It was transferred lock, stock and barrel to Imperial Airways – who turned it into the first sector of their projected Cairo to Karachi air mail service. A government subsidy of £93,600 was allocated for the construction of new aerodromes, hangars and accommodation and, after a survey flight had been completed by the legendary Captain Charles Wolley-Dod, Imperial's ace pilot, the company launched its inaugural service in October 1926 with Sir Samuel aboard as principal passenger.

They used machines specially commissioned from de Havilland, the three-engined Hercules designed specifically for operating in desert conditions and equipped with a powerful radio and state-of-the-art navigational equipment. The Hercules pilots could thus dispense with the Furrow, but they tended to follow it anyway in case they needed its emergency fuel dumps. The dumps were the subject of a long-running tactical battle between Imperial and the desert nomads, who robbed and pillaged them like tombs. The nomads had no interest in the petrol, which they poured away into the sand, but they prized the tins, because they could be made into knives, cups, mirrors and water bottles. When Imperial put the dumps underground the nomads simply dug down, shot the locks off and carried on looting. Eventually London devised heavy-duty bullet-proof locks for which special keys were issued but the pilots, made absent-minded by the heat, forgot them so often that a further modification was required: the fuel dump key also became the key with which they unlocked their aircraft doors first thing each morning.

Whenever they made an unscheduled refuelling stop the passengers were expected to roll up their sleeves and lend a hand, helping to lift and pour perhaps 60 tins of petrol, a dozen cans of benzol and a couple of five-gallon drums of oil. There were few complaints. On the contrary, though sweating, dirty and dishevelled, they usually scrambled aboard again suffused with feelings of satisfaction and camaraderie. Sometimes they were obliged to spend a night far from civilization – all Imperial machines carried emergency water and desert rations – and they invariably made light of that as well. 'Passengers took the whole thing in a spirit of adventure,' recollected Captain Roger Mollard who, having been forced down beside a deserted, roofless fort one evening, sent his charges out to collect dried camel dung in their hats. Doused with petrol, the stuff burned well enough to warm them through the night. Months later they met for a reunion dinner at the Trocadero and sent Mollard a signed menu 'From the Camel Dung-Burners Club'. The scheduled nightstops were made at the first of Imperial's famous custom-built forts, Rutbah Wells, located roughly three-quarters of the way between Cairo and Baghdad, guarded by armed sentries and administered by an English manager and his wife. They had access to an unlimited supply of cold, sweet, artesian water but were obliged to truck in all their food, fuel and supplies from Baghdad 240 miles away.

The emergency landing drill was inherited from the RAF who, after many years of desert operations, had devised a list of good and bad things to do. These were regularly published in volume form. The 1943 edition, titled *Air Route Book – Cairo to Karachi* and distributed to all flying personnel in the Middle East, carried the same advice that the company's pilots had learned by heart. A characteristic section headed 'Some Points on Conduct When Meeting the Arabs in the Desert' offered these tips: 'Remove footwear on entering their tents. Completely ignore their women. If thirsty drink the water they offer, but DO NOT fill your waterbottle from their personal supply. Go to their well and fetch what you want. Never neglect any puddle or other water supply for topping up your bottle. Use the Halazone in your Aid Box. Do not expect breakfast if you sleep the night. Arabs will give you a mid-day or evening meal. REMEMBER, NEVER TRY TO HURRY IN THE DESERT, SLOW AND SURE DOES IT!'

A section called 'Don'ts' said:

'Don't flap. Keep calm and methodical.

Don't waste your strength; be slack and lie up in any shade there is.

Don't drink the compass alcohol or radiator liquid. It weakens you and will give you appalling stomach pains.

Don't use the liquid in the fire extinguisher on your skin, it produces burns.

Don't use urine for any purpose. Used externally it produces sores. Used internally, the high salt content in it draws water from your body and makes you thirstier than before. It has the same effect as drinking sea water.

Don't walk along any road or railways; you may walk the wrong way. Send someone to sit beside it.

Don't threaten natives. They are friendly.'

On the Airbus, meanwhile, a supper of sorts was being served. Kristin and I surveyed our slices of cold, curling, tripe-coloured meat without enthusiasm; any inclination to try the stuff was dispelled by a man across the aisle who unexpectedly put a finger to his nose and emptied it on to the floor. I blanched. Kristin shrugged and said, 'It could get worse.' It did. A few minutes later the plane struck turbulence of the kind normally found in the core of a thunderstorm. It was brief but violent, and left the air polluted with sewer smells. The flight attendants hurried aft, faces bleak, carrying antiseptic cleaning materials to deal with the vomit and excrement fouling the seats and carpet. I reached for the depleted whisky bottle and filled our cups. 'You didn't measure those in fingers,' Kristin remarked approvingly. 'You measured them in hands. Like with a horse. You know?'

I looked through my notes and found the Hoare account of Imperial's Baghdad inaugural, flown in the first of the new Hercules trimotors with Captain Wolley-Dod at the controls. 'A flash of blue water showed that we were over the oasis of El Azrak, once the most famous duck shoot of the Middle East, and now the encampment of many refugee Druses, whose arrival has not only created a political problem, but also destroyed a paradise of wildfowl. It was about half past three when we first saw a great brown city built on either side of a wide river, and dotted about with the dark green patches of palm groves.'

Our own approach was surreptitious, sliding down a dark glide slope with the spoilers giving us enough of a buffeting to slosh the whisky around in our cups. We saw the first ground lights on finals, only a minute before making an impeccable touchdown at Saddam Hussein Airport. 'Foreign airlines may only use the airport at night,' Kristin reported. 'We are told it is a precaution because of the possibility of Iranian rocket attacks, but many of us think it is to stop foreigners seeing the military installations around Baghdad. This city, you know, is a real armed camp.'

She enunciated that without slurring a single syllable and moments later, when the exhausted cabin crew let us off first, she managed to reach the tarmac without falling down the stairs. I fell down some of them, but felt no pain and waved away a mechanic in white overalls who offered to help me up. Inside the terminal I told Kristin that she had very good legs. She said I had good legs as well, though they were maybe a little on the short side. We ambled up to Passport Control, leaning on one another for support while she told me a story about a distraught midget threatening to commit suicide by jumping off the carpet. Then, all at once, I was waylaid by a thin, sombre man in a three-piece suit who asked my name and, before I knew what was happening, had snatched me from under her very nose and whisked me out to a waiting car. He radiated disapproval at the state I was in and, except to intimate that he was from the Ministry of Information, which had arranged my visit, he barely spoke. I was taken to a modern, highrise hotel beside the Tigris – 'All foreign journalists stay here' – and told to meet him in the lobby at 8 a.m. next morning. In the lift I glanced at my watch. That was in only five hours. He'd be lucky.

I looked through a printed list of airline departures on my bedside table, seeking a means of escape. My eye fell on an entry announcing the existence of a service from Baghdad (BGW) to

Southend (SEN), with a change of planes at Amersterdam (AMS). Baghdad to Southend! I fell asleep reflecting that this was even more remarkable than the famous Leeds (LBA) to Casablanca (CAS) service operated weekly, via Heathrow, by a 727 of Royal Air Maroc.

IV

At the Iraqi Information Office in London a helpful, overworked official had approved my requests for visits to Rutbah Wells and Basra, important staging posts on the Imperial route. 'No problem,' he assured me. 'I will telex Baghdad, and also inform them that you must have a three-day visa.' In Baghdad, though, they knew nothing of these arrangements. I was taken to the Ministry of Information, a cool, airy building set in parklike grounds planted with eucalyptus trees, and given coffee and watermelon. The Ministry was staffed by dapper young men in three-piece suits, all looking like my minder, Mr Karim, who, by the light of day, and despite my having been an hour late for our appointment in the lobby of the Al-Mansour Melia Hotel, turned out to be charmingly affable, with sad, romantic eyes and a little moustache that sat astride his upper lip like a bristling brown centipede.

He and his colleagues were welcoming, but seemed bemused by my requests for internal travel. They went into committee, talking softly, murmuring into telephones, eating watermelon and toying with their worry beads. I glanced through the English-language *Baghdad Observer* – 'Arab Doctors Praise Iraq's Peace Moves' announced the page 1 headline – and waited for their verdict. It came after an hour and was delivered by Mr Karim who, spitting seeds into his hand, announced apologetically that Basra and Rutbah Wells were out of bounds to foreigners.

I showed him an advertisement on the back page of the paper. It announced tours of Basra and the beautiful adjoining marshes, with daily departures from Baghdad. 'Ah,' said Mr Karim. 'Yes. Well, just now the tours are discontinued. The Iranian aggressors have cut the road *and* the railway line to Basra. Our heroic soldiers will soon drive them away, of course, but probably not until after your visa runs out.'

I accepted the logic of that, and asked whether the Iranians had also cut the road to Rutbah. They most certainly had not, he said. So why couldn't I go?

'It is more than 300 kilometres,' Mr Karim advised.

'Then we must set off early. I'll hire transport and we'll leave at 6 o'clock tomorrow morning. We can have lunch in Rutbah and be home in time for dinner. Five hours there, five hours back.'

Mr Karim was appalled. '6 *o'clock*?' He shook his head decisively. 'Tomorrow I will take you to Babylon. It is not far, the road is good and we go at 10 o'clock. After breakfast.'

'I don't want to go to Babylon. I want to go to Rutbah.'

Mr Karim was beginning to look discomfited. Noting that his colleagues were exchanging smiles he stood stiffly. 'Babylon is famous place, you will have gorgeous time!' he snapped. 'Now we are making tour of Baghdad war monuments and housing projects!'

He stalked out. I followed him with a sinking heart, realizing that I had been put in the care of a city boy who would no more contemplate crossing the wilderness to Rutbah than going to his office with untrimmed nails or mismatched socks. In the car he sat beside the driver, a burly, uncommunicative man in faded army fatigues. As we moved off Mr Karim pulled down the sunshade and examined himself closely in the vanity mirror. I asked him whether he ever went into the desert and he assured me that it was the best possible place to acquire spiritual refreshment, the silence and solitude being good for the soul in much the same way – he seemed to imply – as a particular shampoo might be good for putting shine into lifeless hair. As he spoke he stroked his moustache in the mirror and, catching my eye, smiled and asked where I had bought my tie.

The city was an undistinguished sprawl, though the monuments were suitably heroic and the housing projects just as impressive as Kristin had promised. They were being built by an army of South Korean guest workers, thus releasing the Iraqi men for service in their Holy War. 'We have workers from many countries here,' Mr Karim told me. 'Also Egyptians, Pakistanis, Filipinos, Chinese and Yugoslavs. Yes, and Irish nurses, who are so nice and pretty. Now everyone likes very much to be sick.'

We were speaking in a traffic jam, one of the hot, noisy, ill-tempered affairs in which we had spent much of the morning. Mr Karim sat contentedly breathing in the fumes, humming as he perused his cologned chin in the mirror. He eventually returned me to the hotel where I spent the remainder of the day trying to make alternative arrangements for getting to Rutbah Wells. The clerk at a car hire agency in the lobby agreed to supply a vehicle and then changed his mind. I spoke to several taxi drivers who said no, emphatically. In the coffee shop I met a Pole who owned a Skoda and offered him $200 for the journey, but he just laughed. I made an appointment to see the British ambassador the following morning and then, obsessed by Rutbah and coming painfully to terms with the fact that I would probably never get there, went to my room and gloomily read through my notes on the place.

First I looked it up in the *Air Route Book*, which reminded pilots that the surrounding high ground was sometimes obscured by low, heavy cloud, that the 'irregular-shaped' landing area had a gravel surface, a wind sock on the Fort and goose-necked flares for night landings. Rutbah endured periodic duststorms and, though water was available, there were no repair facilities, no hangars and no medical help. The passengers had demonstrated mixed feelings towards Imperial's remote stockade, specially built for the company by the Iraqi government and defended against bedouin attacks by a company of Iraqi infantry. 'Just a brick fort,' sniffed one, while a contributor to the Austin Reed house journal wrote of 'the absurdity of coming down to an English ham and egg breakfast in the middle of the desert'. But the Reverend P. B. Clayton found it 'unforgettable' while our old travelling memorialist Mr W. D. H. McCullough thought it 'the most desolate and extraordinary hostelry in the world. It is practically 300 miles from any sign of civilization and is stuck right in the very centre of the Syrian desert. Yet when you arrive out of the sky and taxi up to the gate you pass in through the guards and enter a most pleasantly equipped restaurant in which you can have bacon and eggs, coffee, iced drinks, toast and marmalade and electric light.' One creature comfort not available was heat. 'The only detail that the architect had forgotten,' noted one disgruntled transit passenger, 'was the provision of fireplaces. Rutbah must be nearly 3,000 feet above the sea, and it is often bitterly cold in December; we dined in overcoats and had a very shivery night in the Hotel.' Men and woman slept in separate quarters and, after a dinner of pilaf and barbecued chicken, an armed sentry would lead the passengers up a circular stone staircase to the Fort's flat roof. Captain Patrick Tweedie, who flew into 'the Wells' innumerable times, remembered the view as 'breathtaking, the dark sky covered with millions of stars sparkling in the clear desert air'.

In the cocktail lounge of the Al-Mansour Melia that evening I leafed through the *Baghdad Observer* – 'Tunisian Daily Warns Iranian Aggressors' – and talked to a Yugoslavian engineer who said the city authorities were expecting an Iranian rocket strike during the night. The lounge was packed with Iraqi men drinking Ephesus Turkish Pilsner at one dinar, or $3, a bottle, and staring at the delicate little Filipino waitresses who wore ankle-length skirts slit seductively to the thigh.

In the morning, from my balcony, I inspected the city for signs of damage. Everything seemed intact. It was a crisp, sunny day and the Tigris flowed beneath my window like milky coffee, the bridge downstream from the hotel clogged with the same honking traffic jam that, as far as I could tell, had been there the night before. I found a taxi and went to see Mr John Campbell Moberly, CMG, Her Britannic Majesty's ambassador, a likeable, donnish man in shirt sleeves who occupied a spacious office with a garden view. He was puzzled by Mr Karim's refusal to take me to Rutbah Wells. 'It's a perfectly innocuous little place,' he said. 'I went through it last year after picking up my new Range Rover in Amman. Rutbah's quite a way inside the Iraqi border, but it's the first bit of civilization you come to and it now forms the frontier post, where you deal with the entry formalities. The paperwork needed for bringing in a new car is pretty formidable, and I had to hang around for several hours. All I remember is a hot, dusty little place with a few roadside shacks selling sticky drinks, perhaps a date palm or two, and precious little else. The Imperial fort isn't there any more, and neither is the landing ground.' He picked up his phone and said, 'Let me call one of my contacts at the Ministry and see if we can't get your Mr Karim overruled.'

But the Ministry contact, to whom Mr Moberly spoke in fast, fluent Arabic, could not help. Before taking my leave I asked about getting down to Basra instead. Mr Moberly advised me to put that notion right out of my head; they wouldn't let me anywhere near it. The fighting along the Basra road was so serious that he had been obliged to suspend the Embassy truck's monthly run to Kuwait to collect staples like apples, potatoes and beef. The legation larder, he said, was now almost bare. I said goodbye and made my way back to the gate, pausing a moment to admire the imposing elegant premises built in the opulent days of British rule when Gertrude Bell was resident Oriental Secretary, and the Iraqi royal family were among those eager to be summoned to the famous parties held in the great walled garden beside the Tigris. (Sir Samuel and Lady Hoare, after their arrival, went along to 'a small dinner attended by King Feisul'.)

Less exalted travellers found their amusements elsewhere. Though the Imperial passengers stayed at the Hotel Maude, they were able to use the facilities at Baghdad's three main clubs, the British, the Railway and the Alwiyah. The Alwiyah had a swimming pool and squash courts but, if something more demanding was required, the local company officials recommended polo and pigsticking. For those who always travelled with gun and rod the Imperial Airways *Gazette* thoughtfully itemized the prey available at each stop. Baghdad offered 'some sport with jackal, gazelle, hare and hyena. In the Euphrates carp weighing up to 220 pounds have been caught and there is plenty of fishing in the upper reaches of the Tigris. The season is from November to June. The fish are taken by fly or with spoon and live bait.'

After lunch Mr Karim and the driver treated me to another tour of the traffic jams. I was starting to warm to the driver. He never spoke to me directly but, instead, relayed information through Mr Karim, whose own interest in the city went back no further than 1968, when the ruling Ba'ath Socialist Party finally emerged from the mayhem of the 1958 revolution and the bloody overthrowing of the monarchy. Now he gave voice to the driver's affection for Baghdad, pointing out the ancient corners that had not yet been torn down by the dictates of the Polish Redevelopment Plan: venerable mosques, gates, shrines, even a medieval khan, or hostel, which once provided beds for travellers and stabling for their camels. 'Old Copper Market,' called Mr Karim. 'Old Needlemakers' Wharf.' He cared nothing for any of this, wishing to speak only of Iranian atrocities and the gallant conduct of the Iraqi forces, but that day he allowed the driver to invest his grey, formless city with a significance that had not been apparent before.

In the cocktail lounge I read the *Baghdad Observer* – 'French Daily On Situation in Iran. The situation in Iran is the worst and most horrible in the world, said a French daily' – and talked to a West German engineer who said, 'Iraq is a paranoid police state, just like Iran, and this crazy war goes on because of the personal animosity between Saddam Hussein and the Mullah Khomeini. They are both megalomaniacs and, if you ask me, they deserve each other.'

Next morning I went to meet a senior pilot of Iraqi Airways. The motorway ran across flat, featureless country covered by an opaque milky haze. Massive gun emplacements stood along the airport's perimeter fence, earth pyramids 30 feet high each topped with a sandbagged anti-aircraft weapon manned by a single soldier in a fur-lined combat jacket. The barrels were all pointing east, towards Iran. We drove through a guardpost and, beyond a wrecked car dump and a shed housing Boeing flight simulators, came to the Iraqi Airways administration block.

In the tiny lift two gnarled and frail old men carrying buckets murmured 'Peace and the blessings of God be upon you' and then directed us to the sparsely furnished office of Captain M. R. Jassim, Assistant Director of Flight Operations. He was large and bearlike, with an easy charm and a deep, rumbling laugh. An elderly woman in a black shawl and felt slippers brought miniature glasses of sweet tea as he told me that he had learnt to fly in Perth, Scotland. 'It was a very happy time for me. I like the Highlanders, such open, generous people, not complicated by civilization. Our pilots still go to Perth for their basic training.'

Captain Jassim joined the airline in 1960 as a First Officer on Viscounts, but went up in anything he could get his hands on, familiarizing himself with the terrain, the conditions, the peculiar and sometimes frightening vagaries of desert flying. 'It was the best possible training, specially doing summer runs down to Basra in one of the little De Havilland Doves. You'd get dust devils swirling up to 6,000 feet and, in the spring and the autumn, the sandstorms, very bad in an open cockpit. You came home looking like a bedouin.'

His favourite airport was Jeddah, which serves Mecca and, during the Haj, becomes the busiest in the world. 'It's so magnificently equipped that taking my 747 in there is always a pleasure. For my crew also, specially the stewardesses who know their parents would approve of such a place. Stewardesses are actually a problem for us. We put out recruiting announcements on television but there is never any rush. We are still a deeply conservative people, and in any family there is resistance to the idea of a daughter being exposed to the world outside without a chaperone. This is where the captain comes in. He must become a substitute father for them. He is their moral guardian, responsible for their virtue. They may be wearing make-up and short skirts, but they are still good Muslim girls at heart and, if he sees one being exposed to temptation, he must quickly step in with a firm warning.'

It was time to leave. We shook hands and went speeding back to Baghdad. Mr Karim spent several minutes examining his right eye in the vanity mirror, pulling down the lid to get a better look. It was bloodshot, and he frowned at it with his left eye.

'You'll have to lay off the drink, Mr Karim,' I said.

'I am strict teetotal,' he pointed out but, perhaps pleased by the implication that he was a man about town, smiled at me in the mirror.

That evening I chatted to an Italian engineer who told me that Khomeini, though 83, enjoyed a remarkable sex life. 'He has two women a night. The news is being suppressed here, on the grounds that it would be bad for the fighting spirit of the Iraqi troops.' The engineer and I went down to the river to eat mazgouf, freshly caught Tigris fish grilled on tamarisk wood fires. I told him about Rutbah and he gave me a funny look. 'I have heard rumours about that place,' he said.

'What rumours?'

He hesitated. 'Well, they say the Iraqis are working on a secret plant for making poison gas. It will be used against the Iranians. The plant will be located in underground caves, and my information is that the place chosen is this oasis you speak of, Rutbah Wells.'

I left Baghdad the following afternoon. As I got out of the car at Saddam Hussein Airport the driver suddenly seized my hand and spoke emotionally. 'He asks God to bless you and your journey, and hopes that his work has not been too poor,' explained Mr Karim. 'He says you are probably used to much better drivers than him.'

Surprised and moved, I assured him he had been an outstandingly good and considerate driver, and then followed Mr Karim into the terminal where, brandishing a Ministry chit, he got me through the formalities in the blink of an eye. But I was too bemused by my surroundings even to bid him a proper farewell. Baghdad's new terminal (I had arrived at the old one) was astonishing, a vast petrodollar extravaganza with acres of marble floors and a great vaulted roof, its soaring lines cunningly emphasized in glowing neon and hung, unexpectedly, with thousands of dangling white pipes; they achieved a mosaic effect as soothing and cool as snow crystals. It was the grandest building in the country and now, on the very point of leaving it, I felt I had at last come to the city of the Thousand and One Nights.

But the terminal was empty. But for a sprinkling of soldiers and staff I had the place to myself. I wandered through it like a deposed caliph confined to his palace, my footfalls echoing as I made my way past the deserted duty-free shops – stuffed with silks, scents and jewellery – to the departure lounge, a mosquelike ante-room furnished with deep leather armchairs. There was only one plane on the tarmac, the Iraqi Airways 727 rostered to fly the 1600 hours service to Kuwait. The runways, shimmering in the heat, merged with the desert at roughly the point where a tiny horseman, opaque as glass, moved slowly along the misty mauve line separating earth and sky.

People began trickling into the departure lounge. They spoke in whispers, as though overwhelmed by the size and opulence of their surroundings. Flight IA 121 was called and, aboard the 727, I settled into my seat and took out my copy of *Ma'ak*, the inflight magazine, published in English and Arabic and reading from back to front. It opened – or, rather, closed – with a message from Mr L. Al-Obaidy, the Editor-in-Chief, which read, 'Dear Passenger. Gold is the adornment of women since the ancient times. Today, the glorious Iraqi woman donates her gold jewellery to support the war effort, Saddam's Qadissiya, which is waged by the barbarian rulers of Iran against our country. Her slogan is, OUR HOME IS MORE VALUABLE THAN GOLD, she grants it to have Iraq always safe and glorious under the leadership of the knight Saddam Hussein.' That was followed by a message from the Minister of Transport, who wrote, 'May I seize this opportunity to present my compliments to all passengers traveling [sic] on board Iraqi Airways Fleet. Our Party and Revolution, headed by the President – Leader Saddam Hussein – strongly support the Civil transport sector. This patronage represented by increasing the fleet with the most developed airplain' [sic].

The 727, boarding families and a sprinkling of army officers, took on the air of a holiday charter. Everyone heaved and pushed and shoved, stuffing bedding, pillows and packages into the overhead lockers as they shouted at their spouses and absently cuffed the children who scampered about, having races. Four rather stout, plain stewardesses in shapeless green uniforms – Captain Jassim's good Muslim girls – watched impassively. The engines started up and a tape of 'Amor' was played on the PA, sung by an Iraqi baritone who turned it into a series of barked commands, like an RSM drilling recruits. Everyone rushed for their seats. The one next to mine was occupied by a plump, powdered woman who, perhaps unaware of her obligations towards the war effort, wore heavy gold earrings shaped like crescent moons. Her face reminded me of an over-ripe fruit and when she looked at me her protruding green eyes narrowed with distaste.

A black and yellow car pulled up in front of the plane and switched on its left indicator light. It carried a notice saying FOLLOW ME. We trundled after it, the driver punctiliously signalling his intentions to the pilots by flashing the appropriate indicator as he led us through an empty landscape. The 727 swung on to the runway and instantly accelerated, the thunder of its three tail-mounted Pratt & Whitneys drowned by the RSM, now teaching his men hand-to-hand combat.

As we rotated and rose through the butter-coloured light my neighbour screamed. A bee was circling a couple of feet above. It sank towards her and she scrambled into the aisle, clutching at the seats for support against the Boeing's acute angle of climb. A stewardess told her sharply to sit down, but she paid no attention. The bee made a leisurely pass by her ear then, swatted with a handbag, flew unsteadily away towards the front and stung a brigadier. He too sprang into the aisle, one hand pressed to his neck, the other clasping a set of ivory worry beads. Two flight attendants, responding to an urgent shout from the steward, seized a first aid box and hurried forward, scrambling up the slope like a pair of rock climbers.

We levelled off and someone, mercifully, stopped the baritone in mid-roar. There was a little roughness as the 727 passed through a few scattered fragments of alto-stratus. The desert below was crosshatched, mysteriously, into neat, orderly squares. The Euphrates had the dull, oily glitter of stagnant water and the earth and sky were bonded at the horizon in an impenetrable haze known to Imperial pilots as 'The Blue'. We sailed on into the blue across a landscape the colour and texture of ash. It seemed featureless, but closer examination revealed an unending succession of deep valleys and high rock buttresses flowing onwards like a petrified tide of smoked glass.

I didn't want supper – the cold sliced meats and sprigs of pickled cauliflower that seemed standard fare on desert flights – and leafed through my copy of *Ma'ak* again, noting a message from the editorial staff headed 'When The Aircraft Engine Runs!' It said, 'Dear Passenger. While you are sitting in your comfortable chair on board one of our planes during your pleasant journey, looking out through the windows over the silver colour wings on the engines running, to thrust the plane to take-off and reach the sky thousands of feet over the clouds, we know for sure that you understand that there is a power and efforts behind the mechanical power of the engines that makes them run. It is the active power of the Man and his creative thinking and skill that make the machine to obey his will.'

We were flying on a curving westerly track that would take us well clear of any Iranian anti-aircraft batteries set up on the disputed Basra road, and south of Lake Habbaniyah, once a staging post for Imperial's Empire flying boats and the spot where one of them, the *Calpurnia*, crashed during a night sandstorm in 1938, killing several members of the crew. The low-level run from Baghdad to Basra had been one of the most memorable legs of the Imperial journey, passing over the great arch of Ctesiphon, then Babylon, Ur of the Chaldees and the great marshes between the Tigris and Euphrates where the people, a resilient warrior race, lived on islands of floating reeds. It was here that Sir Alan Cobham, flying a De Havilland 50 seaplane to Australia in 1926 to demonstrate the feasibility of a commercial service, was forced down to 40 feet by poor visibility and fired on by an unknown Marsh Arab. The bullet pierced a petrol pipe and a Foreign Office dispatch box intended for the Governor-General of Australia before entering the lung of A. B. Elliott, his mechanic. At first Cobham thought one of his rocket pistol cartridges had exploded, and it was only when Elliott passed him a scribbled message saying he was 'bleeding a pot of blood' that he began to comprehend what had happened.

Elliott died of his wounds in Basra that night so the RAF gave Cobham another mechanic, A. H. Ward, who was equally familiar with the workings of the Siddeley-Jaguar engine. (Cobham went on to complete his remarkable out-and-back journey, landing in triumph on the Thames beside the House of Commons, welcomed home by the Lord Chamberlain and the Speaker, Mr Whitley.) Basra had plenty of spare mechanics. A major base serving both military and civilian flights, it was situated, according to the *Air Route Book*, 'on the W. bank of Shatt-el-Arab, opposite small island known as Coal Island'. Pilots were warned to keep a wary eye on the steamers tied up at the Margil Wharfs, some of which were likely to be fitted with 170-foot-high masts, while the field and its four tracked runways had to be approached on a 'normal left-hand circuit'; the airspace over Basra itself was strictly off limits.

The Hoares called there for lunch ('I sat next to the Civil Administrator') and afterwards the RAF officers presented Lady Maude with 'a beautiful Amara tea service'. Imperial's passengers stayed near the airfield at the Iraq Railway Rest House – quantities of duck, geese, snipe, sand grouse and wild boar could be conveniently shot nearby – where, by all accounts, they were well looked after. One anonymous traveller in 1934 reported that, after landing in a gale at dusk, everyone relaxed around a crackling log fire in comfortable club chairs before going in to dinner. 'The servants are Iraqis; they are prompt and eager to help. They stay up all night, and in the morning as the weather conditions are still unfavourable, they wake us at 5.15 with a good cup of tea and biscuits and fruit, rush up the hot water, hustle us over our packing and have us all ready before the lounge fire at 5.45.'

The 727 dipped and began sliding into a purple twilight haze. At 3,000 feet we crossed a deserted twin-carriage motorway running down from the Iraqi border, the road along which Mr Moberly's truck travelled in more peaceful times to fetch the embassy supplies. Then, still descending, we saw the motorway rise above the desert and turn itself into an elevated interchange of quite bewildering complexity, the road splitting, multiplying and flowing off into the wilderness like a confluence of tarry rivers. With flaps extended we whistled over a gaudy orange bus abandoned in the sand then followed a line of wrecked cars all the way in to the runway threshold. The 727 flared, touched down and rushed through a radiant dusk, roaring as the thrust reversers opened the engine deflector doors and closed the clamshells to direct the Pratt & Whitneys' efflux thunderously the wrong way. We parked some distance from the terminal which, two months earlier, had been bombed by terrorists. Boarding a giant space-age bus I suddenly felt apprehensive. My visa had not been ready when I left London and the Embassy had advised it should be collected on arrival in Kuwait. But as the bus pulled away – braking sharply to avoid a speeding Kafko Jet-Al fuel tanker driven by a frowning, bearded man in a red baseball cap – I had a strong hunch that it wasn't there.

V

Imperial began flying into Kuwait in December 1932, the first airline to do so, its lumbering Hannibal biplanes landing on the hard, impacted sand outside the walled town in swirling clouds of dust. Then it was an impoverished little sheikdom subsisting on pearls, smuggling and a bit of dubious entrepot trade. Now, however, that desolate wasteland had been transformed into one of the largest airports in the Middle East, the terminal standing like a great white citadel overlooking a 5,436-acre asphalt and concrete plain that reached away until it seemed to dip over the horizon. I thought of the anonymous Imperial passenger who, landing on this spot 50 years earlier, gazed upon a town 'surrounded by a wall with towers at intervals. The towers have loopholes for rifles, but the whole structure is only of mud. A string of camels, roped nose to tail, files slowly into the gate of the town, and an Arab in flowing robes cycles over the sand up to the plane. Pedlars offer knives and carpets for sale, but find business rather dull.'

Some years later Kuwait was found to be straddling a fifth of the world's known oil reserves; the size of a spacious English county, it had more oil than the United States and the Soviet Union put together and today it is the pedlars who are flying in to do business with the locals. I watched a British Airways Tristar touch down, bringing even more, then turned and headed into the terminal through a bright white tunnel like a gallery in a salt mine. At the far end was a shallow step over which I tripped, sprawling at the feet of a coal-black security guard who looked at me with astonishment, placing a wary hand on his revolver as I hobbled away on an ankle that had turned like a tap. The Arrivals Hall was white too, staffed by immigration officials dressed like New York cops. Queues were forming at the desks. An imperious old Saudi standing in a neighbouring queue caught my eye. 'Stand behind the yellow line!' he barked. He wore a well-cut jellaba copiously stained with food. 'You hear me, English? Get back! Only one person at a time may speak with the officer.'

Awaiting my turn, I identified the stains as egg, yoghurt and a rich greenish sauce, possibly cream-based. Then the Immigration Officer beckoned me foward, heard my story and directed me to the Visa Collection Counter, a wooden stall erected in the centre of the floor. It was manned by a young official who had lines of strain deeply etched about his eyes. He heard me out courteously, asked me to wait and hurried away. An emaciated old Indian in ragged shorts and a soiled shirt lolled on a nearby chair, cross-eyed, slack-jawed, face contorted in a wild idiot's grin. We were joined by a dapper American carrying a fancy calfskin briefcase with a plastic Concorde tag on the handle. He said he had spent a week drinking apple juice in Riyadh and now faced the daunting prospect of three more days of apple juice in Kuwait. Then he was going to Bahrain, a wide-open town not yet taken over by the Muslim fundamentalists where, he advised me, he aimed to create a Scotch whisky shortage single-handed. I remarked on his Concorde tag, and he said it was an indispensable accessory for anyone doing business in the Gulf, conferring upon its owner the kind of status that opened doors and got you noticed. 'Not that I've ever been in the Concorde,' he added. 'That plane is dangerous. You know if a window blows out everyone vaporizes? I got the tag from my mother.'

The Visa Collection Officer returned and said my name was not on his list. I explained that I had put in my application more than two months earlier and, after many delays and evasions, was told the visa would be telexed to await my arrival. He shrugged and said, 'Yes, maybe, but it hasn't come.' Told you so, I said to myself and asked whether he would phone my only Kuwait contact, the local manager of British Airways, Bob Lee, and tell him of my position. He agreed to try.

The American said, 'This guy Lee your sponsor?'

'No. But I'm working on a project his airline knows about.'

'In Kuwait you got to have a sponsor.'

'I'm in transit. Just here for the night.'

'My sponsor can't wait to see me. I'm travelling in perfumes. The women here are crazy about the stuff. So are the men. My sponsor will order my most expensive lines the way other people buy gasoline.'

The Visa Collection Counter was suddenly besieged with edgy, anxious businessmen just off the BA Tristar from London. The Officer returned and, before taking their particulars, quietly advised me that Bob Lee would come as soon as he could get his plane ready for its onward leg to Dubai; meanwhile, I should speak to the Immigration Officer, who might be prepared to issue me with an overnight transit permit. I thanked him and, as the businessmen began clamouring for his attention, walked across the floor to the Immigration Officer's room. He sat reading a newspaper, a stout, fleshy man with a sharply receding chin and pouches under his eyes like spent balloons. He wore a frayed brown jellaba and a chequered pink Hashemite headdress, and he looked up, scowling, as I approached.

'Could you possibly spare me a minute?' I asked.

He licked a finger and turned the page.

I sat on the squeaky supplicant's chair before his desk and launched into my plea. He looked at me blankly then called to a man passing his door. The man said something that caused the Immigration Officer to throw back his big head and give a high-pitched yelp of laughter. Turning to me he waved both hands in my face and shouted, 'No visa! No visa!'

I explained that I only wanted to spend the night in Kuwait, and showed him the dated booking form issued by the Kuwait Hilton and the confirmed ticket for my onward flight to Bahrain at 0700 the next morning.

'No visa!' he yelled, banging the desk with a plump fist.

'So where am I supposed to sleep?'

He pointed to the mad old Indian who sat grinning wildly at us. 'On chair. On floor. Anywhere. You go now.' He flicked his fingers at me. 'Out! Out!'

I lost my temper then, telling him he was no better than the Iranian terrorists all this was presumably intended to discourage, but I knew I was locked into an inextricable nosedive situation, and so did he. Absently sucking his teeth, he returned to the sports pages of his paper.

The British businessmen had heard our raised voices and, when I arrived back at the Visa Collection Counter, there was little sympathy in their looks. The White Man's Burden, I realized, had become the salesman's samples case, and the baleful glances being directed at me made me understand how heavy the load had become. The official returned with a sheaf of visa forms and began calling names. 'Patridge S.'

'Here!'

'Brownlow J. G.'

'Present!'

'Goatley P. L.'

'Yes!'

They seized their prizes and hurried off, beaming with relief, chattering like schoolboys. The American said, 'Don't let the bastards get up your nose,' before following them down into the gilded city where everyone was clamouring for his $100 bottles of body splash. I sat beside the crazy Indian and gave him a cigarette. He smoked it with a kind of demonic energy, head wreathed in swirling clouds, as I consulted the *Air Route Book* and found that, even in 1942, Kuwait still had no airport. The planes continued to land on the sand, which was safe in dry weather only, while the only signalling aid was a primitive wind indicator stuck on the city gate. Fuel was not available and neither were repair facilities; and anyone needing medical attention was advised to approach the British Political Agent, who had custody of the iodine and aspirins. The only way out of the place if you couldn't fly was along 'the desert road to Basra' or by hitching a lift on a pearler's dhow. Kuwait, it advised, was 'a large walled town' which endured thunderstorms from November to April and sand and dust storms throughout the year; the latter were specially fierce during the blistering months of summer.

A trim, bearded young Indian with a walkie-talkie came hurrying towards me. He introduced himself as Ram Menen of British Airways, and said that Bob Lee was now making phone calls on my behalf. Noting that I was carrying an Australian passport he murmured this information into his radio before leading me up a white staircase to the white departure lounge. There we were joined by Mr Lee, a smiling, youthful-looking man who said, 'Not much success so far, I'm afraid. I gather you're an Australian national employed by a British newspaper, so I've been in touch with the duty officers of both embassies. The Brits said you were the responsibility of the Aussies, the Aussies said they only sponsor people travelling on official government business. Now I've got calls placed to the ambassadors; I'll ask them to talk to the Immigration Ministry and persuade them to issue your visa. Then we'll get you around to your hotel.'

Before I could thank them he and Mr Menen had dashed off to supervise the departure of their service to Dubai and Karachi. I propped my throbbing ankle on a spare chair and gazed at the Tristar's giant floodlit tail which, with its Union Jack livery, looked like a jet-age version of the Cenotaph. The airfield lights beyond merged into a black sky blazing with stars. One constellation detached itself from the rest and fell slowly to earth revealing itself as a Kuwait Airways 747; another became an Aeroflot Ilyushin I1-62, its four rear-mounted Soloviev turbofans humming as it turned off the runway, landing lights dazzling when they swung across my line of vision. Then the Tristar started up its three Rolls-Royce RB 211s and began pushback. A few minutes later, the pre-taxi checks complete, it lumbered slowly away into the darkness until its lights merged with the others to become part of the glittering Kuwait solar system. I looked at the billions of dollars of technology out there and thought of the place as it was when the Kuwait writer Khaled al-Farag described it at the turn of the century. 'Imagine a vast expanse, offering nothing but sand over which wild beasts roam, with no water to temper the torrid heat except that hidden within the earth, without a tree to give protection against the desert, against the clouds of dust blowing from the distant horizon.'

Bob Lee and Ram Menen returned to report that neither ambassador could be contacted. 'Must be a big diplomatic sheep-roast on tonight,' Mr Lee remarked. We were descending the stairs to the new Immigration Officer's room, led by Mr Menen who said that a man had come on duty, younger, more approachable, certainly more senior; this one was a captain and Mr Menen had talked him into seeing me. The captain, however, proved to be just as intractable as his colleague, but he at least took the trouble to tell me why. 'Transit visas have just been abolished,' he said. 'If you had come a little while ago, maybe even yesterday, I could have admitted you. But now the only way is to find a sponsor.'

Mr Lee said he would write a letter here and now, accepting full responsibility for me, but the Immigration Officer ruled that this would contravene the proper procedures and that, being *persona non grata*, I must leave the country on the first available flight. 'Rule number one when you're kicked out,' said Mr Lee as we trudged back up the stairs, 'is to make sure they keep kicking you in the right direction. There's a Gulf Air 737 leaving for Bahrain at 9.45, the last plane going that way tonight. We'll get you aboard.'

As Mr Menen made the arrangements Mr Lee, looking like a man who had endured a long day, drank a coffee and told me that Kuwait Airways, his chief rival on the profitable London run, was the only airline in the country allowed to advertise. 'And they do,' he said wryly. 'They even get the day's prime TV spot, right after the evening news and weather. But, despite that, we consistently get better loads – possibly because, by orders of the Ruler, all Kuwait planes must fly dry.'

He walked me to the departure gate, waved aside my apologies for the trouble I'd caused and headed home. It was only a chance remark by a heavy-set Canadian travelling in chemical dyes that made me realize the flight departing from this gate was bound for Dubai. I looked at the televised indicator board and saw that the Bahrain plane was boarding at the other end of the vast concourse, going from a gate that, as I hobbled off at top speed, turned out to be halfway to Egypt. The last passenger on, I ran full tilt into a glass door at the entrance to the telescopic loading jetty and entered the homely cabin of the little Boeing 737 with blood running from my nose and my skull full of gun flashes. The stewardess, a tall, pretty English girl in a smart trouser suit and a curious wimple-like headdress, gave me a startled look. 'Blimey!' she said. 'Are you running away from a jealous husband?'

I tidied myself up in the toilet and got back to my seat shortly before we moved away towards the threshold of Runway 33 Left. There, as the skipper held for an incoming Ethiopian Airways 707, I dipped into the Imperial *Gazette* which described 'the town of Koweit, outside of which Imperial Airways' liners land' as 'a mass of Arab dwellings built closely together. On one side there is the waterfront with breakwaters and the many dhows used for pearling.' The local currencies had been the Austrian Maria Theresa dollar and the Indian rupee which must have tickled the fancy of His Highness the Maharajah Gaekwar of Baroda who called there en route to Alexandria in 1937. 'At 11.30 we landed at Koweit to refuel,' wrote one of his aides, 'and found that we could not see the town on account of a wall seven miles long which encircles it on the landward side. This wall has watch towers and loopholes and was apparently completed in forty days. There was nothing to see except camels, donkeys and old cars in various stages of senility, a customs house at which an *ad valorem* duty of 5 per cent on everything is charged, and a junk shop in which Arabia and Woolworths seem to be equally represented. It would be interesting to know the history of the battered King George V Coronation mug which figured in a place of honour.'

The 737 rushed down the first quarter-mile of 33 Left and climbed away from the city, glittering like a rhinestone carpet, where real estate now changed hands for £1 million an acre. My neighbour was a Scottish businesswoman travelling in leisurewear. She had chubby features and pale eyes that contrasted sharply with her crisply assertive voice. When I had told her of my brief stay in Kuwait she said, 'Nothing would surprise me about that place. I know an English family there whose two children, a boy of 11 and a girl of 9, arrived home for the school holidays just a few days after the Iranian bombings. The Immigration Officer was not satisfied with their visas either, and locked them in a cell for the night. Next door they were questioning a suspect. You understand? This man was being beaten. He screamed a lot. In the morning the frantic parents finally got the kids out, but they were in such a terrible state that the little girl is still having psychiatric treatment.'

The stewardess brought a whisky, which helped to anaesthetise my aching face and foot. Oil rigs dotted the dark sea below; they had names like Cyrus, Lulu, Dorra and Umm. Across the aisle three Bahraini youths, their voices barely broken, were drinking whisky too. They began showing excessive high spirits, banging their folding tables up and down, fooling about with their reclining seats, scattering cigarette ash over the carpet. The Bahraini stewardess who had sold them the whisky smiled timidly at the trio, uncertain what to do, but her English colleague came racing aft and gave them a piece of her mind. 'Nice Arab boys aren't supposed to drink and carry on like hooligans,' she said crisply. 'So cut it out or I'll get the captain to talk to your fathers.'

That did the trick. They folded their tables and handed over their glasses, solemn as owls. As we filled in our landing cards I saw, far beyond the starboard wing, the lights of El Jubayl and Ras Tannurah twinkling along the looming Saudi Arabian seaboard. Somewhere out there Captain Tweedie, flying his Hannibal from Basra to Bahrain, ran into the worst weather ever recorded in the area and, his compasses malfunctioning, hopelessly lost, unable to raise anyone on the radio, was finally forced to put down on a salt flat. He ordered the bar to be opened and waited for the storm to blow itself out but, as he prepared to restart his engines at dusk, found that his wheels had sunk deep into the sand. Wondering where he was going to find help in this silent, terrible wilderness, he suddenly saw a party of Arabs leading laden donkeys towards the stranded plane. They halted, erected a large tent nearby and made it comfortable with carpets and cushions. A crackling wood fire was lit and a lamb roasted on a spit. Then Captain Tweedie, his crew and male passengers – but most pointedly not the women – were invited to a feast of lamb stuffed with pistachio nuts, roasted chicken, pilaff served from gleaming copper trays, Arab bread, vegetables, fresh fruit and coffee. To add to the gaiety of this extraordinary occasion Captain Tweedie turned on all the aircraft's lights. The meal over, his host, an official from a nearby village, packed everything back on to the donkeys and vanished into the darkness, returning next morning with ropes and a gang of able-bodied men who pulled the Hannibal out of the sand. Captain Tweedie presented him with a box of 100 'Passing Clouds' cigarettes and, several months later, Imperial sent the official an inscribed gold watch from London.

We began descending towards Bahrain and I recalled that I had last landed here on one of Concorde's first commercial flights in 1976, the narrow cabin crowded with British businessmen who, as the bulkhead machmeter indicated we were through the sound barrier, broke into wild applause, cheering like an audience at a rock concert. Now we whistled in to Muharraq Airport and, moments later, I stepped into the bright, cheery Arrivals Hall, sleepily anticipating my first meal of the day and several uninterrupted hours in bed. But the Passport Office frowned at my documents and took them into a small room, returning a moment later. 'You go in there, please.'

'What's wrong?' I asked.

'You go in there.'

I went at once and found a plump, balding man, mournful as a bloodhound, pondering my papers. He wore a black tunic, like a fireman, and, tapping my passport, he said, 'Your visa is wrong. On your landing card you say you are a journalist, but your visa is a normal business type, not the special press permit you must have to get into Bahrain.'

I stared at him. He had a heavy moustache and limpid brown eyes that were filled with melancholy. Framed Kodachrome prints of neat, smiling children stood at his desk. I took a deep breath and explained that the people at his London Embassy knew I was a journalist and fully understood the nature of my business in Bahrain: this was the visa they had issued. Furthermore, I had a sponsor, none other than Gulf Air, whose headquarters were only a few minutes' drive from this very airport.

'I am only doing my duty,' the official explained. 'About this matter we have strict instructions. It is expressly forbidden to admit a journalist without a valid press visa.'

I nodded wearily, recalling Bob Lee's advice: make sure they keep kicking you in the right direction. Was there a night flight down to Dubai, my next port of call? And would they let me in? The official suddenly reached across and patted my hand. 'Don't worry, my dear,' he said. 'You go and sit down outside. I will make some phone calls.'

The Arrivals Hall was now empty. Old men with buckets shuffled about mopping the floor and emptying the ashtrays. The 737 that had brought me from Kuwait stood outside on the deserted tarmac with its windows darkened, powered down and locked up for the night. If Dubai also refused to admit me I was going to have problems. From there I planned to head for Muscat in Oman where, since I had already been curtly denied a visa, I would be obliged to skulk in the transit lounge before making an absolutely crucial connection, the weekly Fokker Friendship flight across the Gulf of Oman to Baluchistan. But it didn't go for four more days, so if

Bahrain chucked me out and Dubai bounced me on I would head for Karachi, where I had been promised a welcome of sorts and from where, presumably, I could backtrack to my original destination on the Baluchi coast.

The official called to me. He held a telephone in a hand embellished with a large gold ring. 'I have told the man in charge at the Ministry of Information about your case. He would like to speak to you.'

'Have we woken him up?' I asked.

'I think so. But he is not angry.'

He handed me the phone. The official on the other end was infinitely courteous, leading me patiently through my story, putting the occasional question, seeking clarification on this point or that, finally asking to be handed back to the Immigration Supervisor. He took the phone, spoke a few words and hung up. 'I am instructed to admit you,' he said with a broad surprising smile, 'and to apologize for giving you such a poor welcome, my dear. We hope you will understand it is just because of our damn red tape.'

Outside the night was balmy and starlit, its silence broken by the thunder of some Far East-bound 747 alighting to take on fuel and provisions for the long trans-Indian Ocean hop ahead. My youthful taxi driver, wearing a spotless white dishdasha and headdress, took off at speed, pleased when I commented on the electronic compass built into the dashboard of his fancy new Honda. On the outskirts of Manama he whizzed around a roundabout twice, beaming as the compass spun wildly through 360 degrees. When we arrived at the Hilton he politely returned my tip. 'Not necessary,' he said. He waved, banged his car into gear and howled away on a rough north-westerly bearing.

Indoors I explained to the receptionist that I was not actually due until tomorrow; could I have my room a day early? Of course, he said. And something to eat? The coffee shop, he assured me, never closed. My room was cool and quiet, an oasis in which to unscramble the events of the day and arrange them into some kind of order for my notebook. In the coffee shop I sat for a few moments, just savouring the welcoming, non-hostile surroundings of Bahrain. A young Indian waiter came to take my order and wept as he wrote it down. Another waiter said, 'His father died today. He only just heard. Everyone is very sad.' I grew sad too. Later the waiter dried his eyes with his knuckles and took a call at a phone adjacent to my table. 'Yes, Auntie, I will come if I can but the formalities here are very complicated. They may take time. Pray for him, Auntie. And don't cry.'

The only other customer in the coffee shop was a drunken young woman in a low-cut dress. When the bereaved waiter brought her more gin she teased him coquettishly and, presumably unaware of his personal circumstances, urged him, in heavily accented English, to cheer up. 'You look as if you have seen a ghost,' she said. The waiter burst into tears again and rushed for the sanctuary of the kitchen. Then, unexpectedly, a burst of clapping came through the wall and a group of young people surged into the coffee shop, led by a stocky, smiling girl whose hair fell in curling ringlets. She caught my eye and smiled. 'Why don't you pull your table up?' she called in a commanding Lancashire voice. 'It's my birthday. We're celebrating. You too, Monika!' she said to the tipsy woman. 'Come and join us. They've made me a cake!'

The lady was called Magi. She was a singer, working with her husband, a bony, taciturn Paraguayan named Leo who played a wide selection of stringed instruments, including a 38-stringed pine and caoba wood harp. Calling themselves Los Arribentos, they did traditional South American stuff, and were providing the cabaret in the Cavalry Bar next door. The other members of the party, friends, fans and fellow-musicians, smiled affectionately at Magi, who bristled with vitality and benevolence, and who was buying the drinks. Monika, her eyes slipping in and out of focus, told me she was a Swiss from Zurich, here on vacation. 'I am illegitimate,' she said. 'All I know about my papa is that he was a banker and a prince, how do you say, among men.' She attempted to put a flame to her cigarette but couldn't get the two synchronized; I took the lighter and did it for her. The party warmed up. Magi said that, back home, she and Leo had played Camberley, Birmingham, Glasgow and the Golden Garter, Wythenshawe. Now they concentrated on the Middle East because the money was so good, working the hotel circuits in places like Kuwait, Baghdad, Teheran, Beirut, Ankara and Cairo. They had played Damascus for two years and once gone to Amman for the night to do a command performance for King Hussein of Jordan, who was very keen on their kind of music. She told me they were saving up for a small bar on the Costa Brava, where they planned to offer their customers country wine and lots of good songs.

Before going up to bed I talked to a bearded French doctor recently returned from Upper Volta, where he had been working with a Red Cross medical team. He flew out of Gorom-Gorom several days earlier and the only other passenger boarding the little Twin Otter of Air Volta was a native woman who, he said, paid for her seat with a calabash of wild honey.

VI

In the morning I went to see Mr Hussein Yateem, reputed to be the richest man in Bahrain. His monseignorial status, which brought him in just under the Ruler's immediate family, had been achieved by a combination of wisdom, sound judgement and consistent good luck – the qualities most admired in Bahraini financial circles. He was also renowned for his simplicity and, when I caught a taxi to his office, I noted that it did not take me uptown to the fashionable high-rise business and banking district, but headed instead for the noisy, bustling quarter where the bazaar is located. Here Mr Yateem started his business and had been content to remain ever since, surrounded by other merchants selling pearls, old jewellery, lace fashioned from beaten gold, intricate model dhows, rare carpets, handmade copper artefacts, crocodile skins and locally raised produce such as grapes, bananas, mangoes, lemons, figs, aubergines, sweet potatoes, melons, giant onions as juicy as apples and the sweetly succulent Nabi Salih dates for which Bahrain is celebrated.

In the midst of all this munificence sat Mr Yateem, inhabiting a new but modest office block – the Yateem Building – with special holes in the pedestrian precinct roof to accommodate each of the venerable palms that were growing there before the foundations were dug. His ground floor office was large and shadowy, containing a desk and several well-upholstered sofas and armchairs. Grave Indian clerks in the ante-room painstakingly wrote letters and bills of lading by hand. Out in the narrow street honking cars, bicycle bells and a ceaseless cacophony of human voices provided Mr Yateem with the familiar, homely counterpoint to his working day. He had a full face and a grey moustache under close-cropped grey hair, and wore the comfortable white cotton dishdasha that is the uniform of the souk. His manner was courteous to the point of courtliness and he leaned forward slightly when he listened, giving the speaker his complete and undivided attention. A servant padded in to pour coffee boiled with cloves and Mr Yateem began talking about aeroplanes. They were one of his passions, and he spoke with the intensity of the true enthusiast. He saw his first as a child, the old sycamore-strutted machine of some itinerant barnstormer who landed beside the Ruler's palace with his wheels axle-deep in mud and his tail high in the air. He was enchanted by this visitation from the sky and when, some thirty years later, another adventurer arrived in Bahrain under more or less the same circumstances, Mr Yateem took him under his wing and became his patron.

'His name was Freddy Bosworth,' he said. 'He arrived here in 1950 and he was broke. He had an old war surplus Anson bought cheap from the RAF and he had come to Bahrain with some vague idea of starting a flying club. But he had no money and no spares. There weren't any banks in Bahrain then so I gave Freddy his capital – at the insistence of my chief clerk, who was much more far-sighted than I was – and then we discovered that the Arabian American Oil Company in Dharan had a large stockpile of Anson spares. They were happy to sell so we took a dhow across to Saudi Arabia and loaded it up. Next, we applied to the government for a licence to take people on joyrides. Freddy charged his passengers 10 rupees a head and did remarkably well. Flying was suddenly the in-thing here. Everyone wanted to try it and I was now convinced, like my wise chief clerk, that this was where the future lay. A few of us got together and formed a company. Charles Belgrave, the British Financial Adviser to the Ruler of Bahrain, was chairman, and Freddy became managing director. Mrs Bosworth was on the board, together with the Kanoo brothers of Bahrain, and myself.

We began doing scheduled runs to Dharan and Sharjah – where we connected with the BOAC service to India and Australia – and a lot of charter and survey work for the oil companies, and we soon needed a new aircraft. Freddy wanted a pretty little eight-seater called a De Havilland Dove and went home to buy one. But one day, while getting his Dove accreditation in England, he crashed the plane and was killed. No one knows why, and the memory of it still bewilders me. He was such a *good* pilot. His place was taken by Captain Bodger, an expansionist in the Freddy Bosworth mould, who went ahead with the purchase of a Dove and proved that, as Freddy had anticipated, it could make us money. One trick we learnt was that if you took the toilet out on the 15-minute run across to Saudi Arabia you could cut costs by 10 per cent. So, before each flight, we invited our passegers to pop behind a date palm if they wished to avoid potentially embarrassing consequences in the air.'

Mr Yateem grinned and called for more coffee. He told me that he had been educated at Brighton Grammar School on the edge of the Sussex Downs. 'The only thing they managed to teach me at Brighton was how to talk,' he said. 'At Brighton I learnt the art of persuasion – though I had already been given a good grounding in that by my father, a very clever and resourceful man who traded in pearls and ran a chemist's shop here in the souk. Each year he went to Bombay to sell his pearls and stock up on medicines like quinine, aspirin and worm seeds. On at least one occasion his experience in one field led him to profit greatly in the other. He had gone to an important pearl auction in Abu Dhabi but, because he was a stranger, they refused to let him bid. Later he happened to hear that one of the other merchants was suffering from severe stomach pains. My father gave him a large dose of Dr J. Collis-Browne's Mixture and very soon the man was feeling as right as rain. Next morning the sheik who ran the auction sent for him, folded back his sleeve and displayed his arm. It was withered. My father saw at once that the sheik had polio and told him he must go to Bombay for treatment. But what the sheik wanted, of course, was one of my father's wonder drugs. What he got was a very large dose of Eno's Fruit Salts. The effect was so dramatic that the sheik, purged and deeply impressed, welcomed my father into the privileged buyers' circle and announced that, from now on, the Bahraini doctor could bid for all the pearls he wanted.'

Gulf Air, the little company that Mr Yateem, Freddy Bosworth and the others began with their war surplus Anson, now had 4,200 employees, operated a fleet of nine Lockheed L-1011 Tristars and nine Boeing 737s and carried more than two and a half million passengers a year. The Chief Pilot, Captain A. R. Al-Gaoud, worked from a tumbledown single-storey building beside the airport tarmac and, when I met him (with a Bahrain Air Force Hercules parked just outside his office window) he wore Arab robes and headdress and heavy gold cufflinks shaped like daggers. A large, watchful, reserved man, he told me that student pilots were recruited by placing advertisements in the newspapers of the four states which jointly owned and administered the airline – Bahrain, Oman, Qatar and the United Arab Emirates. The matter of selection unavoidably assumed political overtones because, though Bahrain's long-established, British-founded educational system consistently yielded the most applicants with high scores in maths and physics, the required subjects, there could be no discernible bias in favour of Bahrain; the susceptibilities of the other Rulers, who would protest vehemently if their brightest and best were allowed to slip down the admissions table, had always to be taken into account.

Captain Al-Gaoud delicately explained the philosophy behind his mixed ability intake. 'If we realize people haven't had enough schooling we ask them about practical matters instead. What must you do if your car stops? Can you explain the principle of gear ratios? How do planes fly? What can you tell us about thrust, drag and lift? If they demonstrate a real grasp of these matters we will give them extra education before packing them off for pilot training in the United States. They used to go to England, but the English weather is terrible and the English instructors are too slow; it takes them three years to teach what the Americans can teach in two. The boys come home with their commercial pilot's licence and instrument rating for a multi-engined aircraft. Then we train them for two more years. They do theory, safety and survival training, and at least 48 hours in the 737 simulator. They must take the Civil Aviation exams and, of course, start their cockpit familiarization. For this the cadet is handed over to a Line Training Captain and a senior First Officer working on normal day-to-day operations. For the first 25 sectors the cadet sits in the jump seat and answers questions. For the next 30 sectors he helps prepare the aircraft for departure. For the 30 after that he takes the controls after the aircraft has climbed through 3,000 feet but hands them back before it has reached decision height during the approach. Then he does 75 take-offs but no landings. After that there is another long session in the simulator. Then, with his Training Captain, he practises take-offs and landings in an empty plane until he is judged ready to do them with passengers aboard. He does this for a minimum of 400 sectors and 500 hours and then, in theory, is competent to take his Final Line Check with the Fleet Captain himself. If the Fleet Captain is completely satisfied with every aspect of his performance the cadet becomes a lowly junior co-pilot. If he's not, he doesn't.'

The radio on Captain Al-Gaoud's desk crackled. An English voice, harassed but deferential, explained that a Dubai-bound Tristar was half an hour late off the blocks because a couple of off-duty pilots wished to travel as flight deck supernumeraries and the captain was making a fuss; a stickler for correct procedures, he refused to start his engines until the proper authorization had been granted. Captain Al-Gaoud took me into a neighbouring office, introduced me to Captain Pat Higgins, a trim, affable, grey-haired Englishman, then said goodbye and dashed off. Captain Higgins told me he had begun flying around the Gulf thirteen years earlier in DC3s. It is a period he looks back on without nostalgia. 'The quality of life improved the day they brought in the first jet,' he said. 'From June to September you get severe sandstorms in this area, thick dust swirling up to 12,000 feet and terrific turbulence, specially around noon. A jet just sails clean over the top of that. What still trouble us are thunderstorms which get so violent that they can even be active up around 35,000 feet – or more.'

Captain Higgins was first employed flying personnel and equipment out to desert oil camps. 'They'd burn old tyres to give you their position,' he recalled, 'or, if they had a generator, they might be persuaded to fire up a primitive radio beacon for you. The landings were usually made on dried salt pans marked by 40-gallon oil drums. When we carried bedouin they came aboard armed to the teeth with swords and loaded rifles and liked to spend the flight, including take-off and landing, strolling about chatting to their friends. There are even stories of fires being lit in Dakotas to roast a sheep or heat some coffee. That never happened to me, but it's one of the more enduring legends of early Gulf aviation and I don't doubt that there's some truth in it.'

Bahrain's Muharraq, the home base of Gulf Air, takes regular scheduled services from 30 international airlines and is one of the most important staging points in the Middle East. The present airport was built for Imperial Airways after disputes with the Persian government over the company's right to operate along the northern shore of the Persian Gulf. Imperial's India-bound flights had called at the Persian coastal settlements of Bushire, Lingeh and Jask since the service's inception in 1926, but when Teheran announced that the company was to switch to an inland corridor which would take its fragile machines over 14,000-foot mountain ranges, fever-ridden swamps, salt deserts notoriously swept by storms and even, in the vicinity of Bam, a stretch of jungle with tigers in it, the British Air Council secretly began making other arrangements. Noting also that the Shah's proposed new route would take the planes through territory which the Russians were expected, daily, to invade, they ordered Imperial and No. 203 Squadron, operating Rangoon flying boats from Basra, to survey possible landing grounds along the Trucial Coast.

The change to the southern service (through Kuwait, Bahrain and Sharjah) was made in November 1932 and the *Gazette*, appreciating that the only aspect of the new route likely to interest the travelling public was whether you could do good crash landings along it, provided reassurance. 'The Arabian shore is a kindly one, in the sense that it would be possible to put an aeroplane down safely on most parts of it, and on most of the islands. Generally speaking, it would be preferable to land on an island in case of need.' This preference had been expressed not by the pilots, but by 'the King of the Hedjaz and most of the sheikhs' who, 'though quite friendly, are rather conservative gentlemen, and fear that their people would not be too enthusiastic about the advent of such a modern innovation as a regular air service'. In other words, any stranded aircraft containing an unsupervised rabble of gin-sodden infidels was to be kept as far from the mainland as possible.

At first, 'Bahrain off Arabia' merited attention only because the passengers stopped there for lunch. 'The island is the centre of the group, which are under the protection of the Government of India. Bahrain is the centre of a large pearl fishery. It is a pleasant place, possessed of many vineyards and natural wells which yield water of 84 deg. all the year round. After lunch the journey is resumed.' A later issue of the *Gazette* noted with surprise that 'there are cars on these islands' and advised of local industries such as 'the manufacture of reed mats, date cultivation and the breeding of very fine white donkeys'. It failed to report that, in midsummer, the heat was so great Imperial's mechanics had to carry their tools around in buckets of water.

When British Airways held a dinner at the Bahrain Sheraton in May 1982 to commemorate the fiftieth anniversary of the first service, their invitations carried a sepia photograph of a grave young Arab and a middle-aged English couple standing beside an Imperial Hannibal on the sandy wastes of Bahrain aerodrome. The couple, who are both wearing tweed hats and heavy shoes, look as though they are about to go blackberrying in an Esher wood, while the Arab, in big sunglasses, burnous and suede desert boots is . . . Hussein Yateem! 'What I remember most vividly about the Hannibals,' he had said to me, 'was the way they could bump you around even in perfectly calm air. The "terminal" here was a baresti, or thatched palm shack, with a signpost outside, one arm pointing to London and the other to Karachi. Imperial's big brass bell hung outside with a plaited rope lanyard. Four bells meant an aircraft was approaching, six that it was ready to depart.'

In January 1933 the *Gazette* boasted that the new Trucial Coast route was 'already proving of great use to merchants in the area. This district is the centre of the pearling trade in that part of the world, and the sheiks find that they can now, by means of Imperial Airways' services, arrive at places in a few hours which it took them several days to reach by the older forms of surface transport.' And when the Marquess of Londonderry, Secretary of State for Air, made a brief stop in Bahrain in 1934 he too mused on the improvement in communications. 'We landed at midday, and I enjoyed a short walk in the sun, under a cloudless sky, with Colonel

Loch, the Political Agent, and Mrs Loch. They told me what a vast difference the coming of Imperial Airways had made to their lives. They were within a week of London instead of five weeks. They were in the world instead of out of it.'

Many transit passengers commented on the limited choice of souvenirs. The *Madras Mail*, for example, reported, that the only local 'curiosities' on offer were 'blister pearls and the pegs the pearl divers put on their noses', while an anonymous traveller arriving in Bahrain after breakfasting 3,000 feet over the Gulf on corn flakes, scrambled eggs, tea, bread and butter, noted that 'Bahrain is a fairly large town with walled courtyards and flat-roofed dwellings, but the aerodrome some distance away is again a flat sandy waste, with a small woven grass shelter to keep out the stinging and rather cold wind. Here we are set upon by pearl vendors. The pearls are not particularly good, but are interesting as souvenirs.'

In 1937 the Maharaja Gaekwar of Baroda called at Bahrain during his aerial progress to Alexandria. 'Though the air is lovely,' wrote his aide, 'the island looks completely bare and the aerodrome buildings consisted of tents and huts in a vast sandy waste. Fish abounds – it formed the basis of our excellent breakfast –but in the absence of fodder it forms the basis of cattle cake with the result that the inhabitants complain that even the milk tastes of fish. It is curious how Baroda subjects are to be found nearly everywhere in the East, for we were informed before leaving that the leading general store in Bahrain is managed by a Mr Ashraf of Baroda.'

I read all this in the Cavalry Bar at the Hilton, a cool, dimly lit room with swords hanging from its panelled walls and deep leather seats polished like saddles. A woman entered, hesitated at the door then advanced towards me. It was Monika, my Swiss acquaintance of the previous evening. 'Hullo!' she said, sitting down and asking for a large gin and tonic. She wore a simple yellow sun dress. Her bare arms were very white and the skin was showing the first signs of slackness; her face, smooth, pretty and flamboyantly painted, belonged to a woman ten years younger.

During her first drink she told me what a fine place Bahrain was for a holiday, and then she described her apartment in Zurich, situated so close to the zoo that she could hear the lions roaring at feeding time. During her second she confessed that she hadn't come to Bahrain for a holiday at all. She had sold the apartment and come to stay. Maybe she would find herself a job. She had been personal assistant to a senior confectionery executive at home, and was confident that someone would pay well for her organizational skills and general business acumen. Midway through her third she finally told me the truth. 'I am here to find an Arab,' she said simply. 'They like white women. It is not hard. Tonight I am going out with a banker, very good-looking, very successful, *very* wealthy, a real sweetie. He is married already but he says maybe he will fix me up with a nice little flat. Of course, my dear, the really super-rich Arabs are in Saudi Arabia and once I went there, to Riyadh with my Swiss boss for business, but I found it was not a good place for getting boyfriends. Everyone was frightened of the Religious Police. They are the ones who chop off the heads of married people who make adultery. They hate white women because they think we have a very bad influence on Arab men.'

I told her a tale I had heard in London about the Religious Police raiding the British Council Offices in Riyadh after someone had put a photograph of St Paul's Cathedral on the wall. A jeepload of these loonies barged in with paintbrushes and erased the cross on Wren's great dome.

'Oh, yes, crosses make them crazy,' said Monika. 'Even the Swissair cross has been banned in Saudi Arabia; when it appeared on advertising posters crowds used to gather and throw stones at it. But what really got everyone in a state was when some Religious Policeman realized that in the logo of Saudia, their own airline, a space between two characters of the Arabic script made the shape of a cross. What a crisis! The King himself said this shocking space must go. A new logo was designed and, when its spaces had been carefully examined by a committee of mullahs, all the planes were repainted, new tickets and baggage labels were printed, the glasses and cutlery used on the planes had to be changed, all the advertisements and promotion were done again, also the notepaper and even the office memo forms. It cost them *millions*!'

She chuckled then rose to prepare for her tryst with the banker. I urged her to bargain hard and negotiate good terms, and she left me, a sad solitary woman in a cheap yellow dress. Back in the lobby I was waylaid by a hotel executive whose duties seemed to include PR and who, whenever I saw him, liked to give me fresh items from his stock of interesting local facts. Now, as we stood at the front door enjoying the salty evening air, he said, 'Did you know Bahrain gets a lot of its sweet water from springs on the sea bed? It's beautiful water, some of the best I ever tasted. This town still has two ice-making factories and in the summer they work 24 hours a day. The hotels operate their own equipment and, when we can't keep up with demand, we have to lend and borrow from each other; in Bahrain, during a heatwave, ice cubes can become a form of negotiable currency that just about has parity with the dollar.'

I knew his previous posting had been in Jeddah and asked whether he had ever been visited there by the Religious Police. 'Yeah, they used to come and check that we were observing the law against women swimming or sunbathing. I believe that all happened because some dumb Air France stewardess went topless by her hotel pool one afternoon. The ban was imposed the same day. Later, to avoid a mutiny among the airline girls who stayed with us, we had to arrange a special sunbathing place up on the hotel roof. It was the highest building in town and, unless the Religious Police were operating a helicopter check, there was no chance of them being spotted. The girls had to climb up through the elevator machinery to get there, but we issued them with special keys and told them to keep their mouths shut, and everyone was happy. We have crews here at the Hilton also. Our biggest customer is Singapore Airlines, who operate two 747s through Bahrain each night and have 52 rooms permanently reserved, but we look after a number of European carriers as well. We offer the airlines extremely competitive rates because, in this part of the world, having blonde girls sitting around in the lobby and coffee shop is very good for business.'

I went for a stroll. The evening sky was the colour of oranges and lemons and the diesel-powered dhows throbbing away towards Saudi Arabia left rosewater wakes. Manama Island is only a few feet above sea level and the dhows seemed part of the traffic on Government Road, bustling through the red lights then heading away past the highrise offices, the luxury hotels and skyscraper banks – one of which, I had been assured, contained the personal current account of King Fahd of Saudi Arabia who, each day, deposited several million dollars in it by telex. On the decks of the dhows sat rows of black-robed Saudi women over to visit friends or, perhaps, buy some sexy underwear and drink a little champagne.

It wasn't always thus. In 1943, long before Bahrain became a chrome and crystal petrodollar citadel, the *Air Route Book* warned, 'There is quite a lot of sickness here – malaria, dysentery and ear infections – so be on your guard. The air conditioning plants are not yet working. When they are, make full use of them. They rest the body and mind. It is a mistake to think it is not worth the trouble to spend a night sleeping in an air conditioned block. Be careful about the native bazaar in Bahrain. Food purchased there is sure to be filthy.' Provisions available in the mess, however, were judged to be safe. 'At Bahrain iced drinks and ice cream are supplied. They are prepared under medical supervision and may be eaten without fear. But don't take too much of them, especially on an empty stomach. Don't drink alcohol until sundown.'

I caught a mid-morning flight to Dubai. At the check-in desk a plump young Englishwoman with a plump little girl in a pushchair was arguing about two seats to London. The clerk said there were no seats; she had not confirmed her bookings. The woman said she had confirmed by phone. The clerk told her he had no record of any confirmation and, anyway, the aircraft was full. The woman said, 'Well, what are we supposed to do? Where are we supposed to go?' She began crying and so did the child, their tone and timing so precisely synchronized that they were weeping in harmony. I left the clerk with his head in his hands and boarded the Gulf Tristar. The stewards were all young, clean-limbed and English and, in their smart orange blazers, looked like members of a travelling cricket team. My seat was located beside a mural depicting some traditional views of the Arab world – date palms, dhows, camels, minarets and a European guest worker in a protective hard hat whose huge salary and watertight tax avoidance arrangements doubtless contributed to his look of deep contentment.

A trouser-suited stewardess held up a section of safety belt with a buckle on it and, as a recorded announcement said 'The belt is closed like this . . . and opened like this . . . and loosened like this' she gracefully pantomimed the actions while scores of buckles clicked like triggers up and down the plane. My neighbour, an elderly, liverish-looking Englishman with a skin as brittle as a Dead Sea Scroll, muttered peevishly, 'Good thing she isn't trying to show them how to put on bloody parachutes.'

We began taxiing out towards Bahrain's 13,000-foot runway. The Tristar's massive double-slotted Fowler trailing-edge flaps were lowered, activated not by the muscles and sinews of the pilots, but by a multiple redundant servo actuator system powered by four separate hydraulic sources. On the threshold, beside a solitary windsock and a small field filled with vivid green plants, the three Rolls-Royce RB 211 turbofans began to roar. Seconds later we rose over a palm grove and a white beachside villa, our shadow whizzing across an aquamarine sea and growing steadily smaller as we climbed. It slid over a reef with a large shark basking in its lee and chased a couple of dhows that were going like destroyers, their wakes spreading behind them like lacy bridal trains. My neighbour noted them. 'The one on the right's a sambuq,' he said. 'Bahrain-built I should think, and traditionally used for pearling. The other's a bum-safar, general cargo, probably smuggling Scotch whisky across to the Saudis. Or he would be if he's got any sense. They're playing $80 a bottle for the stuff.'

Across the aisle a veiled, black-robed woman sat clutching a blue plastic bucket. Only her hands were visible, the fingers ringed with diamonds, the nails painted a wild, lurid crimson.

We were already far out over the Gulf, unlike the Hannibals which were required, whenever possible, to keep within gliding distance of the coast. The *Air Route Book* advised that 'on this stage maps are most unreliable'. For the first 60 miles 'occasional small villages about water holes are passed but none provide a distinctive landmark. The next pin-point should be the small town of DOHA. This is quite distinct, lying as it does in a bend of the coast, also because of its light-coloured fort. The landing ground as mapped is incorrect. From DOHA the track lies across sea to YAS ISLAND. Course is now set for ABU DUBAI, several very badly mapped islands being passed en route. The town of ABU DUBAI is conspicuous as a small walled coastal town with a noticeable minaret. An emergency landing ground lies to the SOUTH. From this point track lies just off the coast to SHARJAH. DUBAI town, easily recognized, is the first fair-sized native town built on either side of a wide and conspicuous inlet. Nine miles further along the coast is the town of SHARJAH at the mouth of Sharjah creek' – and it was in Sharjah, at the company's famous port, that the Imperial passengers dined and slept.

My neighbour told me he was in shipping, London-based but no stranger to these parts; the Middle East had long been his particular patch and, though Imperial's early days in the Gulf preceded his own by a decade or so, they were still adjacent enough for him to know about the pilot of one of the Hannibals – the *Horsa*, he thought – who took off from Basra late one night in 1935 without telling Bahrain that he was coming. 'As a result, Bahrain didn't light up for him and he missed it and came down in the desert 100 miles to the south. When the rescue party got there next day they found that a crowd of bedouin had ordered the passengers and crew off, hitched a team of camels to the plane and were towing it away for scrap metal.'

We were descending. On finals we passed over a tanker and a number of oil platforms and then the seat belt signs came on and we hummed in over a discoloured sea to a perfect landing at Dubai.

VII

My visa was issued on the spot, without fuss, just as the United Arab Emirates Embassy in London had promised. The airport terminal was small and extravagantly pretty, built around rows of slender columns with their tops spreading like date palms. In its cylindrical tower, reminiscent of a sturdy minaret, Dubai's air traffic controllers sat 92 feet above the desert calling like muezzins to their pilots on 118.3 megahertz. The runway, built of impacted sand until the first Viscount turbo-props arrived and blew it all away, was shared by the Dubai Police Air Wing and the personal Air Wing of the Ruler, Sheik Al-Maktum, who owned a fleet of Boeings which ferried him and his horse-mad sons around the yearling sales and race tracks of Europe.

The town centre lay three miles away across a flat, dusty landscape flooded with white light, the route passing the offices and mosque of the Lootahs, a leading mercantile family, and, at a roundabout, a skeletal concrete tower with a four-faced clock suspended beneath its apex. Three faces of the clock told different times but, by averaging them out, I knew I was on schedule for a lunch appointment with Mr David Lawford, Dubai's British Airways manager, and Mr Nasser Abdul Latif who, in 1931, translated the first air services agreement between Britain and the tiny state of Sharjah into Arabic. We headed on down Al-Maktum Road and, at the Sheraton, I found Mr Lawford and Mr Latif waiting for me.

Mr Lawford was a youthful, engaging man whose enthusiasm for flying – he once thought of becoming a commercial pilot himself – reached back to the early days of aviation in the Gulf. This ability to view the industry with a historian's perspectives was clearly something of which Mr Latif approved. A spry old gentleman in elegant robes, he fizzed with energy, ideas and information, though everything he said was delivered in a voice as quiet and measured as that of a family solicitor. Our table overlooked the Creek, a broad waterway that bisects the town like a minor Grand Canal and, moored directly below us, was a fabulous ocean-going yacht with spotless teak decks and paintwork that shone like glass.

'It belongs to a Saudi businessman,' said Mr Latif, 'who made his fortune growing vegetables in the desert. In the summer he sails up the Red Sea to the Mediterranean and spends the season at the fashionable resorts – St Tropez, Monte Carlo and so on. The rest of the year he keeps it here and comes down in his private 707, flown by a crew permanently seconded from British Airways.'

'Two crews, actually,' said Mr Lawford. 'He has a standby one as well. And his private suite is ready for him here at the Sheraton 52 weeks of the year.'

Mr Latif chuckled. 'And all because of carrots.' He ate a little grilled fish then got down to business. His involvement with the Imperial negotiations, he told us, had been due simply to the fact that his father, at the time, was the British Political Agent. 'My family's association with the British was almost a dynastic one. The Resident was originally stationed across the Gulf at Bushire, in Persia, and one of my ancestors managed to get himself appointed Assistant Political Agent there in 1850. A later ancestor became the Political Agent proper – a kind of consular role, open to Arabs, though the Resident himself was always an Englishman – and we held the post, through successive generations, until 1935, when my brother finally relinquished the job to concentrate on business. We shipped the first car to Dubai and brought in the first telephones. We also started the first electricity generating concern.'

He took a sip of Perrier. 'Negotiations on the British side were conducted by Sir Hugh Biscoe and Colonel Dickson, who had come out on the gunboat HMS *Lupin*. It was moored off the Sharjah coast and, each morning, Sir Hugh and the Colonel were brought ashore in a navy pinnace for their meetings with the Ruler of Sharjah, Sultan bin Saqr. This was the culmination of a lengthy and complicated process. After the Persians had made it impossible for Imperial to continue operating along the north of the Gulf, the British came and talked to all the sheiks along this coast, seeking landing rights for flying boats – they planned to use Calcuttas – because flying boats were thought necessary to cope with the long overwater leg to Gwadar in Baluchistan.' He looked at me. 'You are going there, I understand? They are letting you in?'

'The day after tomorrow,' I said.

He nodded slowly. 'One hears such very strange stories about that place.' Before I could seek elaboration he continued, 'The British met stiff local resistance because the sheiks believed that, if the company came, their women and slaves would slip away to the Imperial manager's office and ask for asylum. The Ruler of Sharjah finally said yes because a friend from Paris, who was wise to the ways of the world, assured him that Imperial would put Sharjah on the map – and that the local manager, having no diplomatic status, couldn't give asylum to anyone. So Sharjah relented and agreed to accept the flying boats. But then Imperial abandoned the flying boats idea and switched back to landplanes. The eastern versions of the big new HP 42 Heracles were now available, their colonial seating arrangements (they carried fewer passengers), extra tankage and greater range specially developed for this route. They could make the trip over to Gwadar without risk and the Ruler was persuaded to allow Imperial to construct an aerodrome instead. But the night before the agreement was to be signed Sir Hugh suffered a fatal heart attack in the wardroom of the *Lupin* so Colonel Dickson, despite his personal distress, signed instead. Work on the fort and aerodrome began almost at once, supervised by Flight Lieutenant McKay of the RAF and his Indian assistant, Nattah Singh. Because Sharjah was a notoriously unstable area Imperial wanted a defended fort, similar to the one at Rutbah Wells in the Iraqi desert. First, though, they had to erect a palm frond barasti for the construction workers to live in and, for that important task, I was made Clerk of Works.'

Mr Latif smiled faintly, pushed aside his fish and nibbled some grapes. 'The fort was built with local stone and cement shipped from Basra. The first Imperial manager appointed to Sharjah was an Anglo-Indian named Mr Jameson. His Iraqi wireless operator, Abdulla Dhafei – whose radio was the first ever seen in Sharjah – also lived at the fort and wanted to bring his wives out to join him. Permission was denied by the British Resident because Sharjah was a bachelor posting and it was felt that Dhafei's wives would cause tension among the rest of the staff. Then Mr Jameson recruited two cooks from Karachi and a staff of Persians from Jask to be the waiters and cleaners. No local people were employed inside the fort. Arabs did not know this job. The only work considered suitable for them was fighting and, from the Ruler, Mr Jameson recruited 25 Omanis and bedouin, gave them old British Army Lee Enfield rifles and formed them into a guard. Shortly before the first plane was due Imperial's engineer, Mr Barnard, took up his post, arriving with his assistant, a Jew, whose name I do not remember. Finally all was ready and on 6 June 1932 the inaugural flight arrived from Bahrain, the HP 42 *Hanno* under the command of Captain Alcock. It landed in a cloud of sand and taxied right up to the fort, where it was locked up by the guard inside a special barbed-wire entanglement.'

Mr Latif went on to describe the fort's impressive range of modern conveniences, but I had already learnt about these from the *Gazette* which announced that the new staging post, 'although it is far from civilisation, contains modern accommodation, electric light and fans, refrigeration, hot baths and showers. The Rest

House is constructed in the form of a fort and the Sheikh provides an Arab guard as a protection against the possibility of raiding bedouins. There is a European staff of five, as well as a trained staff of Indian servants. Passengers are not permitted to visit the town of Sharjah without special permission from the Sheikh, for which previous notice is required. The Residence of the Sheikh is easily discernible by his flag (red panel with white border) which always flies from one of the towers when he is in residence.'

I recounted this to Mr Latif who said yes, the trained staff of Jask Persians may well have been succeeded by Indians, but that now I should really go and see the place for myself. 'Sharjah is next door to Dubai, only half an hour or so by car. The fort is still there, and remarkably well preserved.'

Mr Lawford volunteered to drive me over directly we had finished lunch and soon afterwards we rose from the table, said goodbye to Mr Latif and set off, the car's air conditioning going full blast and filling the interior with frosted clouds of vapour. Mr Lawford told me that though the relationship between Dubai and Sharjah had, historically, been an uneasy one, the two states were now on good terms. But I guessed that traces of the old rivalry remained. While bustling, successful Dubai had become famous for its energetic pursuit of wealth, Sharjah remained a backwater, known chiefly for its profound lethargy. And nothing better exemplified the contrast between them – the predator and the ruminant – than the matter of their respective international airports.

Filled with the best equipment money could buy, they were situated so close to each other that, from time to time, pilots became confused and landed at the wrong one. But while the world's leading airlines clamoured for operating rights into Dubai, few expressed any interest in Sharjah. Its sprinkling of clients included a couple of carriers from Yemen – Alyemda-Democratic Yemen Airlines sent a tourist-class-only 707 from Aden on Wednesdays while Yemenia Yemen Airways provided a non-stop Friday service to Taiz – and China's CAAC, which offered a weekly 747 to Frankfurt with direct onward connections to Baltimore. The true nature of Sharjah's position could best be understood by a perusal of the *ABC World Airways Guide*. At the time of writing, a mere

14 column inches were devoted to flights in and out of Sharjah International, while Dubai got 515 column inches or, in operating terms, almost 37 times more traffic. (Even Sharjah, though, could afford to feel patronizing towards the tiny Emirate of Ras Al Khaimah which achieved only 5½ inches in the *ABC Guide* and whose splendid new international airport had no flights on Mondays, one on Tuesdays and two on Wednesdays; the Emirate produced dried sharks' tails for the Malaysian pharmaceutical industry so, apart from an occasional apothecaries' charter from Kuala Lumpur, little happened to disturb the sea eagles nesting among the glide path antennae.)

We were approaching Sharjah. There were still a few acres of open desert between the two states but it was clear that the sprawling outer suburbs of each would soon meet and merge. Running along the grimy Sharjah Creek I looked out towards the city, a random collection of highrise buildings silhouetted against the hot, white sky, as though someone was trying to recreate downtown Croydon in the middle of Death Valley. It was a dreadful place. At the Al-Khan Lagoon Mr Lawford swung right past the silent airport into an industrial estate littered with shacks and warehouses. A hoarding advertised 'HAPPY COW – The Ghee That Tastes Like Butter' while a rusting sign peppered with bullet holes said, 'Smile You Are in Sharjah'. Empty soft drink cans glittered in the sand. A bony dog, blind in one eye, was crapping by the highway. On a long, broad stretch of tarmac road morose kids in burnouses were testing new Datsun saloons to destruction. Mr Lawford nodded at them. 'They're on the old Imperial runway,' he said. He waited for a Bluebird to go howling past with smoke streaming from its bonnet, then crossed the runway and halted beside a heavy, square concrete structure that reminded me of an abandoned provincial prison. 'And this,' he said, 'is the fort.'

We got out. Mr Lawford told me he thought we were standing on the spot where the HP 42s had parked for the night inside their protective barbed-wire entanglement. I nodded abstractedly, waiting for some manifestation of the thousands who had come to this strange little fastness to bathe, eat dinner and snatch a few hours sleep. But there was nothing. I was aware only of the volcanic heat of the sun and the racket of good Japanese engines being reduced to scrap metal on the road behind us. At one corner of the fort was a roofed turret, part control tower, part look-out post. Here the guard had scanned the horizon for invaders while Mr Dhafei, the Iraqi wireless operator, talked to the inbound pilots and monitored the high-intensity rooftop beacon which, on a clear night, could be seen 80 miles away.

The face the fort presented to the world was closed and anonymous – a few barred windows and, set around the lip of the tower, a line of armoured gun ports. These were probably used in earnest only once, during the Dubai-Sharjah war of 1940 when the Imperial guard was almost certainly taken off aerodrome duties and pressed into active service by a Ruler whose armoury, according to David Holden's book *Farewell to Arabia*, included an ancient Portuguese cannon 'used to fire pistons plundered from abandoned motor engines. Cannon balls generally were in such short supply that a truce was declared after sunset prayers every night to enable both sides to comb the battlefield for old balls that might be used again next day.' Today the faded, sand-toned fort had assumed the colour and texture of the desert around it.

We walked through the main entrance, once sealed by heavy steel doors, into a quiet, shadowy courtyard. A clump of well-watered trees grew from a walled earth dais in the centre, sparrows were chirping and, coming from one of the old bedrooms, I heard the sleepy whine of an electric saw. The atmosphere was contemplative, reminiscent of a small Middle Eastern monastery. I went looking for the famous shower bath, the only one available to air passengers between India and Iraq and quickly entering the vocabulary of the seasoned traveller; the Sharjah Bath became an institution almost as celebrated as the Raffles Long Bar, but there was no sign of it, or its thunderous copper plumbing. The bedrooms, each opening on to the courtyard, were now musty, filthy and empty, with scorpions scuttling around the floors and cobwebs hanging from the discoloured ceilings like fragments of mosquito netting. On the courtyard wall was a rusting iron hook from which, Mr Lawford said, a brass bell had hung to summon guests when their aircraft was ready for departure.

The passengers, by and large, seemed well disposed towards 'this real Beau Geste fort in the desert'. The Marquess of Londonderry reflected the prevailing attitude when he called it 'a triumph over many difficulties'. While acknowledging that 'there are no luxuries' he nevertheless appreciated the fact that one could have 'a good bath and a dinner before retiring for the night'. (A correspondent of the *Madras Mail* even enjoyed such homely diversions as 'playing with the Station Superintendent's black and white rabbits'.) In its heyday, according to the Dumbarton *Rock*, Sharjah was 'an hotel and fort combined, built in the form of a hollow square. At two diagonally opposite corners a well-protected turret is built, and the whole fort is strongly roofed and walled, being fitted with loopholes for rifles. There is a large sliding steel door built of plate ¾ inch thick. Right round the fort, at about 80 feet from the walls, are barbed wire entanglements, excepting two gaps, where the 'plane can enter and leave. We landed on the desert outside and taxied into the door of the fort. Bedouin soldiers with rifles guard the whole station against attack by local thieves, and passengers are warned not to walk beyond the barbed wire. After a bath and a good dinner, had a walk around, and so to bed.'

Another anonymous author, writing in the *Tisco Review*, recalled the 'huge steel doors' which were shut and bolted each night. Just before lock-up time 'I walk through these to get a book I left on the plane; there is a click of a rifle as I leave the fort; a guard of five men in black robes is on duty at the gate. I do not know which is the more disturbing, the unknown danger from which they are guarding us, or the scallywags themselves. Back in the lounge we find the passengers from the Karachi-bound plane, and over our cocktails muse on the fact that tomorrow we shall be two thousand miles apart. The lounge, the bedrooms and other conveniences in the fort are clean and comfortable and well arranged . . . and the dinner, whose materials are presumably brought from Karachi or Baghdad, is first class. Each evening one received a printed form giving information as to the arrangements for the night, rate of currency exchange, hour of call and meals for the following day. We find we are to be called at 5 to-morrow, and the lounge empties very early in the evening.

'*Friday, 23 February, 1934* – 5.30 a.m. There is a faint glow of dawn to the east as we walk over to the plane and take our seats. The morning air is cold and fresh; the fine silty sand of the landing ground pleasant to walk on. At 5.40 the engines start and we taxi to position. Punctually at 5.45 we rise into the air. In the increasing light of dawn the coastline draws away from us, marked by a few lights from fishing villages. We settle down on our cushioned seats to finish our sleep, whilst the plane steadily forges on up the Persian Gulf.'

Now, as we stood in the courtyard, the electric saw fell silent and a man emerged from one of the rooms carrying a plank on his shoulder. He had a shaven, veined head, wore a stained dishdasha and trailed a fragrant cloud of Paco Rabanne aftershave as he walked out the gate. We wandered after him. Standing there in the broiling sun I tried to imagine the dusk arrival of Imperial's IE (Indian Eastbound) flight 367, the Australian service, touching down from Bahrain in a swirling cloud of dust, the Holt magnesium flares burning on the wingtips if the light was fading, its four Bristol Jupiter air-cooled radials rumbling as it taxied towards the fort, the sound of the propellers swishing to a stop after the Jupiters had been switched off and then a couple of bedouin dragging the set of wheeled wooden steps up to the open door before grabbing their guns and hurrying off to fall in with the rest of the guard.

Did the disembarking passengers, stiff and cramped after their flight, express surprise at the looming fort, the armed Arabs, and the homely smells of Brown Windsor Soup and roast mutton being prepared for their dinner? (Captain Tweedie recalled being served giant bowls of oysters, good wines and sickly-sweet pastries.) As we examined the outside of the building I tried to imagine the animated English voices carrying in the stillness as they made jokes about Ali Baba, the Foreign Legion and belly dancers in the casbah. The fabric of the fort was still sound, and following its high wall we found, round the back, a derelict passenger aeroplane sitting mournfully on its fuselage. It was small and high-winged, and its wheels had been stolen. Though clearly nothing to do with Imperial, it had operated from the same strip and so formed a bond of sorts. It too had doubtless often negotiated the notorious 7,000 foot littoral up by the Straits of Hormuz and been forced low enough by the weather for its occupants to have seen 'the hundreds of sharks, stingrays, sea snakes and tortoises' that had been remarked on by travellers aboard the HP 42s. The cabin of the little plane was stripped and gutted, but the two propellers were still in place, and so was the control column. It bore a small badge saying Aero Commander.

'I know who this could have belonged to,' said Mr Lawford, pointing to a weathered wooden sign nailed to the wall. It bore the legend Orient Irrigation Services but those faded words had been painted over others, now barely legible, which said Royal Air Force. 'They were here from 1940 until 1968,' he said, 'based at the fort until they moved over to Qasimia, where the airport is now.' We returned to the car. The Datsuns had gone and it was very quiet. The fort looked desolate, and it was suddenly hard to imagine that it had once been a place of such bustle and consequence.

Mr Lawford started the engine and we drove slowly along the old runway of which the *Air Route Book* had remarked, 'Good hard sand, liable to flood for 24 hours after rain.' The boundaries were 'marked with alternate black and white tins' and the L-shaped landing area possessed 'one natural surface strip 1,400 yards' though pilots were free to make a 1,000 yard headlong run in any direction. The terrain had a slight west to east slope, all approaches were made on a 'normal left-hand circuit' and a windsock flew from the tower of the fort. Though accommodation was plentiful, communication with the outside world − 'Track to Dibai. No telephone' − remained rudimentary. In its general remarks the book said, 'A very uncomfortable station. A shower, change of clothing and dusting with talcum powder will help prevent skin infection. Avoid exercise. Rest in bed in the afternoon when you are not taking off.'

Mr Lawford and I headed thoughtfully back through the long black shadows of late afternoon to Dubai which, by contrast, seemed an oasis of order and enlightened development. We went to the Creek and stood on the low, sandy bank overlooking the 1,800 yard reach where Imperial's first Empire flying boat had splashed down in 1936, the company paying a five-rupee landing fee to the Ruler and a further four to the watchman charged with guarding the boat during the night. (Passengers and crew slept at the Sharjah fort from where, simultaneously, the landplane service continued to operate for several more years.) The Creek was calm in the twilight. Fish were jumping. A green ocean-going dhow with two white

Mercedes lashed to its deck chugged past, its diesels laying down a misty blue haze. The sky was the colour of persimmons. We drove past the wharf where scores of dhows were loading and provisioning. When the price of gold had been high these vessels ran illicit bullion into India, making the skippers important members of Dubai's financial community. Now they shipped motor vehicles, freezers, air conditioning units and livestock to ports throughout the Gulf and the Arabian Sea.

Mr Lawford dropped me at my hotel, waved aside my thanks then rushed off to collect his children from a birthday party. In the lobby a sale of Oriental carpets was in progress. A dozen expatriate English, the men in shorts and sandals, their wives in sun dresses, talked earnestly to the young Lebanese salesmen. A couple of Arabs looked at the carpets too but, when they saw the prices, walked out laughing. Later, in the coffee shop, I fell into conversation with some of the carpet buyers. I told them about Sharjah and they groaned aloud and said it was a place to be avoided at all costs. 'God made Sharjah on a wet Monday morning,' said a plump, dark-eyed woman from London, 'while suffering from a hangover and a sore head.'

Everyone laughed. I remarked that no one seemed to have a good word for Sharjah. Everything one heard about it was bizarre. For example, the only pilot I knew who, years before, had flown into Sharjah reported that the air traffic controller was a Pole who owned a dog with only half a head. The other half had been bitten off.

'Sharjah is full of dogs like that,' said a man wearing a Snoopy T-shirt.

'The Pole liked to invite the pilots up to his tower for a cup of tea,' I continued. 'But instead of adding sugar he stirred in heaped spoonfuls of salt.'

In time the conversation got around, inevitably, to Arab pilots and everyone settled back happily. In this part of the world expatriates exchange Arab pilot stories like they swap gossip or interesting recipes. I had already heard about dyslexic Arab pilots and stupid Arab pilots and Arab pilots having fits at the controls and even very devout Arab pilots being grounded for criminal negligence then reinstated by 'committees' of their Muslim peers. The man in the T-shirt said, 'I know an English flight engineer who was seconded from British Airways to Kuwait Airways on a two-year contract that was worth a *lot* of money. At the end of his first flight with a Kuwaiti captain and First Officer he staggered off the plane and resigned on the spot. That evening he returned to London and, according to his wife, when he arrived at Heathrow he was still looking very shaken.'

I said I had flown with a number of Arab pilots in my time, and all seemed perfectly competent.

'Trevor isn't really talking about competence,' said a man in denim shorts. 'He's talking about something else. Let me give you an example. A friend of mine is a co-pilot with Kuwait Airways – who actually employ 60 British pilots – and recently he was rostered to take a flight down to Abu Dhabi. But the Kuwait met office told him there was a heavy sea fog over Abu Dhabi and the airport was closed. The alternatives, which I suppose would have been Dubai and Sharjah, were fogged in too, and it wasn't due to lift for at least three hours. He reported the delay to his Kuwaiti skipper who said, "There will be no delay. We will go." The co-pilot said, "But we can't land." The skipper said, "We will go." So off they went and, when they got to Abu Dhabi, it was locked in solid, as were the alternatives. The co-pilot said, "What do we do now?" and the pilot said, "We go back, of course." When they got home the captain went off to have his lunch and say his prayers, looking pleased with his morning's work. You see? It isn't competence we're talking about.' He looked at me earnestly. '*It's a state of mind.*'

That night I fell ill and was obliged to spend the next day in bed. The room service waiter said I had a touch of sunstroke. I looked up 'Heat Stroke and Heat Exhaustion' in the Health Hints section of the *Air Route Book* and found that the condition occurred 'most commonly in stout people, older men, especially new arrivals, those inclined to indulge in alcohol, those who have had malaria, dysentery, or other debilitating disease, those who work for long hours or are fatigued by other things.' Much of that certainly applied to me but the symptoms – 'dizziness, hot skin and lack of sweating' – didn't fit at all. I was lathered in sweat so I looked up the bit about sweating and learned that 'wearing stockings soaked in perspiration predisposes to skin diseases, and these are, in fact, common on Persian Gulf stations. Carry your topee, and a silk handkerchief is a good thing to cover the nape of the neck and help absorb sweat. Talcum powder will assist in keeping the feet and crutch dry after a shower, so carry a box of that, too.' The only complaint that tallied with my symptoms seemed to be sandfly fever.

Early next morning, though, I was fit enough to set off through a misty February overcast to catch a Gulf Tristar to Muscat. Imperial hadn't flown to Muscat but they had, of course, called at Gwadar, and the only way into Gwadar now was aboard the PIA Fokker Friendship that went up from Muscat every Saturday morning. On the Tristar I sat next to an old man with a fierce, proud face. His sightless eyes were milky with cataracts and in his arms he clasped a giant inflatable toy gazelle. Clouds of condensation spilled from the air conditioning vents in the ceiling. There was a brief delay while the cabin crew tried to get the passengers' head count to tally, clicking counters as they marched agitatedly up and down the aisle, smiling with relief when the Flight Services Supervisor finally switched on the PA and said, 'Will the cabin crew engage all doors, please.' She told us the flight would take 40 minutes and that we would be travelling at 21,000 feet. Then we began to taxi, the flaps going up and down with a noise like a dentist's drill, the six metal spoilers opening and closing like strongroom doors. We trundled out past cargo sheds and an orange windsock with the word 'Shell' on it. As the engines began to trumpet on the runway threshold the First Officer's flat London voice said, 'Cabin crew please be seated for take-off' and, a moment later, we were airborne, climbing over a colony of trim white houses as the undercarriage retracted and thumped into the fuselage wheel-wells.

Almost at once the gardens and trees of Dubai were gone and we were crossing an undulating cinammon desert, the sand rippled and ridged like an estuary at low tide. Passing an isolated settlement with a twin-towered mosque set in orchards and fields, the Flight Services Supervisor came back on the air to say, 'This crew speaks English, Arabic, Greek, Hindi and Urdu.' We were still climbing, heading towards unending ranges of smoky blue hills. Beneath us the burnt brown rock had been cut by the weather into an astonishing perspective of sculpted gulleys, canyons and mesas. We saw an occasional threadlike track, the only signs of life in that stone landscape. There was plenty to please the eye, though, the colours changing from copper to coral here, from bronze to mulberry or saffron there, sometimes merging to look like veined onyx.

It was only 9 a.m., but the heat came off the earth four miles below with the force of a solar wind. The Tristar lurched and juddered so violently that, at one point, the blind man next to me cried out and seized my hand. I thought of the turbulence the Hannibals must have endured as they skimmed these peaks, running north for the sanctuary of the Gulf and the calm crossing to the Persian coast. 'Leaving SHARJAH,' said the *Air Route Book*, 'the track strikes EAST across undulating light-coloured desert. In bad visibility aircraft should immediately commence to climb, as 70 miles ahead mountains 20 miles to the NORTH of track rise abruptly to 6,000 feet. The desert changes to red sand, and then darker sand, and courses of waterways immediately before the mountains are crossed. The mountains are very precipitous, and in any case of doubtful visibility no attempt should be made to cross at less than 8,000 feet. Track crosses the coast just to the NORTH of a very distinctive well mapped bay. Every effort must be made to check ground speed in order to ensure an accurate ETA for landfall on the Persian coast.'

The blue ranges ahead were doing a slow dissolve into luminous mist. Light began to ripple along the skyline which, all at once, turned into a glittering plain of silver. We swung out over the dazzling Gulf of Oman and started running down the coast, passing a cluster of white houses set in date gardens with a fleet of fishing dhows sitting becalmed a mile offshore. Fifteen minutes out of Muscat we descended past a high, craggy maritime range, its sheer sides dropping like a medieval moated wall into the calm green sea. Small waves lapped and splashed along its base. A humped island floated by like a basking whale. The turbofans were varying their pitch and volume like the bass pipes of an organ as we banked steeply over a long ribbon of beach, made a leisurely, low-speed pass across Muscat, which looked impermanent, like a giant construction camp, then touched down at Seeb International, its hot, sandy little airport. Outside the white terminal stood a gleaming Vickers VC10 with the Omani flag painted on its tail. 'Is that the Ruler's private plane?' I asked a stewardess.

'Sir, that is *one* of the Ruler's private planes,' she said.

We disembarked. The old man with the gazelle was led away by a ground hostess who treated him with a gentleness bordering on reverence. The gardens around the terminal were cool and green, bursting with bright flowers. I felt edgy and pessimistic. In London the Omani consular officials had rejected my visa application fast and emphatically. They didn't want me here but, I reasoned, unless I declared myself at the Immigration Desk, they wouldn't know I had come. All I needed were the temporary squatter's rights of the transit passenger and I prayed no one would demand identification. If so, would I be accused of stealing into the country like a cat burglar and locked up? Or simply marched back to the Tristar? I joined a straggling queue that spilled out across the tarmac. Something was going on. I peered forward and saw everyone's baggage being subjected to an X-ray security check. 'Gwadar,' I said to the pretty Omani policewoman who put my bag through the scanning machine. She wore an ankle-length blue skirt and a London Metropolitan policewoman's hat with a chequered black and white band. She looked at me curiously. '*Gwadar*?'

'Yes.'

She pointed. 'Departure lounge,' she said and, with a sigh of relief, I thanked her and hastened off towards the door indicated by her slim brown hand.

3
DOING THE
(SUB)-CONTINENTAL

From Muscat to Dhaka

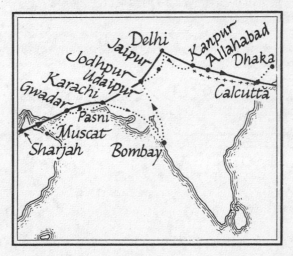

There was only one other traveller in the lounge, a thickset, claret-faced man who sat sucking at a large cigar and scowling over a book called *Ogilvy on Advertising*. First class BA labels festooned his luggage like crimson prayer flags, and a hip flask protruded from his jacket pocket. Along one side of the lounge stood four small adjoining stores. Business was slack. The youth behind the counter of the Khimji Duty Free Shop, which was offering bargain prices on National steam irons and an assortment of twin-speaker ghetto blasters, glanced at his watch then ducked under the counter and went for a coffee, lowering the grille behind him. Another passenger entered the lounge. He was a handsome Indian in a well-cut safari suit who walked up to the counter of the Shanfari Trading & Contracting Co. Gift Centre and began buying fast and decisively. Within minutes he had acquired a battery-operated toy pink rabbit that banged a drum, a cymbals-playing panda, a bear driving a car with a tooting horn and working headlights, a Showbeam torch, a giant blue Thermos flask and three containers of Sunsilk shampoo. Then he moved next door to the Aiman Bookshop and purchased a tin of Quality Street chocolates, several jumbo-sized Yorkie Bars and two tubes of Smarties as big as sky rockets. His failure to buy any books may have been due to the fact that the shop had none in stock. The Indian was paying for his purchases in crisp US dollar bills when the Khimji Duty Free Shop assistant returned from his coffee break. He saw his competitors counting their money and looked stricken. 'You like perfume, Dunhill lighter, nice gold watch?' he asked.

'No,' said the Indian.

'Whisky? Cigar?'

'I am buying present for daughter,' said the Indian. 'What the hell she want with whisky and cigar? She three only.'

He lugged his purchases back to his seat while I went to the ticket counter. The PIA rep wasn't there, but a small, wiry, nervous clerk offered to issue my boarding pass. He had a prominent Adam's apple that, each time he swallowed, plunged deep into his ribcage then bounced up again so high it seemed to vanish between his ears. My destination was making him swallow now. 'I do not think it is to Gwadar you will be going,' he said. I assured him it was. It was there on my ticket and also clearly spelled out in a TO WHOM IT MAY CONCERN letter given to me by the Pakistan Embassy in London. The clerk slowly read the contents, then took the tickets and hurried from the room. I returned to my chair. The Indian had switched on his pink rabbit and sat beaming as it played a wild tattoo on its tiny drum. The red-faced Brit took a long swallow from his hip flask, looked at me and rolled his eyes. A moment later the clerk came back. 'Your seat on Gwadar Fokker confirm,' he said, handing over my tickets and boarding pass. Then he sat and, staring abstractedly at the rabbit, said 'Good, good' in an oddly pleased way. He suddenly patted my hand and asked how I spoke my name. He nodded and walked back to his counter.

A moment later another man approached. He wore a heavy black beard and white robes and a white cap embroidered with gold. He said, 'Are you Alex, going to Gwadar?'

'Yes,' I said.

He smiled. 'I am a Gwadar man, but no work there for skilled technician. So I must stay here.'

He told me his name was Ahmed, a telex operator, and asked about permissions. If Gwadar was famous for anything, he implied, it was for being off-limits to foreigners. Actually, I had been told much the same two months earlier at the Pakistan Embassy in London by its Information Minister, Mr Qutubuddin Aziz. 'Oh, they won't let you go there,' he said at our first meeting then proceeded, with a certain glee, to turn the ban on its head. An old campaigning journalist who thought my project worth supporting, he got on to Islamabad and pulled strings, badgered his contacts, expertly worked the system right up to Cabinet level and, three weeks later, called me jubilantly with the news that I was in. Unexpectedly, he had warned of Russian agents in Gwadar, promising that my photograph and personal details would reach

Moscow within five days of my arrival, and did I mind? I was giving Ahmed a brief account of all this when another man approached. 'This chap is brother-in-law, Alex,' Ahmed said.

The brother-in-law was tall and gaunt, the uneven hem of his green robe revealing electric blue socks and worn brown shoes. He looked at me shyly. Ahmed said, 'He live in Gwadar and also go on the Fokker, bouncy bouncy over sea.' He laughed. 'In Gwadar he will look after you. He a tailor. Now he offer you cold drink.'

As the brother-in-law hastened off to the refreshment counter I explained that, if all went to plan, someone was going to meet me on arrival. Ahmed said in Gwadar things hardly ever went to plan. The brother-in-law would take me to the town's number one man, an administrator working for the Pakistan government but an Omani like all the rest of them. Did I understand the curious relationship between Oman and Gwadar? Gwadar was now part of Pakistan but, for almost 200 years, due to the friendship between an eighteenth-century Muscat prince and the Khan of Kalat, it had been a tiny Omani colony and, to this day, all true Gwadar men still thought of themselves as Omanis. The bond manifested itself in certain practical ways, such as the weekly scheduled PIA flight up from Muscat, and four further trooping flights made by F27s of Oman Aviation Services to ferry Omani soldiers to and from their Gwadar training camp – itself a monument to the old ties.

The brother-in-law returned with cans of chilled lemonade and said the Fokker had come. We heard the whine of its Rolls-Royce Dart turbo-props as it taxied in. An elderly man whose cap and gown were embroidered like altar cloths walked up and said, 'You are Mr Alex, going on this plane?' He was skinny and stooped, and carried a National steam iron and a large flaxen-haired doll with a tiny hole drilled between its pouting pink lips.

'Yes,' I said.

'My name is Mohammed. I am an Omani, from Gwadar.'

He extended a thin hand, inadvertently moving the doll to an upright position. It made a mewing noise and its vacuous blue eyes shot open with a clatter. Mohammed, said, 'Mr Alex, what can I do for you? Tell me.'

Ahmed explained that the brother-in-law had assumed responsibility for me. Mohammed said, yes, he understood that, but he was also at my service and, tonight, would like me to dine with him and his three sons. The room was filling with our fellow-passengers, richly robed men whose dark faces, shaggy hair and full beards were reminiscent of images from icons; their eyes, as they noted me, were cool and appraising. Mohammed indicated that I should come and shake hands with them. As I did so the PIA pilots walked in, two young Pakistanis in shirtsleeves and rumpled blue trousers. They went to the refreshment counter, gulped down cold lemon squashes and hurried out again.

It was time to go. I said goodbye to Ahmed and, flanked by Mohammed and the silent brother-in-law, made my way through the security check and on to a bus, marshalled by a breezy young dispatcher who spoke English with a marked American accent. 'I heard about you,' he said. 'You're the only European I seen catch this flight.' I asked him if he had ever caught it himself. 'To *Gwadar*?' He laughed then lowered his voice confidingly. 'Man, believe me, that place is strictly for the fuzzy wuzzies.'

Out at the green-tailed Fokker Friendship sweating baggage handlers were loading cabin trunks, battered suitcases tied with rope, and bundles of coloured bedding into the hold. We ascended the rickety steps and found all the available floor space piled with cabin baggage. I made my way past a brass pot, bunches of peacock's feathers, a sewing machine, an orange football in a string bag, a wind-up gramophone, a tooled leather camel saddle, an antique wood-framed mirror, its glass all bubbled and cracked, and a model dhow with a broken mast; each bore a PIA cabin baggage label saying GWD.

A harassed young stewardess with big hips and a bad skin was trying to get everyone to sit down, but the men took their time, exchanging pleasantries like customers in a coffee house. A pretty girl seated by a window caused a certain unease among the men, none of whom wished to occupy the adjoining seat. I claimed it happily. She had fine green eyes and a full figure and, when I observed that I hadn't seen her in the terminal, she explained that she worked for Pakistan airport security, body searching female passengers at each of the embarkation points. She had travelled up that morning with the Fokker from Karachi, jumping off at each of the little country halts that were too remote for a resident woman officer. At Muscat she had stayed aboard; they had their own staff here and, anyway, the passengers on this leg were all men. That morning she had been to Turbat, Jiwani and Gwadar. After Gwadar they would go on to Pasni before heading home.

The pilots started the engines and, with a whoosh, the two Rootes blowers working the cabin air conditioning system came onstream – but, lacking the optional bootstrap cooling device, they simply recycled the baking desert wind and directed it straight into our faces. Moments later we rose slowly into the hot sky. I watched the main wheels retract backward into the engine nacelles then turned to see how Mohammed and the brother-in-law were faring. They nodded gravely but looked bored. Flying was clearly no big deal for them.

The big-hipped stewardess, who wore the *shalwar kameez* – a tunic and baggy trousers – distributed cellophane-wrapped pastries and paper cups of orangeade. My neighbour took a drink but refused the pastry. 'Aren't you hungry?' I asked.

She laughed. 'You will see.'

It took a long time to remove the wrapping and I realized, too late, that it had been sealed that way because what was inside was not supposed to get out. I had ignored a coded warning from the packer and, after a single mouthful of something tasting nauseatingly of rancid cheese, hastily parcelled it up again and asked the security lady whether she had found any interesting or unusual objects of contraband while body searching the women of Baluchistan. 'No, nothing,' she said, shortly, but I didn't believe her and recalled a story told to me by an old Navy petty officer who once patrolled this coast. He said that, during a tribal uprising, a rating had been blown to bits while detaining a woman on suspicion of assisting the rebels. Both died messily, the petty officer said, after she or the rating – who may have sexually assaulted her – inadvertently detonated the hand grenade she was carrying in her vagina. 'Them Baluchi women got cunts like duffle bags,' he recalled.

There were supertankers strung out along the pale blue sea below, steaming hard for the Hormuz Narrows 100 miles to the west despite the dangers they faced from Iraqi bombers at the other end of the Gulf; a Liberian-registered 80,000 tonner had been severely damaged only the previous week. The security girl said, 'This morning our flight was almost cancelled. In Karachi they are saying the Iranians will close the Straits and put military squadrons at Bandar Abbas.'

I looked down at those smooth, troubled waters. A naval patrol boat rushed past a plodding, black-funnelled tanker, going like a train. The Fokker droned on at its statutory cruising speed of 259 knots and then, almost imperceptibly, a ghostly white land began stealing towards us out of a milky sea. We crossed a silvery beach to make our Baluchistan landfall at Jiwani, a coastal settlement almost within sight of the Iranian border. Its houses were built from the same pale grey clay they stood on, and made distinguishable only by their own angular black shadows. The dry watercourse of the Dasht River slid through grey mudflats behind the village, with groves of grey date palms visible along its banks. 'The British air force once had a flying boat base down there,' said the security girl. 'One of our Fokker captains has seen it. He says it looks as if the men only left yesterday. In the mess there is a blackboard with English names written on it – the flying roster. You could still read them.'

I craned to look down at Jiwani more closely, but it had vanished under the tail's black rubber boot de-icers and all I saw was our small Cross-of-Lorraine shadow sliding over the plain of ash below. A few miles to the west, just beyond the Iranian border, was the town of Jask where Captain Tweedie, as a young pilot working the original Persian coast route, stopped for the night. After dinner he and his passengers would walk to the bay from the Imperial guest house to observe shoals of flying fish leaping across the narrow peninsula on which they stood, arcing through the darkness like flames. In the highlands of Kalat, beyond the misty northern horizon, were stands of juniper, ash, pines, poplars and willows. Leopards and black bears lived up on the tree line, together with small, scrambling mountain goats like the Sind ibex. Below us now, in the desert, there were wolves, wild asses, skinks, tortoises and crazy horned snakes, but all I could see was a lifeless terrain that had begun to look like discoloured ice. Gwadar field, when it appeared, was just an isolated smudge in the sand. We sank towards it, banking steeply and skimming across the face of a 300-foot-high biscuit-coloured cliff before touching down on the 5,000-foot asphalt strip. The apron had parking space for only a single plane. Mohammed and the brother-in-law were beaming, delighted to be home. Several hundred robed and bearded men formed a heaving semi-circle around the Fokker, like spectators at a tribal wrestling match. They looked a pretty villainous lot to me, and I recalled that Gwadar lay at the heart of 'ball-chitty territory', where strangers were advised to carry reward notices in Baluchi stitched to their coats, promising a £20 cash payment if the bearer was returned alive and without his testicles stuffed in his mouth. A Foreign Office acquaintance in London told me that, during their last uprising, the Baluchis had castrated members of Pakistan's counter-insurgency forces, dumping them back at camp in the early hours bound and gagged and choking horribly on their own severed parts.

As I disembarked a perceptible hush fell. The eyes of the men glittered in the sun. There was no welcome in them, but nor was there discernible hostility. I was simply being appraised. When Mohammed, clutching his steam iron and pink doll, touched my arm companionably and said, 'There are people here from my *qawm*, my tribe, Mr Alex; what binds my *qawm* is sadness and woe,' I thought I sensed a slight easing of the mood. But something was happening. The crowd began to eddy and sway and then, with a convulsive heave, ejected a pair of Pakistanis in silk shirts, club ties and three-piece worsted suits. I stared at them. Back in London Mr Aziz had promised I would be met, but said nothing about sending along a couple of high-profile Karachi superjocks who were clearly as alien to the place as I was.

'S.K. Siddiqi,' said the first, who was tall and assertive and had plainly led the running maul. His shoes were dusty and sweat beaded his forehead. He did not look happy.

'K.N. Haroon,' murmured the second, a slight, bespectacled, soft-voiced man.

'We must first deal with formalities,' said Mr Siddiqi. 'Customs and immigration. This Saturday Fokker from Muscat give Gwadar aerodrome international status, you know.'

'World smallest international airport, I should say,' volunteered Mr Haroon.

I looked around for Mohammed and the brother-in-law, but they had slipped away; I had been publicly claimed by the authorities so they would want nothing more to do with me. We approached a small building site where some kind of structure was being fashioned from breeze blocks. There was a flat roof and three walls and a painted sign saying GENT WAITING ROOM propped beside the space where, eventually, the fourth wall would be. It was thronged with people.

'Terminal,' murmured Mr Haroon.

Mr Siddiqi allowed himself a hollow laugh.

We went inside and I remarked that I couldn't see a waiting room for women. Mr Haroon said it was round the back and screened off with sacking, as custom demanded. The customs officer drew a handsome chalk ideogram on my bag and presented it to me with a flourish. 'Bag is pass!' he said. Then he asked how much foreign currency I was carrying in cash. I told him about £100 and he instructed me to enter the amount in my passport. But I hesitated, never having been required to do this before, and he clicked his tongue. '*On blank page*,' he snapped, snatching it from me. 'Here, I will write.'

He popped a school pen into a bottle of black ink, carefully inscribed '100 f in cash', dated and initialled it, had it counter-initialled by his boy clerk and finally, with great force, crashed a large rubber stamp on to the page. It displayed the star and crescent moon of Pakistan and the legend 'Custom House Gwadur'. Mr Siddiqi said we were to be driven into town by the General Sales Agent. 'But I do not know where hell he is. Out at Fokker, probably. He must get it ready for Pasni flight, check cargo, take ticket and so on. We will wait in his jeep.'

The interior of the battered little vehicle was hot enough to roast a goose. We were being microwaved where we sat and Mr Siddiqi, groaning, cranked down a window. But a desert wind had sprung up which raised the temperature even further so I jumped out and strolled across to look at the Fokker. The pilots were listening to a hockey match from Lahore while the wind caught the plane under the wings and rocked it from side to side. The air was filled with chalky white dust. I slipped off my jacket and loosened my tie. A masked woman staggered by beneath a shiny metal cabin trunk while her man stalked a pace or two ahead of her, carrying a pink pillow and a portable radio in a fitted brocade cover so gorgeously embroidered that it might have packaged the relics of a saint. The men I had met at Muscat now avoided my eye and I stood, unacknowledged, as they all streamed past, their richly beaded and braided caps glowing like halos.

The General Sales Agent returned to his jeep clasping bundles of unsold tickets. He was small, dark-skinned and birdlike, with lined features and thick, dark hair, brilliantined and impeccably combed. His name was Haji Ali Mohd and, looking enviably cool in a flapping lime-green jacket and trousers, he manoeuvred the jeep past the armed sentry at the gate and, peering over his steering wheel, set off down the narrow, nine-mile switchback road to Gwadar. The faces of our two companions had assumed the consistency of melting toffee but they kept their ties and jackets resolutely on. It occurred to me that they might be wearing shoulder holsters. 'Are you from security?' I asked. 'No,' said Mr Siddiqi. 'We are PR.' The wind was blowing sand on to the road and teams of men with brooms were slowly sweeping it off again. Every few minutes a bus came howling past, causing the General Sales Agent to wrench at the wheel and take off into the desert. The buses seemed to be fashioned from beaten silver and glass mosaics, and were fabulously painted with gods, demons, birds, animals and magical landscapes; one had a bonnet embellished with PIA 747s and DC10s, another with F-16s firing streams of tracer, and they thundered through the landscape like gaudy, smoking meteors.

I asked the General Sales Agent what freight he sent down to Karachi. Lobsters, he said; they were the only thing anyone wanted from Gwadar. Once deepwater ships en route to the Gulf hove-to in Gwadar Roads and officers came ashore to buy fresh lobster for the crew. Now few ships passed, none stopped and all the catch was taken away in the Fokker. The flat, hard light made the landscape incandescent. A pale blue haze lay over the desert's middle distance, while the horizon was bounded by lofty battlements of pale rock, cut by the wind into stunning and wonderful shapes. The undulating road rose and fell like an ocean swell and, as we clattered on into town, I recalled that the first vehicle ever brought to Gwadar had been for the Imperial station manager. 'Its appearance,' reported the *Gazette* in 1933, 'created wild excitement among the inhabitants of the village who had never previously seen a motor car. After unloading from the ship, as the van was being pushed from the beach to Imperial Airways' headquarters, it was surrounded by a delirious crowd of men, women and children. Imperial Airways' Station Superintendent reported that when he first saw the crowd he thought it was a fanatical movement and he had a few anxious moments, until he saw the cause of the excitement.'

We were drawing closer. The road was now lined by low, shrublike trees with foliage as green as a parakeet's feathers. We slowed. In a little copse a uniformed man sat barefoot at a kitchen table. He nodded and waved us through.

'Security check,' said the General Sales Agent.

'This is sensitive area,' added Mr Siddiqi.

'Highly so, highly so,' murmured Mr Haroon.

We motored through the outskirts of an impoverished, tumble-down little town, passed the ice factory, swung along a beach and halted beside the vast sparkling expanse of Gwadar West Bay. Before us stood a handsome old building behind a high wire security fence. A notice said '3 BN Pakistan Coast Guard Officer's Mess'. It was guarded by a slim, dreamy-looking young soldier wearing a pale blue beret, cravat and shoulder flashes, who swung open the gate and threw us a real guardsman's salute.

'This is Government Rest House,' said the General Sales Agent as we lurched through. 'The colonel sahib is in Karachi. You will have his room.'

'Also his bearer,' said Mr Siddiqi, with a laugh.

Mr Haroon laughed too. 'Har har,' he went.

The single-storey mess had a deep, shadowy verandah running along its length. A terrific profusion of white and mauve bougain-villaea scrambled up stout Coastguard-blue pillars and spilled over the top so vigorously that the flat roof had become a wild, untended garden. We halted in a dusty, walled courtyard containing a flagpole, a basketball court, dusty palms and tamarisk trees. A huge, menacing man shambled up to the jeep and seized my bag with a grunt. Clumps of knotted veins stood out on his shaven head and his deep-set eyes had a wild, dark glow.

'This is colonel sahib's bearer,' said the General Sales Agent, 'now bearer for your good self. You must go with him.'

The bearer, scowling, led me on to the verandah and into a

cavernous, shadowy room containing a double bed stripped to the mattress, a mother-of-pearl inlaid table, two giant ceiling fans, a wall lined with empty glass-fronted display cases, and enough sofas and armchairs to convene a meeting of the Joint Chiefs of Staff. The bearer, who wore an embroidered cotton top and peasant trousers, unzipped my bag and began unpacking it at terrific speed. Everyone had come in to watch. 'You travel light,' observed Mr Haroon.

'Is best,' said Mr Siddiqi. 'For busy people always on move travel light is watchword.'

The bearer extracted my pyjamas, arranged them neatly on a coathanger and hung them up in a glass-fronted display case where they assumed the weighty significance of a museum exhibit, like the uniform in which Nelson died. In neighbouring display cases he hung a pair of trousers, a shirt, two pairs of underpants and a single blue sock. Then he glared and began making low, furious noises in his throat.

'He want to know where other sock,' said Mr Siddiqi.

I told him I had mislaid it in Egypt. This information was relayed to the bearer who managed, with difficulty, to contain himself. He put another question, translated by Mr Haroon. 'He say have you got any dhobi?'

I said my laundry had all been done the previous day, in Dubai.

The bearer rolled his eyes, stepped up to me and half raised his huge hands. His chest was hirsute and massively barrelled. He spat some words out like broken teeth and I thought, bloody hell, he's going to break my neck.

Mr Haroon said, 'Now bearer want to give you nice shave.'

'What I'd really like,' I said, 'is a cup of tea.'

'Chai for sahib!' snapped Mr Siddiqi.

'Yes!' shouted the bearer, exiting so fast that the heavy, drawn curtains billowed in his wake.

'Give him something to do,' observed Mr Haroon as we trekked back to the verandah and sat ourselves down in creaking cane chairs. It was cool and, but for the agitated crashing of pans coming from the cookhouse, marvellously quiet. The light filtering through the bougainvillaea had the translucent quality of stained glass. The General Sales Agent glanced at his watch and begged to be excused.

'Now I must return to office. For paperwork. For me it is go go go, seven day a week. I must drive to airport to meet every plane, issue boarding pass, check freight, make trim chart for pilot, nine mile out, nine mile back. When plane go on to Pasni, Panjgur, Turbat or Muscat I must go twice, three time. But I will return here later and show you people town.'

'He work too hard, that fellow,' observed Mr Siddiqi as the jeep, its broken exhaust booming like a gun, lurched back out the gate. 'Hasn't had holiday since who know when.'

Tea came on an ornate silver tray in yellow glass cups. It was sweet and milky. There were ants in the sugar bowl. Some of these were transferred to my cup and, as Mr Siddiqi cleared his throat and announced the time had come for my 'briefing', they began swimming energetically up and down. 'Gwadar,' said Mr Siddiqi, crossing his legs and folding his hands, 'has very unusual history. In 1784 a son of the Ruler of Oman fled here after trouble at home and became chummy with the Khan of Kalat, who give him Gwadar and surrounding territory for winding sheet, or burial ground. It was local custom, and all it mean is that Gwadar was his for ever, in perpetuity. The prince build fort here and later return to conquer Oman, but he leave soldiers behind to administer town as dependency of Oman. It remain so until 1958, when Oman sold Gwadar to Pakistan for £3 million. Six years later the first civil air service was start – a Cessna four-seater of the Karachi Aero Club, with two seats allocated for Gwadar and two for Pasni. That replace by weekly DC3 and then, after the sand runway was asphalted in 1966, Fokkers took over. In 1969 Muscat was added to route by popular demand. Today Gwadar has 18 flights a week total and aerodrome staff of 20.'

I was trying to spoon the ants from my cup. Most were now floating belly-up, but two survivors continued to paddle wearily back and forth. I retrieved one, but it staggered to the tip of the spoon and hurled itself back in.

'Aerodrome elevation,' continued Mr Siddiqi, 'is 96 feet above sea level, load classification is 10 and it never close due to weather.'

'Hardly ever,' said Mr Haroon, judiciously.

'It never close *as such*. There is constant south-easterly blowing 15 to 20 knots and sometimes it get up a bit and make sandstorm with visibility under required four-kilometre limit. Then pilot just have to stooge around until wind drop again. These storms only temporary.'

I offered him a cigarette and asked about the man sitting at the table in the copse outside town. 'You said he was there for security,' I reminded him. 'Security against what?'

They glanced at each other. 'Gwadar is very sensitive spot,' murmured Mr Haroon. 'Some Baluchis want autonomy from Pakistan. There has been trouble. The army had to come. Also, this place is famous for smuggling. Why you think Coast Guard keep battalion here? That is no secret.'

I put it to them that perhaps Gwadar was a sensitive spot because the Russians had designs on it. Possession of Gwadar West Bay, a vast natural anchorage which could easily accommodate the entire Soviet battle fleet, would give them absolute control of the Hormuz Straits and the Gulf itself. Since the time of Peter the Great Russia had nurtured the dream of a warm water port, and Pakistani diplomats I had met in London believed that Gwadar was the one Moscow had finally chosen. Gwadar, they argued, therefore numbered among the Kremlin's reasons for invading Afghanistan. It lay only 300 miles from the Afghan border – a mere 20 minutes by MiG – across desolate country difficult to patrol; if they decided to make a pre-emptive strike south the Pakistanis would be hard pressed to contain them. From Gwadar the Soviets could subdue Iran's mischievous Muslim revolutionaries and, if their own fossil fuels ever ran low, even absorb the Gulf oil states. Little Gwadar was being drawn, willy nilly, into the Great Game.

But the United States, I continued, would quickly counter any Soviet move against a friendly power. B52s from the Indian Ocean island of Diego Garcia could be overhead within hours, the subsequent combat making Gwadar a tinderbox that could ignite the Third World War. That, anyway, was what my Pakistani friends believed, and their view was shared by Admiral Thomas H. Moorer, Chairman of the US Joint Chiefs of Staff from 1970 to 1974 who, writing in the *Strategic Review*, recalled that Prime Minister Zulfikar Ali Bhutto had once offered Gwadar to the United States as a base in return for a lifting of the arms embargo to Pakistan. The Admiral regretted Washington's rejection of this 'ideal spot' and warned that 'Gwadar is in a remote part of Pakistan, where Baluchi tribesmen are seeking greater autonomy from Islamabad. The Soviets have obvious designs on this area in their drive for direct access to the Indian Ocean. Their ensconcement in Afghanistan leaves them now only 350 miles from Hormuz and the Arabian Sea, and an "independent" Baluchistan under Moscow's control would provide them with that corridor of access. Indeed, there have already been unconfirmed reports from Turkish intelligence sources that Soviet forces are giving military training to Baluchi tribesmen in southern Afghanistan. At relatively low cost, Gwadar could be made into a naval anchorage. The major needed components would be a crane for lifting supplies, fuel tanks and a barge to bring fuel to the ships if they could not move in alongside.'

Mr Siddiqi and Mr Haroon listened without comment to my résumé of their own case, smiling faintly when I recounted Mr Aziz's breezy assertion that my picture and particulars would land on the Baluchistan Desk of the KGB in Moscow; any white face in Gwadar, he had said, would be assumed by them to be CIA.

Mr Siddiqi stood and stretched. 'Heat has gone out of sun. I think I will go for stroll and check out this famous bay superpowers are going to war about.'

I went with him. The mess stood at the head of the beach. To the left was a towering anvil-shaped headland jutting far out into the Arabian Gulf, a massive structure shaped like a Gothic nave and throwing a half-mile shadow (Imperial's passengers called it Cathedral Rock), while the bay's other arm was barely visible far away on the western horizon. The area of sheltered water between the two was so vast that in it you could probably anchor not just the Soviet Navy, but all the other navies of the world as well. Gwadar West Bay glittered and flashed, so suffused with heat and light that it seemed about to bubble and vaporize. The tide was low, a broad band of dark steaming mud separating the sea from the sand. A group of uniformed coastguards were whitewashing a druidic circle of stones very slowly. We asked the corporal what the stones were for. 'Chopper landing pad,' he said.

The sound of distant gunfire signalled the arrival of the General Sales Agent's jeep. He was ready to show us the town. The tiny main square where we parked was the location of the bus depot. Without warning one of those gaudy folk art vehicles started up and leapt forward, horn going like a klaxon. Everyone jumped wildly and, when it had passed, instantly resumed the normal rhythm of their lives. Mr Siddiqi and Mr Haroon asked for directions to the bazaar, hastening off as soon as the General Sales Agent had indicated where it lay. 'What's the hurry?' I asked him.

'Shopping,' he said. 'Gwadar is only 40 miles from Iran border. Iranian goods very cheap here, specially dinner plate and pistachio nut.'

We walked down narrow, muddy lanes past dwellings of unglazed brick, daub and rusting corrugated iron. The main bazaar, a single alley lined with small open-fronted shops, was barely wide enough to allow passage for a goat cart. At any point one could pause and haggle for freshly caught skate, shark, pomfret and sole, partridges, ghee, maize, wild rhubarb, cumin, hyssop, liquorice, onions, saffron, peaches and apricots from the highlands of Kalat, rice, sweetmeats, sandals, Chinese hurricane lanterns, betel nut, kerosene, ribbons, eggs, wire-framed spectacles, fish hooks, dahl, secondhand dentures, patent medicines, flyblown red meat, used glass eyes, tea and, of course, Iranian pistachios as plump as walnuts and garish Iranian Tupperware decorated with poisonous-looking botanic specimens.

Mr Siddiqi and Mr Haroon were suffused with the excitement of the chase. Urging each other on with ululating cries they rushed in and out of the shops selling the Ayatollah's horrible plastic crockery. Mr Siddiqi sprang into the alley to show me a gravy boat emblazoned with something resembling deadly nightshade. 'Excellent value, tip-top stuff!' he beamed.

I offered to carry the two bags of pistachios he had clamped beneath his arms. As he sped off again I remarked to the General Sales Agent that the bazaar people were paying surprisingly little attention to my alien white face. If I was the first European to have visited the town in some years, why was I not being inspected more closely? He gave a brief chuckle. 'Don't you believe it, they are watching you like hawk. Also, you are not first white man here. Last week Australian doctor pass through.'

I stared at him. 'Did he stay at the Coastguard Mess?'

'No. I did not meet him. He hasn't come by plane.'

I pondered his news all the way back to the jeep where, eventually, we were joined by Mr Siddiqi and Mr Haroon, flushed and laughing after their triumphant expedition, arms laden with plates wrapped in old newspapers. They knew nothing of the Aussie doctor either. It occurred to me, as we drove slowly through a wonderful gilded evening, that if Mr Aziz was to be believed, the only people able to tell me who he was would be the Duty Officers on the Baluchistan Desk at Moscow Centre, the headquarters of the KGB.

The General Sales Agent went home while my minders retired to bathe and change. We arranged to meet in the reception room at 7 o'clock. It had thick pale pink walls and I knew at once that this place had been built by the British. There was a handsome fireplace with a polished marble mantelpiece and, hanging from mock-Elizabethan beams, chandeliers flickering fitfully as camp fires. Glass-fronted display cases lined the walls here too, empty but for two regimental crests, one showing a camel standing stiffly under a date palm and inscribed with the words 'Mekran Scouts', the other a heraldic device saying '10th Patrol Boat Group They Only Live Who Dare'. In the drawer of a fine mahogany sideboard I found a visitors' book, the most recent entries a decade old and accompanied by scribbled exclamatory comments from officers with names like Iqbal and Farooqi — 'What a great evening!', 'Jolly good time had by all!', 'First class grub and company!' Before the fireplace stood a Sony television and video recorder. It was connected to an antique bakelite wall plug through three voltage regulators and enough cables and adaptors to hook up a searchlight battery.

Mr Siddiqi and Mr Haroon entered rubbing their hands. They had changed into the *shalwar kameez*, but wore sleeveless woollen sweaters over their tunics. There was a chill in the air. We were all tired. A glass of whisky would have warmed us and lifted our spirits and I ruefully wondered how many bottles of good malt had been emptied in this room before the mullahs put a stop to all that. At a small table in an ante-room we ate roast chicken, boiled rice, tender young goat in a wonderful curry sauce, steaming mounds of chapattis and, finally, a neon-bright pink custard. Three stewards in gold-buttoned white uniforms attended to us, topping up the water glasses and gravely hovering with their fly swats. Wondering what

I had missed at Mohammed's table, and how he and the brother-in-law were spending their evening, I refused coffee and decided on an early night.

The bearer crouched in the darkness outside my door. He ushered me in, lit a hurricane lantern and swiftly made up the bed, folding a blanket inside a synthetic tiger pelt to form a tube, then demonstrating that one entered it as though wriggling into a sausage skin. That done, he stood, arms akimbo, scowling at my feet. Suddenly he bent, seized my ankles and pulled off my shoes, setting upon them furiously with brushes and polish, making them shine like Chinese lacquer. Then he fetched my pyjamas from the display case and indicated, imperiously, that I should remove my suit. I did so at once and, carefully, he hung it up beside the lone sock. Finally he approached and, peering closely into my face, indicated that the shave could be postponed no longer. But the idea of being worked over with a cut-throat razor in this dim light seemed a very dangerous one and I shook my head. He ducked his, gave me a sudden shy smile and slipped from the room. I listened for the sound of his footsteps padding away across the compound but heard only a muffled cough close at hand. He had resumed his watch by the door.

I slid down into the tiger skin, thinking about Mr A. B. Thompson who had been Imperial's station superintendent here in 1932. Gwadar then was administered by an Arab governor appointed by the Sultan of Muscat and entitled to a personal bodyguard of 15 Arab soldiers. Writing in the *Gazette* Thompson reported that the Baluchis were 'an illiterate class of people, eking out a precarious livelihood by rearing and selling cattle, milk, dates, mats, coal, firewood and fish' which were steeped 'in beds of salt for a few days and then baked in the sun'. Mr Thompson lived at the old Political Bungalow, an isolated house a mile from town. Here he installed his wireless station, 'an extension of two rooms being built to accommodate the accumulator and the Diesel engine for charging. At three different periods during the day, Gwadur has to exchange signals with Karachi and Jask. Two days during the week, when the Imperial Airways liners are in flight, the station transmits weather messages and is in continuous contact with the liners.'

Mr Thompson, who spent much of his working day servicing his radio and generating equipment, was preoccupied with keeping fit. He had a tennis court built behind the house and, each evening, played a couple of sets with the man from the Anglo-Persian Oil Company, two merchants from the town and three Indian meteorologists stationed in Gwadar 'to supply the aircraft in flight with upper air and surface observations'. In July and August, when the evenings were too hot for tennis, they played golf 'among the sand dunes. In the winter months the lesser bustard passes through Gwadur on its migratory trek to India, and there is some fairly good shooting to be had.' The only food available locally was 'fish, milk, eggs, scraggy chicken and very inferior mutton'. Everything else had to be shipped in from Karachi. 'A basket of fresh fruit and vegetables is obtained every week by air. A supply of drinking water is obtained once a fortnight from the British India Steam Navigation Company steamers. The local water is used for cooking and bathing after it has been cleaned with alum.'

The highlights of his week were the arrival of the flights, though he rarely went to meet them. The airfield was too far and the going too rough – 'the rugged sandy pathway is only navigable by camel transport' – so he sent his General Sales Agent instead. Here Mr Thompson describes a typical working day. 'A brilliant sunshine ushers in the morning and flies hop playfully over one's face, making further sleep impossible. The servant enters with the *chota hazri*, which is an early snack, and says that the aerodrome has been telephoning, inquiring if any aircraft is to be expected today. Work on the outpost has started. The Imperial Airways' agent arrives on his way to the aerodrome, to pick up my mails for headquarters. Wireless communication is established with Karachi and the 'plane. The aerodrome is informed by telephone and we all go outside to watch the aeroplane coming in. We see it fairly clearly against the skyline, majestically moving to the aerodrome, and, after a graceful turn, descending and disappearing from view. The telephone bell rings and the aerodrome reports that the aeroplane has landed. The information is passed on to the adjacent air ports, lunch is taken, and then the telephone calls again, reporting, "Machine in the air," and the stations are immediately advised of its departure. Wireless touch is maintained with the aeroplane till it reaches the next stopping place. The flight for the day is concluded.'

I put out the light. The silence was profound, broken only by the distant braying of a donkey and the drowsy swish and rumble of the tide rising on the beach. A big plane passed high overhead, possibly a 747, travelling west. There was a radio beacon at Jiwani, and all the Europe-bound traffic from Karachi went this way, right across the top of Gwadar. I felt homesick and thought of my family. It was late afternoon in London. They would be switching on the lamps and having toasted muffins for tea. Outside there was another muffled cough and a sigh. I wondered how you said go to bed for Christ's sake in Urdu, and then, like a condemned man dropping through the scaffold trapdoor, fell abruptly into a dark and bottomless sleep.

II

At 6 a.m. precisely the door crashed open and he came through it sideways, a hurricane lantern in one hand, a large tray balanced on the other. It contained a glass cup, a sugar bowl and two giant silver thermos flasks. In the mess the night before I had ordered early morning coffee and now I watched as he unscrewed one of the flasks and cautiously upended it over the cup. Nothing happened. He banged its base and out shot a substance as dark and viscous as riverine silt. The other flask yielded something of a similar consistency but much paler, like yoghurt. He added a spoonful of ant-infested sugar, stirred the ingredients then handed me the cup and placed his hands together in an attitude of prayer.

It gave off a faint but alarming smell of sulphur. I took a sip. It was dreadful, a poisonous sludge that put me in mind of something found among the bin scrapings of an Indian takeaway. But I managed a smile and, beaming, he bustled out again. I picked up the hurricane lantern – there was no electricity in Gwadar at this hour – went to the bathroom and emptied my coffee down the basin. It caused a major obstruction in the plumbing but slowly, like a draining sump, the stuff dripped away and, before the bearer could return and snatch the razor from my hand, I shaved, quickly and painfully, in cold well water.

We assembled in the mess for a breakfast of rice, fish and sweet tea. My two friends were not in good shape. Their eyes were bloodshot and a slight tremor was evident in their hands as they picked glumly at the food. Mr Siddiqi said he had passed a restless night. The bed was terrible. He was not accustomed to such silence. At 2 a.m. he had heard scratching noises, lit his candle and seen a rat. 'It was big as mongoose,' he reported. Mr Haroon shuddered. I left them and wandered on to the verandah for a smoke. The sun had cleared the horizon moments earlier and poor, impoverished Gwadar was softly back-lit and magically cleansed by the morning. The light stole across the compound and caught the bougainvillaea, making the blossoms incandescent. The dreamy young soldier was still guarding the gate. He hastened across to shake hands then, since we could not speak, smiled, touched his heart and walked back through the long shadows cast by the trees.

A jeep came grinding up to the door. The driver, small with a round, boyish face, jumped down and shook hands too. 'I am Irshad,' he said. 'Aerodrome manager, Gwadar. I am hearing you are interested in aviation matters. Would you like, perhaps, to see my place? I can take you. If you *wish*.' He gave me an uncertain glance then frowned at his feet. I accepted with pleasure and, when Mr Siddiqi and Mr Haroon had climbed shakily aboard, we set off through the town, past the yawning security man slumped over his kitchen table and on into the desert. Tethered camels grazed on thorns. A bearded nomad was shitting behind a rock, robe bunched around his waist, shanks grey and stringy. During the night the wind had changed and the teams of sweepers were now clearing sand from the other side of the road. We arrived at the airport and halted beside a small, two-storeyed yellow building set a couple of hundred yards back from the strip. 'Ground floor is office,' said Irshad. 'Other floor sleeping quarters.'

A single rose tree stood by the door, the dust around its roots darkened by water. I remarked on it and Irshad laughed and grew animated. 'It is my first rose!' he said. 'I plant this morning. In Lahore I live with my parents in small house, three room and garden. The garden is mine. It is where I am most happy. But two months ago I am posted here, so I must start from scratch and make new one. Civil Aviation Authority will send roses, jasmine, zinnia and African marigold from Karachi, and Forestry Department will give orange, eucalyptus and mango tree. First consignment came up on Fokker yesterday, the rest will come next week and then Gwadar aerodrome will be most beautiful garden in Baluchistan! I am forbidden to plant fruit trees along runway because they bring birds and make birdstrike hazard for planes, so beside runway I will put marigold and zinnia, wild caper shrubs, maybe prickly pear cactus. Around terminal I will make a park. Green grass, and everywhere roses and trees for shade – gum and orange, mango and local date palm. I will mark paths with white-painted stones and have terminal walls covered with jasmine and bougainvillaea.'

The two Karachi men were looking at him as though his head had turned into a flowerpot. 'For all this high-intensity horticultural activity you must have water,' murmured Mr Siddiqi.

'Bowser truck come from Gwadar every day,' said Irshad, 'but I am also building underground tank. Water no problem.'

He ushered us inside. Above his office door was a freshly painted sign saying 'IRSHAD UL HAQ AIRPORT MANAGER GWADAR'. The room contained a desk, two chairs and a table with a large Comco two-way VHF radio on it. Graceful metal latticework was set over the windows. We were joined by a young man with fresh earth on his hands. He said something to Irshad who laughed and clapped him on the shoulder. 'This is Khan,' he said, 'otherwise Officer Commanding Vegetable Patch. First seeds come up with the roses on yesterday's Fokker. Khan, tell them what you just plant.'

'Radish!' said Khan.

'Giant white variety. You have tried? It is very good. Now Khan will wash his hands and get us little snack.'

Khan hurried away. 'We are mostly all young chap here,' said Irshad. 'This is Bachelor Airport, no women or family allowed on premises, conditions too hard. I have myself girlfriend in Lahore, also crazy about gardens, but we must wait for wedding till I get promotion to Married Airport.'

A voice issued peremptorily from the radio. 'Gwadar, this is whisky yankee six zero zero six. Over.'

Irshad glanced at his watch. 'Omani trooping flight, due in 20 minutes,' he said, flipping a switch on his Comco and picking up an old sports commentator's microphone. 'Good morning, whisky yankee six zero zero six, this Gwadar. Are you in touch with Karachi?'

'Negative, Gwadar. We're unable to raise them.'

'Roger.' Irshad frowned. 'Now he should be in touch with Karachi ATC,' he explained. 'Gwadar control only extend for five-mile radius. I suppose Karachi radio probably have conk out.'

I nodded bemusedly, paying little attention, because the voice coming from the radio belonged to a New Zealander. Its broad vowels and easy, unhurried diction were unmistakable. At this moment, I recalled with a pang, my daughter was staying with my mother in a leafy Auckland suburb, just down the road from the large, boisterous family of my sister and brother-in-law. What was a Kiwi doing flying an Omani government trooping flight into Gwadar? He gave his position, estimating over Jiwani at O858, maintaining a flight level of one three zero.

'Now he will need airfield information,' said Irshad. He cleared his throat and threw the switch. 'Whisky yankee six zero zero six, here is Gwadar weather. Gwadar weather fair, wind calm, visibility eight kilometres, QNH 1014 millibars, temperature twenty degree Celsius, cloud nil. Use runway zero six.'

'Roger, Gwadar,' said the New Zealander.

Irshad switched off. 'What the hell happen to Karachi?' he muttered, then sighed and pressed his switch again. 'Six zero zero six, this Gwadar. Requesting your position now.'

'Right over Jiwani,' said the New Zealander, 'and commencing our descent. We've just about got your field in sight.'

Khan walked in with cups of tea and dishes of pistachio nuts and pink biscuits. As we tucked in I admired the onyx pen set and rainbow-coloured paperweights on Irshad's desk. There was a pincushion as well and, under a sheet of glass, a red plastic doily and a page torn from an exercise book which bore a Cloud Guide written out painstakingly in longhand. 'Nimbo-Stratus NS,' I read, '600–10,000 ft. Dark, grey, feebly illuminated. Stratus ST. Resembling fog but not resting on ground.'

Irshad reached over for a handful of pistachios. 'He coming,' he said. 'Can you hear?'

I cocked an ear and caught the whine of turbo-props approaching from the west. We stood at the window and watched the Fokker passing a mile away, the sun catching its tilting wings and making it gleam like a daytime comet. It banked steeply to line up with the strip. 'On finals for runway zero six,' said the New Zealander.

'Okay,' Irshad acknowledged. 'Confirm your wheels down and locked.'

'I'd like to meet that pilot,' I said. 'He comes from my part of the world.'

'No sweat,' said Irshad. 'As soon as he has switch off I must visit terminal anyway.'

We reached the Fokker while its propellers were still spinning. The two Europeans on the flight deck looked down at me with surprise. The burly young co-pilot left his seat and jumped to the ground. 'Garth McGearty,' he said, grinning and shaking hands. 'What's a lone white man doing in the middle of ball chitty country?'

As the wiry Omani soldiers disembarked and walked to their waiting truck we swapped the kind of abbreviated personal information people tend to exchange between planes. He was flying F27s for Oman Aviation Services because of the recession back home. 'Air New Zealand suddenly had too many pilots and not enough aeroplanes,' he said, 'but they also had a contract with the Omanis to supply personnel. So, instead of making us redundant, they sent six of us over here. It's not a bad life. Plenty of flying, a liquor allowance worth the equivalent of 10 per cent of our salaries – that buys me nearly 3,000 bucks US of beer per annum – and home leave every eight months. Sometimes more. All the Omani Fokkers go out to New Zealand for major servicing and overhauls and we take them.' He smiled. 'That's a good trip. Plenty of stops. Some interesting characters along the way. Lots of laughs.'

The troops booked for the return began filing aboard and the captain, a solid-looking Englishman with greying hair, climbed down and introduced himself as Jan Bussell from Chipping Norton. 'This is ball chitty country,' he said. 'What brings you up this way?'

I told him of my Imperial safari too and then, as Garth and I chatted about New Zealand, I mentioned that I spent part of my childhood nearby in the Fiji Islands. Garth said a mate of his, a fellow Air New Zealand pilot, had married a girl from Fiji. It had been a beautiful day, that, perfect weather, nice people, plenty of the amber liquid, everyone happy as a box of birds. He mentioned the girl's name and, standing there on the Gwadar strip while a hawk drifted slowly downwind and, for all I knew, the KGB Baluchi spy who met the planes stood lip-reading our conversation, I said, 'She lived across the street from us. She was a friend of my sister's.'

'Time for the off,' said Captain Bussell, glancing at his watch.

'You're kidding,' said Garth, staring at me.

'Come on, son,' said the captain. 'We've got a lot of miles to cover today.'

'Well, I'll be buggered,' he said slowly, clambering back into the cargo hold and taking his seat on the flight deck. The engines fired, the four-bladed black and white striped propellers began to spin and, while the pilots worked their way down the pre-taxi checklist, we hurried to Irshad's office so that he could give the Fokker its take-off instructions, arriving just as Garth switched on and requested taxi clearance. This was granted. Irshad wanted to know at what level they would be cruising. One four zero, said Garth. We watched the Fokker swing about at the runway threshold and heard the clamour of its engines being run up. 'Gwadar, this is six zero zero six bound for Muscat. Are we cleared for departure?'

Irshad said yes, affirmative, and away they went, climbing slowly into the blue until the plane was just a dot of reflected light. Garth's voice continued to boom over the radio long after it had vanished, giving heights and positions, fretting about Karachi's continuing silence. Eventually, passing over Jiwani, he left us – 'Good day, Gwadar' – switched frequencies and began talking to Muscat. Irshad turned off the radio and, in the silence, we swallowed the last of the tea and finished off the pistachios. My mind was suddenly crowded with childhood memories of my sister and her pretty, dark-eyed friend playing in our shadowy Fijian garden. The melancholy those images induced was only dispelled on the drive back when Irshad suddenly swung off the road and went bumping across the desert. We halted at the foot of a slight rise. 'Now I am showing you something *most* interesting,' he said.

We trudged after him, Mr Siddiqi and Mr Haroon sighing as the fine sand spilled into their shoes and perspiration stains darkened the backs of their tailored jackets. Irshad halted at the crest of the slope and threw out an arm. 'Look!' he cried. 'Is Eye of Sea!'

'I of C?' Mr Siddiqi grumbled gently as we toiled on up the slope. 'Do he mean C of E? Or ICI?'

'Don't ask,' panted Mr Haroon. 'Perhaps he mean CIA.'

'I hope CIA,' said Mr Siddiqi. 'They will have cold beer at least.'

We joined Irshad on the bank of a pond. It was circular, the size of a domestic lily pool, and filled almost to the brim with dark, oily water. Near the centre was a small, shiny bubble. It kept bursting with a wet plopping noise then instantly reforming and bursting again. We stood there, Irshad and three men in business suits, the only human figures in that hot, primeval landscape, pondering the thing. I knew what it was. A. E. Thompson, the Imperial Station Superintendent, had been sufficiently intrigued by the phenomenon to mention it in his dispatch for the *Gazette*. 'A mile away to the east of the aerodrome is the amazing spectacle of the "Eye of the Sea". It is a deep circular pool of muddy water, about fifteen feet in diameter, with a perpetual bubble a little away from its centre. Tradition has it that it is connected with the sea, which is about four miles east of it, by means of a subterranean channel. The bubble is a little larger than a cricket ball and is constantly forming into shape and bursting. There is no legend attached to it, but the natives view it with fear and lower their voices in its vicinity.'

I recounted this to Irshad, who said, 'Yes, it definitely connect with Gwadar Bay. Sometime nomad wash pot and pan here. If pot drop in it go underground through tunnel and carry out to sea. These missing pot and pan have been observe by fishermen.'

'They floating along, you mean?' asked Mr Haroon.

Mr Siddiqi clicked his tongue impatiently. 'Haroon, if clumsy nomad drop pot here it must first sink to get down to underground tunnel. Am I right?'

Mr Haroon nodded. 'So pot fill up.'

'Of course pot fill up. So how can it be bobbing through wave when it get there?'

'Ah, yes,' said Mr Haroon.

Irshad cleared his throat. 'Camel too,' he said.

We stared at him. '*What camel?*' asked Mr Siddiqi in a dangerous voice.

'Camel fall in here is also wash out to sea.'

Mr Siddiqi gave a snort of derision. 'Observe by fishermen as it go swimming past for Bombay, I suppose? What is it you have down here? Subway tunnel? For camel to get through, passage would have to be seven foot diameter.'

'Unless its legs are tuck up,' murmured Mr Haroon.

At the Coast Guard Mess Irshad said he would see us that afternoon when we returned to catch our plane, and asked us to excuse him. He was heading back to plant more roses. I settled down on the verandah to write up my notes while Mr Siddiqi and Mr Haroon, looking oddly furtive, announced they were going for a stroll through the town. But I had barely started work when the sounds of a major street riot suddenly burst from the mess. There were shouts, screams and the ugly noises of close-quarter combat. I jumped up and peered through the flyscreen door. The television was on. A chorus of female singers with voices like police whistles was singing in Hindi, bashing cymbals and banging drums, serenading a well-fed youth in a glitter suit who pranced up and down a catwalk yelling 'Oo *bum bum*'; scores of silver mini-skirted groupies shrieked and lunged at his ankles. The scene was being watched attentively by a uniformed man sitting on a sofa. When he saw me he beckoned and, raising his voice above the din, shouted, 'Come and join me! Hope you like this sort of thing!'

I went in. He wore an open-necked khaki shirt and a jungle-green sweater with a major's crowns on the shoulders. His face bore an expression of melancholy so profound that it could have been entered in his passport as a distinguishing characteristic: eyes: brown; hair: black; demeanour: mournful. He was very short. 'Heard you were here!' he roared. 'Want some tea?'

I nodded, and his bearer, wiry and eager, went off at the double to make it. The youth on the screen had hopped clumsily on to a flower-bedecked swing and was now soaring over the heads of the frantic teenyboppers. As they plucked at him helplessly the picture, all at once, disintegrated into a sequence of rolling coloured bars and then went dead.

'*Damn!*' said the major. 'Power cut. Electricity here only available for a few hours in mornings and evenings but every so often the generator go on the blink.' He nodded at the blank screen.

'Indian video. Musical. Absolute rubbish, of course, but it pass the time. If it not up your street we have BBC cassette also, "The Best of Top of the Pops 1981", very good.'

I told him I was quite happy with the musical. He nodded and said we were having fish for lunch. 'Caught them myself, actually, last night, bit like your plaice, very nice shallow-fry. I go most evening. There's a buoy out in the bay I like to sit on. It jolly peaceful, and they always bite around there.'

His speech and manner were a straight parody of Sandhurst, but he had never been there, or anywhere else. 'Never been out of the country, actually, and I never will. Not young enough, not bright enough. Pakistan is very poor, you know. We haven't got money to splash around sending chap like me on overseas courses. Some go, of course, but only if well-connected high-flyers.'

He was a bachelor. Married men were not posted to Gwadar, designated a hardship post by the military authorities in Islamabad. Time hung heavy, he said, but he had his fishing, his videos and his duties. Talking about these at last produced a spark of animation. 'We get two-way traffic around here,' he said. 'Drugs coming down from the interior for shipment out, and goods like TVs, videos, radios, alcohol and tobacco being smuggled in. Bit of gold sometimes, too, though most of that go to the Indians. But last month one of our patrol boat saw a dhow slipping in late at night, without lights, and give chase. It was carrying seven million rupee worth of gold bullion up from Gulf. Most of contraband come from there. The Baluchi coast is sharp end, where you get biggest hauls, but even the posts on Indian border can sometimes provide bit of excitement. Thing here in yesterday's paper, actually.'

He passed me a copy of *Dawn*, the English-language Karachi daily, and pointed to an item about the arrest of 55 smugglers charged with illegally importing '10,327 grams of Indian bidi leaves, 2,662 shirts, 1,293 pants, 7 VCRs, 2 colour TV sets, 17 cassettes of Indian films, one Datsun car, one Jeep, 51 camels, 64 cows, 2 horses and 78 bottles of Indian whisky'. 'Those contraband cow,' he said with sudden feeling, 'can be absolute *bugger*.'

Then the video came on again and the plump youth resumed his song, though his delivery was now so shrill that the major frowned and shouted for his bearer. 'See, his voice gone high again,' he complained. The bearer knelt and adjusted the controls while I went to wash off the desert dust before lunch and, stepping on to the verandah, nearly collided with Mr Siddiqi and Mr Haroon, creeping by laden with bundles wrapped in newspaper. 'A few last-minute purchase,' explained Mr Siddiqi avoiding my eye. 'Just bit and pieces,' murmured Mr Haroon. Then a treacherous puff of wind raised the corners of the wrappings to reveal more Iranian crockery. When we assembled at the lunch table I was still being assailed by spasmodic fits of laughter. In a somewhat strained atmosphere we ate pilau rice, chappattis, mutton curry and the major's fish, which had been cut into small squares and fried in ghee. It was delicious. Midway through the meal a jeep drew up beside the verandah. It contained a young man and a strikingly beautiful girl, several months pregnant. The major's face was suddenly suffused with the most intense happiness. 'My friends have come!' he cried. He dropped his knife and fork with a clatter, leaving his meal unfinished and rushed out to meet them. They all got into the jeep and drove away, and we never saw the major again.

Later that afternoon we drove away too, in the jeep of the General Sales Agent. The bearer had meticulously repacked my bag, washing and ironing every item of clothing in it, even the things that had already been laundered in Dubai. I thanked him warmly and slipped him some money. He took it with a certain disdain and began walking away but then, as we moved off, turned, smiled and lifted his arm in a Roman salute. Mr Siddiqi and Mr Haroon were in high spirits. That night, as they kept reminding each other, they would be sleeping in their own beds.

There was the usual crowd of wild-looking meeters and greeters at the airport. Irshad pushed through them to say, 'Happy landings. I am pray for you.' The General Sales Agent carefully tore out our tickets and said the Karachi flight would be going via Pasni, a small port just down the coast. Boxes of lobsters were being loaded into the Fokker. I spied a uniformed security girl – a new one – body-searching five hooded, black-robed women behind a sacking curtain in their hot little brick annexe round the back. We boarded after being summarily frisked ourselves and then the stewardess, who looked no more than 17, closed the door and made her cabin announcement. 'The flight time to Pasni, *Insha'allah*, will be 20 minutes.'

I looked at Mr Haroon, who was sitting next to me. 'What does she mean, *Insha'allah*? Is something wrong with the pilot?'

'No, no. PIA girls always say that. You know, God's will. Is routine thing. It just mean if God want us to get to Pasni in 20 minutes then okay, no problem. But if He doesn't we must not blame her.'

We took off on the 70-mile leg, flying fast and low along wide, empty, surf-rimmed beaches and landing a quarter of an hour later. It was too hot to wait in the plane, so all the transit passengers tumbled out and stood in the shade of the wing. Imperial had not called here, but gone direct from Gwadar to Karachi. The *Air Route Book* warned that Pasni, with its brackish aerodrome well and unmaintained dried mud surface, should 'only be used in extreme emergency'. This strip, though, was long, broad and laid with heavy duty asphalt, and my suspicion that it had been prepared to take combat aircraft became a certainty when I noted a colony of blast-proof concrete fighter pens tucked discreetly away at the far end. If the Soviets ever made their push down from Afghanistan this would clearly be a front line base for the Battle of Gwadar.

At Pasni more lobsters were loaded aboard. Mr Haroon, looking distressed, said some were still alive and waving their claws through the cracks in the boxes. A man carrying a newspaper-wrapped bundle called up to the flight deck. The captain, who was young, with fair skin and reddish hair, jumped down as the man laid the bundle on the runway and opened it to reveal six mullet. The captain crouched and inspected them closely, then gave the man some rumpled rupee notes and scrambled back aboard, throwing his purchase in before him. The girl stewardess appeared at the door and called to us, 'Come along, come along!' Moments later we were back in the air, climbing over the desert on an easterly track. The flight time to Karachi, God willing, would be one hour. She brought us water in paper cups. There was so much fish aboard the Fokker that it smelled like a trawler and, for all I knew, might even be towing clouds of gulls along, squalling, in its wake.

III

The terrain below looked very queer, like sea frozen at the height of a storm and turned into blinding white permafrost. The thermals rising from it described precisely, a couple of miles up in the sky, the contours of the ground beneath, causing us to negotiate the troughs and shoulders of those petrified waves like a tramp steamer bucking through a typhoon. Mr Haroon was not enjoying this. He muttered, 'Oh, God, oh God,' and clasped the armrests of his chair. Then, with a final mighty heave, Baluchistan picked us up and threw us out, sending us skidding across a deserted beach and over the sea where, all at once, the plane quietened and grew steady. Mr Haroon sighed and opened his eyes. The water was the colour of limes and shot through with refracted sunbeams. Half a dozen boats tending lobster pots seemed buoyed up on pillars of light. Mr Haroon, after some urging, talked about himself, keeping his voice low. For him government PR was just a means of paying the rent and getting a pension. He was really a poet, essayist and short story writer. I remarked that these must be difficult times for writers in Pakistan, but he would not be drawn. He agreed, though, that the military regime of General Zia-ul-Haq tolerated no criticism of any kind, even if it was covert and indirect. 'Could you get away with it in a poem just using allegory?' I asked. 'No, no,' he said. Zia employed hardline fundamentalist scholars who sniffed that kind of thing out.

He fell silent and stared through the window, unwilling to say more. We were passing Ras Omara, another anvil-shaped headland jutting into the sea. The *Air Route Book* had advised pilots to make a 'coast crawl' along this stretch which, 40 years later, was what we were doing too. We had now switched back on to the track of Imperial's earliest India flights, routed along the Persian side of the Gulf. This was the way Sir Samuel and Lady Hoare had come in 1927 in their travelworn De Havilland 66 trimotor, blazing a trail that the company would follow for almost seven years, heading north from Basra towards the 'Persian town of

Bushire' where, drawn up on the dusty plain, the Hoares found 'the two tiny Moths of Messrs. Stack and Leete, who were flying to India'. The two young aeronauts deeply impressed them by mentioning that, for emergency landings, they carried nothing but a packet of biscuits in one plane and a ukulele in the other.

The De Havilland moved on to Lingeh which, from the air, 'has the appearance of an Italian town. On all sides there is an effect of small domed churches.' The British Vice-Consul told Sir Samuel that 'they are built-in wells for the preservation of surface water. Lingeh has two inches of rain in the year.' But Jask, the next stop, got only three-quarters of an inch, 'and the cows, when they cannot get fish, live on the waste tape of the Indo-European Telegraph Office.' When they landed at Jask 'a black-coated Persian installed a wooden table on the desert, and proceeded with the hand of a trained calligraphist to make curious signs, as if of the zodiac, upon our passports.' They stayed with Mr Janes, the representative of the Telegraph Company, who told them it grew so hot in summer that flies died on the wing and dropped lifeless from the sky. They flew on to Baluchistan 'over the white plain of Pasni' and landed at Quetta where they were met 'by Colonel Keyes, the British Resident in Baluchistan, a Baluchi Guard, and the Air Force officers from one of the Quetta squadrons. In the distance was a tent containing luncheon. I received two interesting presentations. The first was an Afshar carpet sent by the Khan of Kalat, the ruling prince of Baluchistan. With it, enclosed in a bag of gold brocade, was a letter of welcome. "I have asked my Political Agent to greet you on my behalf and entertain you and Lady Sahiba and to offer you from me a carpet as a symbol of your conquest of the air – a conquest such as King Solomon made when he flew over these regions on his magic carpet." The second gift, offered to me by the Sardar Bahadur Mir Bahi Khan, the Gichki Sardar of Kech Makran, was a magnificent sword with a Shiraz blade and a scabbard of blue and white Kalat enamel.'

Now the sun was setting, making the looming, shadowy heights of the Makran Coast Range a misty mauve and our propeller arcs spinning circles of rainbow. In the galley the lights had been switched on. It was cosy and peaceful aboard the Fokker and Mr

Siddiqi, seated across the aisle, stretched and said, 'On most other airline now you could get a drink. Wouldn't it be nice?'

'PIA is dry,' murmured Mr Haroon.

I already knew that.

The teenage stewardess was walking slowly towards us down the aisle. Mr Haroon suddenly giggled and nudged my arm. 'Ask her.'

I stared at him. 'What?'

'Ask her for alcoholic beverage. For joke. Just see what she say. Go on. Go on.'

So, as she drew level, I said, 'Could you bring me a Scotch and water, please? A large one. And no ice.'

She froze. Her hand went to her mouth and her eyes widened. 'Oh no! On this plane . . . sir, PIA is Muslim . . . the management, no, no, it is forbidden. It is . . .'

Mr Haroon, staring fixedly out the window, began to laugh. So did Mr Siddiqi. Then the girl began to laugh too. Her face, animated, was beautiful and as she turned away Mr Haroon called, 'Remember, no ice!'

Ten thousand feet above us the wind was fanning a jet contrail into the intricate pattern of a veined leaf, russet in the twilight. We began our descent opposite Ras Karachi and dropped slowly down past Sonmiani Bay, approaching the city over the calm water and flat green islands of the harbour. There were docks and railway marshalling yards and then a crowded urban sprawl, its harsh contours softened by the dusk. Karachi ATC put us into a holding pattern that sent the Fokker tracking backwards and forwards over rolling brown hills, quartering a 20-square-mile area as though doing a low-level reconnaissance. The Hoares had faced no such delay when they flew in. 'I do not deny that as we neared Karachi I was feeling not a little excited,' Sir Samuel confessed. 'Lady Hoare and I had reached India. A woman had for the first time made the journey [George V, on her return, appointed her a Dame of the Order of the British Empire] and a Minister of the Crown had, for the first time, flown to a distant part of the Empire. The citizens of Karachi . . . came in their hundreds to welcome us. Amongst the letters that were awaiting us I found one addressed to me as Sir Samuel Hoare, "Aeronaut of Renown". My Indian correspondent was the first collector of air stamps in India.'

The Fokker concluded its final sweep, banked steeply and sank through the gloaming towards the green threshold lights of Karachi Civil Airport. The approach to Runway 25 Right was marked by a high-intensity lit centreline, white with crossbars, which flickered beneath us before we came to earth with a single gentle bounce and then braked at the taxiway leading to the domestic terminal. The stewardess, positioned by the door, grinned as I disembarked. I told her I was still thirsty and she chuckled. 'I hope you are patient type, sir,' she said.

Mr Siddiqi announced that we would await our luggage in the VIP Lounge and, showing a pass at the door, sneaked us into a large room furnished in the severe, formalized manner I had last seen in Peking's Great Hall of the People. It was empty but for a delegation sitting ponderously on overstuffed sofas, drinking tea. I questioned our right to be there, but Mr Siddiqi quelled my doubts. 'No problem,' he said. 'The woman in charge here is BA BCom. She know me,' He jumped up and fetched a sheet of paper. 'Look,' he said. 'Warrant of Precedence for use of Lounge, numbered 1 to 20.'

The President stood at the head of the list and the Secretary of Central Government at the foot. Provincial Governors came fourth, ex-Presidents eighth and Envoys Extraordinary and Ministers Plenipotentiary eleventh. The ninth category had been deleted. Mr Siddiqi muttered, 'Oh, they just maharajahs or something, not VIP any more.'

We piled into his small car and set off through dimly-lit streets bursting with traffic, dodging those folk art buses and jousting with the drivers of the auto-rickshaws who, like Roman charioteers, were trying to tear each other's wheels off. Then, in the manner of an archaeologist pointing out the notable relics of a bygone civilization, he drew my attention to the places where you had been able to get a drink before the mullahs closed everything down in 1977. 'That place over there used to be nightclub,' he said. 'Another down that road. A bar was once here. There was a casino on this corner. And a nightclub on that one. Now you can only get drink if you have contacts and can pay black market prices. The authorities know all this but turn blind eye. When my son say, "Daddy, when I am big I want to be very, very rich, shall I be doctor or lawyer?" I tell him, forget all that nonsense, you just be good Karachi bootlegger.'

He dropped me at my hotel. 'I wish I was back in Gwadar,' I said. Mr Siddiqi and Mr Haroon laughed loudly and drove away. I entered the hotel, an anonymous glass Holiday Inn that belonged everywhere and nowhere, registered, and rode the lift up to my room. It stopped at the second floor and a wedding party got in. The bride, in white silk, returned my smile with one so dazzling that it almost made me buckle at the knees. Later, during supper in the coffee shop, I called the waiter over and raised the delicate matter of a cold beer. 'Ask at desk,' he said. At the desk they said, 'You must go back to your room and ask room service.' So I went up and called down for a cold beer. It came a quarter of an hour later, together with a document upon which I was obliged to enter my full name, home address, nationality and passport number. When I ordered another beer a new form had to be completed. The laws of Pakistan oblige the visiting foreigner to drink in his room, secretly and alone, and it made me depressed. If Mr Siddiqi and Mr Haroon had left their phone numbers I would have called and asked them over.

Karachi, for those heading east in the years before Partition split the sub-continent, had been the gateway to India. It was, by all accounts, a pretty dull place. Apart from the massive 201-foot-high hangar destined to house the R101 airship – which crashed in France on a 1930 trial flight for a new Empire service which was then abandoned – the city had little to recommend it. Travelling memorialists merely recorded the fact of their arrival or departure, sometimes dutifully mentioning the hangar (it was the tallest building in India) before moving on to other topics. Charles E. Ward, for example, flew in towards the end of 1931. 'I got my first glimpse of India in the early afternoon – a study in brown and grey, extending inland for miles, with the docks of Karachi in the foreground and the airship hangar rising like some giant tent from the desert. A small crowd of English people had gathered to watch the "Mail" arrive or meet friends and I was soon on my way to the city.'

Passengers spent the night at the Killarney Hotel. A free taxi was provided to take them to the aerodrome, where their plane usually waited near a signpost saying 'London 4,093 miles'. The correspondent of the Dumbarton *Rock* wrote, 'We had breakfast in the rest house, and afterwards "passed" the doctor and had our passports examined. We took off from Karachi at 9.30 in the large bi-plane *Horsa*. Smoking is strictly prohibited, the penalty being £200 and six months' imprisonment.' And Philip S. Rudder, making the run from Singapore to London, also boarded an HP42 at Karachi. 'The first sight we had of the great *Hanno* was at 2 a.m. There she stood ready on the runway, with half a dozen spotlights focused on her. She looked magnificent, her size accentuated by the blackness of the background, and her long lizard-like fuselage shimmering like beaten silver. We took off at 2.30. As soon as we were in the air the steward came round and turned off the lights and, as it were, tucked us in for the night.' And an anonymous Australian, making for Croydon from Brisbane, wrote, 'At Karachi, where a comparatively cool breeze was blowing, we had breakfast and then boarded this flying hotel, the RMA *Hengist* – a four-engined 22-seater with a large pantry and bar between the two cabins. The sight of the ice chest through the open door was too much for me so I rang the bell and ordered a round of drinks – an orangeade for a young kinsman of the Maharajah of Jodhpur and lime squashes for a planter from Assam and myself. This athletic-looking young Indian, who speaks perfect English with a low musical voice, has just been back from England for ten days' holiday. As we flew out to sea the planter from Assam told me it was his first view of it for seven years – he is a Scot, and so is the Indian High Court judge and ex-Conservative MP sitting behind me.'

Mr Siddiqi was late. He appeared at 9.40 a.m., looking edgy and frazzled and talking abstractedly of traffic jams. He said he had arranged some meetings for me, and he wasn't joking. The first was with Air Vice-Marshal Khurshid Anwar Mirza, Director-General of the Civil Aviation Authority, a good-looking, plausible man who had got his wings in Australia and who spent half an hour lecturing me on Soviet plans for the invasion of Gwadar. The Russians, he said, were making no secret of their intentions; Pakistani agents in Kabul had seen published documents which made it clear that Gwadar was to be the warm-water port they had coveted for centuries. The Air Vice-Marshal's aides frowned at their watches. Mine was supposed to be a five-minute courtesy call, squeezed in before a conference with a high-powered American delegation wanting to sell him a new instrument landing system. The aides had given me some dirty looks when I innocently referred to Gwadar, unaware that any mention of the place instantly lit his afterburners and made him loop the loop. He jumped up, talking a streak, and it was only when he reached the bit about plucky Pakistani defenders being nuked by the Ivans that the orchestrated throat-clearing of his aides finally brought him down to earth again.

Mr Siddiqi, ignoring my pleas for a coffee break, bundled me into his car and set off at high speed to keep an appointment with Group Captain Wasim Khan, Manager of Karachi Civil Airport. His office was in the ancient terminal building, a circular edifice like a giant Victorian folly. We climbed a grimy spiral staircase, walked down a tiled passageway lined by doors marked with swinging pub-style signboards and, passing the sign of the Asst. Aerodrome Officer (Admin.), came to one saying: 'Airport Manager Magistrate First Class'.

We knocked and went in. A very small man sat at a large, untidy desk. He had a trim black beard, hornrimmed spectacles and sparse hair carefully centre-parted. One hand held a telephone while the other agitated the documents piled on his desk. 'Yes?' he roared, glaring through a blizzard of flying paper.

'Sir,' said Mr Siddiqi. 'This Mr Frater from London. I tell you about him on blower last night.'

'Park your bum on chair!' shouted Group Captain Khan. 'How are you? Give me one minute. I am trying to find missing chitty. . . .' He pounced on a pink carbon and scowled at it. 'Ahmed?' he said into the phone. 'Yes, I have damn thing here.'

While they talked I looked at a varnished wooden honour board on the wall. It was headed 'Airport Manager Karachi Airport' and the names beneath were inscribed in gold leaf. '1. J. MacDonald 14.8.1947 to 22.10.1949. 2. F. M. Khan 23.10.1949 to 11.12.1952.' The fifth entry interested me. It said 'G/Capt. Wasim Khan 1.6.1961 to 24.9.1963'. Could this be the same man? When he had concluded his conversation I asked him.

He beamed. 'Of course. But then I succumbed to lure of Civvy Street and went off to the Amin Jute Mills at Chittagong as Resident Director. After that I became Finance Director of the Muslim Construction Company but always I missed hustle and bustle of airport, and when they ask me last year to return to Karachi Civil I jump at it. Aviation's in my blood. I flew Hurricanes and Spitfires in combat in '43. Not in your show. In *our* show, Burma. Didn't like the Hurricane. It was too tame. But the Spit was another matter. My God, what an aircraft! It was only damn thing with true-blue fighter qualities. When the Nips saw Spits coming at them their spectacles all mist up.'

He picked up the phone and yelled for tea. 'And now here I am back in old hot seat, dealing with 6,000 passengers a day. Freight too. Karachi ship a hell of a lot of beef, fruit and vegetables to the Middle East, and many, what you call it, *towel*. I work a twelve-hour day and stick my nose in everything. Otherwise you are flying slightly too high and do not know what is going on at ground level. Sitting here you have a lot of fight and row with people.' He looked at me happily. 'But I have age and experience so I can cope.'

An attractive middle-aged woman came in and Group Captain Khan introduced her as the manageress of the airport duty-free shop. I asked whether she sold liquor and she said, 'Yes, but only at my personal discretion. I will not sell to Muslims or anyone with a Muslim name. If they start making trouble I march them straight up here. Khan, remember, is also our magistrate. He is judge and jury all roll into one. Khan dispenses instant justice!'

'Can you lock people up?' I asked the Group Captain.

'The only thing I can't do is hang 'em!' he shouted affably. 'This place is like small city state, you know. I have staff off 1,100 and thousands of passengers, meeters, greeters and so forth here each day. You are bound to get troublemakers. Some just get ticking off, others I fine or stick in chokey. The really naughty boys are sent off to be dealt with by higher court.'

Mr Siddiqi said it was time to visit the control tower. I bade goodbye to Wasim Khan and the duty-free lady and hurried after him as he loped down the corridor and took the stairs two at a time.

'For God's sake, Siddiqi,' I gasped. 'Do we *have* to?'

'It will be interesting for you,' he said grimly, leading me out on to the terminal roof. We teetered along precarious catwalks and up a rickety uncovered staircase to a small glass-sided structure not unlike a rural signalbox. Though the exterior needed a coat of paint and the old door wouldn't close properly, inside it was as smart as a frigate's bridge. Its half dozen youthful occupants jumped up and shook hands. Apart from one who murmured into a radio and moved indentification slats about a board little was going on. The apron and runways were empty and, in the sky, I could see only clouds and crows. A skinny, earnest girl in red overalls told me she was the first female pilot employed by the Civil Aviation Authority and, in a couple of hours, would be taking her Beechcraft to Bahrain to calibrate the airport instruments. 'We have airport calibration contracts with seven or eight countries,' she said. 'It earns much foreign currency for Pakistan.' A young man showed me the brilliancy controls for the runway lighting. 'We can make it fade or bright as anything!' he said, laughing. Another produced the flare gun, a sawn-off blunderbuss with a mahogany stock so lovingly oiled and polished down the years that it gleamed like glass. Then he demonstrated the Aldis lamp for emergency communications with aircraft, airport vehicles and even the teams of sweepers who were out brushing down the runways by hand 24 hours a day. Could the sweepers read morse? 'Every sweeper team have morse-reader with it always,' he assured me.

I asked the supervisor, who was quiet and wryly funny, about the great airship hangar. 'It was dismantled in 1961 because it was structurally unsound,' he said. 'Karachi's biggest scrap metal merchant got the contract, so the hangar will have been recycled and, one way and another, is probably still being put to good use. After the R101 crash Imperial Airways kept their aircraft in it. They were still operating through Karachi in 1938 when the terminal – and this tower – were opened by the Governor of Sind. In those days we were talking down Handley Page Hannibals and now, from exact same tower, we talk down 747s.'

Mr Siddiqi looked at his watch and gave me a frown. We descended the staircase and sidled along the catwalks and I thought of Sir Samuel Hoare who, unaware that the hangar would one day be turned into cooking pots and bicycle frames, wrote, 'With the background of the Sind desert and the clouds of blowing sand, its form loomed up mysterious and even frightening. When we entered it the cranes were working, and huge girders were being swung into their places, whilst workmen from Lancashire and the Clyde were supervising the operations. Would the airship that this shed is to house bring Karachi as near to London as Edinburgh was to London a century ago? Whilst only the future can answer these questions, the present can at least justify the wisdom of an attempt.'

In the car, battling through the airport perimeter traffic, Mr Siddiqi said, 'Now we have lunch at Midway House.'

'Great,' I said. 'It's on me.'

'No, no. This, um, quite a formal affair. You told me in Gwadar you want to meet some old-time pilots. Well, that is what we do now. One dozen are coming.'

I stared at him. 'How did you organize that?'

'Persuasion. It what PR all about. Anyway, you ever hear of pilot who turn down free lunch?'

We arrived at the Midway, a hotel once famed in the annals of flying but now struggling slightly to keep up appearances. Its name was a monument to the fact that Karachi stood at the halfway point between Amsterdam and Batavia – as the Dutch called Jakarta – on KLM's legendary 1930s high-speed run to the Indies. This was where Captain Ivan 'The Turk' Smirnoff, a dashing White Russian who had been a Tsarist Air Force ace before escaping from the Revolution in a cattle truck and coming to the Netherlands, allowed his exhausted passengers a few hours' rest while his Fokker 18 'Pelikaan' was fuelled and serviced during his record-breaking four-day, four-hour, 35-minute blinder out east in 1934. (He got home again ten minutes faster.) They had all stopped at the Midway – Smirnoff, Parmentier, Beekman, Blaak, Geyssendorfer and Evert van Dijk, household names in Holland, celebrated as movie stars, even courted by the Queen herself. It was they who trail-blazed the eastern routes, turning large tracts of the southern hemisphere into their own personal fiefdoms, and leaving Imperial so far behind that Britons made jokes about their own airline and MPs complained angrily of national humiliation in the House.

The Midway had been their hotel. They had their own tables in the dining room and their own corners of the bar, amply stocked with good Dutch beer and high-octane Dutch gin. Now I sought some sense of their robust presence in the echoing, shadowy lobby, but all I got was the aroma of stale cabbage and a faint whiff of beeswax. Mr Siddiqi bustled me upstairs. He seemed a little tense. I was too. The prospect of entertaining a dozen toothless Pakistani aeronauts as they quaveringly recalled forgotten mail runs was slightly intimidating. We got ourselves orange juices and waited. Moments later we were approached by a delegation of chartered accountants, a dozen sleek, well-groomed men in expensive suits and handmade shoes. I noted them absently, and it was only when Mr Siddiqi jumped up and adopted a posture of deep respect that I realized he was greeting his luncheon guests. But these men were at the peak of their powers and I realized, with some dismay, that what Mr Siddiqi had produced for me was nothing less than the PIA pilots' High Praesidium.

Introductions were made. I shook hands with the Chief Pilot (Training), the Chief Pilot (Safety) – who was an Imam – the Chief Pilot (DC10 Fleet) and the Chief Pilot (747 Fleet), then followed them bemusedly into the dining room. Mr Siddiqi, familiar with the company pecking order, seated everyone according to the minutiae of corporate seniority then flopped down and flapped a weary hand at me. 'You are in chair,' he said.

The meeting was not a success. I opened with the subject of the most difficult and dangerous scheduled flight in the world. It lies on the PIA domestic network, from Rawalpindi to Gilgit (subject to weather), a hair-raising sortie through a succession of steep-sided Himalayan valleys and – according to Mr Siddiqi – the fire in which the company's best pilots are forged. Only the elite were chosen to make the Gilgit run, he had assured me, only those who accomplished it flawlessly got to the top in later life. But when I suggested to the party that they must all be Gilgit graduates they responded with derision. *Everyone* did Gilgit. You didn't even get command of a Fokker until you had a few dozen Gilgits under your belt. The man who had brought me back from Gwadar would have been a Gilgit veteran. Mr Siddiqi frowned at his roast chicken and avoided my eye. Though the service was operated by agile little F27s and belonged to the youngsters, the Senior Common Room reminisced a bit, the Chief Pilot (Training) saying, 'I suppose it gave one a certain confidence,' and the Chief Pilot (Safety) agreeing that, in retrospect, it had been jolly good fun. The Chief Pilot (747s), who had made headlines in Pakistan when he took a big, heavy Super Constellation into Gilgit, recalled, 'What makes it tricky is that there are two 90-degree turns, Point Yankee and Point Zulu. At Yankee you go sharp right along the valley, at Zulu you go left.

Except for one critical point where you're pretty well tied in, you can make a tight 180-degree turn anywhere along the way. It really isn't all *that* difficult.'

I wished the Gilgit sector had been on my route. Imperial hadn't flown it and neither had KLM, though pilots like Smirnoff and Geyssendorfer may have occasionally slipped off and done it before breakfast just to keep their eye in. Meanwhile, our meeting was getting out of hand. My companions were jet-age technocrats to whom the Imperial era must have seemed like a chapter from the Iron Age and, though they humoured me – I learned that the Heathrow air traffic controllers were the best in the world and those at Paris Charles de Gaulle among the worst ('Paris is maximum panic; the nastier the weather the faster they talk') and heard what it was like on the flight deck of a DC10 stacked forty-ninth in the queue over Chicago's O'Hare during a blizzard – they were soon chatting animatedly among themselves, employing a mixture of Urdu and English and the abbreviated, gnomic international language of the airways.

They talked about foreign expenses and hotel accommodation in Tripoli, and exchanged dumb co-pilot stories that caused a lot of immoderate laughter. Shortly before they broke up – the Imam, I gathered, had to take a 707 to Peking – I became aware of a certain star quality about them, an element of showmanship and temperament not unlike that found among the old school of ranking actor managers. Then they drifted away, trailing clouds of expensive cologne, and Mr Siddiqi, proclaiming the event a triumph, drove me back to my hotel. He said he would pick me up at 7 p.m. sharp and take me out to dinner. 'We will have *real* Pakistani meal,' he said, before rejoining the traffic like a Formula One driver blasting out of the pits.

That evening, on time, he called me from the lobby. I said I would come down. 'No, no,' he said anxiously. 'We will come up.'

'We?'

'Old chap,' he said, with lowered voice, 'I have brought my friend Mrs Iqbal with me. A widow. You understand? Mrs Iqbal is my chum.'

Mrs Iqbal was a plump, smiling woman in a sari, who shook hands shyly. Then they sat together on a sofa, watching me expectantly, and I suddenly realized what they wanted. 'Drinks!' I said.

Mr Siddiqi beamed. 'Whisky,' he said. 'She will have gin. Also bitter lemon, peanuts and crisps.'

When the waiter arrived Mr Siddiqi instantly took charge, bombarding him with instructions and complaints. 'Put whisky here. Gin there. Where peanuts? They are salted? Why you not bring dry-roast? This soda not cold and look, ice is all melt. You call this whisky a large one? Okay, you can go but stand by for next order.' Then he turned his attention to Mrs Iqbal. 'Find bowl for peanuts and tip them in. Crisps can stay in packet. Pass them round. Mr Frater have no swizzle stick. Give him yours. You have put too much bitter lemon in your gin.' When, perspiring slightly, she had resumed her seat, he began grumbling about his wife. I sensed that I was listening to a long-running saga which was updated each time they met. 'Before I go to Gwadar she give me chick pea for dinner. Last night she give me chick pea again. I get up this morning and, blow me, what you think she put on my plate?'

Mrs Iqbal sighed and clicked her tongue. 'Chick pea,' she murmured.

'That all she cook nowadays. And when she not cooking chick pea she moan moan moan. Non-stop. Blah blah blah. Siddiqi do this, Siddiqi do that.'

After a few more drinks we drove downtown to a little restaurant 'off beaten track'. A party of wild-looking men were sitting at the next table. Mr Siddiqi said they were well-known gangsters. Then he summoned the waiter and ordered, off the top of his head, a meal so delicious that, months later, the memory of it still makes my mouth water. We got through a forequarter of lamb garnished with fiery spices and cooked over charcoal, a selection of spicy masala curries, fragrant pulao rice and then sweets like kulfi and coloured custards flavoured with nuts, saffron and rose water.

I was leaving for Bombay early next morning, and I said goodbye to Mr Siddiqi with real regret. He had been a wonderful guide and companion, resourceful, efficient, funny, endlessly helpful and good-humoured, a marvellous representative of his country. To him public relations was a kind of ministry and when I told him that most PR people in England were just in it for the money, and pretty hopeless too, he plainly didn't believe me; anyone lucky enough to get into PR must regard it as nothing less than a vocation. Back at the hotel I asked him if he wanted one for the road. He said yes but Mrs Iqbal, firmly, said no and led him back to his car. Mr Siddiqi wished me luck. He urged me to take good care of myself and never to piss into the wind. 'Old Urdu proverb!' he said. As he moved off, waving, I caught a glimpse of Mrs Iqbal's shocked expression. Then the car lights vanished round a bend and they were gone.

IV

Mr Haroon came to see me off. It was 5.30 and bitterly cold. He told me there had been student riots in Karachi the previous day and, though the local media had neglected to make any mention of them, a full account had been broadcast on the BBC World Service. That was typical, Mr Haroon said; if you wanted to know what was going on in Pakistan you had to listen to London. Then the flight was called and we said goodbye. The PIA A300 Airbus got airborne at 6.45, climbing over a dark city into a sky tinged with the first glimmer of dawn. We crossed the Indus which, touched by light, rippled away through the sleeping country like a stream of molten metal, then headed down the coast, the heavy cloak of sea mist below parting occasionally to reveal snuff-coloured land and pale green water. The Airbus bumped and wobbled slightly in some small oragraphic lift. Half an hour into the flight the sun began really roaring up over India, making the plane's port windows glow like a row of furnace doors. Inside the Airbus there was a rattle of plastic blinds being snapped down, but mine stayed up so that I could watch the sea mist being burned away to reveal a coastline glittering with water meadows, ponds, creeks and oxbow lakes, all strung out like the letters of some mysterious, primeval script. This was the Great Rann of Kutch, a wetland of swamps and marshes reaching away to the eastern horizon. Smart, affable young stewards distributed breakfast trays of omelette and fried fish but refrained from pouring coffee until the aircraft had negotiated a 20-minute stretch of cobblestone turbulence.

I was making a detour from the Imperial route. They had gone direct to Jodhpur in Rajasthan, not south to Bombay, but today the Bombay connection provided the only means of flying from Karachi to Jodhpur by scheduled commercial services and – just as important – I had an appointment in Homi Mody Street that morning with a man described to me by Mr Siddiqi as the Greatest Living Indian. Meanwhile, I listened to my neighbour, a small, round, fastidious Bombay lawyer who had been visiting relatives. 'All the top military men in Pakistan are millionaires,' he said enviously. 'Their fortunes come from defence contracts, from the "commissions" which the foreign salesmen must pay them, and now they spend their days racking their brains for new things to buy the Armed Forces. As soon as you've thought of something – it could be a missile system or a new Army boot – you open a file on it and persuade your colleagues, in return for a percentage, to write memos supporting your case. When you have enough memos you take your file to Zia and persuade him that he needs this new thing. If Zia signs the chitty – and I have seen one of these famous chitties; it was just a small piece of cheap brown paper, an ordinary bit of bumph – it makes you a very, very rich man.'

The lawyer asked me to take some of his bottles through Indian customs. At the Karachi duty-free shop he had suffered a brain-storm, he said, and pointed ruefully to the crop of plastic bags planted around his feet. They contained sherry, port, whisky, gin, cognac and Sambuca Romana. I told him I was prepared to carry in my legal quota and, looking out, noted that we were now crossing the Gulf of Kutch. At its head, a hazy smudge of land on the skyline, was the Little Rann of Kutch; moments earlier we had crossed the Tropic of Cancer. The sea looked like polished chrome, and I glanced at the *Air Route Book* to see what it said about ditching. After advising survivors that the average man could go for six days without water – though 'a few exceptional individuals can last 10 or even 15 days' – it warned sternly against the fatal consequences of poor morale. 'Almost everything depends on the captain of the aircraft. It is he who should ensure that there is no panic and keep the rest cheerful. If the cause of the forced landing is due, some think, to the carelessness of one or more, don't start grumbling or airing your views on the subject until you are rescued. Save all your energy. You may need it. For the same reason, don't start singing or whistling. It not only wastes energy but makes you thirsty more quickly, and water is valuable. Don't drink sea water and, above all, don't drink urine. Spirits are not thirst quenchers. As regards food, fat is the best if there is any. With little food there may be some constipation, but this is no cause for alarm.'

We headed landwards across the Gulf of Cambay and began our descent along a curving creek, the sun bouncing off it and tracking us like a searchlight. The Airbus drifted down past a high, conical hill and then, wreathed in mist, another hill with the silhouette of a pig's head. Banking gently to the right it hummed over a broad horseshoe of bright water bisected by a long pylon-lined roadbridge that led towards a marsh of flooded rice paddies. On finals we whizzed so low over a shanty town that dogs in the puddled lanes ran from our giant shadow and, with the wheels almost brushing the rusting tin roof of a small factory bearing the faded legend MUKAND IS STEEL, we landed at Bombay, taxiing to the terminal past a row of Air India 747s parked with their flaps fully extended. This gave them a slack-winged, drooping look, like dead turkeys.

I carried the lawyer's bottles ashore for him but airside of customs there was a duty-free shop for arriving passengers and now, suddenly seized by the same madness that had struck him at Karachi, he turned and rushed towards it. 'I must just quickly get a watch,' he said. 'Is Seiko or Citizen best? Oh, and an electronic alarm. Cigars for my brother. Oh, oh, and perfume for my wife.'

He stood fussing at the counter as I anxiously noted the time. Eventually, lugging his cut-price loot, the lawyer professed himself satisfied and we completed the formalities and headed through the echoing, grimy old terminal to the taxi rank. I joined the queue while he took back his bottles, scrambled into a waiting chauffeur-driven Merc with air conditioning and tinted windows, and purred off towards town. Creep, I thought. The taxi queue was long, slow and bad-tempered. Then a child snatched my bag and stuck it into the back of a battered old Hindustan. I shoved a rupee note in his hand, got in and asked the driver to take me to the Oberoi Towers at Nariman Point. He was a small, taciturn man, painfully undernourished, whose limbs were bone and sinew sealed in dusty black skin. The engine fired after many attempts and, making a noise like a barking seal, the Hindustan lurched out of the airport and headed away from Bombay. I recalled a friend telling me that these airport taxis once operated a lucrative sideline taking incoming visitors into the countryside where waiting dacoits robbed them and cut their throats.

'Where are we going?' I demanded.

'Ghaz,' he said.

I was explaining that I didn't want to go to Ghaz when he pulled up at a garage and took aboard 15 litres before setting off to join the first of the traffic jams that reached all the way into town, many of them curiously formalized, structured affairs, the personal fiefdoms of legions of beggars. There were maimed men, limbless children and grim-faced women with babies, all working the jams methodically and expertly, scuttling like monkeys through the seething traffic to present their deformities or crying infants to the occupants of the cars. The journey occupied the better part of two hours.

In the lobby of the Oberoi Towers groups of Arabs, mostly men, sat around looking indolent, purposeless and deeply contented, and I recalled that Bombay had become one of their favourite watering holes. This was where rich Saudis and Kuwaitis came to let their hair down, and their effect on the hotel's internal economy was evident from the curl of the porter's lip when he noted the size of my tip. I caught another taxi and asked to be taken to Tata Sons Ltd at 24 Homi Mody Street in the Fort district. Very soon the driver, a monosyllabic young man in a turban, began frowning and muttering to himself and I realized that he didn't know where Homi Mody was. For half an hour we cruised around, pausing to ask for directions which were freely given but invariably conflicting. When, eventually, we drew up beside a discreet doorway in a quiet, tree-lined street, I rushed inside and was met by a forbidding man who glared through his spectacles as I made my excuses. He said, 'You are *very* late. The appointment was for 12 noon. It is now 12.22. Mr Tata has many claims on his time. I do not know whether he can see you now.'

But he did. I was ushered through a busy outer office into a large, cool, shadowy room containing a desk big enough to accommodate a championship snooker match. On it stood a scale model of a high-winged Puss Moth monoplane, fashioned entirely from silver, while a giant map of the world occupied much of the wall behind. Facing it was a painting of a long-haired nude girl executed entirely in soft, leafy greens. Mr Tata rose and walked briskly around the desk to meet me. He was a trim, quiet-voiced, soldierly-looking man with a firm handshake and a diction reminiscent of Eton and the Guards. He smiled briefly when I apologized for my lateness. 'You mustn't concern yourself with that,' he said. 'I have plenty of time. Come and sit down.'

Jehangir Tata – JRD to the world at large, Jeh to his friends – led me to a comfortable sofa and asked about my flight from Karachi. I said it must have been rather less eventful than the trip he had made two years earlier, going the other way. Mr Tata assured me that, on the the contrary, the run had been entirely uneventful. We were talking about the occasion in the autumn of 1982 when Mr Tata climbed into the cockpit of the same tiny Puss Moth (the original of the replica standing on his desk) in which, exactly half a century earlier, he had pioneered the route, took off from Bombay before cheering crowds and flew solo to Karachi. He was 78 on that occasion two years ago and carrying his original licence, the first pilot's licence – No. 1 – ever issued in India.

Now, a little older, but clearly not even contemplating retirement, he fetched his battered log book from a drawer, the cover inscribed with the words 'Record of Flights', its pages meticulously filled with entries in fading ink. Then Mr Tata, head of the largest industrial empire in India – his chairmanships included, or had included, Tata Sons Ltd, the Tata Iron and Steel Co. Ltd, Tata Ltd London, Tata Inc. New York, Tata AG (Switzerland), Tata Burroughs Ltd, Tata Industries Ltd, Tata Oil Mills Co. Ltd, Indian Hotels Co. and Air India (which he founded) – told me that his interest in aviation had first been aroused during a childhood holiday near Le Touquet. Though he is a Parsee, descended from one of the 100,000 Zorastrians who emigrated from Persia 13 centuries ago and now dominate the Bombay business community, his mother was French and so was his education; he retains those links today, and is a Commander of the Legion d'Honneur and honorary patron of the Indo-French Chamber of Commerce and Industry.

'We spent our summer holidays at a little Channel resort called Hardelrod,' he said. 'Monsieur Blériot and his family were neighbours. Blériot was a rather unprepossessing chap, with a big bushy moustache and absolutely no charm. He was also a rotten pilot. That famous crash landing at Dover was just a case of bad flying. Though I didn't like him I got on very well with his son, who was an outstandingly good pilot. In fact he had set his heart on making the first solo crossing of the Atlantic. I'm convinced he would have done it – *and* beaten Lindbergh – but then quite suddenly the poor fellow got appendicitis and died. The Blériots had a little hangar at Hardelrod and their chief pilot, Monsieur Peglod, would sometimes land on the beach when he came to visit. Once he nose-dived in and broke his hickory propeller. I managed to claim a bit, and even got Peglod to sign it. It became a cherished memento because he was the first man in the world to loop the loop.'

Mr Tata learnt to fly when he returned to India to join the family business. 'Sir Victor Sassoon had donated a couple of Gipsy Moths to the Bombay Flying Club and I persuaded a British naval pilot named Cummings to instruct me. I must have shown some aptitude because he let me go solo after just three and a half hours. I got carried away with excitement, raced up to 8,000 feet and started doing aerobatics. Mr Cummings had taught me how to go into a spin and, after I had started one, I suddenly remembered that he hadn't yet taught me how to get out again and I only avoided a crash by the skin of my teeth. The experience left me with a respect for the proper procedures that has been with me ever since.'

A young clerk walked in with cups of tea. Mr Tata thanked him and continued, 'Then the Aga Khan, the one who was weighed in diamonds, offered a £500 prize for the first Indian to fly solo between England and India. I bought a Gipsy Moth for £1,200 and set off.' He paused and consulted his log. 'Yes, here we are. Aga Khan Prize Flight, first leg Karachi to Jask on 3 May 1930. I got to Croydon six days later, and I was beaten by a 19-year-old Karachi boy named Engineer who, 25 years later, became Air Chief Marshal of the Indian Air Force. Also at Croydon was a gloomy Sikh who flew in a turban and was trying to make it in the other direction. He kept setting off, getting lost over the Continent and coming back again. Whether he ever got past Marseilles, let alone to India, I never discovered, but I had a sneaking sympathy for him because I had had directional problems of my own. Before leaving Karachi I asked a red-headed man named King to check and set my compass and, after setting off, I realized it was taking me too far to the right. I managed to get to Rutbah Wells by dead reckoning and spent the night in the Imperial fort. I told one of the Imperial pilots about my problem and he reminded me that even the roughest westerly heading would eventually take me to the Mediterranean. I said yes, but how would I know which bit of coast I was over? He gave me a pitying look and said, "You go down and ask." So that's what I did. I landed in a place that was full of anthills and sat under the wing until a farmer came along in a cart and told me I was near Haifa. When I finally reached Alexandria I had the compass checked, found it was 45 degrees out, pressed on to England, sold the Moth and came home by Imperial Airways. As we droned across the Iraqi desert the captain sat reading the *Illustrated London News* with such intense concentration that he flew right past Rutbah Wells without even noticing. I wondered whether I should say something, but I was young and shy and he clearly did not wish to be interrupted. He only looked up when the plane began to run out of fuel and, quite calmly, landed on the sand, broke into one of the RAF's emergency dumps and stole enough petrol to get us back to Rutbah in time for dinner.'

Mr Tata laughed and drank some tea. An elderly clerk hurried in to ask his advice about a charity matter, reminding me that his non-business interests and responsibilities range from being President of Honour for Life of the Aero Club of India and Honorary Air Vice-Marshal of the Indian Air Force to trusteeships of bodies like the Jawaharlal Nehru Memorial Fund, the N.R. Tata Family Trust, the Bai Navajbai Tata Zoroastrian Girls' School and the N.R. Tata Poor Relations Trust. He also holds honorary doctorates from Bombay and Allahabad.

When the clerk had gone Mr Tata said, 'I learnt to fly simply for pleasure and excitement but in 1929, soon after I had got my licence, I received a visit from a tall Englishman named Nevill

Vintcent. After a distinguished career in the RAF he had been barnstorming around India with a friend in a couple of De Havilland 9s and had been struck by the huge potential for civil aviation here. What he said to me was: let us start an airline. I thought it a marvellous idea. Bombay and Delhi had flying clubs, but no one was providing any kind of scheduled service – though for a few months in 1932 the little Delhi Flying Club, with a couple of borrowed Puss Moths and one young Indian pilot, took over the mail run between Karachi and Delhi from Imperial Airways. The pilot reported his position by buzzing railway stations. They then telegraphed his whereabouts to the next station up the line. It was a very professional operation, the only mishap being a crash landing in the desert after he collided with a buzzard. Anyway, Nevill Vintcent joined Tatas and began work on the creation of India's first airline. In 1932 the government finally gave us permission to operate a regular mail service from Karachi to Madras via Ahmedabad, Bombay, and Bellary. I went to England and bought two aircraft, one of which I planned to fly home with my wife. But I landed in Naples with flu so the Puss Moth had to be towed through the streets to the docks and loaded aboard the same ship on which they had loaded me. Eventually, though, we were ready to go and on 15 October 1932, I picked up the first mail consignment from the incoming Imperial flight at Karachi and flew it to Bombay, via Ahmedabad – where a Shell bullock cart was waiting to refuel the Moth with two-gallon tins of petrol. Nevill, in white buckskin shoes, a tie and pith helmet, took over at Bombay for the flight on to Bellary and Madras. We were finally in business. The assets of Tata Airlines consisted of one Puss Moth, one Leopard Moth, one palm-thatched shed, one full-time pilot assisted by Nevill and myself, one part-time engineer and a couple of apprentice mechanics. And Bombay 'airport', our home base, was actually a dried mud flat beside the sea. It was quite serviceable for eight months of the year, but when the monsoon high tides flooded it to a depth of several fathoms we moved inland to Poona and a little grass strip beside the Yeravda Jail, where the British were always locking up Mahatma Gandhi.'

Karachi, he recalled, had primitive radio and night landing facilities but there were no flying aids over the remainder of the route so all operations had to be carried out in daylight. Though the 1,300-mile run from Karachi to Madras took the tiny planes – which maintained an average speed of 40 m.p.h. – across 5,000-foot ranges, deserts, swamps and areas which, during the monsoon, got 300 inches of rain in the space of four wild, waterlogged months, in the first year of operations they clocked up 160,000 miles with an unbroken record of regularity.

'The basic rule for monsoon flying,' said Mr Tata, 'was to keep low. There were tremendous convection currents and colossal turbulence. It could get rough enough to make even an experienced pilot airsick. Once I became so violently ill that I took the Puss Moth up to 18,000 feet just to find calm air. But it was even worse up there so I had no choice but to make a forced landing in a forest clearing. It was very calm and peaceful and I sat for two hours, waiting for the sky to calm down. Farmers brought me bananas. Children gave me sugar cane. I still recall the tranquillity of that place. By dusk conditions aloft had improved enough for me to give it another try. I took off and flew on through the darkness to Bellary, following the light of the quarter moon shining on the railway line. Once we were well and truly familiar with the route Nevill and I were ready to branch out. We got a Fox Moth with a spacious covered cabin and began carrying passengers, adopting for ourselves the slogan of Aero Postale, the French outfit that operated the South American mail service: 'Mails Can Be Lost But Never Delayed, Passengers Can Be Delayed But Must Never Be Lost.' It was a time of excitement, anxiety and optimism but then, in 1942, Nevill died somewhere off the Spanish coast aboard an RAF bomber, presumed shot down. He was returning from a visit to England in connection with a Tata project for building military aircraft in India.'

A small plaque fixed to the base of the silver Puss Moth on Mr Tata's desk announced that it had been made for J.R.D. Tata by the Air India engineering department. It was built precisely to scale, perfect in every detail and, as he ran a finger affectionately along its fuselage, I asked whether he enjoyed his fiftieth anniversary flight in 1982. He said it had been great fun. The old aeroplane, regarded in India as a museum piece, was returned to England to be made airworthy and then on 15 October, 50 years to the day, he set off from Bombay, doing his original run in reverse. 'The Indian government was so worried about a frail old man flying alone in such a primitive aircraft that they insisted I be accompanied by a twin-engined Beechcraft full of doctors and medical equipment. I had no choice but to agree and off we went, travelling in a loose kind of formation. At Ahmedabad I was charmed to find that the man who had driven the Shell bullock cart in 1932 was waiting, on an identical cart laden with more two-gallon tins, to fill my tanks again. It was a delightful reunion. Then we set off for Karachi but, unfortunately, the Beechcraft suffered sudden engine failure and was obliged to drop out and make an emergency landing.'

Mr Tata allowed himself a faint smile. 'Deprived of my powerful twin-engined companion I was obliged to carry on in a state of splendid isolation. The flight actually went very well – so well, in fact, that I made a faster time than I did in 1932. Having arrived early I rendezvoused with a couple of Pakistani Air Force helicopters and stooged around Karachi air space until the reception committee below were ready for me. The most irritating thing about losing the Beechcraft was that it contained my suitcase and personal effects. I had to borrow pyjamas from the Indian consul and a toothbrush from the managing director of PIA.'

Mr Siddiqi, at Karachi Airport to witness the arrival, was struck by Mr Tata's modest and unassuming demeanour. During our dinner the previous evening he recalled that Mr Tata had gone to the VIP Lounge for a press conference carrying a small mail bag containing first day covers specially printed for the flight. He placed it on a table and, when the buzz of excitement had finally ceased, said simply, 'As you see, gentlemen, I am but a postman.'

When I reminded Mr Tata of that he remarked, 'It was no exaggeration. In the old days my job was to deliver the mails. But your friend was quite right about the first day covers. I believe there is still one left. Would you like to see it?'

The chief clerk brought in an envelope on which small watercolour sketches of an Air India 747, an Indian Airlines A300 Airbus and Mr Tata's little crimson Puss Moth flew across a pale blue sky. The words '50 YEARS OF INDIAN AVIATION 1932–1982' were printed in Hindi and English, and the commemorative 3 rupee 25 anna stamp showed a youthful Mr Tata, in white slacks and an Aertex tennis shirt, standing with a mail bag in front of his plane. There was a special postmark, too. Mr Tata said, 'What tickled me was that this is the first such stamp issued while the subject was still alive.' Then he unscrewed his fountain pen and inscribed my name on the envelope in a flowing hand. 'What is your home address?' he asked.

I told him and he wrote it out in full, slanting it diagonally in the old-fashioned way, then signed his own name across the postmark and added the flight date.

'A souvenir,' he said, handing it to me.

I was tremendously touched and pleased to have it but, concerned that I might be keeping him from his work, said I really ought to be going. He said yes, of course, and observed, without any irony, that I must have a great deal to do.

He ordered his car around to run me back to the hotel and I asked if he still did any flying. He told me that, apart from isolated sorties like the Puss Moth trip to Karachi, he had given it up back in the days when Tatas operated a converted Dakota for their company plane. Tata executives on their way to Cochin or Bangalore grew accustomed to the boss going forward and taking over the controls. They travelled secure in the knowledge that they were being flown by the Founder and Chairman of Air India – which is what Mr Tata's little 1930s outfit became in 1946 (later it grew into Indian Airlines as well) – and, for good measure, the President of IATA too.

Just before I left he recalled the excitement he felt when his airline took delivery of its first jets. 'We had placed orders for Comets in 1953 but, after the accidents, we had to go to Boeing instead. But we specified – and Air India was the first airline in the world to do so – that our Boeings should have Rolls-Royce Conway engines. Our first 707 went into service on our Blue Ribbon run to London on 19 April 1960. A few months later, in February 1961, one of our 707s, in the course of a delivery flight, made the first non-stop run from London to Bombay. We averaged 600 m.p.h. and completed the trip in precisely eight hours and five minutes. I had the good fortune to be aboard and I recalled, somewhat nostalgically, that almost exactly 30 years earlier it had taken me the same number of days and hours to cover the same distance, when I flew solo from Bombay to London in eight days and five hours.'

That afternoon, while writing up my notes among the Arabs in the lounge of the Oberoi Towers – which had succeeded the Karachi airship hangar as the tallest building in India – I was approached by a portly old man in a grey cotton jacket who dropped wheezing into the next chair and said, 'My dear sir, forgive me for disturbing you.'

He had a pale skin, rheumy eyes, wispy white hair and a big, toothy smile. 'I am a supplier of pineapple products to the main hotels of Bombay,' he announced. 'This morning, having made a delivery of juice and segments to the Centaur Hotel, I was making my way home by bus with the ten 100-rupee notes I had received as payment when two young fellows came up behind me and, quick as a flash, seized the money. I cried out but they jumped off and were gone. The police said, "Old man, you must forget the money. You will never see it again." Though I am 70 I am blessed with a good wife and a good son who lives in New York and unfailingly sends his mother a cheque for $50 each month. He owns an agency supplying models for certain, uh, specialist photographs and films. Now, my dear sir, could you see your way to perhaps giving me a little money for a taxi home? $20 would suffice. Even $10. To save time I could come up to your room and collect it.'

I said I had no dollars and offered him some rupees instead. This proposal fell on stony ground. He was morosely considering the matter when a young house detective in a business suit approached and threw him out. 'He won't go far,' said the detective. 'In 20 minutes he'll be back. What was he trading in today? Pineapple products or jam?'

'Pineapple products.'

'It's the Arabs he's really after. When he gets up to their rooms he shows them dirty pictures. They give him a lot of money because sex is one of the things they come to Bombay for. Some of them stay for months, and afterwards the rooms are in such a state that we must fumigate them, burning all the carpets, furniture and so on. They are even shitting in the washbasins.'

That evening I went to a small restaurant nearby for chicken pulao and a bottle of Guru beer. A couple of Qantas stewards from the hotel sat at the next table. They were called Shane and Gary and looked like ageing tennis pros. We got talking. Gary said he wanted to see the Cages in Grant Road so afterwards we jumped into a taxi and headed downtown. The elderly Sikh driver said the occupants of the Cages were poor peasant girls sold into slavery by their parents. He let us off in a dark, narrow, malodorous street lined by countless small brothels. Hands reached from the darkness and plucked at our hands, arms and clothes. The girls were young and undernourished, and made soft pleading noises. In the doorways, dimly illuminated by oil lamps, sat the madams, corpulent old women with hard old men's faces. The windows of the Cages were barred. One of the houses was parading its girls in the street. They wore the uniforms of drum majorettes, high white boots, short skirts, jackets of crimson silk, and they stood stiffly in line, as though mounting guard. Men loitered in the shadows, watching us. It was a silent, sinister, spooky place and I knew that Gary and Shane, like me, were feeling the hairs starting to prickle on the backs of their necks.

But I wanted to see inside a cage and, when a skinny, wild-eyed girl seized my arm and, displaying demonic energy, yanked me off balance and indoors, I didn't resist. 'Wait for me!' I shouted to the others. The girl led me into a dark open courtyard chanting, 'Full open, ten rupee,' like a litany. The courtyard stank of raw sewage. I followed her into a cubicle furnished with two curtained plastic-covered benches, like old hospital examination couches. The girl leapt on to the nearest bench and tore off a pair of loose bloomers tied with a cord. Her pubic hair had been shaved and there was a blotchy rash on her thighs. She began jumping up and down on the bench, yelling, 'Fucking! Fucking! Fucking!' She looked crazy. I told her I had to go. She sprang to the floor and seized my arm again. 'You give five rupee for rent!' I gave her ten and left that place like someone exiting from a burning building.

V

Slumped in the back of a taxi as we rattled through the outer suburbs at 4.45 a.m. I noted a pair of dogs fighting in our headlights. They were some distance ahead and I waited for the driver to slow. He motored steadily on at 40 m.p.h. and struck them with a thud that sent a small shock wave through the car but did not interrupt our progress. The dogs were thrown to either side of the road and lay there, screaming. I shouted at the driver but he just carried on imperturbably down the airport road, head sunk between his shoulders, while the indescribable noise from behind grew fainter and fainter then died away altogether.

A dozen Japanese were waiting for the plane to Udaipur and Jodhpur – where Imperial had flown direct from Karachi. Despite the hour they looked alert and interested and, though the bare, airless terminal was furnished with manual indicator boards that nobody could read and a tannoy which kept making strange gobbling noises, their beaming good humour remained intact. Not so the Indians, who were as baffled as I was and beginning to hold angry exchanges with the officials posted at the gates. Then the Japanese, responding to no discernible stimulus, suddenly stood, picked up their bags and began to move. The Indians jumped up and followed. So did I.

We marched across the dark apron, past a row of red-tailed Indian Airlines A300 Airbuses lined up like a bomber wing for the day's operations. The apron perimeter was strewn with rusting junk – lengths of tubing, abandoned baggage trolleys, old axles. Our little 737 was reached after a brisk five-minute walk, its cabin lights lit, the ground support system humming away comfortably. The tannoy played tabla music and two good-looking, unsmiling girls in saris offered us candies, liquorice-flavoured fennel seeds and tiny sachets of cotton wool for stuffing in our ears.

The 737 taxied out through the pre-dawn shadows towards the threshold of Runway 09. The Airbus fleet was on the move too, and we slotted into a queue trundling in the direction of the Juhu mud

flats from which Mr Tata had once operated. Though the authorities laid bitumen runways at Juhu in 1936 and turned it into
Bombay's official airport, they were still obliged to retreat to Poona
whenever the monsoon flood tides began lapping round the wind
sock. After the war operations were transferred to Santa Cruz, the
present site, which was adjacent to Juhu but drier. Sometimes the
proximity of the two fields caused problems. The skipper of a
BOAC Comet inbound for Santa Cruz mixed them up and landed at
Juhu instead. Several days later, after the plane's interior had been
stripped of all items not essential for flight, he scrambled off the
little strip by the skin of his teeth, scything through the treetops at
the end and climbing away with vines trailing from his wheels. A
JAL DC8, though, was not so lucky. It came heavily to earth at Juhu
and never flew again.

The 737 swung on to 09 and accelerated. Black cloud obliterated
the bases of the hills that had been flattened – by hand – for the
runway's approach. Soaring into a delicate pink sky I noted that
down below the lights were going out. A small township switched
off its street lamps as we passed overhead and instantly rendered
itself invisible, vanishing into the dark landscape as though it had
never existed. But the Mahi River, when we crossed it, reflected
brightly and precisely the strawberry tones of the sky above. The air
was full of small, gentle bumps, as though we were passing through
flocks of high-flying, heavily feathered geese. Somewhere out to the
left was Ahmedabad, where J.R.D. Tata had refuelled from his Shell
bullock cart, while Ratlam and Indore lay in the shadows beyond
the green light on the starboard wingtip. The patchwork fields
turned into barren, shallow hills that, from 23,000 feet, looked like
wrinkled brown paper. We saw a power station or perhaps a big
factory with smoke streaming from its twin chimneys and joining,
several hundred yards downwind, like the confluence of two rivers.

Udaipur was approached over more hills, steep ones thrown up
like defensive earthworks and casting long shadows in the morning
sun. We sank earthwards, whizzing low over a scummy tank with a
set of ornate stone steps leading down to the water, and landing at
the little airport in a flurry of dust. The Japanese, still smiling,
disembarked as soon as the steps had been wheeled up, and I
followed them off to stretch my legs and warm myself in the sun.

The terminal was a small, twin-storeyed building crowned by a control tower with a revolving light on the roof. The terminal wall bore the words 'Udaipur Airport' in English and Hindi, together with its height above sea level: '509 M (1,670 F)'. A faded red flag hung limply from a pole set in a neat garden planted with flowering trees, dwarf palms and bougainvillaea bushes. In the centre of the brown, unwatered lawn a well had been sunk. I was approached by a grey-haired soldier with an ancient .303 rifle slung from his shoulder. A bulging pot belly hung over his belt like a pouch for scattering seed corn.

'What are you doing?' he asked.

'Waiting for the plane.'

He looked puzzled. 'What plane?'

'This plane.'

'If it is for this plane you are waiting you must wait *in* plane, not out of plane.'

I retreated to my seat. Among the joining passengers was a small, dark-haired Swede who took the place next to mine. The doors were closed and the stewardesses distributed their candies and fennel seeds, but the engines remained silent because there was no one in the control tower to give us start-up clearance. Then a yawning man wandered into the tower and dropped heavily into a chair, followed by a companion who stood talking and knotting his turban. The turbofans roared into life as a cyclist wobbled unsteadily on to the apron. The fat soldier halted him with a raised hand and, with the other, waved on the Boeing, like a cop directing traffic. We raced down the short runway, using its entire length to get airborne. A stewardess told us the flight to Jodhpur would take 30 minutes and warned that under no circumstances were we to take photographs from the air. This was a restricted military area and anyone disobeying could expect to have his camera confiscated.

The little 737 tore out across the Rajasthan desert, keeping low and rushing exuberantly along as though the pilot was flying the sector manually and letting his hair down. The green fields of Udaipur had quickly given way to parched perspectives of sand and rock. We passed so close to a solitary hilltop fort that our slipstream must have rattled its roof tiles. My Swedish neighbour said, 'All the military activity around here is because Rajasthan borders with Pakistan. Sometimes it gets very tense. At Jodhpur the Indians keep squadrons of MiGs to go down and support the Camel Corps on their border patrols.' He told me he was based in Delhi and had spent three days in Udaipur buying mica. It was, he said, one of the most beautiful cities in India, an enchanting place of lakes and palaces, and I regretted it had not been a stop on the Imperial route.

A line of sturdy brown hills ran west, their geometric proportions giving them the look of battlements. We sailed smack over the top of a high, solitary hill with a sunlit monastery gleaming on its summit. Dry river beds wound through the landscape like patterns scratched in the earth with a stick and, though there were no visible signs of water, here and there the wilderness suddenly yielded small fields of a lush, dazzling green. My neighbour said they could be pearl millet, maize, pulses, sorghum or mung, an edible Asian bean seed, probably irrigated from artesian sources. On the horizon a long, high strip of purple cloud ran as straight as a chalk line drawn with a ruler. We were crossing the desert called the Marwar, or Region of Death, but suddenly there was a large industrial estate below, set beside a curving creek and, further on, a marshy lake the colour of soapstone. Then we passed a watercourse as broad as the Thames at Westminster but so dry that the wind had blown its bed into a series of neat, concentric patterns. The contrasts went on. The 737 began its descent over a harsh wilderness of red rock which, as the spoilers popped out, abruptly gave way to tree-lined roads and a flowing river flanked by wheat fields.

A dozen MiGs were warmed up and ready to go when we arrived at Jodhpur. The pilots had their tinted visors down and oxygen masks on, and sat impatiently waiting for us to vacate the runway. The apron and terminal were crowded with soldiers, the officers sporting swagger sticks and combed moustaches and exchanging such violent salutes that their upper bodies seemed to go briefly into spasm. I walked through a bedraggled garden to the gate where a small meek-looking man in tattered shorts and a T-shirt saying 'Roar Like a Lion!' took my bag and led me towards a motorized trishaw with a fringed canvas roof. It could only be got going with a running start so, like tobogganists on the Cresta Run, we both pushed and ran and, when the little lawnmower engine finally clattered into life, jumped aboard and set off at 10 m.p.h. along a road so pitted and potholed that we were obliged to throw our weight from side to side to counteract the yawing of the rickshaw as it plunged wildly through the craters. We chugged through a long village. Women were sweeping their courtyards with bunches of twigs, raising fountains of dust which combined with the smoke from the breakfast fires to turn the light a curious milky gold. Mounted on the front of the rickshaw was a silver horn activated by a rubber bulb which, to clear the goats and children from our path, the driver pumped endlessly, taking us through the village like a small cavalry charge. We came to the foot of a hill. At its crest stood a fantastic domed palace fashioned from pink stone. Crouched over the handlebars the driver urged his tiny, ageing conveyance up the steep, winding road until, triumphantly, he arrived at the top and put-putted down a grand driveway towards the palatial folly built by India's most celebrated flying maharajah.

But something was going on here. Beside an elegant canvas pavilion a brass band in white uniforms and crimson cummerbunds were making noises as loud and discordant as Egyptian funeral music, watched by two laughing women wearing Victorian gowns. As we stopped a young Indian with a clipboard hastened up and stared at me intently. 'Galloping Major!' he exclaimed, then turned and shouted, 'Eric, I have found our man!' To me he said, 'Welcome to the Bengal Lancers.'

'Thank you very much,' I said. 'Is this a reunion or a recruiting drive?'

'No, no, we are making a movie, a six-million-dollar production with Michael York, Trevor Howard, Christopher Lee and others. Tonight we shoot the big ballroom scene but we are short of certain people. We need a major. You look like a dancing man to me. Would you like to make a small guest appearance with Christopher and Trevor? It might amuse you.'

Before I could ask for details we were joined by Eric, a morose, overweight Englishman who eyed me coldly. '*Him?*' he said.

'Yes,' said the Indian eagerly. 'I saw him drive up and thought, haha, the very chap we. . . .'

Eric sucked at his teeth. 'Oh dear, oh *dear*,' he said.

'But, Eric. . . .'

'He's not right,' pronounced Eric, turning away. 'And he's too *old*.'

Disliking Eric more for embarrassing his young assistant than itemizing my own limitations, I went inside and registered. 'Place is like absolute madhouse today,' observed the friendly clerk. Other Englishmen, willowy boys with public school accents and tinted highlights in their hair, were rushing around calling to each other, seeking someone named Stephen. As Trevor Howard walked briskly from the breakfast room one of them slowed briefly.

'I say, Trevor, have you seen Stephen?'

'Out front with the band, I think,' said Mr Howard.

'Oh, brill,' the young man said. 'Thanks so much.'

'Morning!' said Mr Howard, heading past us.

'Morning!' I said. I asked the clerk if the Maharajah of Jodhpur was at home and, if so, whether I could see him.

'Maharajah has gone away for two days. But his great-aunt is here somewhere. You are wanting to talk to her?'

'Yes, please,' I said.

Then the breakfast room door swung open and out marched Christopher Lee, looking cheerful and well-rested. The clerk watched him stride away towards the front entrance and murmured, 'That chappie was best damn Dracula in the business.'

'Is the Maharajah a pilot?' I asked.

The clerk looked puzzled. 'A pilot? You mean like his daddy and granddaddy? No, no. I think His Highness is not.'

A porter picked up my bag and led me away beneath a great dome, past a stuffed tiger and along endless corridors to my suite. It was the size of a modest suburban bungalow and an Arctic chill came off the marble floors. On the wall above the empty fireplace hung a large framed and tinted photograph of Umaid Singh, the flying maharajah himself, taken as a young man. His face was long and sensitive but his eyes were narrowed in anger – caused perhaps by the fact that, for the picture, someone had made him put on pink pantaloons, heavy diamond necklaces and a gold lamé robe with bustles.

I made my way to the coffee shop, pausing to look out across the city to the great fort that sits astride a lofty, isolated rock like an eastern version of Edinburgh Castle executed entirely in complementary shades of copper, mustard and rose. Umaid Singh would have regarded it both as an ancestral home and a major flying hazard and, if aircraft warning lights were not available, probably had fires lit on the battlements each night. The coffee shop, set on a pillared terrace overlooking the rear garden, was thronged with film folk talking intently about the duplicity, dishonesty and perverse practices of other film folk. I drank some lemon tea and eavesdropped, mystified by the fact that the speakers never mentioned or acknowledged their presence in India. India, it seemed, was just the set on which they presently happened to be working; and I sensed that the only impressions they would take away with them would be those that survived the cutting room floor and made it into their movie.

Then some Indians came on to the terrace, two pretty women in saris who sat at the next table and ordered lime juices. The face of one seemed familiar. Her companion was talking about friends in the diplomatic service. 'He is our most intelligent ambassador by far. Did you know he had PhD?' she asked but, instead of answering, the other woman reached over and touched my arm. 'Excuse me,' she said. 'Weren't you once in Nauru?'

I suddenly remembered. 'You're the Harbour Master's wife!'

'And you're the journalist who came to write about us.'

It seemed very odd to be sitting in Umaid Singh's sumptuous pink palace recalling a hot little island far away in the Central Pacific. I had visited the place two years earlier and spent a most interesting day with her husband, a charming ex-Captain of the Indian Navy, who was trying to bring in a bulk carrier to load the high quality phosphate that had made Nauru, with a total land area of only 8.2 square miles, the world's smallest and richest republic. The problems he faced were phenomenal. The south equatorial current flows past the island at such speed that fishermen whose boats break down can be swept 1,000 miles to New Guinea. The bulk carriers are shackled to the deepest moorings in the world by a cat's cradle of chains and plates fastened to massive staples in the reef. Held by eight hawsers as they pitch and roll in the mid-Pacific swell, the ships load from two giant cantilevers in 12,000 feet of open, unprotected water. But on the day I called a boisterous westerly was making the bulk carrier wallow like a trawler as it waited 100 yards offshore and, when the sun began to set, the Harbour Master waved it away for the night, drove home to collect his wife and took us off to dinner at the 'Star Twinkles' restaurant.

She said she had left him in Nauru, still trying to get his ships alongside, and come home to be with the children. But there was a constraint and uncertainty about her manner that puzzled me. She seemed to regret her approach and I made desultory conversation with her friend, who told me that Jodhpur produced the best ink in India and also jolly fine bicycles. The Harbour Master's wife, as they got up to go, finally came clean. 'That was a very naughty article you wrote about Nauru. It caused much trouble. I heard the government was going to sue you.'

I'd heard that too, but nothing had come of it and, after the ladies had gone, I sat there among the gossiping film people and remembered Nauru and the way its strange, secretive administration had taken exception to the *Observer* publishing details such as the horrifying rate of diabetes prevalent on the island (estimates went as high as 90 per cent, people's resistance being lowered by universal obesity and heavy drinking; the 7,000 population were said to consume eight million cans of imported Australian beer each year) and the huge losses incurred by the jewel in little Nauru's crown – its all-jet airline.

Air Nauru operated from a runway that ran clear across the island. After rain people lay in puddles to cool off, making them a hazard to incoming pilots. 'Several times I've had people scrambling out from under my wheels as I was touching down,' an Australian complained. 'I've also picked up drunks in my landing lights, standing there waving cans of Foster's at me during finals. One of these days there's going to be an accident, but none of us have much faith in the emergency services. They've got a very fancy airport fire appliance, the best money can buy, but the last time we had an incident it got halfway across the runway then conked out. The firemen had drained the fuel tank to top up their motor bikes.'

I arrived aboard the Boeing 727 'Chief Nabob' in the company of the Nauru President, Hammer DeRoburt, who had boarded at Guam with his secretary and ADC. Reverse thrust was applied between the wooden government buildings and the Onion Main Store. Then the captain took a dusty Nauruan flag from beneath his seat and, following procedures laid down by the President, held it out of the window as he taxied in across the main road, the waiting traffic banked up on either side behind malfunctioning level crossing barriers which were stuck in the upright position. In front of the terminal the Cabinet stood in line, waiting to welcome their leader home. The pilots pulled on their caps, ran down the steps and saluted as he disembarked.

Though many Air Nauru services flew near-empty and the airline, during my visit, was anticipating a deficit of $18.30 million, its officials were talking of adding new wide-bodied Airbuses to their existing fleet of six 727s and 737s. One of the stewardesses hoping to be assigned to the Airbus was a coal-black Solomon Islander who told me she was having sleepless nights because a colleague had put a curse on her for refusing to take over an inconvenient weekend shift.

That afternoon I explored Umaid Singh's palace. Film unit carpenters were erecting plywood walls and sealing off whole sections of the building, but I managed to slip into a shadowy drawing room hung with photographs of the Delhi Chamber of Princes. Those pictured with the Viceroy in 1924 included the Maharajah of Gwalior, the Pant Sachiv of Bhor, the Thakur Sahib of Limbdi, the Rana of Baghat, the Raja of Mudhol, Raja Sir Harry Singh of Kashmir and, looking solemn in a turban and simple white jacket, the young Maharajah of Jodhpur himself. The room had a cavernous marble fireplace and an array of mahogany sideboards inset with scores of miniature mirrors. A blonde girl in a white ballgown entered behind me and was transformed into countless tiny bright images of herself. I turned.

'Sorry,' she said. 'I was looking for someone. This bloody dress keeps tripping me up.'

'Are you in the ballroom scene?' I asked.

'Yes,' she said. 'Are you?'

'They turned me down,' I said. 'Michael York couldn't stand the competition.'

She laughed. 'Perhaps they'll let you hold his musket,' she said, and dashed out again, holding the hem of the gown above her knees.

Later, as I stood at the heart of the palace looking up into the great central dome, a slim, graceful old lady approached and asked if I was the man who had inquired earlier about the Maharajah. She said, 'As you know, he is away on business. But I am his great-aunt. Can I help in any way?'

I told her about my project and said that I was anxious to learn something about Umaid Singh. She smiled. 'The Maharajah would probably have referred you to me anyway. He never knew his grandfather but I remember him very well. Shall we talk here in the rotunda? It is the coolest spot in the building.'

As we walked to some silk-covered chairs she told me that the palace, completed in 1943, had been designed by Lancaster and Lodge, the London architects. 'Lancaster worked with Lutyens on his great Delhi project. A Mr Goldstraw and several Indian architects supervised the actual site work here. The building contains over a million square feet of pink marble. It has 300 rooms – 47 of which are open to paying guests – and is one of the world's largest private residences.'

When we were seated she continued, 'First Umaid Singh built the areodrome, then he built this place on a sandstone ridge overlooking it so that he could always see what was going on. I've always felt the aerodrome was his true home. That's where he seemed happiest and, when he had built his Flying School – now used for Air Force pilot training – he insisted that all his male relatives and friends enrol for courses; suddenly there were so many Jodhpur men whizzing around the sky there was barely room left for the birds. The Flying School became the place where we all met and spent our days. The best lunch in town was served there, and the afternoon teas were legendary. It was very jolly and relaxed and, in the middle of it all was Umaid Singh who, when he wasn't up in the air, chatted and told jokes and quizzed his students about procedures and navigation and weather. Then in the evenings he would sometimes take us off to dinner at the State Hotel, which he had built beside the aerodrome to accommodate the crews and passengers from the KLM and Imperial flights, and of which he was immensely proud. The building is still there – it's become the Air Force officers' mess – and so is his big sandstone hangar. Today they keep combat aircraft in it, but in the 1930s it housed his collection of planes. He owned a dozen, including a big Lockheed, and he flew them all. It was because of him that Jodhpur became an international airport before Delhi.'

The highlight of the week at the State Hotel was Friday, or KLM night. 'That was when the Dutch flights came through, and on KLM night the hotel traditionally served the most wonderful chicken curry. If Umaid Singh was with us we would even get to meet the KLM pilots. Those men were real celebrities. They sat at their own tables, fussed over by the waiters, treated like millionaires. Everyone was in awe of them. The Imperial pilots were much more democratic, dining with their passengers and taking coffee with them afterwards, but the Dutch tended to distance themselves. Smirnoff was probably the most memorable. He was a stocky man with enormous presence and courtly manners, very correct and old-fashioned. Smirnoff never said much, but that just added to his air of mystery. To us he was a legend. So was Geyssendorfer. And Parmentier. My younger brother once travelled back to school at Sherborne after the holidays in Parmentier's Fokker and he told us it was a real feather in his cap. Even the senior boys treated him with respect – he was the kid who had flown with Parmentier. KLM gave each passenger a special case in which to keep his bits and pieces in the plane. They were so well made that many are still in use around Jodhpur today.'

The Dutch, she said, held Umaid Singh in such high esteem that they were prepared to discuss flying matters with him on equal terms. 'He was as great as J.R.D. Tata, you know, but also someone of genuine modesty and simplicity. When he was made an Honorary Air Commodore of the Indian Air Force for services to aviation quite late in life he used to cycle off to his own Flying School early each morning to take lessons with the young Air Force trainees. His qualification was a civilian one and he insisted on winning a Service pilot's licence so that he could wear his wings. It was no hardship, of course – anything to do with aviation delighted him. When the war came he volunteered at once for active service, but he was much too old and, anyway, maharajahs were not permitted to join up. So he did what he could to make life more agreeable for the others. As soon as this palace was finished he threw it open to all servicemen based in India, for rest and recreation. And he gave two famous parties. At each a thousand people sat down to dinner in this very spot, right here beneath the rotunda. There were New Zealanders, Australians, British, American and Indians. My father was here, too. He said the soup was hot at the start of the meal and the coffee hot at the end and everything was perfect in between. WAAFs had flown in from Delhi and there was dancing in the ballroom until breakfast, when everyone was served bacon and eggs. For those who got a bit worse for wear during the night there were relays of trucks to take them home to bed. Guests who stayed the course received an engraved pewter mug when they left in the morning. But, as I said, he was really a very simple man. Apart from flying, what he liked best was to put on a pair of old khaki shorts and go shooting.'

Just one month after the present Maharajah completed his education – Eton and Christ Church, Oxford – the Indian Government summarily abolished the hefty state subsidies traditionally paid to the princely class. 'He was suddenly left with this white elephant and no Privy Purse, and found himself with a real fight on his hands. He had to put on a new roof and replace all the plumbing and wiring – no simple task since it's all buried in marble and sandstone – so he began taking in paying guests and opening the place to the public; a thousand people a day now pay to come in and look around. The poor love simply hasn't the time for flying – nor, perhaps, the inclination. His father, being the son of Umaid Singh, was a pilot. He fought in the 1952 General Election and won after a very hard campaign. As soon as the result was declared he jumped into his plane and came rushing back to Jodhpur to celebrate with us, but, on the way, he buzzed a tonga – it was just high spirits – and crashed into telegraph wires beside the road. He was killed instantly. I still grieve for him. He was only 28, and a man of such energy and promise, very much his father's son, a chip off the old block.'

Around us there was the soft rustle of silks and taffetas as dozens of girls in ballgowns flitted by like moths in the fading light, going from their makeshift fitting room to their makeshift dressing room. The Maharajah's great-aunt clapped her hands and cried, 'How pretty you all look!' Then she was summoned to deal with a complaining customer in the coffee shop and I thought of Umaid Singh driving to the airfield to welcome Sir Samuel Hoare, inbound from Karachi. Sir Samuel wrote, 'We landed upon the aerodrome that the young and progressive Maharajah had recently prepared for visiting machines. As I descended from the machine I was handed a telegram. "I hope that you and Lady Hoare enjoyed your journey – George R.I." I will not stop to describe the interesting evening that we spent with the Maharajah, and our visit to the Fort, where are stored jewels and arms of incalculable interest and value, or our drive through the game preserves, where the Rolls could scarcely avoid running over the great numbers of chikara and pig.'

The Marquess of Londonderry, calling at Jodhpur in June 1934, was also welcomed by Umaid Singh. 'There was a wonderful sunset, and we finally landed in the dark by flares at the Jodhpur aerodrome. The resthouse, which is maintained by the Maharajah of Jodhpur, is palatial. The Maharajah himself, who is a great air enthusiast, entertained me to dinner there.' Everyone was impressed by what Umaid Singh had achieved. Philip S. Rudder, describing his flight from Singapore in the Imperial *Gazette*, remarked, 'Jodhpur from the air looked a very fine city, good buildings and well laid out. The aerodrome itself is very good, most modern and well equipped; the main hangar is an elaborate place built of red stone. Afternoon tea at a large and very comfortable hotel adjoining the aerodrome, and then we left for Karachi.' And the correspondent of the *Tisco Review* reported approvingly, 'About 400 yards from the aerodrome the Maharajah had built a truly palatial State Hotel. The walls are of red sandstone; the architecture satisfying. We are conducted to a large room with dressing and bathrooms adjoining. The carpets and curtains are of beautiful design and taste; the furniture modern and made of fine woods. We sit on the balcony and sip our tea, watching occasional camel riders swing by silently in the gathering dusk. We could not ask for more comfort at the end of our first day's flight.'

But the most effusive account came from an anonymous Australian writing in the *Gazette*. 'Jodhpur impressed me considerably – the Maharajah's Palace and the new palace that will not be completed for years – the attractive city, beautiful green polo grounds, truly magnificent airport and the State Hotel, the most comfortable place yet stayed at during the trip. On the short drive to the Hotel we passed a perfectly kept earth practice ground – smooth as a tennis court and damped by hand to lay the dust – and a string of magnificent ponies waiting for a practice. The State Hotel was built by the Maharajah regardless of expense for the convenience of air travellers and must be run at a considerable loss. The furniture, carpets and curtains are of the very best and chosen with really good taste, the silver, china and linen of the sort one might expect in a well run private home and spotlessly clean, dignified Indian servants. One, seeing me lying down on arrival, asked if he could bring me dinner in bed.'

When the Maharajah Gaekwar of Baroda, aged 73, embarked at Jodhpur in 1937 for his first long-distance flight Umaid Singh, who had perhaps gone for a nocturnal spin in his giant Lockheed, was not on hand to tell the old man about the system of whistles and lights he had devised for Jodhpur's night departures – the procedures described here by one of Baroda's devoted British aides. 'A solitary arc light shone in front of the control buildings, but in the distance twinkled the aerodrome demarcation lights. A whistle sounded as soon as the door had closed behind us and we had barely settled in our seats. A searchlight threw a solitary broad ray along the ground. The engines roared deafeningly as we sped along and gently rose. Through the windows we could faintly see farewell waves for a short minute. A half turn over the aerodrome as we rose, the lights grew faint, then complete darkness below and a few twinkling stars above. We adjusted our chairs and settled to sleep. His Highness' great adventure had begun.'

Now, as the evening drew in, Umaid Singh's astonishing palace was full of bustle. The girls, their gowns finally fitted, faces made-up and ribbons in their hair, flitted through the great shadowy halls towards the ballroom. Mr Trevor Howard, resplendent in piped trousers and crimson mess jacket, was joined by Mr Christopher Lee, wearing white tie and tails, and, with hands clasped behind their backs, they stepped smartly away past the stuffed tigers, the antique teak and ebony furniture, the life-size portraits of portly maharajahs in rubies and plumes. I followed, keeping an eye peeled for anyone wearing a major's crowns. It was my intention to wish him luck, which you must never do to people so deeply superstitious as actors. In the ballroom confusion reigned. People milled about between the portable klieg lights. The young Englishmen were shouting instructions which nobody appeared to be heeding. Mr Howard and Mr Lee, still with their hands clasped behind their backs, stood together, looking morose. Nothing was happening so I retired to my rooms and, as Umaid Singh would have expected, changed for dinner.

It wasn't a Friday but I ordered the chicken curry anyway. It was delicious. After coffee I went outside for a stroll. The sky was cloudless and the moon full, suffusing the night with a radiance so tangible that I felt my passage through the gardens must be leaving the kind of rippling phosphorescent wake you get in tropical seas. The sandstone and marble palace looked as though it was fashioned from coral. On the dome there were red aircraft warning lights. From the airport below came the roar of engines at full throttle and, a moment later, a MiG flitted like a bat across the face of the moon then banked steeply and raced away over the desert towards the Pakistan border. Later, in bed, I lay listening to the lonely whistles of railway engines, the occasional whoop of steam trumpets recognizable among the diesel horns. The Imperial passengers down at the State Hotel, always woken at 3.30 a.m. for their flight to Delhi with tea, toast and fruit, would have heard those sounds too, the homely noise of locos chugging away down the old Jodhpur Railway branch lines to destinations like Merta Road, Balotra, Samdari, Luni, Raniwara, Plialodi, Pipar Road and Marwar. I drifted off to sleep, soothed by the whistles and wondering how they were getting on with the ballroom scene, unaware that only a couple of weeks after I got back to London I would read an item in *Screen International* announcing that after viewing the first week's rushes, the producer of *The Bengal Lancers*, Mahmud Sipra, had abandoned the project because the film was out of focus. Stephen Weeks, the director, claimed that 'only some 3% of the rushes' were affected by a 'slight camera defect', but

Sipra was junking the enterprise anyway and planned instead to take two of his stars, Trevor Howard and Christopher Lee, off to Pakistan to make another North West Frontier story called *The Khyber Rifles*. The news, frankly, didn't surprise me at all. I had known that production was doomed from the start.

I was woken early by the harsh screams of peacocks outside my window. There was a heavy morning mist and, somewhere beyond the palace walls, cattle were lowing. Later, as the mist lifted, a motorized trishaw took me back to the airport, clattering down the hill, through the long village and past the old State Hotel, a handsome, freshly painted building with its original name still in place. Air Force officers were emerging from breakfast and chatting in its tree-filled garden, smoking and wiping their moustaches with the backs of their hands. The small terminal was thronged, the steady roar of conversation reminding me of a publisher's party in full swing. Near the refreshment stall I noted a sign advising that 'Members of the public who have any grievance should contact the Aerodrome Officer' and went to persuade three yawning, inactive Indian Airlines clerks to check me in.

A 737 suddenly pulled up at the door. Someone said it was the Bombay-bound plane so I paid it no heed. Then the Delhi-bound 737 pulled up beside it and, as a woman security officer painstakingly examined every item in my sponge bag, I felt the tension beginning to rise. She peered at a can of shaving foam. 'Lime fragrance,' she observed grimly, as though lime was an exotic illicit substance that could be smoked or sniffed. I arrived in the departure area as the Bombay plane started its engines. The dispatcher reached up and slapped it hard on the nose and, obediently, it taxied away. Moments later we boarded the Delhi plane for the 20-minute hop to Jaipur. An army captain unwisely passing behind our roaring turbofans had his peaked cap blown off. It went bowling away across the apron and the elderly private standing guard over the Boeing was ordered to fetch it. He left his post with reluctance, scowling as he jogged past us. When we turned and lost him to view he had slowed to a walk and the cap was just a spinning dot on the horizon.

The 737 taxied past Umaid Singh's stone hangar, now battleship-grey, and, half hidden in a tangled wood nearby, an extravagantly domed and turreted building like a Black Forest cuckoo clock factory. The MiGs, supported by a squadron of venerable Canberras, were lined up and waiting with their canopies raised. We climbed away past the palace and set off across the desert, the rust-coloured sand below punctuated by the long morning shadows of isolated trees. Periodically a township slipped by, bounded by green fields. A heavy blue haze reached to the horizon, delineated by a long line of bubbling white cumulus. Then the nose went down and we began a turbulent, high-speed descent over a landscape as pretty as Somerset, coming to ground with a thump beside a walled meadow full of tall grass and shady trees, and braking by a field of yellow rape seed. The elegant little terminal was yellow too. A shadowy verandah extended along the first storey, supported by ochre pillars, and a white sign bore the word JAIPUR in blue capitals with some additional information – '09 C ELEV 1263 FT 385 M' – inscribed on the tower wall. It stood in a trim, well-watered garden filled with marigolds, cannas, zinnias and honeysuckle, all so lambent in the gentle light that, sitting in the 737, I could almost smell the scents and hear the lazy droning of the bees as they made their morning rounds.

VI

The 25-minute sector to Delhi took us over a coffee-coloured river towards a looming range of blue hills. The 737 climbed hard to clear them, its shadow growing steadily larger as it raced up the flanks of the hills until, at the moment we met at the top, the shadow's dimensions almost matched our own. We looked down on a succession of steep, sunless valleys, deep as mines, some with whitewashed villages at the bottom, hidden away from the world like stalagmites. The hills descended to a flat plain patch-worked with fields and pastureland. My neighbour, who had been watching me jotting details of the topography in my notebook, suddenly said, 'Sir, I think you are either a spy or one of these writer chaps.'

He was a heavy-set man in a well-cut dark suit. When I admitted to the latter he told me that a very famous English writer chap was staying in Jaipur as a house guest of the Maharanee herself, a man who, though crippled and chairbound, had crossed the Sahara and written a book about it. My informant called him Kwinting Crewe.

'I think you mean Quentin Crewe,' I said.

He nodded. 'Yes, yes, Quentin Crewe. I was speaking with him just two days ago. I am in Jaipur police and I sometimes call on the Maharanee to see all is well. I was describing to Mr Crewe my travels in the South Pacific. He was most interested. I am a real sucker for that part of the world.'

When I said he could count himself lucky that Jaipur's most wanted men absconded to such nice places, he told me proudly that it had been a family trip, made with the kids during the school hols. 'This summer we shall go to Los Angeles Olympics. Via Dublin. Our ambassador there is a dear friend.' Then, astutely reading my mind, he added hastily, 'The money is just a matter of husbanding available resources. Salary and legitimate expenses. Just good housekeeping.'

The seat belt sign flashed on. We were tracking along a river which abruptly darted off to the left. The 737 approached Palam International over a small mudbrick township and touched down on a runway flanked by grass as high as sugar cane. Outside the domestic terminal a big red Ashok Leyland fire engine had been left unattended with its engine running. Inside I walked past a banner saying 'XII International Leprosy Congress Welcomes Delegates' and a door which, though clearly marked NO EXIT, was jammed with a ruck of people heaving to get out. Beyond the door were an access road and a giant billboard reminding backsliders that 'Prompt Payment of Taxes Ensures Smooth Take Off of the Nation's Economic Plans'. I moved on, seeking the Endorsements and Reconfirmations Desk so that I could corroborate my flights for the following day – a matter of crucial importance to anyone plucky enough to throw in their lot with Indian Airlines – and, when I spotted a couple of dozen businessmen rioting at a small counter staffed by a single woman, I knew I had found it.

She was small, plump and middle-aged and she gazed up at the baying men with a helpless, terrible calm, like an adulteress about to be stoned. Something was clearly wrong and I stood on a chair better to ascertain the situation. Then I understood. All the endorsements and reconfirmations were made on a single battered telephone and it wasn't working. To demonstrate this she periodically picked it up, put it to her ear and shook her head. Nothing. But the businessmen, unmoved, continued to press and batter and furiously shake their tickets at her.

I jumped off the chair and went outside. There was an eight-rupee bus service into town provided by the Ex-Servicemen's Airlink Transport Services Ltd but, after half an hour, no bus had come and none of the ex-servicemen lounging around the embarkation point seemed to know when the next was due. A taxi came by so I stopped it and asked to be taken to the Maidens Hotel. As it pulled away a middle-aged man with a beaky nose and wavy, heavily oiled hair jumped in beside the driver. 'Good morning,' he said. 'I am guide. I will show you many interesting thing.'

I told him I didn't want a guide, but he was already talking animatedly to the driver, with whom he seemed to be on excellent terms. At the airport gate a policeman tapped on my window and shouted, 'What is your name?' We drove through a rural landscape, slowing for convoys of military vehicles and a white zebu bull which was plodding along the middle of the highway, swishing its tail. The driver and the guide continued to converse like old friends, the latter turning at one point to address his only remark of the journey to me: 'The Maidens is very poor hotel. Very old, no glamour, bad food.' There seemed little point in telling him it was where the Imperial passengers had stayed and, anyway, he was now recounting some tale that made the driver laugh immoderately. The guide's hair was so intricately waved and scalloped that he might have slept in a jelly mould. We got stuck in a traffic jam at the junction of Original Road and Faiz Road and then, eventually, arrived at a stately old building set in a quiet, tree-lined back street. I paid the driver and got out. The guide got out too.

'My charge is 20 rupee,' he said.

'Your charge for what?'

'Service as guide.'

I was torn briefly by the conundrum that faces all travellers in India, where one's own relative affluence must always be weighed, often painfully, against the pleas of the hungry. Did this bloke deserve pity or a knee in the groin? I concluded the latter and asked, 'What service?'

He grabbed my wrist then released it as the Maidens doorman, a huge Sikh with boulder-sized fists and a back like a banyan tree, emerged and told him to clear off. In Reception two weatherbeaten old women sat clutching embroidered hessian jiffy bags hung with labels saying Thunder Dragon Air. Their eyes, slanted and buried in brown wrinkles like chips of flint, were fixed anxiously on a slim girl of 19 or 20 who stood at the desk filling in registration forms. She wore a long quilted kapok coat of the kind issued to the Chinese Army but her face, pale as alabaster, exuded a nunlike serenity. As I completed my own form I asked her where she was from.

'Bhutan,' she said.

'Up in the Himalayas?'

'Yes.'

'Is Thunder Dragon the airline of Bhutan?'

'Yes. The planes are very small. And when there is a storm in the mountains . . .' She laughed and returned to her task.

The old hotel wore its years with an air of regret, as though now obliged to live mainly on its memories. The public rooms were musty, dim and silent, the bedrooms, built around three sides of a spacious courtyard in the style favoured by colonial architects, echoing and austere. I looked through the Delhi phone book for the Indian Airlines Endorsements and Reconfirmations number. The airline occupied several pages, but all the numbers I tried were either engaged or unobtainable. I finally made contact with a harassed female voice at the main booking office who told me that reconfirmations were not her job and, anyway, they had to be done in person. I said I was doing it in person. She snapped, 'No, no, you must present yourself in person *with ticket*,' and hung up. I cast a final glance over the Indian Airlines numbers, noted that the Chief Air Hostess was a Miss F. Latouche and went to get some lunch.

The little restaurant was empty, and permeated with an aroma of stale food so heavy and pervasive that it seemed to possess a kind of formal historical structure, as though each smell might be isolated and identified like the rings in a tree. The place was supervised by an old man and a boy, who seemed surprised to see me. I asked for a small mutton curry and some beer. The old man brought a bottle of Rosy Pelican wrapped in a starched napkin and filled the glass with extreme care. He said he had worked at the Maidens for many years. Did he remember the airline passengers who stayed here before the war, travelling on the old planes between England and Australia? He did not, but said he knew an older man, an ex-employee who had worked at the Maidens pre-war, and would ask him. Was I coming to the restaurant this evening? He would tell me then what he had learnt.

After lunch, at the suggestion of a helpful lady in Reception, I hurried off to an Indian Airlines office near Connaught Place. The cab drew up in an open-ended concrete cube like an abandoned car wash. Dingy concrete steps led up to a dark landing posted with signs advertising the building's tenants. Indian Airlines was there among the lawyers, loss adjusters, astrologers and accountants, a large, low-ceilinged room with a man sitting at a curious little desk near the entrance. He wore loud checks and a flash tie and, peering through heavy spectacles, cocked a forefinger and beckoned, as though hoping to sell me a lottery ticket. I told him I'd come to confirm some flights.

'You mean reconfirm.'

'Yes,' I said. 'Actually, I was looking for Endorsements and Reconfirmations but the notice outside says this is Reconfirmations and Adjustments. It's the same thing, I suppose?'

'Reconfirmation is reconfirmation but adjustment is not endorsement.' His voice was hectoring, his manner combative. 'So what is it you are wanting? To adjust, endorse or reconfirm?'

'Reconfirm. Some flights for tomorrow.'

'How many flights?'

'Five. And one for the day after. That's six.'

'How can you be taking so many flights?'

I showed him the tickets and, with a sigh, he drew a chitty pad towards him, wrote '6' on the top one and drew a careful circle around it. 'They will never reconfirm six,' he said with absolute certainty, and handed me the chitty which had the number 145 stamped in a corner. 'Counter 24,' he said. The room was lined with counters, most manned by solitary clerks who, with nothing to do, dozed or gazed vacantly into space. Only Counter 24, surrounded by a jostling scrum of men clutching tickets, was trading today. Above it a device showed an illuminated red number. It said 122. When it changed to 123 a magnified gong went 'boing!' and one of the three clerks in attendance shouted, 'One two three!' It was going to be a long wait so I leant against a neighbouring counter and watched the clerk painstakingly mending a bicycle bell with his nailfile. When, eventually, my number was called I pushed through and handed my chitty to a plump lady in an orange sari.

'*Six?*' she exclaimed. Her lipstick was smudged and perspiration beaded her chin. 'Golly, I cannot reconfirm all this.'

'But I'm making five of them tomorrow. Delhi to Kanpur, Kanpur back to Delhi, Delhi to Allahabad, Allahabad to Varanasi then Varanasi to Calcutta. Calcutta to Dhaka is the day after. I *have* to reconfirm them now.'

'I can reconfirm Delhi–Kanpur only,' she said.

'What about Kanpur back to Delhi?'

'Kanpur–Delhi you must reconfirm in Kanpur.'

'But I'm returning on the same plane. It's only there for half an hour.'

'Then you will have to reconfirm double quick. Look, in Kanpur you must confirm for Delhi, in Delhi for Allahabad, in Allahabad for Varanasi, in Varanasi for Calcutta. And so on. Each flight must be reconfirm before each flight.'

I stared at her. 'Can't you just do it all on the computer?'

That got a loud laugh. Everyone joined in, including the customers. '*What computer?*' she said. 'There is no computer. All this reconfirmation business must be done manually by telephone and written chitties.'

Then she picked up my tickets, walked into an inner office and returned five minutes later to tell me that Flight 415 to Kanpur in the morning was full. 'But you are wait-listed. Be at Palam by 0700 and maybe you will get on. Also, your flight Delhi–Allahabad –Varanasi is cancel. It does not go tomorrow. It goes on Monday, but Monday flight is full. You wish to be wait-listed for that?'

I shook my head. She pushed the tickets back at me and pressed a button. The gong went 'boing!' and her male colleague shouted, 'One four six!' A burly Sikh reconfirming for Madras pushed past me and I walked out of the building, wondering what to do next. I had to be in Dhaka in 48 hours to catch the weekly Bangladesh Biman 707 to Bangkok that would put me down – briefly – in Rangoon, where my visa application was still being gravely considered by officials of the Burmese Ministry of Home and Religious Affairs. It was thus essential to get to Calcutta in time for the Dhaka flight but, by the same token, I had to make my way there via Kanpur and Allahabad, both Imperial fuelling halts. The taxi was approaching Connaught Place when a familiar logo suddenly emerged from the jumble of shop signs. British Airways! Well, all my abortive Indian Airlines sectors were written on BA tickets, so I stopped the cab, went in and asked to see the manager. The ante-room outside his office was crowded with pretty girls all dressed up to the nines. They said the company was recruiting stewardesses and they were waiting to be interviewed by criss-cross.

I advised them to go to the police at once, but they laughed and told me it was the manager's name. I should have known that. Didn't I work for BA? Well, yes, I said, I fly Concorde as a matter of fact, but we don't come through here very often. The girls weren't fooled. They began horsing around, claiming to be lion tamers, concert pianists and astronauts until a secretary popped her head in, gave us a funny look and said the manager would see me now. Chris Cross, who turned out to be stocky, energetic and likeable, listened to my tale without surprise. Then he gave me tea and summoned one of his colleagues, O.P. Anand, a quiet orderly man who took notes. When he had gone to talk to contacts at Indian Airlines Mr Cross remarked, 'Getting on flights here is only half the battle. The other half is staying on. If someone important turns up demanding a seat they'll throw you off again. I was on a 737 recently that was on the point of departure when a party of French tourists suddenly appeared and a dozen passengers were told to leave the aircraft. There's no argument. The cabin crew just walk down the aisle, pointing. If a finger points at you, out you get. What you must do in these situations is feign sleep. The old hands can be chatting or reading their papers one minute and the next they're lying there chloroformed. It's not infallible – some of the crew make a point of going for the sleepers – but, on balance, you're more likely to be left alone.'

Mr Anand returned to say that he had managed to bump someone off the Kanpur flight. I was now reconfirmed for that but the onward sectors had indeed been rescheduled so we would need to find some other means of getting me to Calcutta in time to make my Dhaka connection.

'Could I hire a small aircraft from the Delhi Flying Club?'

Mr Cross made a phone call. 'Okay,' he said, hanging up. 'A Twin Beech will cost you £100 an hour, and you'll have to pay for the plane to go there and back, plus a night's accommodation in Calcutta for the pilot. They estimate 12 hours flying in all, so it'll cost you £1,200 plus expenses. And if you're forced down anywhere for repairs you'll be expected to pay for those too.'

I couldn't afford that kind of money. Also, since I was supposed to be travelling by scheduled services, it would have been contrary to the spirit of my journey.

'That leaves the train,' said Mr Cross. 'You can pick up the Rajdhani Express in Kanpur tomorrow afternoon. It gets you into Calcutta early next morning.'

'And it goes via Allahabad,' added Mr Anand. 'The line even passes the airport, so the railway is at least true to your route.'

The idea of falling back on the railways had been forming uneasily since I left the Reconfirmations and Adjustments office and now, dejectedly, I accepted that it was the only way left. I thanked Mr Cross and O. P. Anand for their help, made my way through the ante-room where the girls cried, 'Oh, goodbye, Captain!' and caught a taxi back to the hotel. In Reception I was handed a telex asking me to call my office in London. It took a while to get through and, sitting by the phone, I read Sir Samuel Hoare's account of his arrival in New Delhi. He reported that, after leaving Jodhpur, 'Captain Wolley-Dod could afford to unbend, and show us at his leisure the various tricks and paces of the machine. Sometimes we flew upon three engines, sometimes upon two, sometimes even upon one. As we looked down upon the (Delhi) aerodrome, we gaped in surprise at the crowd that was looking up at us. A public holiday had been declared in our honour.'

They were welcomed by the Viceroy and a cheering public, then carted off to Government House for the banquet that would launch the celebrations. Later Sir Samuel found a little time to reflect on the significance of his journey. 'An ordinary commercial machine with a full load of passengers and luggage had, day after day, carried out its timetable with the precision of a pre-war express train. It was this aspect of our journey more than any other that had impressed itself upon the imagination of India. Ever since I became connected with the Air Ministry in 1923 I had become convinced that the future of British civil aviation lay in the long-distance Empire routes, and not in the short joy-rides between the capitals of Europe.' He added prophetically, 'A service to the Far East could be operated upon a relay system, a British line flying to India, an Indian line continuing the service, and an Australian line forming a junction at Singapore.'

Then it was on with the motley. The day after their arrival the Viceroy and Lady Irwin formally named the Hoares' travelworn Hercules 'The City of Delhi' and, next morning, Sir Samuel flew off to inspect the North West Frontier. At Kohat he stayed in an Air Force mess with a cupboard full of silver cups awarded for 'all the funny flights made by officers of the squadron' and at Peshawar lodged with the Governor who explained peevishly that the reason their conversation kept being interrupted by the roar of low-flying aircraft was because the RAF, when they wished to memorialize him, insisted on dropping their damned chitties in his garden. And at Arawali the Political Officer – who, captured by brigands in Persia, had once spent a year chained night and day to a homicidal Kurdish prisoner – wondered whether Imperial could be persuaded to fly out a consignment of bees, rainbow trout and pheasants' eggs to stock the local streams and coverts and start a bee industry.

Passengers passing through Delhi on Imperial's scheduled services found the place remarkable chiefly for its preponderance of civilian and military brass. The Marquess of Londonderry 'reached New Delhi at 8 o'clock, where I had time to enjoy breakfast with Air Marshal Sir John Steel, Air Officer Commanding, India. Thence we

flew to Cawnpore.' And the correspondent of the Dumbarton *Rock*
landed at 2 p.m. and 'lunched in the clubhouse of the Delhi Flying
Club. We were joined here by Captain Ian Wallace, Civil Lord of
the Admiralty, and his Secretary, Mr Grant Smith, who were given
quite a good send off by His Excellency Lord and Lady Willingdon.
Just as we taxied off from the aerodrome an amusing incident
occurred. We discovered that a Spaniel dog belonging to one of the
staff had crawled into the aeroplane, so, after a bit of manoeuvring,
the pilot brought up, to allow the dog to be given a drop of a few feet
back to earth again.'

Palam had then been just a tract of agricultural land to the west of
the capital. Delhi's aerodrome was Willingdon, named for the
Viceroy who opened it in 1936 close to the Safdarjang Tomb, a
bulbous-domed monument erected to the memory of some Mogul
Grand Vizier. After Independence the Indians renamed the field
Safdarjang Airport and, even though it was soon entirely surrounded by the encroaching city, continued to use it for services
operated by aircraft up to DC3 category. It remains the headquarters of the Delhi Flying Club – and the place where Sanjay Gandhi
was killed early one Monday morning in June 1980 while doing
aerobatics in a tiny crimson Pitts Special biplane. (The Club's chief
instructor, Subash Saxsena, an ex-Indian Airline 737 captain, died
with him. Captain Saxsena had been fired from the airline in 1977
on the express orders of the Prime Minister, Morarji Desai, for
allowing Sanjay to take over the controls of his Boeing during a
scheduled flight with passengers aboard.) Palam, established as a
wartime base, took over international operations when the authorities became concerned at the risk imposed by large aircraft moving
in and out of a heavily built-up area.

That evening in the restaurant I chatted to a young French
anthropologist. He was telling me about Delhi's large, close-
knit transvestite community, most of them dancers, entertainers
and minor criminals who kept their numbers up by regularly
abducting and mutilating male children, when the elderly waiter
approached and said he had spoken to his friend. Though his
friend's memory was fading, he clearly recalled serving drinks one
evening to an Englishman off an Imperial flight. The Englishman
had said 'Look at this,' and taken a ping pong ball out of one ear and

a chiming watch out of the other. 'Then out of his mouth he take flags, flowers and a toy bird.'

'A magician!' I said.

'No,' he said. 'My friend think he was a doctor from Rangoon.'

Palam lay beneath a heavy morning overcast. The apron was clear, but isolated banks of mist rolled around the runways and drifted past the base of a large hangar in the middle distance, turning it into a giant ark becalmed on a ghostly sea. I had arrived at the milling domestic terminal before sunrise to claim my place on the little Kanpur-bound Hawker Siddeley 748 and now, awaiting the flight announcement, sat squeezed between two fat men in Nehru jackets. One, who had a sticker on his briefcase saying 'Praise God!', kept his eyes averted from the magazine being read by the other; it was running an extract from a Germaine Greer book and had the words 'Why Should Sex Be Like Squirting Jam In A Doughnut?' emblazoned across its cover.

Out on the tarmac 20 Dakotas were drawn up in a row, looking as worn and functional as old spoons. After being visited by Indianoil tankers several had now begun loading and I watched as they took on boxes of flowers and perishable foodstuffs, a couple of coffins, crates that might have contained computers or printing machinery, tanks of tropical fish, two sleek Borzois led by a woman in a white sari, and three charter groups consisting of – I judged – a wedding party, travelling musicians and an amateur cricket team bound for some distant fixture with its cheery escort of wives and supporters.

One of the veterans moved off towards the runway, plumes of blue smoke streaming from its exhausts, engines barking like old tractors, and vanished behind a giant Aeroflot Ilyushin Il-76T freighter that had turned up moments earlier. I could see the Russian pilots stretching and talking while, way below in the glass-walled nose, their navigator packed up his charts and ran a comb through his hair. The pilots, whose flight deck appeared to be the size of a farmhouse kitchen, got up and moved about, perhaps throwing birch logs into the stove to keep their samovar bubbling for the duration of the turn-around. The Il-76T, code-named Candid by NATO and designed for long-distance military operations in Siberia (the guns have been removed from those in airline service), holds 25 world records for speed and altitude with big payloads, the best-known being the parachuting record achieved when a team of warmly dressed Soviet jumpers exited from the great rear doors 50,479 feet up.

As the passengers disembarked and walked away beneath the high, drooping wings our flight was called and, moments later, we scrambled up a set of rickety steps into the little cabin of the HS 748. When everyone was seated the two Rolls-Royce Dart turbo-props began whining, the stewardess slammed the door and we drove off across the tarmac like a village bus. The stewardess, who was as beautiful as a movie star, handed out her cotton wool and fennel seeds then hurried forward to the PA to announce, in English and Hindi, that the flight would last 75 minutes; as she explained the function of the overhead air blowers a forest of arms shot up to adjust the nozzles, and the cabin was suddenly filled with a loud, sustained hissing like escaping steam.

The 748 climbed for a quarter of an hour through dense mist then burst clear into a huge, hot sky. My three immediate neighbours were all reading *Idols* by Sunil Gavaskar. The stewardess brought coffee and cake, moving about gracefully even in that restricted space. She had jasmine in her hair and the gold thread in her sari matched the colour of her eyes. 'What kind of cake is this?' I asked.

She grinned. 'Stale cake,' she said, returning to the galley.

I nibbled a few fragments and noted that we were heading down a shadowy canyon formed by sheer cliffs of slate-coloured cumulo-nimbus towering higher than the eye could see. Ahead, drifting loose in the canyon, there were clouds of a vaguely architectural shape and colour – limestone towers, marble domes, sandstone pyramids and arches. The air was calm, but occasionally a wingtip clipped the canyon wall and rolled playfully a few degrees up towards the vertical.

I took the *Gazette* out of my bag and found a piece reprinted from the *Madras Mail*. It was called 'This Flying Business' and set out to allay some of the commonplace doubts and misconceptions associated with aviation in 1934.

'(a) "*I'll be sick.*" Well, it's not impossible; but it's difficult. I *have* seen passengers sick in an air liner, but nothing like the number I've seen sick on the sea. These were people who would have been sick anywhere and they would have been ten times sicker and sick ten times longer on a boat.

(b) *"I've no head for heights; I'll be giddy."* Are you giddy when you look up at the moon? Well, then you won't be giddy when you look down at the earth from an air liner; and for the same reason – there's nothing joining you to either. A cliff or a church tower draws the eyes downward and the stomach upward; empty space doesn't.

(c) *"I'll be deafened by the roar of the engine."* The noise is not much greater than that of a fast-moving train; and as it is steady and unvaried it is much less distracting. In the *Heracles* and *Hannibal* I could talk to the man across the gangway by raising my voice to board-meeting, not public-meeting level. The steward never failed to hear me.

(d) *"It's hot and stuffy."* Much of the flight is done at a level of eight to ten thousand feet – far above Ooty. That is one of the great assets and charms – the cool, dust-free, sweat-free relief.

(e) *"There must be inconveniences.'* Every air liner has at least one complete lavatory which is *always* accessible.

(f) *"You can't see out properly."* You see splendidly. From the huge windows of *Astraea* I could see sixty miles on either side of the Sind desert.

(g) *"You can't carry any baggage."* You can carry any amount in reason, provided you pay for it. I travelled with a man who had £13 excess, and heard of a lady (it would be a lady) who paid £58. A person of normal proportions and weight gets a free allowance of about fifty pounds. Get a big fibre suitcase and put in two changes of raiment and your toilet things and a thin-paper book or two and your writing materials and smokes (you'll need these at halts) and I'll be greatly surprised if the complete outfit scales much more than the free fifty.

(h) *"You get no meals."* The cross-Channel lunch (I have the Menu before me) was Ox Tail Soup, Curried Beef and Rice with Potatoes and Carrots, Stewed Plums and Custard, Cheese and Coffee. And I never tasted a nicer sherry. Later on the collation is mostly cold but on the same lavish lines. And you should see what Athens, Cairo, Jodhpur *and* Sharjah can do in the way of dinners.

(i) "*You get no sleep.*" You spend every night in a bed on the ground except for two that you spend in a first-class wagon-lit. There *are* some early starts. The worst I did was 3.15. That was quite exceptional; but a five o'clock call is no rarity. Well, *il faut souffrir pour être beau*; remember that when you arrive you are not as tired as after a train journey. On one section east of Suez I travelled with five ladies, a little girl of six and two infants in baskets. They all survived.'

When the stewardess came to collect the trays I asked if I could go forward and talk to the pilots. She returned to say they were finishing their breakfast and would be free in ten minutes. As I got to the tiny flight deck they were dusting cake crumbs from their mouths. Captain Dawar was greying, handsome and distinguished, with protruding teeth. His companion, young and anxious-looking, lit a cigarette and gulped down the smoke with a hungry sucking noise. He occupied the left-hand seat but both men wore the four gold rings of command and, when I remarked on this, Captain Dawar said, 'I am 748 check pilot. Today he is being checked.'

'How's it going?' I asked the young man.

'Okay,' he muttered, pulling so hard at the cigarette that it emitted a sudden shower of sparks.

I sensed I had intruded on a domestic scene and, to lighten the atmosphere, asked if they were flying manually. That was a dumb question since they were clearly sitting with their hands off, but my ignorance seemed to cheer and unite them. 'We're on automatic,' said Captain Dawar. 'It does it better.'

The little 748 was still driving on through the canyon, the isolated clouds in our path rushing mesmerically towards us like alien intruders on a giant Space Invaders screen. The Sperry multi-mode autopilot seemed to be playing tip and run with them, making minute adjustments to the control surfaces so that we kept swaying clear and avoiding them by the skin of our teeth.

I remarked that Britain's Royal Flight operated an exclusive executive version of the 748, known as the Andover, which both Prince Charles and his father were licensed to fly. 'But the cabin configuration is probably different from this. The Queen's

Andovers would have sofas and bookshelves and hand-woven carpets, and there would be Constables and Gainsboroughs on the walls.'

'And gole trone,' said the young pilot, unexpectedly.

Captain Dawar gave him a withering look.

'For sitting on,' he gamely added. 'Gole or silver trone would be standard fitting.'

Pointedly changing the subject, Captain Dawar told me that our 748 had been made locally. 'In Kanpur, as a matter of fact. There is a factory there, Hindustan Aeronautics, which has built almost a hundred. Actually, you should be making this flight in a 737 – 737s and 748s alternate to Kanpur, and today is a Boeing day. But none was serviceable. Boeing days for Delhi-Kanpur-Delhi are Tuesdays, Thursdays and Saturdays. All others inclusive are Hawker Siddeley days.'

I had read that Rajiv Gandhi – a distinguished Indian Airlines pilot until he was hijacked into politics to take the place of his dead brother – had flown both 748s and 737s, and this the young man confirmed. 'Also the Airbus,' he said, his voice full of warmth. 'He was very good pilot, so careful, so calm, one of the best. And most modest. In announcements he never use the Gandhi name, just "This is Captain Rajiv".'

Whump! We burst through a large triangular clump of alto-cumulus resembling the summit of Everest and capped by a banner streaming like blown snow. Then, far below, I saw the flash of a river snaking through acres of brown sandbanks.

'Ganga!' exclaimed Captain Dawar.

We looked down at the most sacred waterway on earth and I thought of some of the hundreds of names devout Hindus had given the Ganges through the ages – Daughter of the Lord of Himalaya, Triple-Braided Stimulator, Born from the Lotus-like Foot of Vishnu, The Cow That Gives Much Milk, Mother of the World. When it was obscured by more cloud I made my way back to the cabin. The stewardess was sitting on a jump seat in the galley, frowning over a book no bigger than a matchbox. She smiled at me when I asked her what it was.

'Thought for the Day,' she said. 'There is one for every day of year.'

She showed it to me. Today's Thought read:

> God made the sun
> And God made the tree,
> God made the mountains
> And God made me.
> I thank You, O God
> For the sun and the tree,
> For making the mountains
> And for making me.

We continued tracking along the Ganges, which glittered with an extraordinary intensity. I wondered whether all that human devotion had charged the river with such energy that, from time to time, it boiled up and went critical. On its great alluvial plain they produced rich harvests of wheat, rice and barley. There were mango and mahua groves out there and, somewhere, a solitary, shadowy dhak forest. Then the 748 tilted and began its descent into Kanpur, India's Birmingham, a vast, sprawling conurbation studded with mills and factories all laying down smoke as ferociously as duelling battleships. The largest city in Uttar Pradesh state (with an urban area of 101 square miles it is one of the largest in India as well), it looked as charmless today as it had when Imperial called there. The man from the *Tisco Review* noted that the only features to 'stand out from the air are the Railway Station and Loco sheds and woollen mills', while an anonymous passenger inbound from the Far East was more interested in the icy self-control of the pilot than in anything 'Cawnpore' had to offer.

'Here Captain — got out,' he wrote, 'exchanged papers with the other commander, who is to take us on, quietly bid us goodbye, strolled over to a sister aircraft, and was off on the two-and-a-half days' trip back to Singapore, over scorching plains, sea, mountains and Malayan jungle, before we had time to order and drink our lime squashes in the rest room. Nothing could ruffle him, not even the wealthy district commissioner haggling yesterday with an Indian clerk about a few rupees for excess baggage. And now we are droning on to Delhi – wonderfully cool and comfortable in the air, but one could have fried an egg in the sun at Cawnpore. It is hard to believe that British troops clad in uniforms and kepis designed for England used to march and fight in the same blazing heat – almost as difficult as it would have been for them if told that some day travellers reclining cool and comfortable in lounge chairs would cross India in a day.'

Kanpur was an obscure little farming settlement when the British arrived in 1801 and turned it into a frontier station. They quickly noted its growth potential and 56 years later, as Indian Mutineers butchered the town's British garrison (troops not put to the sword were dropped down a well), the first mills were already operational. Now there are hundreds, served by no less than three railway colonies, and I looked down on a city seamed and veined by railway tracks. The station was the grandest building in town, a great mosque-like edifice roofed with elegant creamy domes and, as the undercarriage rumbled down, I watched a puffing tank engine hauling a freight train towards it along a curving silvery line.

The 748 landed in a wood. Stands of trees flanked the runway and apron and, when we had parked, a man pushed a clanking yellow maintenance stand up to the aircraft's nose, ascended the ladder with a bucket and began slowly washing the windscreen, chatting to the pilots as he worked. The passengers walked past the trees to the little terminal. There were rumours of a bus into town, but these were denied by an official with watering eyes and a racking cough. In the garden a giant kingfisher, brilliantly plum-aged, sat on a notice saying 'Please Do Not Pluck the Flowers'. A plump young taxi driver said he would take me to the station, ushered me into his battered Premier Padmini Pal sedan and tore off down a road crowded with cyclists, trucks and curious little vehicles with flared amphibious noses, the size and shape of a flying boat's floats. 'Slow down!' I shouted but, in his head, this man was chasing fire engines. Tumbledown villages flashed by like images in a speeded-up film and the clamour of angry horns came from all around in full quadrophonic sound. At the station he took his fare, yawned, folded his arms and went to sleep.

It looked even more imposing from ground level, a giant temple of freshly painted ochre brick tricked out with ornamental screens and Moorish windows. At the booking office I asked the clerk for a ticket on the Rajdhani Express to Calcutta.

'AC two-tier or AC chair?'

'I'd like a sleeper, please. What's AC mean?'

'Aircon. Two-tier sleeper on Rajdhani all full, actually, but there is AC chair on Two Down and two-tier non-AC on Mail. Also AC chair on Express.' He cocked an eyebrow and waited, tapping a finger.

I told him I would think about it and come back later. None of the Calcutta trains were due through for several hours so I strolled off down the platform, looking for a timetable to study. Noting a room marked 'Station Superintendent' I went in and asked a solemn, heavy-set man in a shiny blue suit if he could give me any information regarding services to Calcutta. He rose from his imposing desk and, like a courtly family solicitor, indicated that I should sit in the visitor's chair. Then, steepling his fingers, he listened gravely as I explained that I had to get there via Allahabad and would appreciate a bit of sleep on the way. When I had finished he leaned across the desk.

'Will you have tea or coffee?'

I said, bemusedly, that I would like some coffee and an elderly clerk was sent to fetch it. Then another man entered, pulled up a chair, kicked off his sandals and began massaging his feet. The newcomer was chewing pan and the betel nut had stained his lips a vivid crimson but, even as he spat a stream of juice onto the floor, I was struck by his similarity to Clark Gable. He had the same cheeky grin and extravagant good looks and, while he and the Superintendent discussed the day's services to Calcutta, I examined an honour board on the wall. It bore the words 'Station Master, Northern Railway Kanpur' and a list of names – B. V. Borwanker, J. S. Gayatri, S. H. Shepherd (Off Sick) – inscribed in dull gold letters. The elderly clerk returned with a cup of excellent coffee and, as I drank it, Clark Gable suddenly jumped up. 'I get you ticket,' he said.

'That's very good of you. But for which train?'

'Rajdhani Express.'

'Two Down is better,' said the station superintendent.

'Does the Two Down go via Allahabad?' I asked.

The station superintendent shook his head. 'Yes,' he said.

Clark Gable said, 'The Rajdhani is better. It stop also at Allahabad.'

'But Two Down stop longer.'

I told them the ticket office clerk had reported there were no sleepers on the Rajdhani, but my friends smiled and said AC sleepers could always be found if you knew where to look. Clark sauntered out and returned accompanied by the clerk who carried tickets and a wooden pencil box and, after a lengthy conversation with his colleagues, selected a pencil, licked the lead and, in a spidery Victorian hand, wrote out an AC two-tier sleeper ticket to Calcutta Howrah. The train, he announced as he counted my money, was due in at Kanpur at 2.30. Yes, but which train? 'Two Down,' he said. Clark shrugged and the superintendent, allowing himself a faint smile, told me I was welcome to use the first class waiting room upstairs. I started to thank these kind men but they shook their heads and waved their hands self-deprecatingly. Really, it had been nothing.

The waiting room, spotlessly clean, contained bare wooden sleeping benches and a few wooden chairs. A bespectacled old attendant with a woollen tea cosy on his head shuffled towards me holding a battered ledger. 'Fill in book,' he said. In the columns provided I entered my name, destination and time of departure. The final column was headed 'Number'. This I left blank.

'Number! Number!' he said, tapping the page with a horny fingernail.

I said I had no number. He made a brief gobbling sound, snatched back the ledger and retired agitatedly. The waiting room balcony overlooked the station courtyard. Several hundred motor scooters were parked there, together with 20 or 30 cycle trishaws, the drivers all sleeping in the vacant passenger seats with lengths of faded cotton drawn over their faces like shrouds. Beside them a white bull was mounting a scrawny white cow. The bull grunted and salivated over the cow's neck and then, *in extremis*, stumbled against a trishaw, almost upending it. The driver woke, shouted at the bull and instantly fell asleep again. On the far side of the courtyard a row of hoardings carried vivid hand-painted posters for Dinesh Worsted Suitings, S. Kumar's Texturised Suitings, the Hotel Grand Trunk ('Now Kanpur gives you a Grand Welcome') and the Hotel Bliss ('House of Comfort With Modern Amenities'). There was a sudden flash in the sky and a glider appeared, banking steeply above a line of trees not far from the station. It caught a small thermal, scrambled up a few hundred feet then, descending in a series of tight turns, vanished below the tree line. Two women entered the waiting room, wrote their particulars in the book, lay down and within seconds, heads pillowed on their arms, were dead to the world.

VII

The Two Down (if it was the Two Down) pulled in a few minutes early, hauled by a growling diesel with a garland of marigolds hanging from a hook in the driver's cab. People surged about the platform as though word had got around that someone was giving away money, and it took a lot of shoving and heaving to find my AC lower berth. I showed my ticket to four large men sitting on it, indicating that I was entitled to sit there too, but they shook their heads as emphatically as if I had asked for alms so I grabbed a vacant chair in the aisle until an old woman with a seamed yellow face and gold-studded nostrils came along and threw me out. Then, standing spreadeagled against a window while a travelling hockey team clambered past, I heard a deep, melodious voice say, 'My dear fellow, why don't you come and join us?'

A tall, handsome, grey-haired man was peering at me from the next compartment. 'You need the TC,' he advised, 'and he won't be along for ages. There's room over here and we're just going to have some tea.'

Beside him a plump, smiling woman in a green sari was balancing a Thermos between her knees and unwrapping a napkin filled with small pink cakes. She patted the berth. 'See, there is space.'

The man said his name was H. K. Rajaram. He and his wife were bound from Delhi to Calcutta to attend the wedding of her younger sister. 'She is marrying a chap who hires out earth-moving equipment. Only 29 but already running his own firm and making an absolute *fortune*.'

'A bulldozer baron,' said Mrs Rajaram.

'Not like us poor teachers,' her husband sighed, handing round the cakes. 'He will soon be a rupee millionaire many times over. *Everyone* in Calcutta wants their earth moved. His machines are rearranging the whole city. By the time we get there he will even have the Hooghly flowing the wrong way.'

Mrs Rajaram giggled and told her husband to stop being silly. 'He has a feverish imagination,' she explained, stirring a little sugar into my tea. 'Too much reading and not enough exercise.'

The diesel horn blared and the train pulled slowly out of the station, trundling along the edge of a field from which the same glider was being winch-launched. After dropping its towrope it did a series of slow, speculative turns then, perhaps intending to get lift from the train and the heat waves rolling off its baking metal carriages, banked sharply and came swooping towards us. I caught a glimpse of the pilot, a woman with long black hair and a handsome profile, and then we slid between trees and Mrs Rajaram pressed another cake on me. She said she had visited England in the summer of 1977 and seen the Queen in a traffic jam near Broadcasting House, the illustrious occupant of the big black Rolls apparently going unremarked by the other motorists but responding to Mrs Rajaram's frantic waving with a faint smile. Apart from this royal sighting the thing that most impressed her about London was the way the ticket collectors at the Underground stations always said 'Thank you' even at the height of the rush hour.

Our own TC appeared as Mrs Rajaram was packing the Thermos away, a bow-legged man with long, agitated arms, protruding ears and a stained blue beret yanked down to the level of his eyebrows. A pair of broken granny glasses was clamped to his head with elastic, like swimming goggles, and he scuttled towards us followed by an entourage of clerky young men who kept crying 'Ticket ready! Ticket ready!'

The TC perused mine with a disembodied swivelling eye then demanded a 26-rupee surcharge for the AC. The young men examined me sternly. I wondered whether they were trainee TCs or just assorted railway groupies and, before handing over the money, pointed out that I couldn't get to my sleeper because there were four large men sitting on it. He told me they were getting off at Allahabad, the next stop, and the Rajarams said I was welcome to stay with them until I could claim the berth. Then, while Mr Rajaram read a paperback anthology of Len Deighton short stories and his wife dozed, I gazed out at the flat green landscape. From time to time the line slid through small, shadowy woods and copses. In one a man sat fishing by a pond with red birds swimming on it. Beside him a small fire sent a thin column of smoke into the air and all around there were lilylike flowers of such intense colour that their trumpets seemed to contain burning candles. The scene had the intimacy and order of a Mogul painting, and was so beautiful that I envied the fisherman and could almost smell the flowers and woodsmoke. We went past a number of spots like that.

The evening began to draw in. I looked through the *Gazette* and found that in 1937 an anonymous passenger had written, 'At 10 o'clock we landed at Allahabad where we caught up with an Air France air liner that had left Calcutta half an hour ahead of us. The dashing-looking French pilots and their two passengers were breakfasting at the next table. It was certainly impressive to see men drink pints of beer for breakfast in a shade temperature of 110 degrees.'

We ran past the airfield a quarter of an hour later. Mr Rajaram identified the terminal, a small, unlit concrete building partly shielded by trees. It stood silhouetted against an angry orange sky, unlit and devoid of activity or human presence. Allahabad, clearly, was closed and, wondering why the ground between the tracks and the airfield had been bleached white, I suddenly noticed soft white flakes drifting against the window. 'It's *snowing*!' I exclaimed.

Mr Rajaram looked up from his book with a good-natured chuckle. 'Nonsense,' he said.

But Mrs Rajaram confirmed it. 'Look, Hari, it's true!' she cried. 'Snow!'

He hurried to the window to see for himself. Then he laughed and, as we coasted into Allahabad, I took a bottle of whisky from my bag so that we could drink toasts to the snow and each other's health. When the train stopped the four men from my berth rose and got off. I claimed it as a man in a dripping raincoat boarded and claimed the one opposite. 'I am inspecting new tubular trusses at

factory when it is starting,' he said without preamble. 'Now look at
me. I am soaking soaking.'

He mopped himself with a handkerchief then, without ado,
pulled off all his wet clothes, got into an embroidered white shirt
and a loose cotton dhoti and lay back on his berth with a sigh. The
snow gave way to torrential rain which thundered and boomed on
the roof. Two other dripping men entered and began changing too,
so I went next door and chatted to the Rajarams. 'Allahabad is a
tremendously holy place to us,' said Mr Rajaram. 'It is here that the
Jumna meets the Ganges and when there is a mela, or religious
festival, millions come from all over India. The crowd control
measures are pretty rudimentary and often there's trouble. Some
years ago the sadhus were trying to hold a procession but the press
of worshippers was so great that they started laying about them
with sticks and everyone panicked. Two thousand died in the crush
and thousands more were injured.'

I returned to my compartment. My three companions lay on their
berths, smoking and staring abstractedly into space. The cook
wallah's boy, an urchin wearing a tattered Fruits of the Loom
T-shirt, came and took our orders for dinner. There was mutton or
chicken. I asked for chicken and dug into my bag for Sir Alan
Cobham's *Australia and Back*, his account of the epic 1926 flight in
a single-engined De Havilland seaplane which, despite the loss of A.
B. Elliott, his mechanic – shot by a Marsh Arab near Basra – finally
convinced Whitehall that a regular scheduled service between
London and the Antipodes was a realistic proposition. Sir Alan's
arrival in Allahabad caused much local excitement. After splashing
down on the Jumna the plane was surrounded by pleasure craft
packed with sightseers, all jockeying in the racing current to get as
close as possible. 'I shouted at them with all my might to keep clear,
but it was of no avail; all they did was to grin and laugh. At last I
thought of the syringe with which we tested any floats for leakage,
and we proceeded to squirt every boat-load that came within reach.
This was very effective.'

He refuelled at a Burmah Oil Company barge using semi-rotary
pumps, then tied up the aircraft and went to spend the night at an
ancient fort situated by the confluence of the two rivers. 'Having
made sure the machine was safe I had a last look at her from the

balcony and then turned into bed. On the following morning I awoke all fresh to carry on with the job, but found to my dismay that it was pouring with rain.'

Well, the skies had opened above Allahabad again and, as the train finally pulled out of the station with water cascading down the windows, I lay reading about Sir Alan's departure. He got away during a break in the weather but misread the signs, revved up his yammering little Siddeley-Jaguar engine and raced off down wind. The plane refused to unstick – 'We went on, and on, and on' – and nearly hit a bridge before scrambling into the air and heading for Calcutta, dodging storms all the way.

It was almost dark. The urchin brought our food on chipped enamel plates. My chicken leg was as stringy as a rope's end, the rice lumpy and the popadoms glistening with congealed grease, but I hadn't eaten for fourteen hours and wolfed down the lot, neutralizing an odd, troubling aftertaste with a mug of milky tea. My companions showed less appetite, grumbling gently as they held up fragments of bone and sinew for public display, each gloomily laying claim to the most awful meal. When the urchin returned for payment they gave him a piece of their minds but, long accustomed to complaints and abuse, he nonchalantly counted his money and took no notice at all.

'Eight rupees for a meal that is costing four at most,' said the tubular truss inspector. 'The difference go straight into their pockets. Indian Railways! The TCs overcharge also. It is all corruption, corruption. Some TCs are very rich men – two car, foreign holiday in Thailand and suchlike. I know a TC at Howrah who have gold Rolex and big ruby ring. How can he afford such on his wage? Next thing he probably sending his boy to Eton.'

The others sighed. One, who wore copper bracelets around both wrists, said, 'This ring and Rolex probably stolen. Theft is important revenue source for TCs. They use young boys. When the train stops at night the boys are waiting. The TC tells where rich passengers are and they go through train pulling watch, necklace, ring and everything off the sleeping people. Sometimes it is not just robbing. It is murder also. If passenger wakes sometimes they are cutting his throat. This has happen.'

'You must sleep hugging your bag in bunk,' the tubular truss inspector advised me. 'A Westerner travelling alone with money and valuable! That is TC's dream.'

The conversation, fortunately, became more general and I returned to my notebooks, reminding myself that the world's first air mail service had been flown from Allahabad to Naini Junction in February 1911. The six-mile journey, made by Monsieur Henri Piquet in a Humber biplane, took 13 minutes and served to give the Indian government (then controlled by expatriate Britons) such an inflated opinion of its own importance in aviation that when Imperial first got to Karachi in 1929 they were told that all their crucial Indian sectors were to be operated by an entity called the Indian State Air Service. But the ISAS possessed no aeroplanes, pilots, engineers or managers, and a bemused Imperial board, denied a route that the Indians were unable to operate, was obliged to accept the role of sub-contractor and do the job for them. This bizarre arrangement eventually led to Imperial personnel operating Indian Trans-Continental Airways aircraft all the way to Singapore as part of their own Australia-bound service – and sharing the profits with Delhi. The anger in London increased sharply after KLM and France's Air Orient, Imperial's major rivals, were granted free passage across India to their destinations in the Far East. But cynics believed that the Delhi authorities were being realistic rather than devious. When Lord Chetwynd, a senior official at the Air Ministry, asked rhetorically, 'Who'd ever fly with an Indian?' (the question instantly lost him his job), he voiced a widely held populist view. For the passengers the scheme made little difference. Though they had to change planes – and airlines – at Karachi and Singapore, all the legs between were flown by British crews and regarded as part of Imperial's standard eastbound run.

The Depression led to the cancellation of all but one of Delhi's first aircraft orders – four Avro Tens painted in Indian livery – the lone survivor being earmarked for the personal use of the Viceroy, Lord Willingdon. He had been persuaded he needed an official plane by Nevill Vintcent, the young Englishman who teamed up with J.R.D. Tata and whose widow, Mrs Pamela Dennis, remarried and living in Oxfordshire, had told me about the occasion. 'Nevill simply pointed out all the advantages – speed, convenience and the fact that you wouldn't need armed soldiers posted along every few yards of the route, which was what happened whenever the Viceroy went by train. Nevill flew the Avro from the Manchester factory out to Delhi and he took me with him. We knew a crowd would be waiting to welcome us and, before we arrived, he asked me to wear my prettiest dress and cross the tarmac as though I was walking down Bond Street. He wanted to show everyone how easy and relaxed air travel could be. One person who didn't need convincing was Lady Willingdon. The plane so delighted her that she got one for herself and had the interior decorated entirely in purple.'

Vintcent was both a dreamer and a man of action. As a young RAF officer he won a DFC in what his *Times* obituary described as 'unusual circumstances'. After a forced landing in the Iraqi desert he was attacked by waves of Arab horsemen. His gunner couldn't use the fighter's Browning automatic because it had little lateral traverse and, with the grounded aircraft sitting back on its tail skid, was pointing uselessly into the sky. Vintcent lifted the plane's tail on to his shoulder and 'throughout a prolonged engagement' swung the aircraft this way and that, aiming his plane along the lines of advancing Arabs so that the gunner could keep shooting until help arrived.

He decided to take his first civilian job while travelling one day on the London Underground District Line; his mind made up, he jumped off at Turnham Green and headed for North Borneo where an interesting vacancy had been advertised. 'They wanted a seaplane pilot,' Mrs Dennis recalled. 'Nevill had never actually flown one before, but picked it up by crouching behind another pilot's shoulder and seeing how it was done. He must have learned quite quickly because soon afterwards he took the first air mail from Borneo to the Straits Settlements. Then he spent two years barnstorming around India. That was when he met Jeh Tata and told him about his dream of a mail service from Karachi all the way down to Colombo. When the service eventually got there it met stiff local resistance because the Rapides were landing on the first hole of the Colombo golf course. Nevill and Jeh loved sitting down and *planning* things. I even remember them wondering, before the war, whether they should get air hostesses. Nevill was all for it. He

thought it a terribly good idea. And of course when Tatas became
Air India in 1946, four years after his death, they *did* get
them.'

Air India's first stewardesses were recruited in Calcutta and
interviewed at the Great Eastern Hotel, where the Imperial
passengers had stayed and where, tonight, I should have been
staying too. They were trained by Miss Genell Moots of TWA and
dressed in paratroopers' blouses and chic little hats of the sort worn
to Viceregal garden parties. Their names – Peggy Henderson,
Dorothea Wilkins, Ray Salway (later promoted to Chief Air
Hostess), Dorothy Whitaker, Lorna Bainbridge, June Argent, Betty
Walsh, Monica Gilbert, Colleen Robinson and Lorna Halliburn –
indicated that the dead hands of people who asked 'Who'd ever fly
with an Indian?' would take a little time to shake off.

I looked up to see that one of my travelling companions, having
admitted an interest in amateur shadow play, was being urged to
show us what he could do. He protested, saying a performance was
impossible without the right equipment, but the tubular truss
inspector, brushing aside his objections, produced a torch and
doused the lights. The shadow player crouched before the blind,
positioned the torch behind him and ruffled his hair. 'This is marsh,'
he said, indicating that the hair had become reeds. Then he did a
fairly complicated duck-hunting sequence involving a man in a boat
whose downed birds were eaten by a giant fish. When the hunter
tried to shoot the fish it capsized the boat and ate him too.
Encouraged by our applause he showed us a rosebud putting out
petals and then, to round off the entertainment, a pair of mating
elephants that clumsily kept falling over and getting impaled on
each other's tusks. We were still smiling when we wished each other
a good night and climbed into our berths.

My companions slept noisily, especially the shadow play man
who groaned and ground his teeth as though dreaming of unimaginable pain and humiliations. Then, at about 2 o'clock in
the morning and without any preliminary symptoms, my chicken
curry suddenly erupted inside me like a Chinese firework. Doubled
up with cramp I staggered away down the carriage to a cold,
foul-smelling little lavatory with a hole in the floor. A man was
sleeping in there and he complained loudly when I threw him out.

During the next few hours I ejected him so often – there was no lock on the door – that by dawn, when the worst was over, he was gibbering with indignation and weariness.

I lay corpsed on my berth and watched a huge red sun climb swiftly through the early morning mists of Bengal. A magical landscape began to emerge. There were lovely perspectives of ponds, paddy fields and water meadows, and the reflections of the figures walking through the flooded fields made them seem, in my light-headed state, as ethereal as angels. A flight of tiny green parakeets suddenly whirled past the window, tumbling like leaves in the train's slipstream and then abruptly dispersing in all directions, as though shot from a gun. The others woke slowly, coughing, farting and scratching. The tubular truss inspector commiserated – 'Food poisoning is quite usual on Indian Railways; it is just the old Calcutta Quickstep' – and handed me some pan. 'There is opium in it, good for your condition.' The pan, a mixture of betel nut, lime paste, catachu powder and spices wrapped in an edible green leaf, was bitter and astringent. We reclined on our berths, chewing, chatting companionably, perhaps getting very slightly stoned.

Later I popped next door to see the Rajarams. They looked cheery and rested, and said they had slept well. 'We get to Calcutta in less than an hour,' said Mr Rajaram. 'Where are you going when we get there?'

'The Great Eastern,' I said. 'For breakfast and a bath.'

'It is on our way,' he said. 'We can share a taxi.'

Howrah Station (from where, more than a century earlier, India's first train service set out, hauled by the locomotive Fairy Queen) looked like a refugee reception centre. A thousand people slept or sat on the platforms, surrounded by battered cooking pots and small possessions scavenged from rubbish dumps, clearly not going anywhere. The train discharged a thousand more. 'Stay with us!' called Mr Rajaram as we pushed towards the entrance. Five hundred other people queued for taxis in the shadow of the giant Howrah Bridge, a 27,000-ton iron entity arching massively across the Hooghly, built by Tatas in the 1930s. As policemen patrolled the queues, edgily swishing their lathis, I reflected that we must be close to the spot where Cobham landed. His friend, Captain Scott, waiting in midstream on the Burmah Oil Company launch, had shouted, 'Whatever you do, *don't fall in,* for you'll never come up again.' The river, Cobham recorded, was full of eddies, tides and undercurrents which could carry a man submerged for miles. 'We crept about our floats with anxious care, for after all it is no easy matter to hop along the cross-bars and climb about the swaying machine when one's shoes are slippery with oil. As soon as the machine was moored up we went aboard the BOC launch where lunch was prepared beneath a big awning.'

We proceeded slowly across the Howrah Bridge, joining the two million people who use it daily, ran west down Strand Road North then turned up Old Court House Street and halted outside the Great Eastern. I had to argue with the Rajarams to make them accept my share of the fare, and said goodbye with regret. The hotel, looking appropriately seedy, has long been a journalists' watering hole – Kipling stayed here, on expenses, while researching pieces on the Hooghly pilots and the Calcutta Vice Squad for the *Civil and Military Gazette* – and, when the taxi had moved off again, I picked up my bag and went inside.

VIII

I claimed the room that, booked in advance, had been standing empty all night – a forlorn little chamber up on the roof with stained bedspreads, a torn carpet and a tilting wardrobe that wouldn't close. I had promised myself an hour's rest, but the mattress was unyielding and deeply furrowed and I heard the sudden, tinny jangle of wire coathangers as the wardrobe apparently lurched another degree away from the perpendicular. Convinced it was about to topple on to the bed, I got up and took a shower. As I tried to work up a lather with a cake of greyish soap the door opened and a small, wizened man walked in and clicked his tongue sharply at the cast-off clothes strewn across the bed. When he spotted me peering around the curtain he bobbed his head and began folding them up.

'I am room boy,' he said. 'You want I take this to laundry?'
'No thanks,' I said. 'I'm checking out soon.'
'But you just check in.'
'I got held up.'
'Why?'
'They cancelled my plane.'
'Where are you going?'
'Dhaka.'
'Okay.' On his way out he remarked, 'There is soap in your ear.'

I thought of Philip S. Rudder, in transit from Singapore, who 'stayed at the Great Eastern Hotel, which is situated in the heart of the city and is a magnificent place, by far the best hotel on the route. Awakened at 3 a.m., and in trooped a tribe of servants, one bearing a tray laden with breakfast – porridge, fried eggs, coffee, toast. Another prepared my bath, yet another packed my bag and another cleaned my boots. I had my bath and was dressed by an Indian bearer, who would not let me do a thing. It seemed funny to have breakfast and go downstairs and be welcomed by the porter with a bright "Good-night, sir".'

Today breakfast was being served in the Maxim Room, a cavernous, shadowy place reeking of stale beer and cigarette smoke. At one end stood a bandstand containing a drum kit and a white grand piano draped in crêpe paper. The piano stool had a broken leg. One wall was occupied by a huge curving art deco mirror decorated with extravagant gold flourishes and gold lamps shaped like pawpaws. Two elderly waiters emerged from the gloom to take my order. I wasn't hungry, but reckoned a bit of food would set me up for the day and asked for scrambled eggs. Then, as I was trying to decide whether the only other occupants of the Maxim Room were speaking High German or Swiss German, I fainted. When I came to the waiters were holding me up in the chair and anxiously flapping a napkin in my face. The German-speakers looked on with knowing smiles. They thought I was drunk.

I returned to my corrugated bed and, on the verge of sleep, remembered that my flight had not been reconfirmed. Hell's teeth! Minutes later, I reeled into Reception, fumbling for my traveller's cheques, and found a man throwing a tantrum because the switchboard had cut off an important telephone call from his lawyer in Bombay. Everyone gave him their full attention, faces puckered with concentration as though listening to some wild revivalist preacher. Their interest merely served to inflame the complainer even more, and sent his ranting voice soaring off to new heights. The Great Eastern had known anger and conflict before, and not only on the many occasions that Imperial's planes were late. It was here, during the Indian Mutiny, that the British community mustered a volunteer force of armed vigilantes when rumours swept Calcutta that blood-crazed sepoys were coming to murder every European in town. But the rumours turned out to be false (the sepoys had been stopped by a detachment of Highlanders) and people gradually drifted away again. We were witnessing the same sort of anti-climax in the lobby now as the shouting man began running out of steam. His voice faltered and a young clerk gamely asked him to modify his language. 'Sir, there are ladies here. To use words like "all damn day" and "bloody shambles" is very bad, sir. You must stop.'

I paid my bill and asked the doorman to get me a taxi. When he raised his hand four cars roared towards us simultaneously down Old Court House Street, arriving with brakes locked and horns going like trumpets. The driver of the one I chose seemed weighed down by grief. After we had travelled a few yards I understood why. His engine was about to fall out. He tried to reassure me, chanting, 'No problem, no problem', but oily fumes and a noise like a spin drier full of cutlery were issuing from the bonnet and I knew we had a very big problem indeed. Imperial always laid on large, well-maintained limousines for their passengers so Philip Rudder's drive from the Great Eastern to Dum Dum had been 'uneventful but of some interest'; the interesting bit was the way 'many natives sleep in the streets, just casually lying down on the footpath sound asleep with their heads resting on the kerb. Goats and water buffalo stray about the streets and make it most difficult to drive. An amusing thing we saw was an old woman with a sewing machine sitting in the street and sewing by the light of a street lamp at four o'clock in the morning.'

I wondered whether the old woman had noted the sahibs grinning at her from their car and now, seeing for myself a family of seven lying unmoving on the pavement, faces covered with rags, was reminded of the chilling conclusion reached by Geoffrey Moorhouse in his masterly book *Calcutta* – that the dispossessed hordes who must live and die on the streets are an affront to human dignity and one day, driven beyond endurance, may rise up in a holocaust that would horrify the world. The homes, offices, banks, factories and godowns of the second city of the Empire, together with all the great self-glorifying monuments put there by the British – St Paul's Cathedral, the Victoria Memorial, Government House, the High Court (modelled on the Ypres Town Hall) and the massive Writers' Building erected to house the East India Company's army of clerks – would be reduced to a wilderness 'of smoking ruins with a handful of savages who are beginning to destroy one another.'

The narrow, grimy streets gradually widened into a boulevard down which we lurched, now making noises like sporadic gunfire. I didn't think we would make it and neither, I sensed, did the driver. His early agitation had gone. He sat calmly at his wheel, fatalistic as the pilot of a doomed plane that had ceased to respond to the controls. At 25 m.p.h. we chugged through the countryside, past weed-choked ponds in which people were bathing and washing their clothes, the wet saris being spread out to dry like brilliantly coloured markers for parachute drops. It was a fine Sunday morning, crisp and sunny, and gradually, as the distant hangars of Dum Dum grew enticingly closer, I began to feel a guarded optimism. In this area prowling leopards are sometimes seen; a friend in London told me that a baggage handler on his way to work at Dum Dum several years before had been found in a bamboo thicket with his head torn off and his genitals eaten. And somewhere in this vicinity was the site of the small arms factory where, in 1898, Captain Bertie Clay invented the soft lead-nosed bullet designed to spread on impact and inflict a wound the size of a saucer.

The driver and I exchanged broad smiles when we finally rolled to a halt outside the terminal. I felt for him the comradeship that binds climbers who have scaled a difficult peak and, though he added 15 rupees to the agreed fare, and demanded an extra 20 for the bag, I paid up happily, reflecting that he might need a cab home himself. A policeman said the reconfirmation counter was unstaffed but added that Indian Airlines had just opened a desk for Katmandu. I should try that. But even as I joined the crowd milling around the counter I knew these clerks could not help and, when I got to the front and proffered my ticket, a thin, stooped man told me I must talk to the Dhaka chaps. They would be opening for business within the hour and, until they came along, he advised patience.

Back at the edge of the crowd I spoke to a slim, sweet-faced girl with cropped blonde hair who told me she was seeing a friend off to Katmandu. 'Have you paid your airport tax? she asked. 'You must do that before they will let you in.'

The man at the tax desk wanted to know if I had changed my rupees. This also had to be done before checking in and a chitty obtained from the money changer. I paid my 100-rupee airport tax – the price of a bottle of malt whisky – and, armed with chitties from the tax man and money changer, walked back to resume my conversation with the blonde. She told me she was German, a doctor from Hamburg who, each year, flew to Calcutta to spend her annual vacation working at a children's home. The travel expenses came out of her own pocket. A growing number of German doctors now passed their holidays in this way. Indeed, she was at Dum Dum today to say goodbye to a colleague who was going to Katmandu for a few days' rest, and to welcome another, arriving within the hour on a Lufthansa flight from Frankfurt. Her colleague was a middle-aged man wearing denim dungarees. They both looked tired but talked at length about their work at the children's home – the chronic shortage of medicines, official indifference, the terrible state of the kids brought in, the courage of the slum dwellers, the struggle to find food for everyone at the home. Then the girl suddenly cocked her head and said, 'You are not looking so good. Is something the matter?'

I told her I'd had a few problems but was now recovering well. She asked some precise, clinical questions about my symptoms and treatment and, when I mentioned what I was taking, she and her colleague both shook their heads.

'They can be bad for you,' she said. 'There are sometimes side effects. And they give temporary relief only, not a cure.' Fumbling in her shoulder bag she produced some tablets wrapped in silver foil. 'Take one now with a cup of black tea and another one before dinner. Also one before bed.'

'Put much sugar in the tea,' said her colleague. 'For energy. This condition you suffer is very enervating.'

His flight was called and the arrival of the Lufthansa DC10 announced. I shook hands with them then they kissed and went their separate ways. As I swallowed the tablet I noted signs of activity at the next desk. Half a dozen clerks were smoking and talking animatedly behind a counter with the word 'Dhaka' posted above it. I hastened over to speak to them but was told to go away. 'We are not open,' said one. 'You come back later.'

'I'm not checking in,' I said. 'I just want to reconfirm.'

'You reconfirm when you check in. Come back later.'

'But I can't check in if I'm not on the flight.'

His gorge was rising. I knew the signs. He said, 'That is your problem. You should have reconfirm long time ago. This is check-in desk, not reconfirmation desk.'

'The reconfirmation desk is closed.'

His colleagues were now taking an interest. They grouped around their spokesman, eyeing me bleakly. I explained that I had tried two days ago in Delhi and described the circumstances that led me to stand, wretched and unreconfirmed, before them now. They heard why I had to be in Dhaka to catch the next day's onward flight to Rangoon and Bangkok. Then I asked them to tell me if my name was on the passenger manifest for Dhaka. My friend indicated that the manifest had not been delivered. 'You come back later,' he said, dismissing me with a wave.

Other Dhaka-bound passengers were assembling. We stood about in a sea of battered suitcases, bed rolls and string-tied bundles, waiting for the clerks to open their desk. The manifest arrived. I pushed forward to ask if my name was on it and Kumbak Lhater, voice raised, told me to come back later. The assembled travellers were growing restless. Strangers began addressing one another, talking mutinously. Forty minutes before the advertised take-off time the clerks were still smoking and chatting together. The mood on the public side of the counter was turning ugly and then, all at once, in the Indian manner, their patience snapped. People were suddenly swarming around the desk, shouting at the clerks for service, information, boarding passes.

The clerks responded like men trained and conditioned by the bouncers who do customer relations for Aeroflot. They smirked, turned their backs, lit fresh cigarettes and began conversing animatedly, rejecting us in an astonishingly emphatic way. The crowd began to bay and a policeman walked quickly towards the Dhaka desk, perhaps recalling that riots are by no means unknown at Dum Dum. Geoffrey Moorhouse described a good one in 1969 when a couple of local oarsmen who had made an epic journey to the Andaman Islands in the Bay of Bengal flew home to a heroes' welcome. Thousands of cheering well-wishers poured on to the tarmac and surrounded the plane, making it impossible for the stairs to be wheeled into position. Angered by the delay people began throwing shoes at the aircraft and then went rampaging around Dum Dum, smoking in the aviation fuel stores, swinging from the wings of a foreign 707 attempting to take off, and chasing after three Indian Airlines aircraft as they were being taxied hastily towards the sanctuary of the hangars. For several hours the mob took over, so dismaying international operators that several threatened to boycott Calcutta unless measures were taken to improve airport security.

Now the policemen pushed through and spoke sharply to the clerks. An argument ensued but, soon afterwards, they waved us forward and began checking us in. I presented my ticket. 'Are you full today?' I asked Kumbak Lhater. 'Half empty,' he said, handing me my boarding pass. With a silent whistle of relief I hurried through Customs and Immigration and climbed a broken escalator to the security checkpoint. The official there found a pair of nail scissors in my sponge bag. 'This are offensive weapon,' he said. 'I must put in sealed envelope and give to captain. You get back by showing receipt at Katmandu.'

'I'm going to Dhaka,' I said.

He frowned. 'Dhaka flight is not called yet. I am process Katmandu people now, not Dhaka people. You must go out and wait for Dhaka security check announcement.'

'No,' I said.

'I am ordering.'

'No.'

The official shrugged. 'Okay. You must collect scissors from captain at Dhaka.'

'Keep the scissors,' I said.

He suddenly grinned and dropped them back into the sponge

bag. 'Pass,' he said, waving me towards a guillotine frame which emitted a foghorn roar as I went through. The duty officer made me empty my pockets and then body searched me vigorously, like a Turkish masseur. I moved on into the departure lounge and sat down, feeling ill again and badly in need of a brandy. But a notice above the bar said 'Payment can be made in Indian rupees only' and the authorities had already deprived us of those downstairs. I offered the barman dollars and got my brandy with a wink and the offer of a second when I wanted it.

It helped. As I began to take note of my surroundings the German doctor walked across and, with his thumbs hooked into the straps of his dungarees, asked if I was all right. I said I'd live and he hurried off to board the Katmandu plane. The lounge floor was unswept and the ashtrays overflowed with refuse. Only a few of the ceiling fans still turned. At the back of the room stout women dressed like midwives passed in and out of a door marked 'Anti-Hijacking Police International'. Nearby stood a giant glass display case containing groups of model mules with necks like drainpipes. They had the barmy, overblown look of inflatable rubber toys but then I realized they were made from glazed pottery. A neighbouring display case was full of dolls in faded silk costumes positioned around a notice saying 'Chant Hare Krishna and Be Happy!'

Other Dhaka passengers began filtering through to the lounge. Though our flight was already an hour late there had been no announcement or explanation. The only aircraft visible on the tarmac was a blue and white Fokker Friendship waiting to go to Chittagong, across the Bay of Bengal, and I thought of the Greek girl on the TWA 727 to Athens who had come to Dum Dum for a Katmandu flight and finished up in Chittagong and a lively civil war. The afternoon was drawing on. The airport seemed to be hacked out of the forest, its perimeter marked by a dense, unbroken line of greenery. In the forest small fires were burning, the columns of smoke rising in the still air to form a blue pall above the trees. I had first called here in 1969, on a Qantas 707 inaugural from London to Bali, and remembered that, as we left the aircraft, a whiskery old man distributed forms announcing that each transit passenger was entitled to one free drink. A list of the 50 different beers, colas, teas and coffees available concluded with the words

'Passengers must cross out those drinks not required'. I ticked the one of my choice and got a flea in my ear from the old man, who insisted I run a pencil through the 49 I didn't want. That was my first experience of the awesome bureaucratic legacy bequeathed to India by the British.

The Dhaka flight was now running two hours late. Outside the window a crow settled on a radio antenna and pecked at it so savagely that the clatter of its beak could be heard through the glass. I yawned, wondering if it was causing static in the earphones of monitoring pilots. A kind of torpor had settled over the occupants of the departure lounge. Seventeen people, some of them Japanese, filed aboard the blue and white F27. It started up and whined away towards the threshold of O1 Right, the runway on which, probably, the first scheduled Imperial service to penetrate this far east – operated by the Armstrong Whitworth Atalanta *Arethusa* – touched down from Karachi in July 1933. Dum Dum was then a grass aerodrome, though £23,500 had been spent to counteract the effects of monsoonal flooding and give it an all-weather capability. Imperial may have terminated here in 1933 but KLM and the French, characteristically, kept on going, merely staging at Dum Dum en route to the Dutch East Indies and Indo-China respectively. It was a year before Imperial struck out for Singapore, plying from here to Akyab in Burma – a service no longer operating today – bypassing Dhaka entirely.

They called us. An ancient bus stood wheezing on the tarmac but most people ignored it and trailed off towards the 737 which waited a couple of hundred yards away with its ground support system running. The steps of the bus were so high that the men were obliged to haul up their womenfolk as though pulling them on to the deck of a ship. Aboard the 737 a plump stewardess with a heavily powdered face complained about the size of my bag. 'That should be in hold!' she snapped. I told her it was a certified cabin-sized bag and demonstrated that it could fit under the seat. As I was doing so a Dakota trundled by with the Indian flag fluttering from its roof. 'Is Mrs Gandhi in that?' I asked.

She sniffed. 'PM wouldn't go in such old thing,' she said, and went off to make her cabin announcement, telling us that the flight would take 25 minutes and offering no explanation for the two-and-a-half-hour delay. The tangy liquorice smell of chewed fennel seeds was so strong that not even the full blast of the air conditioning could clear it. At the threshold of O1 Right we held while a Piper Cherokee landed blind in dense white smoke from a nearby fire being tended by a woman with a baby on her back. Then the captain pushed his throttles open and we accelerated through the smoke and past two shabbily dressed, bespectacled men from the forest who were strolling along the grassy runway verge with their hands behind their backs, too deep in conversation even to glance up as we went howling by.

The correspondent of the Dumbarton *Rock* took off from Dum Dum at 4.30 on a dark morning in June 1934, 'a motor car having been sent to the far end of the aerodrome to indicate by its headlights the limit of space available' (sometimes the car also had to chase runaway cows), but we had no need of such niceties and went rocketing into the sky like a delayed space shot going for its window. The throttles seemed to be locked in their full-open position and the vibration made the overhead lockers boom like kettledrums. The boy next to me, who sat clutching a plastic bag containing a prayer mat, looked over wide-eyed and shouted something, but communication was impossible. A big bruise-coloured cloud lay ahead and Bhuk Rojahs on the flight deck busted through it, plunging the cabin into darkness and making the wings flutter, as though bent on being the first man in history to take a scheduled commercial service to Bangladesh via the moon. My young neighbour hugged his prayer mat while the cross stewardess sat behind us with her powdered face turned to stone. That Bhuk, she seemed to be thinking, I often wondered about him, the way he carries on during night stops, always talking to himself and sticking peanuts in his ears.

Then, a quarter of an hour after blast-off, he throttled back. The 737 caught its breath and began to cruise. The cabin crew distributed cardboard boxes containing sweet sandwiches and bright yellow custard tarts. My tart had disintegrated, the pastry case smashed by the stresses of the launch. I tried a sandwich, but the filling resembled brown sugar so I put it back and surveyed the northern perimeter of the Sundarbans, a fearful wilderness of mangrove swamps watered by the myriad mouths of the Ganges. It looked peaceful and pretty in the evening light and it was hard to believe that, under the jungle canopy, the great 10-foot-long Sundarbans tigers, among the largest and most ferocious on earth, preyed on monkeys, wild buffalo, hog deer and barking deer; curiously, one of the few species down there that actually frightened the tigers was a crazily aggressive dwarf leopard the size of a cat. The gleam of water was everywhere. My neighbour told me he had been visiting an uncle at an ashram in Varanasi. I asked him whether anyone at the ashram could levitate. He said no, none of them were holy enough for that, but he had heard of an old man in Bhutan who, each morning, rose two or three feet off his bed and then went floating out the door and around the garden, pushed along by his granddaughter. I stared at the boy. Did he really believe that? Yes, he said, he did. True holiness enabled one to transcend the body and render it weightless.

We began descending towards a tranquil landscape of quite remarkable beauty. The fields looked like a jade mosaic in the soft yellow dusk. A man poled a high-prowed wooden boat along a creek that went meandering away through little woods and copses. In the farming hamlets lamps were being lit. Flocks of bright birds spun away below as Bhuk lowered his wheels for a real kangaroo landing, steeplechasing the Boeing along the runway in a succession of giant bounds that must have turned the shock absorbers into coin-sized fragments of scrap. The terminal of Zia International Airport was extravagantly palatial; no sign of Bangladesh's grinding poverty had been allowed to intrude here. Inside gregarious young men in blazers touted for the downtown hotels. One welcomed me as exuberantly as an old friend, so he got my business. We drove off in his minivan, diverting to the Bangladesh Biman office where a smiling girl with a radio telephone reconfirmed my Bangkok flight in two minutes flat.

Later, at the hotel, as I washed down the German doctor's second tablet with a little whisky, I was visited by a man who looked like an Air Chief Marshal. He had commanding features, silver hair and a neat moustache, and wore an elegant grey suit with great distinction.

'Good evening,' he said. 'I just popped in to unpack your bag.'

I stared at him.

'I am your room boy.'

I told him not to worry about the bag. So he turned down the bed and told me, as he folded back the sheet in a precise, military crease, that in this troubled country you were grateful for any work you could get; pride had become a luxury that was now unaffordable. I offered him a whisky which he drank neat, in a single swallow. 'That hit the spot,' he said, and wished me a very good night and left.

4
WHERE THE DAWN COMES UP LIKE THUNDER

From Dhaka to Singapore

I

The room 'boy' who brought me coffee and the *Bangladesh Observer* in the morning was skinny and balding but possessed of a surprisingly resonant, authoritative voice. I discovered this when I asked about the paper's smudged front-page headline announcing the death at the London Clinic of General M.A.G. Osmany. A Biman DC10 had left Heathrow with the body at 1600 hours GMT (2200 BST) the previous afternoon; it was due in Dhaka this morning and the cremation would be held later today. The 'boy' told me that Osmany had been C-in-C of the liberation forces that split Bangladesh away from Pakistan in 1971 and turned it into a sovereign Bengali-speaking state. Afterwards he stood for the presidency of the new nation but was beaten at the polls. Osmany accepted his defeat with characteristic good grace and never again meddled in affairs of state.

'Not like our present leaders. They came along in March 1982, General Ershad and his army, and suspended the Constitution. We are having no human rights. The prisons are full of people being held without trial. In the universities they shoot students and teachers; recently the whole faculty of the Mymensingh Agricultural University handed in their notices on same day. As protest. But resistance goes on, specially in Dhaka, and Ershad has said if it doesn't stop the air force will bomb the campus.' He smiled. 'That is classic Ershad "solution". And he is managing economy so brilliantly we are now second poorest country on earth. Out in the provinces there is starvation. All the people with the brains and ability to save us have been locked up.'

I guessed he had been an academic himself, but before I could ask there was a knock at the door. A man entered, gave my friend a quizzical look then asked if I had any laundry. I said no. The room 'boy' addressed his colleague. 'He is just asking what to buy here.

I told him Dhaka muslin at the Chawk bazaar. And, of course, the famous Bangladeshi pink pearl.'

'I can get you pink pearl,' said the laundry man. 'I give you better price than you are getting in town.'

I said I was checking out in a few hours and they left together. Flight BG 70 was due to depart at 1415 and, on the way back to Zia International, I looked for signs of trouble in the streets. General Osmany had been a great freedom fighter and the circumstances of his homecoming might have provoked some kind of anti-Ershad demo. But there were hardly any citizens on the airport road, just columns of smart, well-fed soldiers who, man for man, looked a stone heavier than the civilians. They had classy uniforms, good boots, guns, free transport and the sullen, edgy watchfulness of an army obliged to fight the resentment within rather than the enemy without.

The check-in staff at Zia were eager and affable. I was through the formalities in the blink of an eye and, climbing the stairs to the departure lounge, contrasted the procedures here with those in India. If Ershad really wanted to break the universities, I reflected, he should appoint Indian Airlines counter clerks to all the Vice-Chancellorships. He wouldn't need bombs or bullets then — the demoralized academics would spend their days in queues having breakdowns and major personality changes. I reached the head of the stairs and passed the shadowy prayer room. A row of shoes was laid neatly by the door and, inside, three prone men murmured in a corner. The restaurant at the end of the departure lounge was clamorous with the chirping of sparrows. When the waiter brought soup and rolls half a dozen alighted expectantly on my table while scores of others swooped and chattered in the high vaulted ceiling. It was like sitting in an aviary and, noting that the premises were sealed tight for the air conditioning, I asked the waiter how they had got in. 'Through Customs, Immigration and Currency Control,' he said. 'Same as you.'

As the sparrows and I tucked into our lunch I saw the DC10 that had brought General Osmany's body from London standing on the far side of the apron, deserted but for a crow sunning itself on the roof. A Bangladesh Biman 707 parked nearby was being fuelled and readied for departure and, watching a mechanic tinkering with the number three engine, I felt my spirits lift. After many days spent heading due east – Dhaka lay on virtually the same latitude as Muscat, and I had crossed and recrossed the Tropic of Cancer several times – I was now about to strike south towards Australia. On the public viewing balcony a young woman and her two small daughters were crying and tapping at the glass that separated them from a man sitting in the departure lounge. He was puffing at a cigarette and, when he saw me watching, smiled and rolled his eyes, embarrassed by his weeping family.

At 2 p.m. the flight was called. Fifty or sixty of us walked across the apron to the 707. It had *City of Tokyo* painted on its nose and, as we filed aboard, I wondered how many other names the old plane had carried down the years. The first Boeing 707 made its maiden flight on 15 July 1954 and close to a thousand more were built before the last model, ordered by the Moroccan Government, rolled off the production line early in 1982. If one placed all the 707s ever made end to end they would reach from Marble Arch to Maidenhead – 28 miles of 707s, a mile for every year of manufacture. A burly, fit-looking Englishman wearing a copper bracelet and a blue T-shirt strapped himself into the seat next to mine and looked around with a nostalgic smile. 'Must be ten years since I flew in one of these,' he remarked. He said he was going to Bangkok to pick up a Thai International 747 to London. A BA flight engineer out on the bi-weekly Tristar, he had received news the previous evening of his father's death; at Speedbird House, the airline's Heathrow headquarters, the procedure for this kind of contingency was already being followed and, as he headed home, a standby engineer would be flying out to join the Tristar for the return sectors. The Boeing's four veteran Pratt & Whitney turbofans started up and he fell silent and listened, head cocked like a piano tuner. What he heard made him frown faintly and tighten his belt.

Moments later they lifted us slowly into the hot, hazy air. The old aeroplane settled comfortably into its climb, taking us up over yellowing chequerboard fields and a treacle-coloured river running sluggishly between ash-grey sandbanks. We tracked along a sugary white beach towards Chittagong and Cox's Bazaar, the Bay of Bengal glittering in the afternoon sun on the right, to the left a long range of serrated cinnamon hills running away to the Arakan Yoma range, the blue spine of western Burma now standing massively ahead, mistily filling the horizon.

Peter, the flight engineer, began to relax. Though he still periodically craned to look back at the portside turbofans the deep unease that often characterizes professional flight deck personnel being flown by strangers was less evident. 'I began my career in one of these,' he explained, 'a boy engineer on Old Spread Legs, the first 707 to cross the Atlantic. When BOAC bought her from Pan Am she was just a flying junkyard, only good for cheapo charters to places like Tel Aviv and Cairo. But that aircraft taught me my trade.'

I glanced at my watch, worried about missing Akyab, the small Burmese trading port on the Arakan Coast to which Imperial had flown from Calcutta. Several months before I had applied to the Burmese Ministry of Home and Religious Affairs for permission to visit both Akyab (also known as Sittwe) and Rangoon. Burma is one of the most difficult countries in the world for a journalist to enter, but I had spent two weeks there a couple of years earlier and made a point of observing all the courtesies, customs and solemn proprieties expected of one. The Foreign Office in London kept assuring me that Rangoon was viewing my new application with sympathy but I realized something was bothering the Burmese and I guessed it was Akyab. Though the *ABC World Airways Guide* advertised daily Burma Airways Corporation F28s from RGN to AKY, each carried the qualifying clause 'Subject to confirmation'; I knew this was a coded warning that the flights were likely to be misplaced, forgotten or cancelled without explanation. The methods of the Burma Airways schedulers indicated a direct link with the old Royal Corps of Astrologers, and I reckoned the authorities were reluctant to admit me to the secrets of timetables written on palm leaf and dictated by the movements of planets. Though I was now resigned to not visiting Akyab (the visa was approved weeks later, when they knew I was safely back in England; that was the well-mannered Burmese way of saying yes when they meant no) I guessed that our flight today must pass close to it, perhaps even affording me a distant glimpse of the place. I asked the purser, a tall, elegant four-striper who looked like a destroyer captain, if I could visit the flight deck and told him why.

He returned a moment later, beckoning urgently. 'Hurry!' he said. I went forward and found the pilots nibbling cashew nuts from a pink glass dish propped behind the throttles. Both wore the four gold stripes of command. Captain Zaman was portly and reserved but Captain Nazrul, small, intense and thin-faced, talked a streak, admiring my suit, offering me a nut, introducing me to Mr Emanuel, the bony, dark-skinned Sri Lankan flight engineer (and another four-striper) who had the deeply pessimistic look of a man obliged to nurse some of the oldest jet engines still smoking along the world's air routes.

'The purser say you want to see Akyab,' remarked Captain Nazrul.

I told him I wanted to see it very much indeed, and outlined my reasons.

'You are just in time,' he said, pointing. 'It is over there, about 17 miles. On tip of point.'

'Which point?' Akyab lay hidden in a lovely perspective of hilly blue islands and archipelagos set in a sea fashioned from crushed mirrors.

Captain Zaman dusted the cashew crumbs from his hands. 'Hang on. We will take you over the top, give you a proper look.' He disengaged the automatic pilot and banked the 707 gently to the left. 'There!'

And then I spotted it, pale roofs huddled beside a bright harbour and spilling on to a small arrowhead of land. The harbour drained into the Bay of Bengal through the broad green estuary of the Kaladan River. Offshore stood the Baronga Islands, the dazzling light making them so ephemeral they might have been giant shadows cast on the sea by clouds, and a set of notorious reefs called the Terribles. Along the back of the little town a creek meandered; Cobham, I recalled, had landed at its mouth. A small, red-funnelled coaster was moored at the wharf. Nothing moved anywhere. Akyab, its brown buildings baking in the sun like biscuits, looked abandoned and I thought of the days when its large British population held dinners, dances and fancy dress parties at the opulent Akyab Club under the patronage of the writer Maurice Collis who, from 1923 to 1925, was the town's Deputy Commissioner. In *Into Hidden Burma* he said he had lived in a large house situated on the tip of the arrowhead which afforded him fine views of both the ocean and the anchorage; from his verandah he had once observed a small aeroplane inbound from Calcutta falling into the harbour. Now, looking down from 21,000 feet, I saw no sign of either the house or the Club, an institution unique in the country because it admitted Burmese as full members. I assumed the buildings had been destroyed in the battles that had raged around Akyab during the war. Both sides wanted it for its harbour and airstrip, a broad black asphalt smudge set between the town and the sea. It looked as empty and lifeless as the rest of Akyab.

The pilots told me the asphalt had only been put down a year ago. Before that it had been surfaced with perforated steel plates, very slippery in the wet, laid by the Japanese in 1943. Neither man had ever seen a plane at Akyab. I asked about a lone tree, a large, bushy casuarina that had once grown at the eastern end of the strip and had often been remarked on by transitting passengers. One, writing in the *Gazette*, dismissed Akyab as 'a drab-looking hot spot where we refuelled, picked up the local commissioner and drank tea under a casuarina tree which, like a sheoak, seems to attract a cool breeze however hot and still it may be around it'. There was a small government rest house with punkahs that stirred the sluggish air but, if it wasn't raining (250 inches fall on Akyab during the monsoon), most travellers preferred to linger outside in the shade of the casuarina.

Captain Nazrul had never seen the tree, or the rest house, and said they had probably been blown down in a storm. The weather around here in May and June was just unimaginable, with turbulence throwing the 707 all over the sky and cu-nim reaching up to 60,000 feet. Or more. He made a graceful heavenwards gesture indicating that the cu-nim above Akyab boiled off, like liquid oxygen, into the very fringes of space itself. 'We try to go around,' he said, 'but sometimes the way is closed. And you cannot go through. There are forces inside cu-nim that would break a plane to pieces, snap snap, like sticks. So you apologize to passengers, make 180-degree turn, give big sigh of relief and get the hell back to Dhaka.'

Akyab was sliding away beneath the wing. Cobham's creek

vanished first, and I thought of all the pioneer aviators who had come to this obscure little place – Amy Johnson during the 1930 solo flight to Australia that made her, for a time, the most admired woman in the world, Bert Hinkler, Francis Chichester and Sir Charles Kingsford Smith, the Australian pioneer who was perhaps the greatest of them all: today the *Southern Cross*, the famous big-wing Fokker in which he made the first trans-Pacific crossing, stands enshrined behind glass at Brisbane's Eagle Farm Airport while Sydney's airport is named for him and the Australian $20 note is engraved with his portrait. In 1935, while heading for Akyab during a new England-to-Australia record attempt, he came down somewhere in the Bay of Bengal. 'Smithy' was never seen again but, months later, a wheel from his plane floated ashore on the western beach here, just below the airstrip he had been making for. I watched the beach, a hot buttery yellow edged by a black tidemark, disappear under the wing then, all at once, saw signs of activity in Akyab. A launch had put off from the red-funnelled coaster and was heading across the harbour but abruptly it swung about then stopped dead in the bright green water, its wake describing a perfect question mark. That seemed an appropriate farewell from a place that was always likely to remain an enigma to me and, when Captain Zaman asked if I had seen enough, I nodded and thanked him for his trouble. As he eased the Boeing back on course a grinning young steward brought a tray containing two glasses of clear soup, dishes of chopped chives and onions and a green plastic spoon. The pilots stirred the chives and onion into their soup and sipped it, smacking their lips.

'You will have a glass?' asked Captain Nazrul. 'This fellow can make more. He is very good at soup.'

I said no, adding that I thought pilots were never supposed to take the same food.

'This is absolutely true,' said Captain Zaman. 'But we both are happening to *like* this fellow's soup.'

'Soup is quite safe, boil boil, germs all kill,' vouched the steward, lighting up a cigarette. To me he explained, 'Flight deck is only damn place we are being allowed to have smoke.'

Mr Emanuel, the flight engineer, didn't want soup either. 'Then I can fly plane when these two fall down dead,' he said. He asked me to guess where he lived. I tried Dhaka, Colombo, Grand Bahama, Acapulco, Monte Carlo and Port Said. Everyone laughed.

'Redhill, Surrey!' said Mr Emanuel. 'That is my home, and I can go there only once a month, deadheading to Heathrow on the Biman DC10. I have few days with wife and kids then it's deadheading back to Dhaka and slavery on the old 707s.' He sighed. 'When last 707 is phased out I will be forced to take job on Concorde. I will have to go slumming.'

On the way to my seat I asked the destroyer captain if I could disembark at Rangoon. He said the airport authorities always made transit passengers remain in the aircraft. I told him I was very anxious to set foot on Burmese soil and he, clearly assuming I was up to something, winked and promised to speak to the station manager.

The cabin crew were handing out free drinks. As Peter sipped a Heineken and talked about a previous visit to Dhaka when his hotel had charged him £148 for a bottle of modest burgundy (the matter was now in the hands of BA's legal department), the 707 rode on through calm air, heading down the coast towards Kyaukpyu, another small port, before swinging inland and passing between Sandoway and Prome on the way into Rangoon. I looked down on winding bays flanked by convoys of attendant islands. The sea was like polished blue lacquer. It was around here that Cobham had 'hit the Burma rains' and been shaken by their ferocity. 'There were moments when the rain was so dense that my visibility was reduced to about a hundred and fifty yards. Under these conditions it meant flying as slowly as possible at a very low altitude along the beach, where the coast-line was rocky and inundated with bays and inlets. The twistings and turnings required in order to maintain any sort of view ahead made it a most difficult and alarming task. I have memories of plunging into dark banks of rain which became blue-black as we flew deeper into the storm.' Only five miles from Monkey Point, the Rangoon seaplane base, he 'encountered a rain storm of such intensity that it was literally impossible to weather it' so he took refuge on a quiet creek, hailed a passing paddle steamer and asked the captain for directions. But the captain spoke no

English and, when Cobham clambered aboard and showed him his map, gazed at it uncomprehendingly, never having seen one before. Cobham got to Rangoon late in the afternoon, touching down in failing light under threatening skies.

The coast behind us, we cruised on down the Arakan Yomas, a range of tall, steep mountains so densely forested that their slopes seemed cloaked in moss. Somewhere down here two young Englishmen, Eric Hook and his mechanic, Jim Matthews, crashed their Gypsy Moth in 1930 during an attempt on Bert Hinkler's England to Australia record. Hook, from West Wickham in Kent, set off from Lympne aerodrome less than three months after taking his first flying lesson. He had said he wanted no distractions during take-off so his young wife watched from behind a hedge. On 3 July they left Akyab ahead of Hinkler's schedule and, climbing over the 10,000-feet Arakan Yomas, suffered a burst fuel pipe and came down in the jungle some minutes later.

According to *Croydon Airport: The Great Days 1928–1939*, an engaging book published by Sutton Libraries and Arts Services, the crash became a major news story. When Jim Matthews, ten days later, emerged from the trees at the little Irrawaddy port of Prome, the London *Daily News* reported that he was 'haggard, hungry, staggering with weakness and running a high temperature'. Matthews told the authorities that though Hook had sustained serious injuries he had been able to walk. But after several days' march he grew so weak that Matthews was forced to carry him. When their food and water were finished Hook, in a gesture that the *Daily News* likened to Captain Oates at the South Pole, insisted that Matthews carry on alone and save himself. The *Daily Mail* organized an expedition to find Hook and eventually came upon his skeleton, identifiable only by the hair, on the bank of a mountain stream. The *Daily Herald* flew Matthews home and had Mrs Hook waiting for him at Croydon. 'The widow,' reported the *Herald*, 'tears wet upon her cheeks, embraced the man who had tried so desperately to save her husband, who for three days had carried him through the jungle. "Jack, old boy," she said, gripping his shoulders, "you were simply splendid. You risked your own safety for him. I don't know how to thank you." They sat down, holding each other's hands for comfort. She was sobbing and could scarcely speak.' Matthews then passed on Hook's last message: 'If you get through, give my love to all at home.' Later the *News Chronicle* reported that Mrs Hook, determined to fulfil her husband's dream, was taking flying lessons, but she never made the journey. Instead, she married a widowed St Albans dentist named Hopper, whose first wife had died on the very day that Eric Hook's Gypsy Moth crashed in the Arakan Yoma mountains.

We had put the mountains behind us. The Boeing was crossing a dusty plain scattered with villages, each built around a pagoda gilded and studded with tiny mirrors; in the late afternoon sun they signalled us like lighthouses. Then abruptly the 707's nose went down and we began a clamorous, shuddering descent.

The two hydraulically operated aluminium alloy speed brakes had popped up, causing us to drop like an elevator encountering turbulence in its shaft. Moments later they were retracted again and we continued whistling smoothly down towards Mingaladon Airport.

In the fields below farmers were loading stooks of rice on to buffalo carts. The villages on the Rangoon approach looked prosperous, their pagodas endowed with city money and dressed up like funfairs. The landing gear went down. Mr Emanuel's elderly turbofans roared sweetly as we cruised up the Rangoon River, passing Monkey Point and the Twante Canal along which, one wet and blustery night two years earlier, I had sailed in a twin-decked river steamer at the end of a week-long journey down the Irrawaddy from Mandalay. Then, with the fillet flaps and the big Fowler flaps fully extended for landing, we swung on to finals. The anonymous Imperial passenger who had cooled off under the casuarina tree at Akyab wrote of this moment, 'Now we are flying up the river of Rangoon – the water is chocolate, oil tanks everywhere. Mr — has just pointed out the golden pagoda, the Shwe Dagon. It is amazing – in fact this is the most attractive city we have seen so far.' Philip S. Rudder was impressed too. 'When we were as much as 20 miles from the city we could even then clearly see the famous Buddhist Pagoda with its huge tower entirely covered with gold leaf. Rangoon looked very beautiful from the air, well laid out, and with avenues of the beautiful red "Fleur in the Forest" trees.' After breakfast and a passport check at Mingaladon they were joined by a passenger for London who, following the usual procedure, was weighed before boarding to ensure that, with his baggage, he did not exceed the 221-pound free allowance.

Captain Zaman's landing was as gentle as a brushstroke. As he parked 100 metres from the terminal the old Burma hands left their seats and tensed for the off. Mingaladon's entrance formalities are the slowest and most complicated on earth. Visitors must complete not just visa, immigration, customs and currency forms, but also supplementary forms for valuables like American Express cards, cameras, pocket calculators, rings, jewellery, even wristwatches. Everything has to be declared and produced for inspection, each form is painstakingly checked and initialled by officials working at the bucolic pace of tally clerks at some pastoral co-op. The first passengers into the hot little arrivals shed would get processed within the hour, those at the back could expect to reach their hotels after nightfall.

The Biman station manager coming up the steps was nearly flattened by the old hands going down. The purser entered a plea on my behalf and the station manager, a plump, harassed-looking Burmese, said, 'Okay, you come with me.' The old hands, bunched like 800-metre runners on the first bend, were bursting through the Customs and Immigration door while two of their number, overcome by the free inflight hospitality, tried to effect entry to the Control Tower. It was a small, graceful structure built by British PWD engineers in the pre-war days when Rangoon had been the most elegant city in the East. The Tower, embellished with art deco flourishes, had a bright green trellis pattern painted up its white sides. The drunks were seen off by a portly air traffic controller in a blue *longyi* who had popped out for a smoke. Waving a giant green cigar he drove them back like stray cattle so they headed instead for the VIP entrance where a banner reading 'Welcome to the Prime Minister of the Heroic People's Republic of Czechoslovakia' was strung beneath an ornate gold and crimson ceremonial canopy. The station manager sighed and we trudged on past a couple of parked Burma Airways Corporation Fokker 28 twin-jets with grubby, dirt-smeared paintwork and birdlime on the wings.

In the departure lounge there were the same faded posters I had noted on my last visit, and the same glass tanks containing Chinese carp. Two of the fish were dead, floating belly-up in the scummy green water. The room was hot, airless and dim. Nothing had changed. Our joining passengers sat lethargically on hard wooden seats or browsed around stalls selling jade bangles, fake opium weights, silk hats called gaung baungs, wooden carvings, Bassein parasols, embroidered Burmese slippers, silverware, lucky black and gold lacquerware owls. I bought a cherrywood chess set for my son, each piece handmade and delicately painted with the intricate costumes of the Shan tribes. It cost $6.50. I asked the pretty girl behind the counter to make me a special price and she grinned at the language of the market. 'No special price here, mister. This official government shop.'

I looked at the duty-free counter which, due to Burma's chronic foreign currency shortage, was entirely stocked with items purchased from incoming travellers. Youngsters arriving on flights from Dhaka, Bangkok or Katmandu sold their duty-frees for fistfuls of kyats, earning themselves enough for several days' subsistence living, while departing passengers wanting duty-free items had to buy them with foreign money, preferably dollars. It was a classic Burmese arrangement, carried out with courtesy and tact and leaving all parties content.

The Burma Airways flying personnel rostered to work the handful of overseas destinations served by the company did not contribute to the Mingaladon duty-free counter because they got better prices in town. A job with the airline was a passport to riches. Crew members brought in many of the goods unobtainable in Burma, everything from colour film to Western medicines. The country was so starved of the latter that hospital patients facing surgery often had to provide their own anaesthetics. If the burgeoning black market (served by smugglers who trekked up and down snake-infested trails from Thailand) couldn't supply your needs then you approached a pilot or steward. Sometimes they got greedy, the delicate balance was disturbed and there were dismissals. One casualty was the son of Ne Win, the supreme ruler of

Burma. A senior flight captain, he made such huge personal profits that even his old man was scandalized. Now he ran a restaurant in downtown Rangoon.

I had a drink of freshly pressed limes then walked back to the plane with the station manager. I asked if he had heard of Balthazar & Sons, once the Imperial agents in Rangoon, or the Minto Mansions, where overnighting passengers had stayed, but he said the names meant nothing to him. One of the Burma Airways F-28s was being prepared for departure. An antiquated Bedford van drew up beside it and a man slowly carried a hand of green bananas up the Fokker's steps. I recalled that the last time I travelled in one of these aircraft the beefy steward distributing the bananas had scolded me when I waved mine away. But what I had really wanted was a large drink. The armrest had fallen off my seat during take-off, posing questions about maintenance procedures and structural integrity, and reminding me vividly of an incident at the British Embassy the previous day. Visiting a Burmese clerk there I had noted on his desk a pair of bottles filled with a grey, powdery substance. When I idly asked what they were he giggled nervously and said the bottles contained the ashes of a couple of tourists, a husband and wife from Manchester. They had been killed in a Burma Airways crash a few days earlier and their remains were waiting to be flown back to England in the diplomatic bag.

II

We took off from Runway O3, banking steeply during the climb. There were no noise abatement procedures at Rangoon. The engines thundered away at full throttle and laid curving plumes of black smoke across the copses and parklands of this sleepy green city. The astonishing golden finger of the Shwe Dagon was as lambent as flame in the late afternoon light. Started in the Buddha's lifetime and containing, in its vaults, eight hairs plucked from his head, it soared 326 feet above the trees and was clad with 8,688 foot-square plates of solid bullion. Much of the country's gold reserves were stuck up there, topped by a jewel-studded weather vane containing 6,835 precious stones, 5,452 of them diamonds. Before leaving for Mandalay to begin my river trip down the Irrawaddy I had visited the Shwe Dagon with the British embassy clerk who was going to act as interpreter and who, to ensure a safe journey, wished us to gain merit. We bought booklets of finely beaten gold leaf at a stall and clambered up high, rickety ladders propped against the flanks of the temples. Then, following the clerk's example, I tore the leaves from the booklet, licked them and stuck them on the masonry. All around there were random patches of gold leaf put there by other pilgrims, but I could see that this was going to be a short-term arrangement. The clerk had warned that when the monsoon rains arrived our flimsy offerings would be quickly washed away. Then, for a day or two, the water gurgling through the Shwe Dagon's storm drains carried a glittering sediment which, down the years, had probably gilded even the drains themselves.

The Boeing continued its climb over the Rangoon River and the ramshackle outskirts of the city. It levelled off in a purple haze and cruised over a pale, dusty plain then out across the Gulf of Martaban. Peter went forward for a nostalgic chat about Pratt & Whitney JT3D-7 turbofans with Mr Emanuel while I peered down through the gloaming seeking the coastal town of Moulmein where, in 1934, the Irrawaddy Flotilla and Airways Company launched a weekly service from Monkey Point. Two days later, using the same Fox Moth seaplane, they inaugurated their weekly service to Mandalay, calling at Prome and Yenangyaung, a small river port set in the lee of shadowy, biscuit-coloured cliffs. It was at Yenangyaung, centuries earlier, that the Burmese discovered large oil reserves. The wells, operated by hand, were traditionally owned by the same 24 families, who sold their crude up and down the river for preserving wood and lighting lamps. Among the passengers regularly flying to Yenangyaung in the Fox Moth were representatives of the great European gunsmiths who always used – and still use – Burmese oil for polishing the stocks of their best handbuilt sporting weapons. (The Irrawaddy Flotilla management later found themselves embroiled in a major religious controversy when monks chartered the Fox Moth to fly the embalmed body of a pongyi, or priest, seven times around the Shwe Dagon. Ritual decreed that a corpse must be kept in motion before cremation, and the modernists argued that employing the most progressive means of doing it showed respect for the dead; the traditionalists, though, regarded the innovation as blasphemous.)

Aboard the 707 more free liquor was being served. A buxom stewardess in a green sari brought me a Heineken and said, 'You must write your good name, please. Is airline regulations.'

'I don't mind paying,' I said.

'No need. Name *and* address of good self, please.'

I shrugged and scribbled the details on a page torn from my notebook, wondering whether Bangladesh Biman was preparing a file of problem drinkers. She thanked me gravely and moved away down the aisle but, instead of placing it with the ship's papers, popped it into her handbag and gave me a sudden, dazzling smile. Later I talked to an urbane Singaporean Chinese who had joined us at Mingaladon. He was a gem dealer returning from the annual Burmese sales. 'There are dealers from 20 or 30 countries in Rangoon at the moment and you can't get a hotel bed for love or money,' he said. 'I go every year, mainly to buy rubies. The government mines at Mogok and Sagyin produce the most wonderful pigeon blood stones, quite unique, the finest in the world. I also buy in Thailand and sometimes Sri Lanka, though the Sri Lankan gem gravels are pretty well worked out. But I like coming to Burma best. It always surprises me.' He lit a cigarette. 'The man who drove me to the airport today was telling me about an eighteenth-century king who owned a baby white elephant. For the Burmese a white elephant was a mystical, almost sacred thing. It gave the king incredible status and, to keep his baby safe and happy, he kept it in a silk pavilion. Musicians played to it all day long and it was suckled by women with their breasts full of milk.'

Night fell as we began our descent into Bangkok. I looked down on the scattered lights of Thailand then glanced through the *Gazette* to see what Philip S. Rudder had made of Bangkok in 1934. He travelled in the Armstrong Whitworth *Athena* under the command of Captain Mollard whose decision to fly at 7,000 feet caused Mr Rudder to appreciate 'the heavy rugs provided for us. At 4 o'clock we were in sight of Siam, first flying over great salt fields, where the tide is allowed to flow in and the water to evaporate, leaving salt deposits, and then Bangkok – a fine city, but apparently very few roads, only canals. The aerodrome at Bangkok is very large and has numerous hangars – the Siamese officials are very proud of their Air Force, and are only too pleased to show some of their 'planes. We were taken up to the city in a Diesel train. Bangkok station is a fine building, and reminds one of the Gare du Nord, Paris. We stayed at the Oriental Hotel that night; it is an excellent place, and very well run. The next morning, at four o'clock, saw us back on the train to the aerodrome.' And the anonymous Australian aboard the *Arethusa* wrote, 'We are about to land at Bangkok, the capital of Siam, ruled by a regency council since the King abdicated some time ago. Anyway, he now has a lovely country house in England. The palace and temples of Bangkok look rather fine from the air as we pass over.'

The engines surged restlessly as we slid on to finals. Peering ahead I could make out, through thin, hazy cloud, the high-intensity approach beacons of Don Muang Airport. The pilot made constant small adjustments to the heading and brought us down with scarcely a tremor. As we motored to the terminal past brilliant blue and white runway edge lights Peter emerged from the flight deck looking bemused. 'The bloke in the left-hand seat was being checked,' he said. 'The other one held a seat cushion over the window and made him do the entire approach on instruments. He only pulled it away when we reached decision height. With *passengers* aboard. Remarkable.'

We disembarked. He hurried off to catch his London-bound 747 while I went through the entry formalities, purchased some *baht* at the Thai Military Bank and caught a taxi to the Hilton where, thanks to the influence of a friend at the corporation's international press office in Paris, a heavily discounted room awaited me. The hotel was brand new and sumptuous as a palace. The pretty PR girl who took me up in the lift said it stood on the site of the old White Bus Company depot and had cost $40 million US. On the ground floor they had the only fertility shrine in Bangkok. 'It was there from long time back, so we keep it and women still come to pray for babies.' My room was banked with fresh orchids, and there were bowls of gaudy tropical fruit and classy French chocolates.

Lolling on a silken sofa I ate some kumquats and looked at the *Gazette* to see how the Imperial passengers had spent their nights in Bangkok. The anonymous Aussie who visited in 1937 went on the town after dinner when 'unfortunately it was too late to go and see Laurel and Hardy at the pictures'. Laurel and Hardy! In *Bangkok*! Instead he headed for 'a cabaret where the turns were on Geisha lines but not very amusing on account of not being able to understand the words, but even the locals did not seem very amused. Afterwards we went to a roof garden dancing place or nightclub. Some of the Siamese had bright faces and very graceful figures while all seemed to dance very well – we enjoyed it so much that I am ashamed to say we only got to bed two hours before being called. However, it is so restful in the aeroplane all day that it is exercise we lack rather than sleep.'

I reckoned I knew enough about the expectations of Imperial's unaccompanied adult males to guess where, had the Patpong red-light area been operating in the 1930s, most of them would have finished up. Recalling the company bus that had called at various Alexandrian knocking shops on its way to the airport, I caught a taxi downtown and, 20 minutes after leaving the hotel, found myself drinking beer at a wooden table in a shadowy basement room. A plump, motherly-looking woman with a big smile crouched naked on a small stage firing ping pong balls from her vagina. She had at least half a dozen tucked away in there, and dispatched them one by one with such tremendous velocity that they whistled over our heads like grapeshot, crashed against the opposite wall and went bouncing wildly around the room, causing everyone to duck. I was sharing the table with a skinny, bespectacled, preoccupied Englishman named Walter who told me he was from Basildon, Essex, and had flown in that morning on a special package.

'What do you mean, special?' I asked.

'You know. For, uh, bachelors. A fortnight in Bangkok and Pattaya Beach. I saw an ad in a magazine at the barber's. Fuckin' *'ell*!' he exclaimed as a ping pong ball whizzed past his ear. 'You ever seen a 'uman bean do that before?'

The markswoman, her ammo exhausted, bowed and threw out her arms like an opera diva to warm, sustained applause. Most of the audience were middle-aged Thai couples who, during the act, sipped their drinks and whispered animatedly. There were also a party of Japanese men and a dozen assorted Europeans, three of them single women. A tiny Thai girl, nude and spectacularly pretty, jumped on to the stage and, with Little Richard thundering from the speakers, did a wild, gyrating rock 'n' roll solo. Walter peered at her earnestly, as though witnessing some strange ethnic rain dance. The Thais clapped with their hands in front of their faces, like an audience at a school concert. There was a short intermission. The dancer, who had not put on any clothes, came and sat on Walter's lap. 'Hullo, sexy,' she said, removing his spectacles and dropping them in his beer.

'Oh, *dear*,' said Walter. He fished them out and put them on again. His cheeks dripped with golden tears as he sat ramrod straight, hands held stiffly at his sides. He tried to smile at her but the effect was ghastly, a frozen leer, and I reflected that if he really was embarking on two weeks of unbridled promiscuity he would need to loosen up a bit. The girl, sensing that she had picked on a funny one here, got off and jumped on to the lap of a portly, balding Japanese who went 'Nnggh!' and hugged her like a long-lost sister.

Walter wiped his glasses with a white hanky that had a gothic 'W' embroidered in a corner. 'I thought she was goin' for my wallet,' he said, shakily.

'That wasn't what I thought she was going for.'

He gave a long sigh and drank some beer. 'I got jet lag,' he told me. 'A good night's kip, that's what I need. Had a bloody awful flight. That Thai lot. First of all they run out of booze then, when I'm fast asleep, this little yellow joker suddenly wakes me up and gives me bleedin' *jam sandwiches*.'

A woman walked on to the little stage brandishing a bottle of beer. She shook it vigorously then handed it to a spectator and asked him to confirm that the cap was firmly in place. He gave it a tug and handed it back, laughing. The woman, who had a fashionable haircut and bruises on one breast, knelt and pushed the neck of the bottle deeply into her vagina. She tensed, briefly displaying the musculature of an athlete, then grunted and tugged hard at the bottle. It came away foaming, without the cap which, seconds later, dropped into her hand. The applause greeting this feat was suddenly replaced by murmurs of distress as she reached for a paper tissue, dabbed herself then held it up to show us the blood. Walter's face was invaded by doubt. If this was common practice among Thai birds, he seemed to be thinking, then having congress with them would be like placing your equipment in an electric blender. Morosely he watched the woman shoot a peeled banana 20 feet into the air. She repeated the trick several times to laughter and applause, desisting only when one of the Japanese caught a banana, falling backwards in his chair and biting the end off. She concluded the performance by tipping the contents of the beer bottle inside her and holding it there for a full minute, squatting with the veins standing out on her face before evacuating it into a blue ovenware baking dish.

The live show followed a few minutes later. The girl was young and pretty while her partner had long hair and a full, rather womanly figure. But he performed with machine-like efficiency, spinning the girl this way and that, turning her up, down and over, demonstrating so many bewildering positions and such phenomenal staying power that I began to sense a growing resentment among some of the audience. When the couple finally walked off, carrying their airbed between them, the partisan Thais whistled and clapped but from the Japanese corner there was only a brief smattering of applause. Most of them looked badly demoralized.

It had made Walter gloomy too. As we left he sniffed the warm, gasoline-scented air and said, 'Fancy a massage? There's supposed to be a good place down the end of the road. I got *vouchers*.'

I declined, wished him luck and hailed a taxi. What I had seen made any kind of erotic activity seem about as desirable as going over the Niagara Falls in a bucket.

A notice posted by the door of the Don Muang domestic terminal denied entry to 'persons dressed untidily' and banned 'any action which disturbs or annoys the aircraft passengers'. The warning seemed superfluous. Everyone lining up at the desks of Thai Airways, the internal carrier, looked as earnest and respectable as customers in a bank, and passengers and airline personnel alike spoke to each other with great civility. The lavender-scented girl who handed me my boarding pass said, 'You are going to Penang. You are so lucky. It is where my heart flies when I am down on the dumps.'

I promised to give her love to Penang and she smiled and touched my hand. Before catching flight TH 420 I went to find Mr Singkarn, the airport manager, with whom an appointment had been arranged. In the administration offices I learned that he was downstairs dealing with a malfunctioning baggage carousel, but a pretty secretary offered me a chilled Coke and, as I waited, gravely explained the techniques of Thai boxing, telling me about a tiny jockey-sized flyweight of her acquaintance who claimed he could kick a water buffalo senseless. Then Mr Singkarn bustled in, clicking his tongue apologetically and, sipping tea, gave me a quick briefing: Don Muang, he said, was remarkable for the fact that it had two virtually identical runways running side by side. 'One is civil, the other military, and they symbolize the way they have always worked together here. When Don Muang became a listed international aerodrome in 1923 – just a few years after Croydon – it was already the headquarters of the Siamese Royal Aeronautical Services *and* the Army Air Service Flying School. All this was just grass then, very swampy in the rains.'

He added that aviation had come to Thailand during the reign of King Rama VI, a Sandhurst-educated technocrat who was determined that his country should take the heavier-than-air machine seriously. 'The whole Royal Family was flying mad. One of his brothers started the first air mail run, from Bangkok to Korat but then, because he was a prince of the blood, the king grounded him. So he had to stand around and supervise the training of others, watching his students up in the sky like a man flying kites.' Mr Singkarn laughed. 'KLM was the first foreign airline to call regularly. Imperial came next, the old *Astraea* arriving in December 1933 on the maiden run from Rangoon down to Alor Star and Singapore. Alor Star was the main stop, but sometimes they called at Penang instead. When the Empire flying boats came in 1937 they *all* went to Penang. They came to Bangkok too, and the passengers were taken by launch to the jetty of the Oriental Hotel.'

Leaving Mr Singkarn I went to board my Thai Airways 737, a

triangular emblem above the door indicating it had been blessed by monks, its cabin furnished in the colours of a tropical garden. Sunlight streamed through the windows. There were only a handful of passengers and three cheery young flight attendants, a youth and two strikingly beautiful girls, who laughed and chatted as though making preparations for a picnic. Their high spirits pervaded the plane and even the three or four Europeans aboard began to unbend. As the engines started up a bony, freckled Englishman sitting across the aisle cleared his throat and observed that it was a very decent morning.

We moved out to the threshold of the civilian runway and held while a Royal Thai Air Force Hercules took off from the neighbouring strip, roaring past as though overtaking on a motorway. We followed a moment later, climbing steeply away over the smoky, sprawling outskirts of the city then turning south for the 75-minute hop to Hat Yai. The Gulf of Siam was a lustrous Ming blue, its surface scored with the wakes of small craft like fine cracks in a porcelain glaze. The cabin attendants, still full of bounce, brought coffee and seedcake, and the Englishman told me he caught this flight every three months. 'I have to,' he explained. 'My Thai visa is a normal tourist one, valid for 90 days, and the easiest way to get a renewal is to leave the country then come back in and claim another 90. There's never any problem. The Thais are very good-natured about such matters and it's a lot easier than getting a residence permit; lots of the expats here do it, popping down to Penang for a couple of days then heading home again with Malaysian stamps in their passports.'

As the 737 hummed across the Isthmus of Kra to make its landfall near Surat Thani he told me that he had first come to Thailand as a tourist seven years earlier and fallen for it, hook, line and sinker. 'So I decided to stay. It was a spur of the moment decision, actually made on the way to the airport to catch the plane back to London, and I've never regretted it. I was a commodities broker at home and I still undertake a few commissions for people – not many, just enough to pay the rent. I've got a small inheritance and a few shares, and I live pretty well.'

But when the boyish young steward brushed against him while refilling his coffee cup my neighbour gave him a sudden sultry smile that made me realize he had been less than frank about the specific nature of Bangkok's appeal for him. I looked out and noted that we were descending over a muddy bay. Cloud shadows drifted across it like oil slicks. The 737 swung lazily across a vast, dense plantation, the orderly lines of trees – mahogany, I thought – vanishing across the horizon, then turned into the wind and landed at Hat Yat airport. There were cargo godowns and a grassy garden planted with travellers' palms, banana trees, crimson hibiscus, pink frangipani trees and zinnias of many colours. But the control tower, six storeys high and made sinister by blank black glass windows, bristled with advanced military radar and communications equipment. It appeared to be in a state of permanent combat readiness and, glancing at the map, I understood why. Ho Chi Minh City was less than half an hour away by MiG.

III

Three Thai soldiers got off and a large German tour party got on, skins spit-roasted, arms full of carved teak elephants and souvenir lacquerware trays. They were a husky, well-heeled and authoritative crowd who immediately took over the aeroplane, stuffing their souvenirs into the overhead lockers, giving brusque orders to the cabin attendants, glancing at their black Seiko diving watches as they settled into their seats with the confident familiarity of company high-flyers boarding an executive jet. The tour leader, a dapper young Frenchman in a white linen suit, sat just behind me, blinking in the sun, giving off a faint but persistent whiff of violets. He had an interesting casino pallor and I guessed he was not at his best during the hours of daylight. His party had come from Songkhla. 'It is a big resort not far from here. Superb beaches, wonderful seafood and native fruits. I know the responsible people there. Always they look after us well. Why is this plane not leaving? My party wishes to get to Penang and cool off. On the bus they complained much of the heat.'

The scheduled 20-minute stop had now overrun by a quarter of an hour. The cabin attendants and a young dispatcher wearing a peaked cap rakishly blocked to resemble the kind favoured by Second World War USAF bomber pilots were standing by the door, counting and recounting boarding passes. Then the steward switched on the tannoy and told us, in halting English, that we were carrying two unauthorized passengers; those who had boarded without the proper pass should make themselves known. Getting no response, he said that everyone must now produce their tickets for inspection. This was not a popular decision and the men not carrying handbags were obliged to leave their seats and scrabble through the overhead lockers. The offenders – a couple in matching Hawaiian shirts sitting a couple of rows behind me – were located with surprising speed and a stewardess, no longer smiling, peremptorily ordered them off the plane. The man shouted, 'I have tickets, I have good boarding pass!' but to no avail. As the dispatcher escorted them back to the terminal the tour leader said, 'They are Germans, but not my Germans. My Germans would not have to leave. I know the sales manager of this airline.' Five minutes later the couple suddenly returned, the door was closed and we were taxiing almost before they had reached their seats. The tour leader, familiar with the complexities of ticketing procedures, questioned them during take-off and, as we levelled off at our prescribed cruising height, told me, 'It was a misunderstanding. They had tickets, but for a later flight. When they changed to this one their names were not put on the passenger manifest so the boarding pass count showed two too many. In this part of the world such a nonsense is not uncommon.'

The Penang sector took only 30 minutes. As we left the Thai coast and whizzed out over tankers and container ships plodding stolidly between the Andaman Sea and the Straits of Malacca the steward distributed Malaysian entry forms bearing the words 'Be Forewarned. Death for Drug Traffickers Under Malaysian Law.' My freckled friend across the aisle was talking animatedly to a handsome blond teenager whose mother, not bad-looking herself, listened to the exchange with a faint frown, perhaps troubled by the way the Englishman kept touching her son's bare arm. The tour leader leant over my seat and said, 'You have seen what it says on the landing card? I know the Malaysian hangman. I met him at a golf club in KL. I know also the Foreign Minister and a couple of the Sultans. The Foreign Minister recently crashed his plane in the jungle. He is a good egg. Malaysia is a country where you must have contacts if you wish to get any action.'

Somewhere beyond the port wing was Alor Setar, one of the more obscure Imperial stops. In the early days it had been the first halt after Bangkok and I was bound there now but, due to the vagaries of the present schedules, it could only be reached via Penang and Kota Bharu, a township on the South China Sea. To fly from Penang to Alor Star meant crossing from the west coast to the east and then back again, finishing up only a few miles from my original starting point. Now the little Thai 737 descended over blue hills bounded by a shiny hot sea. The flaps were lowered over Butterworth Field, a mainland military base, and we tracked along the new causeway leading to Penang island, touching down at Bayan Lepas airport a few moments later. I followed the Germans through a covered air bridge, had my passport stamped by an amiable but sharp-eyed official and passed into the terminal proper, a lofty, airy, open-ended structure built in the style of a kampong long house. It was cool and elegant, a classy piece of design, with sparrows clamouring high in its shadowy, steeply pitched roof.

Imperial's Empire boats had landed at Glugor, six miles distant, while, periodically, their Armstrong Whitworth Atalantas – wearing Indian livery – called to pick up the mail and passengers down from Hong Kong on the company's branch line. In the *Gazette* an anonymous passenger wrote, 'The first stage today over Johore and the Federated Malay States to Penang, where we breakfasted on the Aero Club verandah, was almost entirely over jungle. At Penang we picked up a passenger and the mails from Hong Kong, brought there by the new Imperial Airways *Diana* class operated service. Penang is an attractively situated prosperous-looking town.'

I asked an exuberant young cab driver to take me to the Eastern and Oriental Hotel and we moved off at high speed while he shouted questions over his shoulder. Where was my family? How old was my daughter? What was my son's name? Was I an Oxford man? Were my children diligent? He himself had not been diligent, preferring car magazines to textbooks, but now he was helping to put his diligent younger brother through electrical engineering at Glasgow University; this helped to make amends for his slackness at school. Penang, he continued, was very pro-British. I would feel at home here and, to prove it, he began reciting some of the street names of George Town, the island's little capital: Turf Club Road, Bell Lane, Jalan Jones, Rose Avenue, Bridge Street, Jalan Brick Kiln, Lebuh Leith, Lebuhraya Scott, Jalan Brother James, Pierce Close, Jalan Edgecumbe and Piggot Road.

The lobby of the old Eastern and Oriental on Farquhar Street was humid and shadowy, without benefit of air conditioning. In 1929 Noël Coward and his friend Lord Amherst, both wearing mono-grammed silk tennis shirts and blue berets, had registered at this same ample desk and, clearly, little had changed since. The lift was a gilded iron cage that groaned up to the third floor, discharging me on to a covered verandah. My room stood at the end of a private passageway where, once, my servants would have slept on bedrolls. In the cavernous adjoining bathroom, before the installation of plumbing, guests slopped water over themselves from tall Shanghai jars. The hotel stood within a few yards of the sea wall and, when I threw open the windows, the room was filled with the sleepy splash of the tide rising in the Straits. The smoke of a distant ship smudged the blue horizon. Across the water the misty hills of Kedah loomed on the mainland. Below my windows was an enchanted garden, a long, trim lawn planted with casuarinas and coconut palms and containing a small pool in which a pretty Malaysian woman was teaching her baby to swim. There was a tap at the door and a bluff, vigorous-looking man walked in, said he was my room boy and shook my hand. He began unpacking my bag. Certain items he set aside for washing, others for pressing. What was the purpose of my visit? Was I married? Were my children at school? Did they work hard and obey their teachers? I said the teachers complained only rarely. 'Good, good!' he beamed and hurried off with a pile of stuff destined for the laundry.

I went for a dip in the pool. The Malaysian girl smiled when I said her baby seemed to be picking up the technique of dog paddling very well. 'He wants to learn,' she told me gravely. That evening, drinking a Tiger beer in the Anchor Bar, I chatted to an elderly

Dutchman who had worked in Penang as a young man and now, widowed and retired, was back for a sentimental visit. In the old days, he said, the E & O had been the centre of the island's social life. 'It was once just a small boarding house but at the end of the last century an Armenian named Sarkies took it over. He was the chap who built Raffles in Singapore and he was a bit of an extrovert. You know? When they had balls here he would always dance a Viennese waltz with a glass of whisky on his head. He never spilled a drop. It was his party trick. I think he probably was a bit of a pain,' added the Dutchman, who was small and neat with a trim moustache. 'His head boy was a Chinese called Hindenburg. This Hindenburg always wore white socks and black silk matador pants and did his hair like a twenties' movie star – lots of oil, combed flat. Even when I was here, just after the war, they still talked about him. Hindenburg could do anything: cash a cheque, get you a woman, call off your creditors, fix an invitation to Government House, even get you out of jail. All the famous English names came here – Kipling, Coward, Maugham, all those writers.' Then, with some reluctance, he left to attend a Malaysian cultural evening for which he had purchased a ticket. 'I expect it will be quite boring,' he said.

Passengers from Imperial's Hong Kong connection stayed at the E & O while awaiting their mainline flights. Hong Kong was incorporated into the company's network after complaints had been voiced in the House of Commons about the slowness of the mails between Britain and China. Letters went out in only 19 days – the Soviet post office expressed them across Siberia by air – but took an eternity to come back because the Chinese post office put them on very slow boats and routed them home via the Suez Canal. So in 1936, as a result of Parliamentary pressure, the company formed a new subsidiary called Imperial Airways (Far East) Ltd. and dispatched the De Havilland 86 *Dorado* from Croydon to Penang to begin route survey work. Mail collected at Penang from the London plane went to Hong Kong via Saigon and Touraine. Later, when the Japanese had occupied part of the territory over which the service operated, the *Dorado* was fired at by fighters and the *Delia* by warships. The unctuous, gimlet-eyed opportunists of the Japanese diplomatic corps answered British protests by proposing that the service be immediately discontinued 'to avoid further friction'. Imperial's response was to paint Union Jacks all over the wings and fuselages of its DH 86s and keep them flying until October 1940. In aviation circles Penang had made its mark.

Cobham called here too, arriving 'just as the sun was going down behind the mountain at the back of the town, so that the clear-cut rock horizon formed by the mountain stood out boldly, illuminated by the great light behind it. We landed in the bay, which was quite calm, and as we could find no mooring we heaved our own little anchor overboard. We discovered that we had come quicker than our telegram and they had been unprepared for us; for it appeared they dared not leave our mooring out, having already had three stolen by the native fishermen during the fortnight that they had been expecting our arrival. However, they soon brought out an anchor and we were quickly tied up in calm waters.

'Penang is a delightful town, deservedly noted for its perfect order and cleanliness. As we left the centre of the city we passed through broad, spacious avenues overhung with magnificent trees. Everywhere there seemed to be an abundance of foliage in which the villas of the merchants of Penang were partially hidden. Government House here is perhaps one of the most beautiful in the whole of the East, with imposing views of the great mountain behind the town appearing above the Residency lawns. It was a wonderful moonlit night and I longed to rest in this delightful spot; instead of which I had to dress in a matter of minutes and dash off with the Governor to an important dinner where, he told me, my presence was very much requested.'

Cobham did not say where the dinner was held but I knew that the only venue appropriate to such an occasion would have been the E & O and, sitting in the dining room, I imagined him being welcomed here by perspiring, gregarious men in boiled shirts and black ties who traditionally subsisted on a high-octane diet of hot curries and cold spirits. But now the dining room was occupied by single business travellers and middle-aged holidaymakers unable to afford the ritzy new gin palaces that had creamed off the upper end of the luxury trade, subdued, rather mournful people who took care not to raise their voices or clatter their soup spoons. Grave young waiters moved about noiselessly, like priests bringing wine and wafers to their communicants. What my waiter dispensed, food apart, was knowledge. While serving up a plate of fish and fragrant boiled noodles he told me that the British had called Penang Prince of Wales' Island but its real name came from Pulau Pinang, meaning Island of the Betel Nut Tree. I wrote that down in my notebook and he nodded approvingly. During the remainder of the meal I got excellent service and a lot more information. I had been an attentive student, and when I left he smiled and wished me sweet dreams.

The Anchor Bar was deserted but for a flabby middle-aged American with thinning hair and a nose like a giant strawberry. He was a drinking man and he plainly wanted a drink now. But he was already half cut and the barman refused to serve him. The American was throwing a tantrum, shouting abuse, pounding the bar with his fist. He wore Bermuda shorts, and the varicose veins running like estuarine maps down his flaccid, marbeloid legs seemed to swell and pulse, as though filling with purple ink. When he shambled out, still yelling, I said to the barman, 'You should have belted him one,' but the barman shook his head and explained solemnly that violence against customers was not a policy the management encouraged.

Later I went to my room and sat for a while by the open window. The narrow track thrown across the Straits by the quarter moon slipped out of focus as an outward-bound coaster chugged through it, all lit up and trailing a mist of diesel fumes. The high tide sucked and rippled softly against the sea wall. There was a small, fitful westerly breeze which periodically rattled the palm fronds like dominoes. I went to bed and, on the verge of sleep, recalled a story the waiter had told me which seemed entirely in keeping with this pretty, faintly eccentric island. When Francis Light, the Briton who persuaded the Sultan of Kedah to allow him to build a settlement on Penang, brought in Indian labourers to clear the site they became disheartened by the thick, tangled jungle, the snakes and fevers. Light realized the men needed some powerful new incentive so one morning he called them together and, as they watched, filled a large cannon with silver dollars and fired it straight into the trees. The

Indians seized their axes and cleared the jungle so fast that, only days later, work could be started on the wharves, roads and houses of this hot little place that had just become the newest fragment of Empire.

IV

Flight MH 350 to Kota Bharu, operated by a Malaysian Airlines System 737, was scheduled to depart from Penang at 1750. During the day I made a number of phone calls, looking for anyone who could tell me about the pre-war local aviation picture, but none of the people I spoke to seemed even to know what I was talking about. In the Anchor Bar before lunch an affable young Malaysian who worked for Wira Kris, a charter company operating a fleet of light aircraft, explained, 'Everyone in the aviation business here is young. Older people like to have a quiet life so they leave. The competition for aviation jobs is very big – for flying or ground duties they take only the best graduates, and students. They must also be good physical specimens, strong and fit, very sporty. It is Malaysia's most high profile profession.'

I decided to go to the airport early and try my luck there; perhaps I would come across someone furtively concealing the onset of a middle-age spread who would at least acknowledge the existence of the past. While packing my bag I decided to jettison half a dozen cotton vests and a heavy woollen sweater brought along for chilly evenings in northern India. I offered them to the room boy who beamed and thanked me effusively. 'But you must write chitty or management will say I have stolen these goods.'

'All right.' I picked up my notebook. 'What shall I say?'

He frowned and cleared his throat. 'Put: "I give six white singlets and a green jumper, army-style, of my own free will to Room Boy Mohammed."'

I dated the document and handed it over. He took the clothing and dashed out, but returned a moment later holding a folding Chinese paper fan delicately painted with swallows and willows.

'It is for your mem,' he said. 'You please tell her it is from Mohammed at E & O.'

Half an hour later I arrived back at the Bayan Lepas terminal, the gaudy tiles on that lofty longhouse roof taking on the patina of silk in the late afternoon sun. Inside I made a few random inquiries, but all the responsible persons I spoke to looked like teenage marathon runners and seemed unaware of any significant airline operations that predated the invention of the jet engine. Out on the tarmac squads of pubescent girl air cadets in short blue tunics were drilling beside three parked Shorts Skyvans, arms swinging, knees scrubbed, faces shining with effort as they wheeled, turned, marched and counter-marched, gravely preparing to become the aircrew and ground personnel of the next generation. I gave up and retired to the departure lounge.

It was only when I reached Singapore, several days later, that I finally tracked down a veteran who had worked in Penang during the Imperial era – and whose memories therefore belong in this section of the narrative. Harold J. Foley, a retired Principal Officer of the Singapore Prison Service, was a tall, shy, courteous man who lived with his wife Milly in a suburban bungalow surrounded by a small, vivid garden. As Milly brought glasses of fresh lime juice her husband said he had been the chief air traffic controller at Penang when it was the only airport in Malaya with night landing facilities. 'At first there was just a gas beacon burning on the hillside above the strip – good for picking up Penang in the dark but no real use otherwise. Then they installed boundary lights and special searchlights for illuminating the runway. I first went there to work on the construction of the aerodrome but in 1936 they sent me to the UK for air traffic training – I did the theory course at Hurn, the practical at Manchester Ringway – then they appointed me ATC officer at a salary of 40 Straits dollars a month and gave me a radio, an Aldis lamp and two local assistants. I was as happy as a sandboy but no slackness was tolerated in my tower. There are dangerous hills around Bayan Lepas and they kept us on our toes. Is your drink sweet enough? Does it need a little more sugar? Milly can bring it.'

I assured him the drink was excellent.

'We like our lime juice tart,' said Mr Foley.

I asked him what other personnel had been employed at Bayan Lepas.

'We had a little Customs and Immigration Department. There were a dozen traffic hands who did the manual work, cutting the grass, loading and unloading aircraft. The refuelling was done by the chaps who drove the old Shell and Esso tankers, and the E & O provided the inflight catering. They sent out drinks and boxes of *excellent* sandwiches. The traffic hands were supposed to put them aboard the aircraft but quite often they took them around the back of the hangar to sample them first and angry scenes with the Imperial and KLM stewards would follow. I am not judging the traffic hands; I have to admit that some of those sandwiches also found their way up to the control tower.' He grinned. 'There were also complaints from a lady. The main user of Penang then was Wern's Air Services, a local company that flew Rapides down to Singapore and employed a Penang girl as an air hostess. The trip took just over three hours. KLM came through twice a week, their overnight service from Jakarta arriving at 0730 hours precisely. It didn't matter how bad the conditions were, those pilots always touched down right on the button. I met them all because they reported to me for their onward weather. Smirnoff was a big solid chap with no small talk and a faraway look in his eyes. In his thoughts he sort of seemed to be somewhere else. You often find that with exiles, but I never knew whether he was dreaming about Russia or about just getting back into the sky again; Smirnoff never looked too comfortable with his feet on the ground. I knew Parmentier, too, and Moll, his co-pilot. Parmentier was always correct, always neat in his white shirt and dark trousers even if he had spent the night flying blind through a typhoon. Once I flew down to Singapore in Parmentier's DC2. It was a stormy day and probably the bumpiest journey I ever made, but I felt no fear. We hit one particular air pocket that seemed to reach right down to the ground. It was a hell of a fall but as we dropped I remember thinking we'd be okay because this man *couldn't crash*.'

I asked Mr Foley about the Imperial men. 'Ah, the Atalanta pilots,' he said. 'Well, there was Captain Alderson, a nice chap who always liked a chat. And Captain Mollard, who knew this part of the world so well he could have flown over it blindfolded. And

Captain Locke – he was like a Dutchman, no fuss, very professional, always landing at 0200 prompt, refuelling, getting his weather and taking straight off again for Singapore – and Captain Paine, who was always late. He flew the Empire boats which landed at Glugor and were also my responsibility. My job was to prepare the flare path for night landings. The flares were kerosene lamps stuck on top of four-foot-high floats. We lit them with matches and dropped them off the back of a fast pinnace along a 1,200-yard stretch with searchlight boats stationed at both ends. We had already picked up the skipper on radio 100 miles out and, when he was overhead, he'd circle until I signalled him with my Aldis lamp. He acknowledged by flashing his landing lights. If we suddenly spotted an obstruction, a fishing junk or a floating log – we always swept the track first, and those last-minute alarms were a real nightmare – I fired a red Very light telling him to abort. The Imperial boats arrived at midnight and left again at 0300 sharp; they had to be in Singapore in time for breakfast at Raffles and, while the Shell tanker launch did the refuelling, Mansfield's, the Penang agents, brought the passengers ashore for a cup of tea. I didn't have much to do with them. All I remember is that they were confident, well-dressed people who behaved as if they had plenty of money.'

Then, gradually, the tenor of life began to change. When an RAF Sunderland flying boat – the Service version of the Empire – was forced down in the sea 60 miles off Penang while searching for survivors from two Wildebeest bombers that had collided near Alor Star, Mr Foley was ordered out in his pinnace to find it. The Sunderland, suffering from overheated engines, was able to follow him home to Glugor, rumbling along through an oily swell under its own power.

As the Japanese invasion force closed on Penang the Singapore authorities ordered him to abandon Bayan Lepas. He disobeyed. 'The Japs had already bombed Butterworth on the mainland so I knew ours was the only serviceable strip in the area and I reckoned it had to be kept open. All my staff left, except for one Indian assistant I had looked after as a boy. They called us fools. Then, at midday on 11 December 1941 – it was my wife's birthday; *everything* always happens on Milly's birthday – a flight of 12 fighters suddenly appeared over the field. We thought it was the RAF and ran out to wave but, of course, they were Zeros. It was very noisy and frightening. They fired several thousand rounds but the only damage they did was to kill a cow. The Indian and I stayed for another six days, living on biscuits, but there were no more attacks. Then someone told us the RAF had gone to Singapore. There was no more point in staying so we went into George Town, collecting Milly from the telephone exchange where she worked, and caught the last train out of Butterworth. I was working in the control tower at Kallang, the new Singapore airport, when the city fell. The Japanese sent me back to Penang. Things were very bad there. Four of my brothers were getting the water treatment in the George Town jail – they made you drink a lot then jumped on your stomach – and one died. I was not sent to the jail but I had to kneel in front of Suzuki, the famous headcutter, who hit me with judo blows. I can remember thinking I must not tell Milly; she hated the Japs and would really have gone for Suzuki. But I survived and thought, well, this is not for me, so I left and went up a hill. I had a friend on the hill and for the rest of the war I just lived there quietly. When we heard the Japs had surrendered I came down again and went back to my tower at Bayan Lepas. Once again it was business as usual.'

Now, almost 40 years later, the passengers for the MAS flight to Kota Bharu were filing into the departure lounge, only a few yards from the site of Harold Foley's old tower. People spoke in murmurs and the loudest sounds were the barked commands from the wiry, bespectacled woman drilling the girls out on the apron. I wandered into the bookshop, its shelves stacked with paperbacks on self-improvement: *How to be a Better Manager, Success in Financial Accounting, Play Snooker Like a Champ, Who Wants to be a Millionaire?, Win at Tennis, Investing Your Nest Egg, How to Make Your Own Luck* and *Get That Job!*

The flight was called. We filed through the airbridge into a 737 where the stewardesses, beautiful, strong-looking graduates of the air cadet training scheme, strode up and down the aisles, checking our seat belts and snapping the overhead lockers shut. The little Boeing took off precisely on time, its port wingtip seeming almost to brush a lofty green hill as it scrambled into the sky. The noise and rush of our passage brought hundreds of startled white birds tumbling out of the forest. They swirled away like confetti as we climbed towards Butterworth, passed Grik and headed out across the green escarpments and bright red earth of Malaysia. The stewardesses brought coffee and sweet yellow cake. We bumped over the dimpled topography of the highlands and, only a few minutes into the half-hour flight, I picked up the South China Sea ahead on the other coast, glassy in the late afternoon sun. The young man in the neighbouring seat, a dental student, told me that Kota Bharu was the home of the previous king. 'He is the Sultan of Kelantan. In Malaysia the king changes every five years. There are nine sultans and they themselves elect the new king. So everyone has a turn. It is very democratic. That way the king does not get too many big ideas.'

With the spoilers out and the engines throttled back we drifted across a bright river estuary scattered with islands, our shadow slipping between those cast by the triangular patchwork sails of small fishing craft. There were settlements on both banks. The estuary split and ran out to the sea through a bewildering number of channels which merged into a watery, palm-fringed horizon as we sank towards Pengkalan Chepa airport. An uncommunicative old man drove me through coconut groves to the Perdana Hotel, its swimming pool filled with shouting, splashing children. I had grilled mackerel for dinner, caught that day, and a pudding made from jackfruit. In the bar a young Malaysian pianist in a dinner jacket was playing requests. An American couple asked him for a Chopin nocturne which he knocked off between 'Amor' and 'Light My Fire'. There were some pretty girls in the bar, looking for action. I talked to a local businessman who said that Kota Bharu had two famous beaches. The first was called *Pantai Chinta Berahi*, or The Beach of Passionate Love, and the second *Pantai Dasar Sabak*. It was here, at 16.55 GMT on 7 December 1941, 95 minutes before the attack on Pearl Harbor, that the Imperial Japanese Forces entered the Second World War, landing with their bicycles and pedalling off down the long road to Singapore. When I left the bar the pianist was playing 'The Moonlight Sonata'.

On the way back to Pengkalan Chepa at 6.30 next morning my

driver suddenly halted his rattling Toyota by a small kampong and wound down the window. It was still dark and the air held a sharp night chill. 'Listen,' he commanded and I heard, coming from the shadowy kampong, a bird singing with extraordinary power and sweetness. Its rich, liquid voice flooded through the car as though amplified by quadrophonic speakers. 'That is a *merbok*,' said the driver. 'We catch them in the forest and train them for big competition in June. Early morning is best time for *merbok* practice. Now they are singing all over Kota Bharu.'

The check-in hall in Pengkalan Chepa's little terminal was open to the road. Half a dozen figures sat sleepily, waiting for the flight to Alor Setar – or, as it is more colloquially known, Alor Star. The terminal signs were all in Bahasa Malaysia and, emerging from the Gents, or *Tandas Lelaki*, I glimpsed through the half-drawn curtain of the prayer room a kneeling man in a smart white suit muttering and agitatedly polishing his spectacles. We were directed to the flight through *Pintu A*. The 737 was sitting out on the empty apron with its lights on, humming comfortably and ready to go.

We took off through rolling banks of sea mist. The atmosphere at the rear of the aircraft, where I sat, was as clubby and convivial as a tea house. My neighbour slipped off his sandals and massaged his feet while he chatted animatedly with his friends. Half the 35-minute flight was made across the protruding southernmost tip of Thailand; we passed back into Malaysian airspace near Kampung Pinang where puddles of fog lapped through the deep, jungled valleys below. They gave way to a prospect of shadowy lakes and islands and, peering out, I noted that the Boeing was cruising just beneath a filmy layer of stratus so shallow that its tail must have been cutting through the top like the fin of a shark.

My neighbour told me he suffered from recurring bunions and said the best remedies were available from Boots the Chemists in the UK. 'They have tip top selection for feet disorders,' he added, 'so when I go to Britain I stock up. I have been many times. I look after overseas student welfare and we have 60,000 Malaysians studying there. My favourite place is Glasgow. That is a hot town!'

The flaps were extended with their coffee-grinder noise and the 737 descended over fields of burnt rice stubble towards the single runway at Sultan Abdul Halim airport. As it touched down the sun broke through heavy cloud and washed the blackened landscape in an eerie crimson light. Thirty or forty red and white Swiss-built Pilatus Turbo-Trainers were parked on the far side of the field where five platoons of uniformed boys and girls marched up and down, doing their early morning drill before dashing off to school.

The drive into town took half an hour. I had hit the morning rush hour and, as we inched through the fashionable new contraflow and one-way systems my driver made his own prolonged contribution to the Alor Setar concerto for two-tone horns and broken silencers. At the highrise Merlin Hotel everyone was having breakfast and, while waiting for a room to be vacated and cleaned, I asked the desk clerk if Alor Setar possessed a museum. He said yes, it had a *State* Museum and invited me to call its curator, Mrs Nabihah, from the lobby phone. Mrs Nabihah sounded brisk and friendly but regretted that her museum contained nothing about the airfield during the pre-war years. 'It is a big omission,' she said. 'I am jolly interested in aviation matters and I will have to do something about this. Perhaps there are some photographs or artefacts you would like to contribute yourself?' I told her that, unfortunately, I had nothing worth displaying and asked if there was anyone in Alor Setar who could help me. She suggested I call Mr Azizan, the present Airport Director. He was young, of course, but he might know something.

Mr Azizan said he would be delighted to meet for a talk. I was at the Merlin? He would be there when he came off duty, at 1400 hours. At 1350 hours he came bounding up the steps, a plump, energetic man with a wispy moustache who told me, as we sat in the coffee shop, that he was the first Malay to manage the airport. He came from Pulau Langkawi, an island just off the coast where the government were building a giant billion-pound tourist complex with an airport that would take 747s from all over the world. Mr Azizan indicated that one day he would like to go home and manage that. 747s! The largest visitor he had welcomed to Alor Setar had been a stretched DC9 on a sales demo, flown by an American astronaut. I asked him which astronaut and he shrugged. 'Not big league fellow, I think, not a moon walker or anything like that.' He drank a Coke and said Mrs Nabihah had called and told him I was an important aviation historian. I laughed and pointed out that I was just an itinerant scribbler hunting for historians myself.

He persisted. 'Well, she think you know about the old days out at Sultan Abdul Halim.'

I ordered another coffee and shared my meagre store of facts with him. He hadn't heard that Imperial and KLM called here for fuel and provisions while travelling along the original trunk route between Bangkok and Singapore. Nor did he know of the occasion in 1931 when the *Southern Sun*, an Avro Ten of Australian National Airways (the airline founded by Sir Charles Kingsford Smith) crashed here on 25 November with mail bound for Britain. KLM offered to take it on but some Little Englander in the local post office declined on the grounds that their Fokker flew the wrong flag; patriotism, to the servants of the Empire, came before punctuality. So poor Kingsford Smith had to hasten up from Sydney in the *Southern Star* and carry the delayed cargo all the way to Croydon. There he picked up the Australian-bound Christmas mail and raced home with such a wind at his back that, characteristically, he broke the record *again*. The Alor Setar aerodrome then was a reclaimed paddy field, notoriously marshy, though the race course could be used by pilots caught short when the field was waterlogged.

And that, I said, was more or less the sum total of my local knowledge, except for the Tweezer Man.

'Excuse me?' murmured Mr Azizan.

I explained that he had been employed to pick dead insects out of the engines. Malaysian airspace teems with them and the old Atalantas, droning along at insect height, sucked them up like hoovers. At Alor Setar he propped a ladder against the wing and painstakingly cleaned up the four Armstrong-Siddeley double Mongoose ungeared air-cooled radials, ridding them of the milled remains of dragonflies, moths, beetles, flying spiders, lacewings, fireflies, locusts, butterflies – including the great rainbow-coloured Malaysian swallowtails – perhaps even migrating booklice, all tweaked out by the Tweezer Man until the grass beneath would have glittered with iridescent fragments like the sweepings from a gem cutter's shop.

Mr Azizan said he would like to show me his airport. It was a fine sunny afternoon. He drove a new Honda and, as we negotiated the traffic systems, told me he was a fan of all things Japanese. An airport management course in Japan had only served to increase his respect. The one thing the Japanese couldn't do was cook. Their food, he said, was so bad it had made him ill. We cleared the town centre and went bowling past the Kompleks Tunku Jaacob, a new shopping mall, and out into the open country, humming along under a huge Vermeer sky speckled with clumps of drifting cloud and several droning Pilatus Turbo-Trainers. Mr Azizan shared the field with the Royal Malaysian Air Force flying school but all air traffic duties were carried out by his civilian staff. 'Our ATC people are the best-qualified in South East Asia. They must all have good degree, plus excellent health and hearing and 20-20 eyesight with good colour vision. Also clear speech, good English and quick thinking.' He pulled out to pass a bullock cart laden with oil drums. 'Last year I almost lost one. I sent him by Airbus from Penang to Kuala Lumpur on educational flight but the plane crashed 1,000 feet short of the KL runway. He survive okay but when he got back he said, "Hey, boss, what sort of education you trying to give me?"'

He laughed and identified the race course, deserted but for two men hitting golf balls down the home straight. 'My total staff is 180, including security personnel who have special training at Penang College. All luggage is now X-rayed *twice*. This has been the rule since a 737 with our Minister of Culture aboard explode just after taking off from Penang.'

We passed a handsome villa standing in a large, shadowy garden. 'That is home of the PM, Datuk Seri Dr Mahathir Mohamad. Before going into politics he was a local GP. Recently the Foreign Minister visited us here too. He was also in a bad crash recently. He is qualified pilot and his Piper 28 came down in the jungle, killing his co-pilot and bodyguard. To get help he had to walk for some days, eating only nuts and wild fruit.'

I observed that Malaysian politicians seemed to lead eventful lives. He said gravely, 'Oh, they are real get-up-and-go people. When the Airbus crash at KL the PM himself was there within a few minutes, helping the rescuers, treating the injured. My chap saw him working in the wreckage and thought, "My God, isn't that the PM?" but he wasn't surprised. In Malaysia we expect such things.'

The road, long and straight, ran past dense plantations of rubber trees. Mr Azizan turned off towards the terminal, a spacious new building set in a pretty tropical garden where, among beds of orange cannas, an elderly piston-engined Provost trainer sat on a plinth with vines growing around its wings. The restaurant, commanding a view of the empty tarmac, was full of families gossiping over soft drinks and plates of cakes. Mr Azizan said, 'The airport is a very popular place for outings. People like to see the planes and equipment. Here they can see that Malaysia is at the forefront of technology. It makes them feel good.' He went to the counter and bought a couple of Cokes. The girl attendants had been slouching and yawning when we entered and, though they now affected a great show of industry, the Cokes they gave us were warm. Mr Azizan frowned and spoke to them sharply, telling them to call the engineer – busted refrigerators had no place here on Malaysia's technological front line.

I remarked on the several dozen Pilatus Turbo-Trainers drawn up on the far side of the field. 'Forty-four have been delivered so far,' he said. 'Only Iraq and Mexico have more. It is the best trainer in the world. The engine is a Pratt & Whitney turbo-prop driving a Hartzell three-blade constant-speed fully-feathering propeller. Swiss delivery pilots fly them out from the factory in Lucerne, two by two. I know them; they are very good chaps. And of course I know also our Air Force instructors. We are forming a gliding club here – I am the Vice President and many of them are joining.'

One of the trainers was on finals. As we watched Mr Azizan said the club would be using powered German sailplanes because the winds on this side of the country were weak and fitful. The really good gliding winds blew over on the east coast, specially during the months when the SE monsoon came whistling down the South China Sea. A skilled pilot could sit up there for hours, secure as a dish on a shelf. Abruptly the Pilatus made a wild kamikaze dive at the ground. Seconds before its constant-speed Hartzell propeller began drilling a hole in the tarmac the instructor hauled it back and set it down with a thump that made it go frolicking along the runway like a spring lamb.

'Ow!' exclaimed Mr Azizan. The plane steadied then gathered speed and took off again. 'He is doing circuits and bumps.' We watched the landing gear retract as it climbed away. 'The gear has a castoring nosewheel with shimmy dampers,' he said knowledgeably. Then, in an unexpected aside, he mentioned that fragments of the old British-built runway could still be seen, though most had been planted with rice. 'The present runway, O4, was aligned and put down by the Japanese. They had squadrons of Zeros and Betty bombers here.'

The late afternoon sky turned silvery. To the south big lavender clouds were massing, heavy with the promise of rain. A small object suddenly emerged from them which, as it came curving towards us, assumed the dumpy profile of a 737. Mr Azizan glanced at his watch and noted approvingly that it was two minutes early. 'Inbound from KL,' he said. 'In half an hour he will return there then, after dark, he will come back to operate the night economy flight.'

The 737 drifted up to the threshold of Runway O4, breasting the breeze like a gull, and dropped gently, the thunder of its reverse thrust booming around Sultan Abdul Halim like a tropical storm. We returned to the Honda. Mr Azizan had discovered that I had never looked closely at a rubber tree and, determined to put that to rights, set off at high speed past small kampongs, translucent bamboo groves, meandering brown creeks and pools with wild water lilies floating on them. We drove through the shadow of Bukit Tinggi, a lofty, jungle-covered volcanic plug rearing high above the plain like an inverted yoghurt tub. 'Bad place,' remarked Mr Azizan. 'Full of snakes. But men go up there to cut the stone. We call it Hill 450; that is its height in feet.'

This would have been the primary landmark for Imperial's pilots, I reflected, craning to gaze up its perpendicular sides but, by the same token, a real hazard in dirty weather. Then, four miles beyond, we coasted to a halt beside a plantation and strolled through dense, shadowy trees while Mr Azizan pointed out the lateral scarring where the trunks had been slashed to collect latex. Most of the trees had their cups in position for nocturnal milking. The plantation was thickly carpeted with damp russet leaves, like an autumnal English wood. Mr Azizan urged me to touch the bark. Wasn't it a miracle that a mere plant could produce such wealth? The nation had been built on its sap. As we returned to the car the

737 went racing overhead on its way back to Kuala Lumpur, the roar of its Pratt & Whitneys agitating hundreds of birds that had been roosting quietly in the treetops.

Driving home through the gloaming he confessed he never imagined he would ever become a person of such consequence. Airport Director, Alor Setar! Malaysia was a country where hard work and single-mindedness paid off. He socialized with the town's top people. He went to their houses, they came to this. 'What unites us is service to the community. That is what matters today.'

The road took us past the palatial residence built for the British District Administrator, now used for housing visiting VIPs, and then the old Planters' Club, an imposing structure looming massively in the dusk. We popped in for a look. The tuans had been replaced by wealthy Muslim teetotallers but the air still seemed scented with the whiff of gin pahits, shag tobacco and Capstans, and the talk still dealt obsessively with world rubber prices – which, Mr Azizan remarked as we slipped out again, were going through the floor. Back in the urban contraflow system we passed two remarkably ornate Edwardian timber structures, the Theatre Royal and the Empire, the former now condemned, the latter serving as a cinema. Here companies of travelling players had performed their Gilbert and Sullivan, their operettas and musical comedies. At the stage doors mooning young expats would have waited with armloads of orchids for the chorus line blondes from *No, No, Nanette* and *The Sheik of Araby*.

We drew up at the Merlin. Mr Azizan had given up a large part of his day for me, but became gruff when I thanked him and shook hands. I took the elevator, marked '*lif bomba*', to my room and looked through the *Gazette* to see what people had written about Alor Setar. There wasn't much. Philip S. Rudder remarked on the country – 'thousands of little squares, water-logged paddy fields, banana plantations and tin mines' – but 'Alor Star, where we arrived at 9.30 a.m.,' was notable only for the fact that, during a brief refuelling halt, 'luncheon baskets came aboard.' I switched on the television and watched a recording of Brighton playing Liverpool in the Fourth Round of the FA cup, a match held in thin, wintry English sunshine. Brighton won 2–0. That was followed by an ad for Darkie toothpaste. I watched a smiling Malaysian family scrubbing their teeth in unison then went down to the coffee shop for supper. A startlingly good-looking girl sat alone at the next table, eating a banana split and scowling over a paperback called *Guerrilla Tactics in the Job Market*.

V

At 0835 the MAS 737 climbed away from Sultan Abdul Halim through a hazy, overcast morning. Though the sky looked tranquil it was full of strange, conflicting currents that made the plane pitch and wallow. The paddy fields far below looked like complex, beautiful mosaics of mirrors and Roman glass. A smooth young banker in the next seat said the flight would last 45 minutes and take us past Taiping, Ayer, Telok Anson and across the Slim River. He had made it several times. The bank paid, of course. For them it was a legitimate business expense and therefore tax-deductible. Then, without preamble, he said. 'Have you ever seen Mrs Thatcher, sir? In the flesh?'

'Only from a distance.'

'She is my ideal lady. She is my pin-up.'

I looked at him uneasily.

'I admire so much. Such leadership! Such courage! And that yellow hair – she is quite dishy, I would say. In Malaysia we think she is definitely the bee's knees.' He lit a Cabin 85 cigarette with a flash gold lighter. 'It is my ambition to go to London to study law, sir. When I come back I will be able to charge 160 dollars Malaysian for my signature!' He gave a sudden yelp of laughter. 'That is what people must pay a British-trained man for putting his name on a document. One six oh dollars!'

Half an hour later we began our descent over a battlefield of ravaged red earth and flooded pits. I asked my friend what was going on down there.

'They are sluicing for tin,' he said. 'The profits are good but it damage the soil, sir. For years afterwards the land is dead. Tin is all very fine but we cannot eat it.'

'I'll bet Mrs Thatcher can,' I said.

He gave me an uncertain smile. I looked down on a great dog's leg of devastated wasteland reaching away through the trees and far up into the hills like a colossal motorway project. It slipped astern and was replaced by a vast palm oil plantation. Here and there in the endless, orderly rows of trees there were small clearings containing houses on stilts; beside one a man was climbing on to a bare-backed horse and, as we came over, the horse reared up and the man jumped off again.

'All the rubber men want to get into palm oil now,' my friend remarked. 'They are coming to see us at the bank. They speak only of palm oil. It is where the smart money is going.'

Moments later, on finals, we skimmed over a dense tract of jungle with the patina of a tapestry worked in matching shades of green silk. 'That is specially protected land,' said my friend. 'Only experts in jungle studies are allowed to enter for research and surveys.' There was a clearing down there too, only a few miles from the perimeter of Subang, the Kuala Lumpur airport, with a venerable stilted house standing in its centre, fashioned from weathered thatch and smoky grey wood. Here, presumably, the jungle studies experts lived, surrounded by the huge, silent trees of the rain forest, and I thought it looked the ideal retirement spot, secluded and peaceful, until I remembered that the thundering noise footprint of our Pratt & Whitneys must be rattling the old building like a tambourine.

We touched down on Subang's 11,397-foot runway with its circling guidance lights and parallel crash strip (pilots inbound with a bad Mayday situation were expected to dump their wreckage in the space provided) and, moments later, I was past the *Kounta Transit*, out of the airport and heading down a broad new motorway in an air-conditioned Toyota *teksi*. Kuala Lumpur is a handsome city cradled in green hills but the combative nature of its traffic jams made the Alor Setar morning rush hour seem as well-mannered as a vintage car rally. I booked into a hotel with a view of the Racecourse then headed for the Far East Freight Conference Association offices. They were within walking distance and, on the way, I bumped into the French tour leader who boarded the Thai Airways 737 at Hat Yai. He had just shipped his Germans home and was in high spirits. Also, the previous evening he managed to wangle himself an invitation to some high-powered reception for senior tourism executives where, to his delight, he had met the King. 'In this country he is the ultimate contact,' he told me.

'What's he like?'

'He is a very good egg,' said the Frenchman.

We shook hands and I hurried on to keep my appointment with Mr William Cook, an exceedingly amiable Far East hand of the old school who, before the war, worked for Mansfield's in Singapore. The company's interests had ranged from ownership of shipping fleets and the Singapore Steam Laundry to the agency for Imperial Airways.

Mr Cook consulted his watch. 'Let's chat over a spot of lunch,' he said. 'We'll go to the Dog.'

He summoned his driver and, in the car, said his youthful Singapore posting had been a very agreeable period of his life which had been terminated by the arrival of the Japanese forces. Before the city fell Mansfield's used the old Imperial pinnace – by then the property of a brand new corporation named BOAC, which had absorbed Imperial on April Fool's Day, 1940 – to ship refugees across the Malacca Straits to Sumatra. Some of Mansfield's own people got away in the last boatload. 'Frank Lane, the MD, was aboard, and so was Oliver Holt, a major shareholder and well-known local eccentric. Oliver loathed commerce and gave it all up to devote himself to Malay scholarship and a pretty little nutmeg plantation on the coast.'

The car pulled up beside a spacious, comfortable-looking white building which, despite a climate that attacks bricks and mortar like flame throwers and water cannon, had clearly stood there for a very long time.

'Here we are,' said Mr Cook, hopping out and leading me briskly indoors and up the stairs to the Long Bar. 'The Selangor Club, otherwise known as the Dog.' He ordered pink gins. 'It was founded a hundred years ago and has been a great KL institution ever since. The Prince of Wales came here in 1922 and scandalized everyone by dancing all night with a beautiful Eurasian girl from Ceylon. Every year there was a great ball on St George's Day when they carried in enormous sides of roast beef surrounded by blocks of ice with red roses frozen inside.' Mr Cook pointed to a balcony overlooking the *padang*, as trim and green as Lord's. 'And Noël Coward wrote *Mad Dogs and Englishmen* while sitting there watching a game of cricket.'

Our drinks finished, we processed slowly to our table, Mr Cook pausing to greet the occupants of all the other tables passed in transit. He greeted the waiter with equal warmth and, when starched napkins had been draped across our laps like vestments, said, 'I never flew with Imperial, I'm afraid. As far as I know the only person left in KL who did is a chap called Tan Sri Dato Mubin Sheppard. He's an Irish Muslim who's been out here since 1928. Before he embraced the faith and took his new name – Mubin means Mervyn – his middle initial was ff. Stood, I think, for ffolkes. So everyone calls him fuffuff. Not to his face, of course, but people will say, "Seen old fuffuff recently?" or "fuffuff was in jolly good form last night". He and I usually meet here for a curry lunch on Sundays and I happen to know he once went to Southampton on an Imperial flying boat. I imagine his recollections will be similar to everyone else's – sitting in a noisy old machine barging through the middle of the cu-nim at 9,000 feet and always finding the most interesting storms.'

We ate magnificent chicken curries washed down with cold Tiger beer and talked about mutual acquaintances and the decline of manners and moral standards in Britain. It was a conversation the Dog had heard many times before – indeed, I had the uneasy feeling that everyone else in the dining room was having it as well.

Later, back at my hotel, I called Tan Sri Dato Mubin Sheppard and asked if I could come and see him. But he said he was wrestling with the constitution of one of the many local societies he chaired; the members, against his advice, wanted the rules changed that very evening and he had a fight on his hands. Could I pop round in the morning? I explained that I had to catch an early plane to Singapore and suggested we talk on the phone instead.

'By all means!' he said in a surprisingly warm and youthful voice. 'Aren't you the chap who's interested in Imperial Airways? Bill Cook said you'd probably be in touch. I went on one of their flying boats. Did he tell you? From Colombo to Southampton after the war. Was it Imperial then?'

'BOAC,' I said.

'Oh, well, same lot, different nomenclature. Anyway, it was one of their *boats*, very spartan with its wartime decor, and dreadfully bumpy. They spilled my drinks all the way home. Usually we impoverished civil servants went P & O but I'd been delayed and had to get back in a hurry. The Japanese had locked me up for the duration – I was in Changi camp and then put to work on the railway – and several members of the Kempeitai, their military police, had given us a specially bad time. After the Surrender I heard they'd done a bunk to a little island off the Sumatra coast so I thought I'd fetch them back to face the music. It took three separate expeditions and I missed the last of the ships going home with the POWs. When I failed to show up my wife started firing off messages asking where on earth I'd got to, so they put me on an aeroplane. We landed on the Nile, I believe.'

'Yes?'

'I haven't been the *slightest* help to you,' he said cheerfully and, realizing that his interest in aviation matters was minimal, I asked about his adopted names.

'They're actually titles, old man. Tan Sri is an ancient one conferred by the Sultans on their chiefs. The first Prime Minister, Tunku Abdul Rahman, whose biography I have just completed, reinstated them for people who had performed a worthwhile service to the state. Tunku is the highest title, the equivalent of an earldom, while Dato is the third-ranking one. I've got two Datoships, probably for organizing the National Museum after independence and writing a lot of books about Malaysia. My field is the decorative arts and crafts – one of my books won a Gold Medal at the Italian Book Fair – but I've also brought out my autobiography. It's called *Memoirs of an Unorthodox Civil Servant*. The other thing perhaps you ought to know is that I'm 80.'

At 5 o'clock that evening Kuala Lumpur was struck by a terrific tropical storm. Thunder boomed over the city and bounced back off the hills while gunflash lightning made the dense monsoonal rain eerily luminous. Across the street a deep pit dug for the foundations of an office block was filling like a bath. Cars inched by with foaming brown water swirling over the bottoms of their doors. A wind sprang up and, on the Racecourse, waves began breaking.

Then, like a monstrous band marching off into the distance, the storm gradually faded away, leaving the mauve hills capped with cloud and wreathed in mist. From my vantage point Kuala Lumpur seemed so full of trees that it looked like a city camouflaged against the possibility of air attack. It was a pretty place and I would like to have stayed longer, but it wasn't one of my primary stops and I was obliged to hurry on. Between now and the end of my journey in Brisbane I had 25 more planes to catch.

An A300 Airbus was assigned to work MH 603 down to Singapore. Only a couple of dozen passengers boarded on this buoyant, sunny Saturday morning. After take-off a morose stewardess in a tight batik uniform brought me coffee and a little carton marked *krim*. As the red and green country slid by below I looked through *Wings of Gold*, MAS's glossy inflight magazine. The cover story was about Malaysian birds like the Asian Paradise Flycatcher, the Treepie and the Fire-Tufted Barbet, while the Customs Information section advised incoming travellers that among the items exempted from duty were 'Not more than 100 matchsticks' and 'Not more than 1 pair of footwear'. A useful six-language double-page spread entitled 'Getting By in the Orient' taught me that 'aeroplane' in Bahasa Malaysia is *kapalterbang* (in Japanese it's *hikoki*, in Tagalog *eroplano*) 'bank' is *bank*, 'book' is *buku*, 'bus' is *bas*, 'coffee' is *kopi* and 'hello' is *hello*. It's *hello* in Tagalog as well.

When the stewardess came to collect my cup I thought of singing 'You're the krim in my kopi,' but she gave me such a truculent look that I let it pass and turned back to *Wings of Gold*. The 'What's Up Doc' column posed a complex sequence of questions. 'Whenever you travel by air do your ears go "pop" or does your world go round and round? Do your ears ache or your eyes water? And do you suddenly find yourself farting and belching, much to your embarrassment and to the annoyance of your fellow-passengers?' If you suffered from any of these symptoms it was because the gas-filled cavities of your body were responding negatively to high-altitude travel. Gas in the gums can cause toothache, in the intestinal tract acute stomach pains; thus anyone prone to flatulence should avoid 'beans, cabbages, turnips and brussels sprouts' before a flight since, at 33,000 feet, they were likely to blow the victim up as explosively as a self-inflating dinghy. I read an item claiming that the 'French empress, Marie Louise, could move her ears at will, even turning them inside out', and then put the magazine away. Its name derives from the fact that MAS – Malaysian Airline System – is also the Bahasa Malaysia word for 'gold', a happy concidence made much of by the company's copywriters. Had they been true to the economic realities of the country, of course, their title would have made reference to wings of rubber or tin.

Our route took us past Seremban and Malacca, then down along the coast over Batu Pahat and Johor Bahru. The A300 rode easily through calm air and a sky cloudless but for a range of cumulus stacked up on the eastern horizon; we cruised almost four times as high and nearly five times as fast as the Atalantas that had travelled the route half a century earlier. They had been introduced in 1933, specially built by Sir W. G. Armstrong Whitworth Aircraft Ltd for Imperial's operations throughout the tropical regions of the Empire and were, according to the *Gazette*, 'a high-wing unbraced monoplane type, equipped with four Armstrong-Siddeley Double *Mongoose* air-cooled engines, of 340 horse power. The specification prepared by Imperial Airways demanded that the *Atalanta* class should have a cruising speed of 118 miles an hour, with an ability to maintain a height of 9,000 feet with any one of the four engines stopped, while carrying a paying load of 3,000 lbs – well over a ton and a quarter.' Each aircraft could accommodate a Captain, First Officer, Wireless Operator and nine passengers. 'One of the leading decorators in Great Britain' had been responsible for the passenger cabin. It had tilting chairs and sound-proofing. The windows were 'large and made of safety glass. Each aeroplane is provided with a lavatory. The luggage and freight space is situated between the passenger cabin and the Captain's control cabin, and there is a special compartment for the stowage of the Mail.' The aircraft was also provided with hat racks and a sliding roof.

A correspondent of the *Singapore Free Press*, who travelled up to KL on an Atalanta, reported that 'the plane remained unbelievably steady, with only very occasional "bumps" when she ran into an air pocket and suddenly lost a little height. On the silver wings the engines kept ticking away, sounding like a number of large sewing machines.' Midway through the flight the sight of the rain forest passing 9,000 feet below inspired him to write some very bad prose: 'One could not help wondering what might be the feelings of the denizens of the jungle when planes passed overhead. All primitive animals, not excluding man, are inspired by an overpowering fear when some phenomenon occurs which they do not understand.' He was bound for Simpang, the Kuala Lumpur Flying Club field to which Imperial then operated periodic services, having transferred from the city polo ground because the Sultans complained that the noise of the machines frightened their ponies.

As we began our descent through scattered wisps of cloud the skipper switched on his PA and gave us a chatty, protracted discourse on the Singapore weather which, by now, we could see perfectly well for ourselves. His self-evident assertion that it was a fine day provoked groans in the rear smoking section. We drifted over blue bays and islands, and saw the causeway bisecting the Johore Strait like a ruled line; the sun caught the windshields of cars making the crossing, Malaysians coming to Singapore for their Saturday shopping, Singaporeans escaping to spend the weekend on Malaysian beaches. Johore Bahru, at the mainland end, was a random scattering of highrise buildings. When the man from the *Free Press* flew over he noted only 'the mosque appearing like a small marble ornament which one might have used to decorate a table on the verandah'. The Singapore end of the causeway, stacked with tall office blocks, was merely a preface to the Lion City itself, an equatorial Manhattan glittering in the morning sun. Even from 3,000 feet it looked freshly scrubbed and polished, clean as a Swiss kitchen. Down there a thrifty, obedient, industrious people were pursuing and, through a selective breeding programme securing, their economic miracle – graduates were being urged to marry graduates – while teaching tidy-mindedness by imposing $500 fines on anyone who dropped a bus ticket in the street. Singapore inspires respect but little affection. We headed out over the Roads, where hundreds of tankers, bulk carriers, passenger vessels, freighters, pilgrim ships and coastal tramp steamers were moored in orderly rows. Away to the right Sumatra, huge and misty blue, loomed like a continent. The flaps and wheels went down, the cabin music system came on and we swept in low over Changi beach, its offshore water stained with effluent, and landed gently at Changi International.

Singapore's latest airport is an extraordinary place, its 235-foot-high control tower crowning a development with the dimensions of a city state. Horizontal travelators raced us through echoing halls to the Customs and Immigration desks, a set of eight race-track conveyor belts bringing our luggage close behind. I asked an official where the barber was. At Paya Lebar, the old airport, a stout woman in white overalls sat phlegmatically by the Immigration barrier with a box of combs and scissors. Any long-haired males wishing to enter Singapore either submitted to an instant trim or caught the next plane out. The official said, 'The barber is still here, but now she has an *office*.'

At a duty-free emporium near the entrance a stern, bony girl with a heavy cold refused to sell me anything; passengers inbound from Malaysia did not qualify for the reduced prices. I went out to Arrival Crescent and caught a taxi. We set off down the East Coast Parkway, a broad new road with flower boxes set between the carriageways. Each contained a brave display of bright blossoms and leaves, carefully watered and tended, and they went on for miles. Bemused, I asked the driver, who wore gold-rimmed spectacles, what they were for.

'Defence emergency,' he said.

I stared at him. 'The Army's going to throw flowers?'

'If we are invaded they will move the boxes to one side. Then the road becomes a runway. It has been specially strengthened and reinforced. 747s can operate from this road.' He turned solemnly. 'So can Concorde.'

Raffles Hotel still stands at Number One Beach Road, though Singapore's formidable land reclamation programme has moved the beach way over towards Sumatra; the sea, visible from the hotel a dozen years ago, is now just a memory. I got one of the cheapo rooms stuck away behind the Arcade then went to the Palm Court for a cold Tiger beer. When it isn't swarming with coach parties this is one of the Seven Wonders of my World. It was empty now, suffused with a heavy morning calm, and I sat and surveyed the airy French Renaissance edifice enclosing an enchanted garden splashed with the inky shadows of 13 species of palm. Doves, kingfishers, black-naped orioles and gaudy Painted Jezebel butterflies barn-stormed through the trees while the scents from the frangipani and bougainvillaea numbed the mind like nerve gas. It was here, working steadily in the cool of the mornings, that Somerset Maugham, a Raffles regular, is believed to have written all, or part, of *The Moon and Sixpence*.

Much of the hotel's faded eminence is founded on the legendary authors who once patronized the place. In *From Sea to Sea* Kipling noted, 'Providence conducted me along a beach, in full view of five miles of shipping – five solid miles of masts and funnels – to a place called Raffles Hotel where the food is excellent, let the traveller take note. Feed at Raffles, when in Singapore.' (His waspish postscript, 'but sleep at the Hotel de l'Europe', is not included in the brochures.) And, according to the authorized version, Conrad was leafing through *The Straits Times* on the balcony after breakfast when he noted a report about British officers deserting a pilgrim ship on its way to Jedda, leaving their charges to drown. An idea took root which emerged, in 1900, as *Lord Jim*. The management cannot prove the story is true but, on the other hand, they are well aware that sceptics would be hard-pressed to prove it isn't. Today it has assumed the status of legend, and is left alone because people know the fabric of Raffles is too venerable to stand the strain of major structural alteration.

I finished my beer and went to see Doris Geddes, a vivacious, doughty Australian I met on my previous visit seven years earlier. For close on half a century she had run a boutique in the Arcade but now it was closed and, taking an early lunch in the Tiffin Room, I consulted a cutting of the piece I had written about her then: 'Raffles was the centre of *everything*. Lord Nuffield stayed here and became a great friend. Such a simple man; people mistook him for a taxi driver. And Noël Coward used to drop in with his four friends to say hullo and look at my batiks. He loved that very English undercurrent of nonsense that was always going on here. I used to put on fashion shows for charity at Raffles, but my greatest success was out in the Roads, on a boat. The Fleet was in and I said to the Admiral, "You must lend me a battleship." He said, "Doris, my dear, you may have HMS *Terror*." It was a great occasion, and everyone who mattered in Malaya was there.'

She had kept the programme. It contained ads for Ho Ho biscuits, for Robert Donat and Greer Garson in *Goodbye Mr Chips* ('destined to be the star sensation of 1939') and Imperial Airways ('England less than a week away'), as well as pictures of all the Archipelago's pretty society women with their untroubled buttermilk faces, the cream of the shires transposed to the tropics.

At a neighbouring table two elderly Japanese men sat with their wives, talking quietly, and I idly wondered whether they had been here during the Occupation and were remarking that the old place hadn't changed much. Shortly before the Japanese forces arrived at Raffles – led by a colonel named Nakajima who, before the war, had sold shirts in the Arcade – the staff buried all the hotel silver (including a large, ornate beef trolley) in the Palm Court and then maintained an obdurate silence about its whereabouts. A senior officer of the Kempeitei became so obsessed with the beef trolley that he spent much of his war looking for it, periodically torturing staff members and summoning them to compulsory beef trolley parades. They also had to assemble in the ballroom each morning, bow to the east and sing the Japanese national anthem; and each evening at dusk the officers fell in naked on the grass to do sword drill.

Raffles was founded in 1886 by three Armenian brothers named Sarkies – one of whom also started the E & O in Penang. They offered 18-course dinners, and breakfasts consisting of porridge, fried fish, mutton chops, devilled fowl, cold beef salad, boiled eggs, cheese, toast, jam, tea and Benedictine, and soon the British expatriates were fondly claiming the place for their own. The Sarkies were able to boast that theirs 'was the only hotel in the Straits lighted with Electricity, Electric Bells, Electric Fans, Spacious Green Lawns & Lawn Tennis'. They also offered free roller-skating facilities, and among those who came to sample these delights were the King and Queen of Siam, Grand Duke Cyril of Russia, the Sultan of Johore and numerous British admirals who, propped at the Long Bar, could keep an eye on their respective fleets through the bottoms of their gin glasses. One of the regulars shot a tiger in the billiards room. Another liked to traverse all the Tiffin Room tables by jumping from one to the other without spilling anyone's wine. And yet another – a French champagne millionaire –

rewarded the staff by mustering them at the foot of a staircase and throwing down handfuls of gold coins.

The first air passengers to arrive in Singapore – and put up at Raffles – were Van Lear Black, the American industrialist owner of the *Baltimore Sun*, and Leo Bayline, his butler. They flew in on 29 June 1927 aboard a chartered KLM Fokker commanded by the great Captain Geyssendorfer who inadvertently damaged its tail while landing on the rutted Balestier Plain. While Geyssendorfer was getting it repaired at the United Engineers workshop in River Valley Road, Van Lear Black told the assembled throng, which included the Governor, Sir Hugh Clifford, and members of the Diplomatic Corps, that he was just making a casual journey around the Far East. He had vague plans to explore a little further – 'If I feel inclined I may take in Australia' – but later, on reaching Batavia, changed his mind and returned to Amsterdam. Van Lear Black had the Fokker fitted with a cocktail bar and a deep pile red carpet and, each morning before departure, liked the cabin to be filled with freshly picked orchids. Mr Bayline supervised the packing and stowing of the luncheon baskets and, when he wasn't serving up their contents, spent the hours aloft inventing and testing new cocktails. He said, 'Duty on board to me is all in a day's work. I go about it just as if I was in a hotel.'

What Black and Bayline thought of Raffles is not known. The passengers who followed on the Imperial services were quicker to go on record. An Australian who spent the night there in January 1937 wrote that 'The Raffles Hotel at Singapore, one of the most famous in the world, well justifies its reputation. The size and comfort of my suite gave me such a surprise that I felt there must be some mistake. It was 17 yards square and furnished with very good modern furniture. Yesterday being the first day of the Singapore races Raffles was packed for dinner and the dancing afterwards. At a table near the one at which Captain Scotty Allan (the famous Qantas pilot who will fly the mail down on Monday) and I sat to watch the dancing were two very dapper Singapore Chinese men dancing with two beautifully dressed Chinese girls.'

And Philip S. Rudder wrote in the *Sydney Morning Herald*, 'Our starting place was "Raffles", romantic and old-fashioned, probably the best-known hotel in the world. At 4 a.m. we were awakened and given an early cup of tea; without delay bags were packed, and before five the cars left the hotel. It was quite dark, and Singapore was fast asleep. Half-an-hour's drive through native villages and rubber plantations and we were at the aerodrome. The usual formalities were quickly over, baggage stowed, good-byes said and all on board. At six sharp Captain Mollard revved up the four engines of the beautiful *Athena*, and soon the great ship was roaring down the flare-lit runway. In 20 seconds we were on our way, heading for Alor Star, and to me almost brand new experiences. We had breakfast on the plane at eight o'clock; a hamper had been packed for each passenger by "Raffles", and we eagerly got to work on the coffee, rolls, sandwiches, hard-boiled eggs and fruit.'

Though it was a week since I had picked up the gastric infection on the Two Down from Kanpur, periodic stomach cramps warned that my terrorist bacteria were still dug in and ready to try more of their human wave-style attacks. I had finished the German doctor's tablets so I set off to find a chemist's shop in the streets behind the hotel. Giant buildings were going up all around, erected by tiny figures working at such altitudes that they must have been able to nod to pilots passing on the way into Changi. This was to be Raffles City, part of an ambitious master plan aimed at giving Singapore more tourist accommodation than any other comparable-sized place on earth – while simultaneously knocking down everything the tourists had come to see. Bugis Street, with its raffish air and famous strolling transvestites, was already demolished, and only a last-minute reprieve had saved Raffles itself. When the development was completed the hotel would be enclosed by tower blocks, looking like an ornate French pastry at the bottom of a cookie jar.

I found a tiny pharmacy, smelling like a herbalist's, where an elderly Chinese woman sold me some tablets but made me sign the Poisons Register first. Outside a man fell into step beside me and offered to buy my US dollars. I said I had none to spare. As we walked I remarked on the construction going on all around and he pointed to the miniature figures working high on the scaffolding. 'Koreans!' he said, and made a rude gesture. 'Animals!'

Back in my room there was a message confirming my meeting with Harold Foley, the man who had worked in the Penang control tower, and another from a *Straits Times* reporter who wished to interview me the following day. I sat in the Palm Court until it was time to visit Mr Foley. An Alitalia DC10 crew were sunbathing on the grass. Both pilots had hairy backs, heavy jowls and gold chains around their necks, and were being ministered to by a couple of tall blonde stewardesses who fussed over them like mothers, oiling them, adjusting the towels over their heads, ordering (and paying for) their iced drinks, whispering to them as they lay sweating in the heat. The pilots grunted from time to time but otherwise made no attempt at speech.

That evening, in the Tiger Bar, I spoke to an Australian who said I had chosen a bad time to travel down through the Indonesian Archipelago. A succession of typhoons were chasing each other away to the east of Java and out into the western Pacific. 'How far are you going?' he asked.

'Timor.'

'Oh, they won't let you into Timor,' he said. 'There's a civil war going on. The Indonesians are killing people. There're even killing journos. A couple of years back the army murdered some Aussie TV reporters.'

I knew that, but pointed out that the Indonesian Embassy in London had promised there would be no problem about visiting Timor. He laughed. 'That's the official line, that there's no problem on Timor and no problem about getting there. There's no problem because they're not going to let you in. They'll just stop you boarding the plane. You follow? Then it's not their problem, it's your problem, so far as they're concerned it's no bloody problem at all.'

I was in the Tiger Bar to meet an Englishman named Mike King, a Singapore Airlines 747 skipper and a friend of one of my neighbours in London. A pleasant, low-key sort of man, recently widowed, he had once worked for British Airways but, several years earlier, decided he wanted a job out East. His daughter, a trainee air traffic controller in England, was consistently coming near the top of her course; recently she had taken her twin-engined pilot's licence. Mike periodically flew the SIA service to London and, one of these days, she would be saying, 'Good morning, Singapore two two, maintain present altitude and heading, please,' then bringing her own father into Heathrow. He reckoned that would be the proudest moment of his life. We strolled to a satay stall near the sea front and had chicken and pork roasted on skewers and served with wonderful savoury peanut sauces. SIA, he said, suited his temperament better than BA. There, when making inflight announcements, for example, he was expected to call himself Captain King, but now he had become just plain Mike King speaking from the flight deck, which contributed significantly to the relaxed atmosphere he urged his crew to achieve. His aim was to give everyone a pleasant, trouble-free ride. If he hit turbulence, for example, he always throttled back to minimize the wear and tear on people's nerves (not everyone did that) and, when things were quiet, liked to go and talk to the customers, specially the ones in Business Class. 'They're hard-nosed, cheeky sods,' he said, 'usually good for a laugh.'

We were sharing our table with a Viennese in the freight business and a young Singaporean who ran his local office. The Singaporean had put away a lot of beer and, overhearing our conversation, alleged truculently that the SIA 747s had to have European captains since Lloyd's of London would not otherwise insure their hulls. What did we think of that? Perspiration beaded the young man's brow. He was becoming tremendously indignant. 'It simply isn't true, my dear,' the Viennese said soothingly. 'My flight yesterday was commanded by a Singaporean, a tall fellow, *very* good-looking. Now drink your beer and don't fuss.'

Mike went home and I called at the Raffles Long Bar for a nightcap. On my last visit here an old planter had told me this was traditionally the place where expatriates came to lay down their White Man's Burden for an hour or two. 'I remember a chap called George,' he had said, '19 stone at least, going on 20, and he always concluded the evening with his impersonation of a dying elephant. "Watch this," he would say after his last gin pahit, and then, very slowly, he'd topple off his bar stool, crash to the ground and just lie there. It used to frighten strangers, who'd assumed he'd been taken ill, but he could fall like a cat and, to the best of my knowledge, George never hurt himself at all.'

The planter had drained his glass of mother's ruin and announced he was off for a curry and a spot of Egyptian PT, and now I noted that he and his like seemed to have departed for good. Tonight the Long Bar was crowded with tourists, many of them Japanese. An unshaven, poorly dressed Indian walked in, hesitated a moment then approached me. 'You like nice souvenir?' he asked and produced, from a hessian bag, a 12-inch-high figure of a monk. It wore a long robe, a hood and an expression of extreme piety, and its hands were clasped in an attitude of prayer. The pedlar pressed a concealed button in its back and a huge penis swung up through the folds of the monk's robe and locked into the erect position. The Japanese, both men and women, clustered around with shouts of laughter and, as I commenced the long march back to my room, fierce bidding for the figure was already under way. I recalled that I had seen one before, on Bugis Street, when the most baffling thing about that pleasant, disreputable old thoroughfare had been not its gorgeous resident transvestites, but a gang of small boys who patrolled the bars and clubs playing noughts and crosses for money, winner take all. They were infallible and unbeatable. On the plane home I sat beside an Edinburgh accountant who, after being thrashed repeatedly, lay awake for hours trying to puzzle out their system. 'I've got a maths degree from Cambridge,' he said, 'and I still haven't a clue how the wee buggers do it.'

Singapore! When those kids grew up and took over the running of this purposeful, ambitious little island the rest of us wouldn't stand a chance.

5
THROUGH THE
SPICE ISLANDS

From Singapore to Darwin

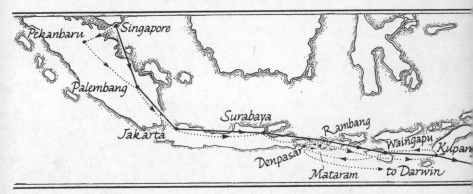

I

During the night successive storms hit Singapore like waves of bombers, filling the sky with noise and rippling flashes of light. I slept fitfully, nagged by worries about Timor, a famous stop on the old route and the launching point for the long overwater leg to Australia; headwinds or tropical depressions had often made this a real wing-and-a-prayer, white-knuckle sector, and being barred would weaken the credibility of my journey. But then I awoke to the optimism of a bright morning and, after breakfast, went to the Palm Court to meet the reporter from the *Straits Times*. Lee Geok Boi was a chic, quick-witted divorcee who asked precise questions and marshalled her material as briskly as a barrister preparing a brief. She began with my reasons for making the journey ('Flying was a great adventure. Even being a passenger was a great adventure,' she wrote in the paper's review front a week later. 'The deputy editor of the Sunday magazine of the *Observer* newspaper in London flew in for 24 hours recently to do part of his research for his book on air travel. "There is a long literary tradition of writing about travel by sea, but there are almost no books about travelling by air," he says. So he decided to write this book. "I'm describing the world I see as I go across it. It's a bird's eye view." ') Then she quizzed me about civil aviation in the 1930s, asked about the logistics of my trip ('Mr Frater's British Airways ticket could well be the longest airline ticket ever written. It has 53 sectors in it, and was certainly the longest ticket BA had ever issued. The travel agent has submitted it to the Guinness Book of World Records') and wondered how I felt about it all generally. ('Doing research for his book has been exciting, but exhausting. He is looking forward to home-cooked meals and being back home with his wife and two teenaged children.')

Afterwards Miss Lee packed me into her car and drove me to the airport. She lived near Changi and told me that, following the government's directive, she had wed a fellow-graduate but it hadn't worked out; brains weren't everything, and the authorities seemed unable to comprehend that there was more to marriage than compatible IQs. As I said goodbye and entered the terminal it began to rain, a solid equatorial downpour that pinged off the windows like buckshot and turned the apron into a flooding estuary. Mechanics in waterproof capes were dismantling the No. 4 engine of a BA 747 parked at a nearby gate, its paintwork discoloured as a tramp steamer's, smoky black smudges staining the humming auxiliary power unit at its tail. Beside a neighbouring gate a gleaming SIA 747, so clean you could have eaten food off its wings, was being readied for departure. Though the grimy, grounded British plane served as a gloomy reminder of cuts and recession back home, it was still a sentimental link and I found myself counting the days till my return. Fifteen to go, and I recalled that, only five hours after the scheduled arrival of my flight at Heathrow, I had to be in the St Paul's crypt for my son's confirmation. I thought of all the things that could go wrong between then and now, and added the St Paul's worry to my Timor worry.

A Thai Airbus splashed down on the sodden runway and the terminal's huge electric indicator board announced that GA 901, the Garuda Indonesian Airlines service to Pekanbaru and Palembang – where the London service stopped for fuel – would be boarding in 20 minutes. Looking around Changi's streaming acres it seemed entirely in keeping with Singapore's bustling ambition that this should be its fourth airport in only 50 years. The first Imperial flights operated into RAF Seletar, on the northeast coast, but switched in 1937 to the Singapore Marine and Land Airport at Kallang. An anonymous Australian, inbound from Brisbane, described it in the *Gazette*: 'Coming in over the town we saw the incomplete but already famous new civil airport, which has already cost over one million sterling and some say will have cost between two and three millions before in use. On landing at the Air Force aerodrome, which is still in use by the airways, I was taken to see Air Commodore Sidney Smith, who has been in command at Singapore for the past two and a half years, developing the wonderful station and advising the local government how to construct the new civil airport. He has very kindly asked me to stay on the way back so that he can show me how the work was carried out and teach me some of the elementary principles of operating flying boats.'

Kallang had a circular grass landing area, a terminal, two hangars and a concrete slipway where the thrice-weekly Empire boats, on arrival from Southampton, could be winched ashore for repairs and routine maintenance. The passengers, after their night at Raffles, transferred to an aircraft wearing the livery of Qantas Empire Airways, a new company incorporated in January 1934 with Imperial holding 50 per cent of the stock. Initially Qantas confined itself to operating the Brisbane to Darwin sectors but, in 1935, using flimsy little British-built De Havilland 86 land planes, they assumed responsibility for the route all the way to Singapore. In April the first joint passenger service set off from Croydon to Brisbane, cutting the journey time to 12 days, a saving of 60 hours. The introduction of the Empires by both companies two years later reduced it to a speedy nine and a half days.

Kallang was closed in 1955 and the new airport at Paya Lebar brought into commission. To build it they felled 30,000 coconut palms, cleared 900 acres, moved five million tons of earth and installed storm drains that could disperse an inch of rainwater in ten minutes. But it wasn't enough. A ground with third division facilities had been provided for a club hellbent on a place in the first, so the authorities commandeered the sleepy military strip at Changi and started all over again. The new terminal, a towering high-tech cathedral, sits astride the most spectacular airport in South East Asia. Inherent in its design is the possibility of virtually unlimited expansion; theoretically, reclaimed land could extend the runways so far out that supplementary windsocks would have to be planted on Sumatra.

The Pekanbaru flight was called. I joined eleven Indonesians and a stooped, bony Dutchman on a bus which set off through the monsoon towards one of Changi's sixteen 'remote' aircraft stands, the wipers merely rearranging the water on the windscreen like swizzle sticks stirring gin. Our little Garuda Fokker Fellowship twin-jet was parked between a dripping Swissair DC10 and an Air Niugini 707 with a crimson bird-of-paradise painted on its tail. We dashed up the Fokker's airstairs into its tiny, puddled entrance lobby. A plump, grumpy-looking stewardess in an incandescent orange uniform raised the airstairs as the two pod-mounted Rolls-Royce turbofans roared into life. The aircraft sloshed through the downpour to the threshold of Runway O2, swung on to the centre line and blasted away as though being launched from a carrier.

Seconds later we were climbing through bright sunshine across a sparkling summery sea. Craning back to see the black clouds sitting over Singapore like tethered balloons, I recalled that somewhere down there Cobham had landed and gone ashore to be welcomed by the Colonial Secretary, who formally received him on the steps of the Yacht Club jetty. That night a dinner was held in his honour which Ward, the mechanic, attended in a borrowed outsize monkey suit so rigorously pinned that the poor man suffered an involuntary tattooing each time he lifted the fork to his mouth.

They flew on to Banka, an island off the Sumatran coast. Our course took us north, across islands like Rangsang, where peaty brown creeks curled down the beaches and spilled discoloured rain water into the sea, and Padang, one of a quartet of interlocking islands shaped like a formalized bird with outstretched wings, the four elements fitting as precisely as pieces of lustrous green mosaic. The hostesses distributed cardboard boxes containing curried egg sandwiches, a small can of Schweppes sparkling orange and a bar of Van Houten Finest Milk Chocolate. Indonesian immigration and customs forms came next, the latter prohibiting the import of pornographic objects or publications and, curiously, all 'printed matters in Chinese charachter'.

The bony Dutchman, with whom I traded an egg sandwich for a chocolate bar, said the Chinese literature ban stemmed from 1965 when there had been an attempted Communist coup, Peking-inspired. It in turn led to an anti-Communist backlash that, with army encouragement, resulted in a five-month-long programme of mass murder. Though I paid my first visit to Indonesia – a Qantas inaugural to Bali – at least four years after the killing had stopped, there were still bullet holes in the masonry and a feeling of unreality in the air. I learned that the open season had not been restricted to killing Communists. It was used to settle personal scores as well – family feuds, quarrels with landlords and neighbours, outstanding debts; the life expectancy of moneylenders who failed to hide in the forest suddenly assumed a mothlike ephemerality. On Bali estimates of the death toll ranged from 50,000 to 100,00. No one had precise figures. Throughout the country it was put at half a million, possibly higher.

My visit coincided with the period when, like patients coming out of shock, people were starting to talk about their experiences. I met an affable young man in a bar who, getting a little drunk, told me that he and two of his friends had gone to the house of their schoolteacher one evening and, as he poured glasses of lemonade for them, cut his throat. It seemed that the teacher, an incorrigible Maoist, of course, had also failed the boys in an English exam. I recounted this to the Dutchman who shrugged and said stories like that could be repeated till the cows came home. Living in Indonesia you heard so many that they ceased to have any real dimension or meaning.

He told me he worked for an oil exploration company and was bringing in a new drilling component that had cost a king's ransom in freight charges. 'Pekanbaru is a real hole,' he said. 'It is the kind of place where people go troppo. You know this expression? The first symptoms are when you start having gin for breakfast and keep forgetting the names of your own children.'

The Fokker crossed the village of Perawang. The country below was a lifeless vista of viridescent swamp punctuated by the occasional oily gleam of stagnant water and small, drifting miasmas of mist. The Dutchman said you got fevers down there that medical science didn't even know about. Then the wetlands gave way to primary jungle and we began our descent, banking steeply over a clearing with a township in it. The houses were roofed with dazzling silver tin that caught and concentrated the sun like giant lenses, stinging the naked eye. The place had a raw, frontier look and, but for a few scraggy palms, seemed almost entirely bereft of shade.

'There it is,' said the Dutchman, resignedly. 'The Jewel of Sumatra. Down there the mosquitoes are so big you need stitches when they bite you.'

I laughed and he grinned at me. 'Ach, it's not such a bad little dorp,' he said. 'At least the natives are friendly.'

We slid over a green-roofed terminal with the word PEKAN-BARU painted on it in large white capitals and made a bouncy touchdown watched by a solitary black ape sitting in a chestnut tree. Midway through the announcement from the Fokker's small forward pantry – 'We have landed at Simpang Tiga airport, Pekanbaru. All passengers must disembark heah; passenger going Palembang on dis plane, flight GA 221 at 1500, must kumbak in one hour' – heavy rock music crashed through the speakers and the stewardess, exasperated, shouted, 'I am make cabin PA!' The two pilots, who had switched on a portable cassette player, sat snapping their fingers and banging their control columns in time. The youthful skipper wore three stripes and his teenage co-pilot one. As we disembarked the Dutchman said, 'That noise is made by Meatloaf. My daughter plays it. It brings on my migraine.'

The heat on the tarmac at Simpang Tiga reminded me that we were only 50 miles north of the Equator. The air shimmered, as though it had spontaneously ignited and was burning with a slow, colourless flame. The Dutchman, supervising the unloading of his drilling component from the forward hold, warned the baggage handlers that it was very, very heavy. They nodded sagely then gave whoops of surprise as it crashed on to the trolley, splintering part of its timber crate. The Dutchman sighed.

Two adjoining pathways, perhaps 150 metres long, led to the terminal. One, shrub-lined, was reserved for VIPs; both conducted arriving passengers towards a giant painting of President Suharto, the general who had vanquished the Communists and now led the nation. The portrait, badly weathered but still the most dominating factor in that steaming landscape, glared straight down the pathways, the eyes fixed as though watching through a gunsight.

At the terminal the shrub-lined VIP pathway led into the dark, empty VIP room, its flyscreen door propped open with a bucket, while the commoners' pathway terminated at the annexe housing the Customs and Immigration desks. This was my Indonesian point of entry, but my passport, with its London visa, was stamped without comment and a small Customs official in a rumpled, sweat-stained uniform said, 'All personal effek?' and chalked a hieroglyphic on my bag before I could answer. I was told to wait with the other half-dozen Palembang-bound passengers in a patio next to the VIP entrance. But first I said goodbye to the Dutchman, who stood frowning, with his hands in his pockets. The trolley containing his drilling component had to be negotiated up a six-inch concrete step, and the baggage handlers were proposing to make a high-speed run at it. Even as he urged them to take it in careful stages they were off, working up such a momentum that, when the front wheels hit the step, the circular component shot off the front, shed the remainder of its timber casing and rolled back down again with a noise like a falling tree. The Dutchman's remonstrations were lost in the yells of laughter from the baggage handlers who, balancing the thing on its rim and bowling it along like an old tyre, finally got it up and over, reducing much of the step to rubble.

The Palembang flight was not called. Instead, one of the passengers suddenly stood and walked slowly away down the pathway towards the Fokker. A moment later a young woman carrying a large basket got up and followed. Then a grizzled, grey-looking man with an injured leg set off too, leaning on the shoulder of his plump, placid wife. I offered him an arm. He hobbled along wordlessly, face furrowed with pain. Blood had soaked through the soiled bandages and the smell of putrefaction was very strong. When we reached the foot of the Fokker's airstairs the wife thanked me with a tranquil smile but did not speak. Rock music was still thundering from the flight deck. The pilots, though, had changed their tape and were now playing the Rolling Stones in concert.

Imperial may have pioneered the Singapore to Australia section of the Eastern route, but the Australian Government insisted on the right to nominate the company which would actually exploit this tract of its own hemisphere. Imperial joined forces with Qantas to tender for the service – to the dismay of Sir Charles Kingsford Smith who, with his airline, Australian National Airways, had carried the Royal Mail between Britain and Australia often enough to believe that the English – always quick to call on him when they required assistance – were acting maliciously. (The controversy was later blamed by some for Kingsford Smith's death; unwell, driven by despair and the need to win back public esteem, they claimed he had undertaken his ill-fated record attempt when wholly unfit to fly.) Imperial and Qantas announced their agreement in the November 1933 issue of the *Gazette* which, as the Fokker started up and prepared to taxi, I opened and read.

'A "concordat" has been established between Imperial Airways and The Queensland and Northern Territory Aerial Services, Ltd. "for the formation of a joint company to tender for, and if successful in the tender, to operate the Singapore-Darwin-Brisbane section of the England-Australia service", and we think that our readers will be interested to know something about this pioneer company.

'The Queensland and Northern Territory Aerial Services, Ltd., familiarly known as Q.A.N.T.A.S., came into existence in the year 1920 when two Western Queensland sheep squatters, Mr Fergus McMaster and Mr A.N. Templeton, and two pilots, late of the Royal Australian Air Force, Mr Hudson Fysh and Mr McGinness, met in a hotel in Brisbane to discuss the idea of forming an air service to serve Queensland. All of them were impressed by the lack of communication in Western Queensland, especially during the winter, for then all travel was impossible owing to the absence of roads and bridges, and although there were three railways running from points on the coast far inland, they were not connected at their heads. This, to the founders of Q.A.N.T.A.S., seemed an excellent place to establish an air transport line.'

Several paragraphs followed describing the company's progress from an itinerant backwoods provider of joy rides to a successful carrier of passengers (2,661 in 1932), mail and freight. The piece concluded with a sales pitch aimed at the Australian Government promising that the new partners, if awarded the tender, would provide 'the best possible air service between Australia and England'.

The Fokker climbed away from Pekanbaru – at which, in fact, neither airline had called – and crossed a broad, sluggish river. The flight deck door stood open and I saw our boy captain exclaiming and pointing animatedly at something below. The stewardess hurried forward to look and returned smiling to say that a tiger had been sighted drinking in the river. A quarter of an hour later we crossed the Equator. It was burning. A straggly cloud of heavy white smoke ran along it for perhaps 50 miles, slowly consuming the rain forest – stands of sandalwood, satinwood, camphorwood, ironwood, ebony, teak, oak, koko and black chuglam. Once I thought I saw tiny tongues of flame bursting from the trees, but the flames suddenly merged and took flight, a flock of parakeets. A stewardess brought me a cup of rich, dark, Sumatran coffee and said the fire had been burning for months. There was no one down there to fight it. She knew of other forest fires, even larger, which had been going so long they were regarded by the pilots as navigational landmarks, like hills or lakes. The fires had been started by careless charcoal burners. I tried the coffee, which tasted tarry and had a kick like rum.

Away to the right another river glinted brassily in the hazy sun. My six fellow passengers slumbered in their seats, the sick old man lying with his bad leg propped on his wife's knees. The girl with the basket muttered in her sleep while, several rows behind, a thin, exhausted child with a pink plastic bow in her lank hair was curled up like a cat, face pressed into her mother's ample rump. Nearby her father dozed with his mouth open, a single gold incisor glittering among a blackened array of stumps. He wore tattered shorts and a stained pith helmet, like an old campaigner from the Viet Cong.

What made their repose remarkable was the level of noise coming from the flight deck. The pilots, unable to play their cassette machine, had diverted themselves by turning up the volume of their radios so that the cabin reverberated with the roar of static and a babble of disembodied voices. I caught odd phrases – 'Seven oh one passing two thousand,' 'Thirty to run to the field,' 'Okay, Jakarta, I accept a six knot tailwind,' 'Seven two six, you are fully establish on glide slope,' 'Report on track clearing 3,000,' and then a deep, theatrical delivery, reminiscent of Orson Welles, saying calmly, 'That's affirmative, we've taken a lightning strike.' A lightning strike! I strained to hear the rest but suddenly an English voice cut in, plummy and self-assured, seeking clearance to climb to a new height. It sounded middle-class and middle-aged, and I was still trying to get the measure of its owner – the Rover, the comfortable detached house in Reading or Maidenhead (handy for Heathrow), perhaps the small antiques business run as a sideline – when he was drowned out by a surge of other voices, like a controversial orator being shouted down by his audience.

The skipper climbed out of his seat and went to the galley for a Coke. I joined him there. He offered me a cigarette flavoured with cloves and I asked if he had ever been struck by lightning. He said yes, once, while flying a small De Havilland Twin Otter from Sumba to Flores in 1977. There was a sudden bang and a fireball passed between the pilots, rolled slowly down the aisle then exited through the tail. It had been about the size of a beachball and left tiny holes in the front and rear of the fuselage. The skipper, who had a smooth, unlined face and deepset eyes, added that a lightning fireball could weld your controls together, turning them into artefacts immobile as cast iron.

The Fokker entered a stretch of turbulence. The skipper stuck the cigarette in his mouth and, head wreathed in clove-scented smoke, returned to his seat, strapped himself in and began singing in a loud, tuneless voice, 'By the rivers of Babylon, where we sat down/And there we wept when we remembered Zion.' He turned down the radios and sang it again at such volume that the stewardesses giggled and made faces. The motion of the plane was frisky but repetitive, like a flat stone bouncing across the surface of a pond. It woke the girl with the basket. She stretched and yawned then undid the buttons of her red blouse and slowly rubbed her breasts. From the basket, resting on the neighbouring seat, she lifted a linen-wrapped bundle and peeled back the top to reveal the pale, wrinkled head of a sleeping baby. It began to drink, but the skittish ride kept pulling the nipple from its mouth; each time, soundlessly, doggedly, the baby retrieved it. Now the Fokker ceased skipping and began steeplechasing through the sky, whipped on by a curious force that kept kicking the tail sideways and making us pitch and yaw. The co-pilot clutched the glareshield to steady himself while his commander sang, 'Let the words of our mouths and the meditations of our hearts/Be acceptable in Thy sight here *tonight*.'

Far below I saw a tin-roofed camp set in a forest clearing. Winding tracks of red earth connected the camp with three low green hills, and I wondered what the inhabitants of that remote little place sought in those hills. Sumatra, an island prodigiously endowed by nature, produces a third of Indonesia's timber, together with an abundance of rubber, coffee, tea, tobacco, palm oil, sisal, betel nuts, copra, kapok, peanuts and pepper. Deeper down the soil harbours vast reserves of oil, tin, coal, bauxite, tungsten, silver and gold. From time to time the Sumatrans, wishing to keep all this munificence to themselves, rise up and declare their island a sovereign state. Jakarta gives them very short shrift. President Suharto shoots the ringleaders and stamps down hard on everyone else. The survivors return to the forest and lie low until the next time. But one day, they think, they will win.

The earth vanished as we flew into thick cloud. Moisture streamed across the windows like barley water. The lame old man had woken, and so had his wife. She gazed at the bandaged leg resting on her lap then prodded the swollen, discoloured foot with a finger, as though testing the ripeness of a piece of fruit. Her husband neither moved nor spoke. His face was grey and beaded with sweat and I reckoned he would be lucky to see out the week.

The skipper had stopped singing and turned the radios back on. We descended, breaking clear of the cloud a few hundred feet over a swampy jungle clearing that gleamed in the dull evening light like copper. There were shallow pits brimming with muddy red water near the runway threshold. The Fokker touched down and parked beside a boxy, businesslike aeroplane being prepared for departure. Two men awaited me at the foot of the airstairs. One wore a natty linen safari suit and had a thin, intelligent, rather ascetic face. He gave me a courtly little bow and extended his hand. 'I am Soebijanto, Manager, Talangbetutu Airport, Palembang.'

His companion, a small man with a bushy moustache and a twinkle in his eye, said, 'And I am Suwarsono, Chief Fire Officer.'

'Welcome,' said Mr Soebijanto.

'And welcome also from Aerodrome Fire Fighter Section!' declared Mr Suwarsono.

They were telling me that Jakarta, acting on advice from the London Embassy, had instructed them to meet me, when the boxy aeroplane started its engines. As the shrieking turbo-props gushed plumes of blue smoke Mr Soebijanto put his mouth to my ear and shouted, 'That is joint Spanish-Indonesian collaboration, 20-seater for operating from short, primitive strips, the Cassa 212.'

'Charlie Alpha Sierra Sierra Alpha!' yelled Chief Fire Officer Suwarsono. 'Cassa!'

He pronounced 'Sierra Sierra' as in the Italian 'Che sera sera', an expression indicating a degree of fatalism that seemed not inappropriate for a heavier-than-air machine designed by Spaniards and Indonesians. The small, low-ceilinged terminal was thronged with sightseers. Mr Soebijanto said there wasn't much else to do in Palembang. 'It makes nice recreation,' he murmured. Out in a deeply puddled yard a new Daihatsu jeep gleamed under the dripping trees. Mr Soebijanto took the wheel and we lurched away through a wood and on to the Palembang road. Neither of my companions were Sumatrans, and both held the Sumatrans in low esteem. 'They are rough, crude fellows,' said the Chief Fire Officer, who came from Bali.

'Very tough chaps,' confirmed Mr Soebijanto.

The drive into town took a long time due to Mr Soebijanto's apparent unfamiliarity with the jeep. The controls seemed to baffle him. When he went to sound his horn he started the windscreen wipers, when he wished to stop them he flashed his lights or activated the blinkers. And he changed gear often and in a very random way, engaging top to climb steep inclines and bottom to coast down the other side. The first mile of the journey was accomplished with the handbrake on and, periodically, he strayed on to the wrong side of the road, causing carloads of rough Sumatrans to shout and brandish their fists at him. Preoccupied with this I only heeded the scenery from the corner of an eye, noting that the outskirts of Palembang seemed prosperous and well-ordered. The Chief Fire Officer said this was the centre of the oil industry and there was a lot of money about.

We lurched on under lowering skies into a sprawling grey city. 'It is not so beautiful,' the men said, and showed it off to me resignedly. We passed the premises of Dicky Metals Ltd, L. Kasoem Optical, Mandjur Apotik and the New Holland Bakery and then, after several diversions caused by Mr Soebijanto's tongue-clicking indecisiveness, crossed an imposing bridge spanning the Musi, another broad, brown Sumatran waterway. On the other side the Chief Fire Officer said, 'There is nothing for you here,' so we turned, with some difficulty, and drove back. He added that it was supposed to be a drawbridge but the mechanism had stuck years ago and now the big vessels up from the sea 300 kilometres away had to moor on the downstream side. One was there now, a tanker loading at the Pertamina oil and fertilizer wharf.

They dropped me at the Sandjaja Hotel and promised to pick me up at 8 o'clock in the morning. That would give us time to talk before the departure of my 1135 flight to Jakarta. Before they left I asked if they knew anything about the situation in Timor. The question produced symptoms of unease in both men and was left hanging. They shook their heads, glanced at their watches and hurried away. I went to my room. It was dim and musty. The rain began sluicing down, scattering some kids stoning a dog in the street. While washing I noted that a new Toto Western-style lavatory had been installed in the bathroom, together with diagrams and comprehensive instructions issued by its Japanese makers. The first diagram showed a sticklike figure standing before the bowl, one hand clasping a demure little member no larger than an acorn, the other resting rakishly on his hip. Black arrows indicated that both seat and lid should be raised for this particular function, while the arrows in the second diagram showed the configuration recommended by the manufacturers when the Toto was being sat upon. Here the stick man perched with clasped hands and bowed head, but there was little repose in the line of the figure. It suggested, instead, a high degree of apprehension and stress, as though he had been suddenly confronted with the possibilty – not covered in the instructions – of a busted flush.

II

In the eleventh century Palambang had been the sumptuous, gilded capital of the Srivijaya kingdom, made rich by thriving entrepot trade with China. The local monarchs, who proudly counted themselves among the 'emperor's barbarian vassals', divided their time between commerce and prayer. So devout were they that the Chinese pilgrim I-ching commended Palembang, with its thousand resident monks, as an excellent centre for studying Buddhist texts. Today, after centuries of decline, oil and fertilizers were causing its stock to rise again – but tenuous links with the past appeared to remain. In the lobby before breakfast a man told me he knew someone in Palembang who claimed descent from the Srivijaya kings.

'Really?' I said, interested.

'Sure. You could meet him. He is a salesman for the YKK Indonesia Zipper Company.'

Mr Soebijanto, this morning, seemed to have got the measure of the jeep. Splashing through giant puddles left by the heavy overnight rain he told me that Talangbetutu, his airport, was the fifth largest in the country and had been built by the Dutch some time back in the 1930s. He knew nothing of Qantas or Imperial (who had called here) and cared even less. His preoccupation was with his single undulating runway, so short that the DC9s couldn't take off with a full load of fuel, passengers and freight. Despite this restriction Mr Soebijanto was still able to dispatch and receive daily an average of 1,200 passengers, 11 tons of baggage, 10 tons of cargo and a ton of newspapers. Much of the outgoing cargo consisted of Palembang river crabs destined for Singapore, and a profusion of beautiful little tropical fish flown to aquariums and collectors around the world. Periodically the airport was closed by smoke from the burning forest. He managed a staff of 326, of whom 60 worked in Security, 54 in the Fire Unit and 15 in Air Traffic Control. The duties of the men in the tower included Approach Control, Aerodrome Control and, for aircraft operating at less than 15,000 feet, Overflying Control. Anyone travelling higher was supposed to talk directly to Jakarta but, occasionally, they called down to ask about the weather or local aircraft movements, or just to pass the time of day. The airport was open from 6 in the morning till 9 in the evening, though they kept a non-directional radio beacon going round the clock. In case of a nocturnal emergency the Fire Unit night shift, made up of fanatical card players, held the tower's master key. With it they could effect entry, pull all the switches and light up Talangbetutu like the Fourth of July.

Chief Fire Officer Suwarsono was waiting in Mr Soebijanto's

office. He slapped my back and greeted me like an old friend. The office was shadowy and fastidiously neat. Mr Soebijanto waved me to a chair then picked up an orange telephone to ask if my flight was due out on time. The Chief Fire Officer smiled at me and said, 'How old is your son?'

'Fourteen.'

'Would he write to me? It will be very good for my English.'

'I'll ask him,' I promised.

'In fire work English is number one language. My best crash car, the Chubb, is English. It is completely automatical. You tell your son I will send him nice photo of my Chubb crash car.'

Mr Soebijanto concluded his call and sprayed the mouthpiece with a can of Love Freshphone. 'The DC9 on schedule,' he said.

'How old are you?' inquired the Chief Fire Officer. 'Excuse me, sir.'

'Forty-seven,' I told him.

'Mr Soebijanto is younger. But he look a lot older. Too much worry. You know why? *Daughters.* Guess how many he got.'

'Suwarsono is Balinese,' muttered Mr Soebijanto, who had pulled a packet of spicy Sumatran tobacco from his pocket and was rolling himself a cigarette. 'They are all mischief.' He licked a fingertip and painstakingly collected the tobacco crumbs from his desk. 'I have seven children.'

'*Daughters*, Soebijanto!' crowed his colleague.

'Four,' said Mr Soebijanto, hoarsely. 'Big ones.' A jet whistled overhead. 'Fokker,' he added.

'From Medan,' said the Chief Fire Officer.

They glanced at their watches in unison. 'Late,' they announced.

It began to rain. The deluge drummed on the broad leaves of the papaia trees beside the little Met. Office opposite, bowing them down and making their plump green fruit gleam like jade. The sparks jumping from Mr Soebijanto's cigarette whizzed through the gloom like fireflies. Then two girls walked in with black coffee and plates of cakes. One was startlingly pretty, the other plain, earnest and plump. Mr Soebijanto jumped up. 'This girls are Admin!' he cried. He pointed to the pretty one. 'She know no English so you are no good for her. But this one has studied. Now she will speak.'

The plain girl gave me a sudden shy smile. She said, 'Sir, de kek is chilly.'

The Chief Fire Officer clapped and shouted, 'Answer! Answer! You must practise her!'

I cleared my throat. 'Why is the kek chilly?'

'Hi megid chilly,' she replied, flushed and smiling broadly. We were having a conversation! 'Hototot,' she added.

I caught her drift then. She had baked chilli cakes hot enough to require a formal health warning. Sensing my mettle was being tested I popped one into my mouth. Within seconds I gasped to the Chief Fire Officer that he must quickly fetch his Chubb crash car to put me out. He laughed appreciatively, picked up the cakes and offered them around. As everyone tucked in, eating them as effortlessly as meringues, he confided that his favourite book was English – *The Truth About The Great Fire of London*.

'Oh, sir,' he murmured. 'I *love* to read about the big blazes.'

The Garuda DC9 'Batam Agam' roller coasted down Mr Soebijanto's undulating runway and climbed straight into a layer of cirrus. A moment later it broke out again then promptly entered another one, ascending through layer after layer until it levelled off in a dense blue haze so impenetrable that it was impossible to tell the sea from the sky. Though the two Pratt & Whitney turbofans murmured away at the rear there was no sensation of movement; the 'Batam Agam' seemed as inert as a dragonfly embedded in ice. The air of unreality grew when the captain switched on the PA and, carelessly shifting a decimal point, said, 'We are flying at 7.2 speed of sound.' 4,000 m.p.h! This astonishing news was received without emotion by my fellow-passengers. He added calmly. 'Our height is 35,000 feet. Prognosis: cloudy all the way,' and switched off again.

During the 50-minute journey two girls served Van Houten chocolate and coffee. The latter part of the route took us over the Sunda Straits, the seaway running between Sumatra and Java. Off to the right, unseen in the haze, was Pulau Rakata, the island domain of Krakatau, or Krakatoa, the most notorious of the 130 active volcanoes that line the Indonesian archipelago like gun emplacements. After rumbling for three months Krakatoa finally erupted at 10 o'clock on the morning of 27 August 1883. The explosion, heard in Australia 2,200 miles away, caused tidal waves off South America and put enough dust into the atmosphere to lower the earth's temperature by half a degree Fahrenheit for several years. The dust clouds were carried by the Krakatoa Winds, a 20-mile-high series of jet streams blowing out of the east at speeds of up to 110 m.p.h. and named when they began painting evening skies everywhere with wild, swirling colours, their glittering clouds of ash and powdered rock providing the world with Pole-to-Pole Hawaiian sunsets. Today Krakatoa continues to agitate the area with rumbling tremors and periodic discharges and now, looking out into that sulphurous blue fog, I wondered if it was surreptitiously stoking up its fires again.

We were heading for Kemayoran airport where pilots on the approaches to Runways 08 and 35 must take note of the fact that 'small paper kites may be encountered at heights up to approximately 300 ft'. Such warnings would have been heeded by the crews on the Australia run. They were flying fragile little De Havilland 86s, fashioned from plywood and built in a hurry, the prototype being commissioned on 23 September 1933 and making its maiden flight, at Stag Lane, a mere three and a half months later. The DH 86 was specifically designed (said the *Gazette*) 'to the order of Imperial Airways and Qantas Empire Airways in order to comply with the conditions of tender for the extension of the existing route from Singapore to Port Darwin.

'She is the fastest 4-engined air liner yet built in any country in the world, and has proved capable of a top speed of over 170 miles an hour. With ample reserves of power, she would be able to cross the Timor Sea (a stretch of open water over 500 miles in length, which presents the main obstacle to air services to Australia from Singapore) in less than three hours.

'Very comfortable accommodation is provided in one large saloon for a maximum number of ten passengers. Special attention has been paid to the question of ventilation, and each passenger has a ventilator under his own control. A totally enclosed control cabin is provided for the crew, a Captain and First Officer. She is equipped with four 6-cylinder Gipsy engines of 200 horse-power which are mounted on the leading edge of the lower wing. With all four engines in operation she has proved capable of flying nearly four miles above the ground.'

Now we were descending, just as the DH 86s would have done, past the Javanese town of Serang, approaching Jakarta over the Roads and the Tanyung Priok dock area. On the run into Kemayoran we crossed slums roofed with warm orange tiles, pretty in the hazy sun. Clouds of condensation boiled through the open flight deck door as we taxied past a grassy meadow stacked with the wrecks of Dakotas, Vanguards, Friendships and a couple of rusting write-offs mangled beyond recognition.

I disembarked and went looking for a Garuda press officer, eventually running one to ground in a rambling administration building behind the terminal. Three men sat in a dim, silent office piled with dusty stacks of files. One rose and presented his card. It read 'A.P. CHR. Tomasow BSc Staff Ground Handling & Facilitation Dept.' When I said I was looking for someone who dealt with the press he gravely retrieved the card, crossed out the job description and wrote 'Public Relation' there instead. He said he knew nothing about me, but would I care for a soft drink? One of his colleagues left the room and returned carrying bottles of Tehbotal with straws stuck in them. It tasted like perfumed hair oil. Mr Tomasow listened patiently as I described the purpose of my visit.

'Suwardi,' he said.

The others nodded. 'Suwardi.'

'You must speak with Suwardi,' said Mr Tomasow. 'He is Air Transport. He can tell you all this thing about local flying past and present. I know little about the matter. It is not my field.'

'Tomasow is Garuda only,' explained the colleague who had fetched the Tehbotal.

'Yes, I am Garuda only.' Mr Tomasow smiled. 'But our story is very interesting, a great adventure of little acorn and mighty oak, derring-do and so forth.'

Urged on by his colleagues he was persuaded to tell it. After a moment spent collecting his thoughts he said it started in Aceh, north Sumatra, during the struggle for independence against the Dutch. 'These Aceh people hate the Dutch. They have been fighting them for a hundred years, and always they are having meetings to talk about how they can fight better. At one meeting someone say maybe they should get an aeroplane for throwing bombs. The Aceh people like this bombs idea. The motion is passed. They collect money to buy a plane for the Republic. Then they ask First Officer Supono, head of the Revolutionary Bureau of Planning and Propaganda, to find the best plane. He is an expert. Once he even built a plane himself. It was powered with a motorbike engine and the pilot had to change gear during take-off, so the Aceh people did not want that plane. They want a proper one!'

What the Aceh people got was a war-surplus Dakota, picked up cheap in India and flown back to Jakarta in October 1948. It successfully ran the Dutch blockades, carrying supplies and ferrying the revolution's leaders around their hidden jungle strips until, back in Calcutta for an overhaul, the Dutch launched a major new offensive and First Officer Supono was ordered to remain in exile with his Dakota and put himself out to charter. He went tramping off to Rangoon and signed a contract with the Burmese government. It was a difficult, unsettled period. Rangoon's authority was being openly flouted and, up and down the country, the Indonesian crew periodically came under fire from opium runners, warlords, even disaffected right-wing monks running a liquor-smuggling operation. I had heard about these monks, believed to have drunk bourbon and carried Schmeisser submachine guns.

'But the boys just patch up the plane and fly on,' said Mr Tomasow. 'They are making so much money from the charter business they can soon buy another two Dakotas. In 1950 we get independence, they come home and buy 17 more. Then they get eight Catalina flying boats for work in the islands. Now it is really an airline. They call it Garuda (it means "eagle") and go international but even today the peasants and fishermen in north Sumatra say it should be called Air Aceh.'

Mr Tomasow, as I left, promised to call Mr Suwardi at Air Transport and make an appointment for the following morning. My taxi took me along Jalan Patrice Lumumba, past Merkeda Square and the grandiose 400-foot-high Freedom Monument topped by gold-plated flames, then the Medan Banteng, with its giant statue of New Guinea Man breaking his chains. My understanding of the position in Indonesian New Guinea – the western half of that great island, known as Irian Jaya – was that most New

Guinea Men regarded the Indonesians as harsh neo-colonialists and longed to see the back of them. We drove on, through foul air and choking, undisciplined traffic. This was a dense, dangerous, charmless city, inhabited by a largely uncountable population. As the rural poor flooded in to seek work so Jakarta continued its unregulated sprawl into the countryside.

At the Hilton I leafed through Cobham's book to see what he had to say about his Jakarta stopover. He had landed in the harbour and tied up at 'a small seaplane base belonging to the Dutch authorities. We had a wonderful reception and as it was mid-day we were in time to motor in to lunch with the British Consul. It was Sunday and the day was a general holiday. I was greatly struck by the gaiety of the Javanese and more so that evening when after a dinner held in our honour we adjourned for a few minutes to the dance that was in progress at the hotel, to find that these people mix comparatively freely with their European administrators.'

I went downstairs for a beer and found the lobby filled with armed security men. The barman, pouring my Bintang, explained that Professor Dr Mochtar Kusumaatmadja, the Foreign Minister, dropped in regularly to buy the air mail edition of the London *Daily Telegraph* and now, as was his custom, had retired to the coffee shop to read it.

Mr Suwardi of Air Transport proved to be a stocky, personable, welcoming man whose large office and solemn secretaries indicated that he was a person of consequence at the Ministry. He waved me to an armchair and said, apologetically, that all he knew about the old British service to Australia was that it had called here; he had made inquiries among his staff and found them equally ignorant. 'Our ancestral memory doesn't go back that far,' he said. 'And I'm just as vague about the early days of KLM. All I can tell you is that they began their service from Amsterdam in 1930, landing at the first Jakarta aerodrome, Tjililitan, a few miles southwest of Kemayoran.'

I wasn't too put out because it had occurred to me that, in the person of Mr Suwardi, I might have found an ally able to pull strings to get me into Timor. He talked on, saying that even the Hollanders understood that the aeroplane was the most rational way of linking 13,677 islands scattered across 3,000 miles of sea: they commissioned the legendary German Dornier DO-24K flying boat, one of the most beautiful aircraft ever built, specifically for work in the East Indies.

'And we have continued that tradition,' said Mr Suwardi. 'Indonesia is a very air-minded country. It is the only way of keeping open the lines of communication. There's more to us than just Garuda, you know. Other airlines operating domestic services are Merpati Nusantara and Bouraq Indonesia, Mandala Airlines, Seulawah Air and Zamrud Aviation. Then there are the charter firms, and the fleets owned by major companies, by the universities, the big plantations and spice gardens and, of course, the missions: Mission Aviation, Associated Mission Aviation, the Regions Beyond Mission and the Yayasan Missi Suku-Suku Terpencil Mission.'

A young male assistant bustled with cups of steaming lemony tea. 'Exactly how many aircraft are registered in Indonesia is unknown to me. But I can tell you that Garuda alone operates 124, including 77 jets. We have 59 official airports and 120 pioneer strips. These have surfaces of grass, sand or crushed coral, and often joining passengers must sit and wait under a tree. The strips are unsupervised and unstaffed so people just turn up and buy their ticket from the pilot. They are in the most isolated places, served mostly by Twin Otters and Cassas. You have seen the Cassa?'

'I saw one at Palembang. It looked like a little Hercules.'

'A plane with an 85-foot wingspan is not so little,' said Mr Suwardi, slightly affronted. 'We designed and built it in conjunction with Construcciones Aeronauticas in Madrid. It is an *excellent* machine, ideal for our transmigration problem. This is an airlift to move families from areas of dense population like Java and Bali out to the empty places in Sulawese, Kalimantan and Irian Jaya. Our intention is to move half a million family heads – five million people in all – to 233 transmigration locations in the east. For this we have a fleet of one dozen Hercules and several dozen Cassas working full-time and non-stop. It is the biggest airlift in the history of the world.'

He sat back and beamed at me. I said that certain elements of the foreign press were reporting that many family heads apparently took exception to being arbitrarily plucked from their villages and flown away to the middle of nowhere.

'Your newspapers have got it wrong,' he said, calmly. 'We are talking about simple peasant types without land or property, a drain on the communities who must feed and house them. When they are transmigrated each family gets nine acres – half an acre for a house, two and a half for food crops and six for cash crops – and full government support for the first year; after that they must be self-sufficient. It is a very good deal and the family heads are queueing up to go.'

But what if the land being distributed to the family heads belonged to someone else? The Papuans of Irian Jaya, for example, were Melanesians to whom the ownership of land was hereditary, inalienable and sacred; the thousands dispossessed to make room for the migrants were now getting guns from the OPM Free Papua secessionist guerrilla movement and turning them on the hapless Indonesian settlers.

Mr Suwardi sighed and said, 'Look, that is a problem for the politicians. It only becomes my problem when they start shooting at my planes. Meanwhile, I have to keep scores of aircraft moving around a couple of hundred destinations, many of them very primitive, with no facilities or back-up. I must roster crews, arrange fuel, supplies, maintenance, spares, security, accommodation. I must also roster standby crews and standby aircraft. My life has become one huge logistical exercise. Sometimes I sit here and feel like Eisenhower planning the Invasion of Europe.' He drank some tea. 'But to answer your question: if those Free Papua rogues became too troublesome we would round them up, send down the Hercs and transmigrate them somewhere else.'

'Like Timor?' I asked.

'Ah, Timor is another matter. But, yes, we are sending migrants to Timor. Maybe a sojourn in Timor would be good for the Papuans.'

I said, 'The day after tomorrow I'm supposed to be going to Timor. Will I get in? Everyone says there is no problem, but I wonder.'

Mr Suwardi looked at me steadily for a moment then scribbled a brief message and some numbers on an office memo form. 'If it is necessary,' he said, handing it over, 'give this to the appropriate person and ask him to telephone me. I have put my home number as well. But I can promise you nothing. Down there others make the decisions.'

I thanked Mr Suwardi, a good man, went downstairs and jumped into a *helicak* motorized trishaw. It went rattling off to Kemayoran where, in 40 minutes, I was due to catch the 1 o'clock Surabaya Shuttle.

The flight had been cancelled. The next was scheduled for 3 p.m. when both Garuda and Mandala would be operating services. As I stood in the queue at the Garuda window a bald, bony Mandala tout plucked at my sleeve and tried to sell me a seat on his 3 o'clock to Surabaya. 'It is jet-propel Super Viscount, full air-con and big dinner, sir. You must take. Garuda give bad service, no food and is all full.'

I told him I had already booked with Garuda who, in the event, had plenty of spare seats. I picked up my boarding pass, went into the departure lounge and instantly regretted my decision. Out on the apron stood a wondrous old aeroplane painted in Mandala's ornate purple livery. But this was no Viscount. A dozen young men in smart purple safari suits were furiously polishing its ample, rounded fuselage, making it gleam. The flight deck was as spacious as a ship's bridge and there were flowers in the curtained cabin windows. Its four engines looked like antique air-cooled radials and even the three-bladed propellers had been burnished by polishing youths standing on boxes. The lofty tail was shaped like a cathedral door and embellished with a great golden mandala, the ancient Buddhist symbol. What was it? A converted Flying Fortress? A restyled Lanc? Or something built locally from bamboo and hammered Capstan cigarette tins? I tried to find out.

But there was bedlam in the terminal. A score of television monitors were showing the Bee Gees with the volume turned up. The marshal on Gate 7 had an electronic bullhorn through which he kept shouting incomprehensibly at us. Behind him two rumbling old DC4 freighters of Bayu Indonesian Air were warming up. I approached the marshal and asked him what the Mandala aircraft was.

'Viscount!' he snapped. He was pale and very wound up.

'That's no Viscount.'

'It is *Super* Viscount! Go back inside till flight is called.'

It was called an hour later. I had put my question to other officials in the terminal and always got the same answer. The young men were still shining their Viscount-That-Wasn't-A-Viscount as we filed aboard our DC9, climbed away over the harbour where Cobham had landed and began cruising east along the Java coast. I decided the old plane wasn't used for scheduled services at all but, like a resplendent ceremonial carriage, only brought out for great occasions of church and state when, in all probability, it was flown by a crew of abbots.

In the misty afternoon light the sea looked as faded as ink on blotting paper; the coastal lands were flooded and wan. Across the aisle a woman of 60, dressed in a coat of heavy, honey-coloured silk and a mantilla of fine black lace, read aloud in Persian from a small, leatherbound book, richly embossed like a psalter. A crystal chandelier rested on the vacant seat beside her, wrapped in an embroidered shawl.

We swung far out over the sea. Java became a distant smudge on the dark horizon, but I realized that we were off Semarang where, on 17 April 1931, the ill-fated De Havilland 66 *City of Cairo* stopped for fuel during Imperial's first attempt to reach Australia. Flown by Captain Jimmy Alger and Captain R. P. Mollard, it had set off from Karachi four days earlier with 290lbs of mail but no passengers, an experimental flight devised to test the feasibility of a regular through service. Semarang was not one of its planned stops. 'On arrival at Batavia it was quite clear that we could not make Sourabaya, our planned destination, before dark,' Alger told the aviation historian D.M.V. Jones. 'Not knowing what night flying facilities there were in Sourabaya, we decided to carry on as far as we could, and we ended up that day in Semarang. We then decided that if we made a night flight to Sourabaya from Semarang we would be back on schedule. The British community at Semarang were marvellous. They turned out in force for our arrival and I was garlanded with flowers on stepping out of the aircraft – this I didn't really like, because I'm superstitious.'

Alger and Mollard took off for Surabaya at 10 o'clock that evening, assisted by the British residents who lined up their cars and switched on their headlights to create a runway flare path, honking their horns and waving as the *City of Cairo* scrambled precariously away over the perimeter fence. It flew into 'extensive thunderstorms' which forced it to edge north, towards the coast, but managed to reached Surabaya without further incident, landing by the first light of the sun.

Now we were making our own approach to Surabaya, over a brown river that went looping wildly across the flooded countryside like crayon whorls scrawled by a fretful child. The DC9 flew into black raincloud and sudden sharp turbulence that dislodged my neighbour's chandelier and dumped it on the floor with a noise like a dropped tray of glasses. She gave a cry of anguish as the crystals scattered up and down the aisle, glittering like giant diamonds. 'Oh, God,' she moaned. 'It was my mother's best thing, an heirloom.' Tears trickled down her cheeks.

There were murmurs of concern from the other passengers, unable to help because the seat belt signs were on. A Fokker turbo-prop idled along a couple of thousand feet below, following us as we turned out to sea then back again, the sea and flooded fields of the same uniform grey, one barely distinguishable from the other. The flight deck ran with rivulets of water, routine condensation which the co-pilot mopped up, swabbing the dripping ceiling and bulkheads with a dirty green towel kept for the purpose. Finals took us over a swamp criss-crossed by hedgerows. Of Surabaya there was no sign, and I wondered whether Indonesia's second city had succumbed entirely to the rains, a drowned metropolis identifiable only by the muffled clang of its bells being rung by the turning tide.

At Juanda airport we parked near seven Dakotas drawn up in a line. As the engines were switched off everyone rose and began retrieving the crystals from the broken chandelier. The captain, who had a wispy moustache and large, protruding ears, came back and helped too. Nobody left until every piece had been found, placed in a carrier bag and handed to the owner. A bus took us down a tree-lined rural road to a small building standing deep in a silent, dripping wood. A notice outside said 'Arrivals'. I went in and bought a 6,000-rupiah ticket for the taxi ride to town.

The car allocated to me was a Toyota, probably left over from the Japanese occupation. I climbed through a broken door and sat in a dusty concavity on the rear axle. The engine worked, but there was no silencer, upholstery or suspension, and none of the dashboard dials functioned. The driver had a huge flattened head and a lowering hairline that came almost to the bridge of his nose. Nine or ten taxis revved up and blasted away from the grid together. My driver took the lead by trying to crash into the back of anyone who got in front, stamping hard on the accelerator whenever an opponent cut across his bows. After they had all given way he turned his attention to the oncoming traffic, his progress marked by the panicky blare of horns approaching and receding rapidly behind us. At the outskirts of the city we found ourselves surrounded by cyclists and for these he slowed, turning to say something that sounded apologetic, perhaps explaining that in Indonesia the manslaughter of cyclists could get you into a lot of trouble.

The narrow road was lined by small, ramshackle, open-fronted shops. The cyclists cut wakes in the giant puddles while pedestrians plodded ankle-deep through mud. Surabaya, one of the most resonant, romantic names in the atlas, inspired Kurt Weill's haunting song 'Sourabaya Johnny' but I guessed that Weill had never actually been there. Even my locally published guide book admitted, with disarming frankness, that 'Surabaya has little glamour, and within the city boundaries, no natural beauty'. It warned, 'Anyone spending more than a few days in the city cannot come to any other conclusion than that it is primarily a centre for trade, finance and manufacturing.' As a postscript it added that certain local manufacturers were still using equipment imported from Britain and Holland during the nineteenth century.

Approaching the town centre the traffic was so dense that, at times, it entirely obscured the road surface. Small boys flew coloured kites beside a graceful little suspension bridge. I had asked the driver to take me to Jane's House, a small hotel near the French Consulate. We turned off the main road into the Jalan Dinojo, a quiet street of spacious down-at-heel villas built by Dutch merchants in the 1920s. Jane's House stood behind a high wall. The driver agreed to wait as I entered a silent, deserted hallway containing a sideboard with an ornamental wooden goose on it. There was a bell, which I rang, but nobody came.

'Can you let me have a room?' I asked the goose.

Then behind me, there was a sudden shriek and I turned to find an elderly female midget furiously waving her arms. Could this be Jane? I inquired again about accommodation but, wild-eyed and squawking, she made to pummel my knees with her tiny fists then lunged to slam and lock the door as I backed into the street. A girl in a purple dress said Jane was away, leaving the hotel closed for a while. 'Try the Bumi,' she advised. 'It's not far and it's quite comfortable.'

We arrived at the Bumi, a big modern place downtown, to find it encircled by armed soldiers wearing vivid blue berets and clusters of bright silk ribbons. They waved us away from the front entrance but I managed to gain access through the back. In the lobby a man raised a warning finger.

'Hush, please, sir! Prince Norodom Sihanouk and party have just arrived.'

I watched as the President of the exiled Coalition Government of Democratic Kampuchea and ex-King of Cambodia, now resident in Peking, walked by. He looked old and overweight. Behind him marched two grave courtiers in lounge suits. One carried the Prince's pillows, held stiffly before him like Coronation regalia, the other a chipped enamelware bowl containing a dozen ripe bananas. Everyone clapped. Sihanouk waved a plump, beringed hand and inclined his head from side to side as he progressed regally to the lift. I went to get a room and, a few minutes later, stepped into the lift too. It smelled of Gucci aftershave and contained a large notice advising that bridal make-up and head massages were available at the hotel beauty salon.

Outside the room next to mine a thin, uniformed man sat in a high-backed chair with his legs crossed. In one hand he held a clove cigarette, in the other an M-16 carbine. 'How you doing?' he said. My room was banked with fresh flowers in crystal vases, bowls of fruit and exotic candies. Each piece of fruit had been individually polished. I ate a guava and stuck a couple of oranges in my bag against the probability of being thrown out again. The room had plainly been prepared for one of the courtiers but nothing happened and, after enough time had lapsed to convince me he had been fixed up elsewhere, I went downstairs for a drink.

The bar was hung with lobster pots. An American told me the nautical motif was supposed to evoke the memory of Joseph Conrad, who had frequently put into Surabaya. Then a plump, nattily dressed Indonesian asked for a light and told me the English had shot his father. 'Two bullets in the head,' he said, cheerily. 'But no sweat. I *like* the English. I am big friend of your country.'

I told him I was Australian.

'They were here also. Maybe they kill my old man. Who knows? There were many soldiers, a big force sent by Mountbatten in 1945 to round up the Japs. But everyone thought it was a trick by the Dutch to get Indonesia back for themselves. So for three weeks we fought the British. The Battle of Surabaya. We lost, but it made the Dutch understand there would be trouble when they returned.'

He told me he was a civilian working for the Navy. Surabaya was the Indonesian Navy's main base. I bought him a Bintang and asked if the Navy was active around Timor. He grew suddenly cool, asking why I wanted to know. Idle curiosity, I said, but our burgeoning relationship was spoiled. He had grown wary of me so I went to the coffee shop for a plate of nasi goreng – rice, pork and eggs fried fragrantly in coconut oil – then returned to my room. The thin security man with the M-16 was nodding off as I passed. He jerked awake and said, 'How you doing?'

I ate an apple and looked up Cobham. 'At last,' he wrote, 'we came to Surabaya, at the eastern end of the island of Java, where there is a vast expanse of shallow water; but despite the fact that we drew about six inches of water our good friends must have thought that we drew about six feet for they placed our moorings at least a mile from the shore, so that we had to be towed this distance to the hangars of the seaplane base, which I believe is the main station for the Dutch Indies Air Force. After this little yachting cruise on the end of two tow-ropes, we came alongside the jetty and were received by the Commandant who had staged a magnificient welcome for us.'

Later I heard strange sounds coming through the wall and discerned the thin, reedy voice of Prince Norodom Sihanouk singing the 1930 standard 'Beyond the Blue Horizon' from the movie *Monte Carlo*. I had read somewhere that he liked the old songs, often giving public renderings at his own birthday parties in

Peking. After the song he gargled. I dozed fitfully till 4 a.m. when I crawled out of bed to catch the 0610 Bouraq service to Bali and Lombok.

III

The Imperial passengers, aboard their little DH86 biplane with its Qantas Empire Airways livery, now flew southeast from Surabaya to the island of Lombok, landing at Rambang, where the grassy strip is no longer operational. Lombok's present airfield lies near Mataram, on the west coast, and I travelled there aboard a Bouraq Indonesian Airlines Hawker Siddeley 748 prop-jet which went via Denpasar, in Bali.

At 5.30 a.m. the morning rush hour was getting under way at Surabaya's Juanda airport. In the murky half light aircraft were taking on fuel, loading freight and preparing to start up. A young Swede, aggressively wide awake, joined me in the departure lounge and said he had just returned from the island of Madura, a brief boat ride from Surabaya, where in August they held bull races. The bulls were reared on a diet of beer, eggs and chilli peppers and, bred for speed, could gallop at more than 30 m.p.h. We agreed that this was pretty fast for a bull, and made jokes about the cows of Madura needing to be even quicker. The Swede told me his uncle had once met a retired British admiral living in the hills outside Surabaya. 'For lunch he always had ship's biscuits and a bottle of amontillado sherry,' he said.

He was going to Ujung Pandang on Sulawesi, on his way to the Spice Islands. I watched his Garuda DC9 trundle off through the mist to join the queue at the threshold of Runway 28, far out in the marshes, then BO724 was called and a dozen of us scrambled aboard an elderly 748 freshly painted in Bouraq's bright green livery. The Rolls-Royce Darts fired and ran at full throttle, filling the cabin with noise and wild vibration. A shiny silver plate set in the casing of the starboard Dart gave its oil capacity in Imperial Pints but the number, worn away by years of polishing, was illegible. After two minutes the engines were switched off and the captain, a portly, anxious-looking man in his early fifties, clambered down from his tiny elevated flight deck and opened the forward cargo door. He spoke to a youth leaning on a small antique fire extinguisher who nodded and walked away, pulling his appliance with its clanking iron wheels behind him. A quarter of an hour later a bus drew up beside the 748. The stewardess, a slim, graceful girl, said we must disembark and wait in the bus.

It took us to a spot only 30 yards away and parked beside an old Bouraq Viscount. A dozen mechanics in blue safari suits sat under its wings, paying no attention to us or our mechanical problem. Several read comics, a couple arm-wrestled, another did press-ups. Then a white-overalled supervisor approached the 748 with a giant screwdriver, removed a manhole cover from its underbelly and stuck his head in. He replaced the cover and spoke to the captain who, picking his teeth in the doorway, waved us back aboard. Moments later we were airborne, breaking through eight-eighths cloud cover into a lovely dawn sky awash with iridescent mother-of-pearl colours. Water began sluicing from the air blower above my seat. The stewardess helped staunch it with a paper napkin then brought breakfast – sweet black tea, hard-boiled eggs and a savoury rice cake wrapped in banana leaf. We crossed the Madura Straits towards the easternmost tip of Java and, back over the island, saw craggy green mountains topped by plump rings of pink cloud. Brown creeks snaked down the sides, some foaming like burns in spate, others dropping over precipices and turning into waterfalls.

Most of my fellow passengers slept, their breakfasts untouched. The stewardess brought me two more rice cakes and a clove cigarette. We followed a winding dirt road to a tiny port where, beside a settlement of thatched houses and a yellow temple, tawny cattle were being unloaded from a blue-funnelled coaster sitting low in the water. We skimmed over the lip of a dormant volcano. The crater, several hundred feet deep, was a secret parkland of trees and grass with paths winding from top to bottom. At the base stood a wood with a clearing in the middle. Blue smoke rose from the clearing and, realizing that people had business in the volcano, I wondered what rare things grew in that wildly enriched soil. Nutmeg and mace? Prime cloves? Marijuana? The intimate, windless, deeply shadowed little world slid away as we crossed the further lip and headed for a small, hilly island set in the bright sea.

Beyond it the 748 began letting down towards Bali, a prospect of high, rocky cliffs looming out of the haze, and coast-crawled half a mile offshore. The skipper, enjoying himself, flew at a height that almost caused the gaudy triangular sails of the fishing canoes in our path to billow in our propwash. Then we banked steeply, whizzed low over a shallow bay lined with mangroves and touched down at Ngurah Rai Airport, a large, functional establishment clearly conceived for the age of mass travel. The Lombok passengers were sent to a Transit Lounge while the aircraft was refuelled. It had modish chairs of yellow plastic and large smoked glass windows through which I watched a procession of F28 twin-jets take off like scrambling fighters. This was the place that Rabindranath Tagore had called The Morning of the World, celebrated for its piousness, tranquillity and beauty, an island in a state of grace, but now I saw only concrete and heard the shriek of engines at full throttle.

Twelve years earlier, during my last visit, Ngurah Rai had been a sleepy little field with a tin-roofed bungalow for a terminal. Then they were just starting their modernization programme and I talked to a Dutch engineer who had been blasting a storm drain along the airfield perimeter. He told me that, the day it was due to be covered over with concrete, he arrived to find all his workers crouching in the drain, busy with hammers and chisels as they emblazoned the rock with intricate carved scenes from the *Ramayana*. He said, be-musedly, that they would not leave until they were satisfied that — though nobody would ever see it — the drain properly reflected their remorseless insistence on beautifying every nook and cranny of their magical constituency.

The hop to Lombok took only 20 minutes. At Ngurah Rai a barking, rabid-looking dog chased the 748 out to the runway where a heavy surf, breaking on the rocks beyond the threshold, splashed the plane. We climbed over a coconut grove and out across the Badung Strait, closing on the islands of Lembongan and Nusa Penida. The Lembongan coast was intricately indented, as though cut with a fretsaw, while the dense concentric whorls and curves of the rice terraces on its hills looked like patterns scraped with a comb in plasticine. A young man wearing a spivvy three-piece oxblood suit tried to engage me in conversation. I was tired and not disposed to help him with his colloquial English, but he persisted. 'Excuse me, sir, are you marry? Excuse me, sir, do you make business in Lombok? Excuse me, sir, you are first time in Indonesia?'

My monosyllabic responses merely served to urge him on. He became loquacious and confiding, telling me he was in import-export on Lombok, planned to marry a Jakarta nurse and once had a female pen friend in Chippenham, Wilts, called Deirdre. He pronounced it 'Dyerdray'. Then he mentioned that the Lombok Strait was full of whirlpools and dolphins and, though I saw no sign of either, as we came in high over a neat, tree-filled town built on a spreading green plain, we were chatting. The 748 commenced a fast, swooping descent and a mountain unexpectedly swung past the window, topped with mist and bathed in a yellow light that made it seem swathed in cellophane.

We skimmed over a pair of water buffalo ploughing the airfield perimeter, making the animals rear and plunge. The field, in the lee of the gift-wrapped mountain and its range of attendant hills, was called Selaparang. As we disembarked I asked my companion if he knew the whereabouts of Rambang, the site of the island's first aerodrome. He said it was on the other coast. Then I asked if he knew about the old aeroplanes that had come to Lombok. He jerked his chin at the 748 and said, look, they are coming still. My laugh delighted him. He threw an arm around my shoulder and, as we entered the tidy little terminal, summoned an old man from the waiting crowd and said, 'This is my father.'

My new friend's name was Tommy. He apologized for his father's lack of English and asked how long I was staying on Lombok. About four hours, I said. This was just a day trip. At 1310 I would be returning to Bali on the Fokker Friendship of Merpati Nusantara.

'I would like very much you come to my house,' he said, 'but it is a long way for such small time. So we will go to the house of my friend in Cakranegara. We will drink tea.'

A battered VW van stood outside the terminal, deeply pitted with rust. Tommy ushered me into the front seat with much ceremony and a good deal of nervous laughter. His father, following silently with Tommy's baggage, clambered into the back. Halfway along the palm-lined airport approach road Tommy paused to chat to the driver of a veteran Mercedes taxi. Its front bumper was held on by bailing wire and its idling engine sounded like broken gongs being bashed with a hammer. I had last seen a car like that in a film about the Gestapo and Tommy, reading my thoughts, said the Lombok taxis were all Balinese rejects, declared unsafe by the Denpasar authorities and shipped over on the ferry. I asked what happened when they became too old for Lombok; were they then sent to Sumbawa, the next island along? Tommy shrugged and said nothing was ever too old for Lombok.

Mataram is one of three settlements virtually joined together. The first, Ampenan, once a great spice port, is now silted up and abandoned. Mataram, the modern provincial capital, comes next, and joins on to Cakranegara, the island's one-time royal capital and presently its major market town. In Mataram we looked at new Government offices and in Cakranegara saw the Puri Mayura gardens where, in 1894, a Dutch expeditionary force led by General Van Ham was slaughtered following an incident in which the entire Lombok royal house, women, children and courtiers included, committed ritual suicide under the Dutch guns.

'The Hollander Van Ham and his army all killed here, one thousand dead,' Tommy grinned as though recalling a famous football win, the day tiny Lombok beat a Dutch team stacked with million pound strikers. 'Van Ham is buried at Karangjangkong. The grave is nice for tourists.'

We saw the bird market and the walled villages of the island's Balinese community, with its drum towers and elegant pavilions. On the way to visit Tommy's friend we passed the Merpati Poultry Shop, Mbojo Tours, Swastika Travel, Astawa Tailor and Modes Beauty. The streets, full of cyclists and little pony-drawn carriages called dokkers, were lined with bright billboards: Xerox Copy Service, Eveready Dengan EMD, Indomie Instant Noodles. The grandest building in town was a bank. We drove along a slow brown river where bamboos grew beside the water. In a vacant lot between two handsome bungalows stood a grave with an imposing headstone. Tommy's friend, a shopkeeper, was out. His wife, a scrawny, watchful woman in a sarong, greeted us with chilling restraint. Tommy, plainly disconcerted, laughed nervously but persisted. 'We will go in,' he said. 'You must see.'

The shop was divided into two parts. One sold groceries and hardware, the other wood carvings. Tommy spoke rapidly to the woman, who gave me a thoughtful glance and cheered up a bit.

'You must buy statue,' Tommy told me, smiling more nervously than ever.

I knew I had been set up, but was happy enough to take home some examples of ethnic Lombok art; it was a subtle, beguiling island, certainly worthy of a souvenir or two. The trouble was that much of the stock on display was erotic – rutting boar, rutting deer, rutting apes, humans copulating in a wide variety of positions, all intricately carved in honey-coloured hibiscus wood.

'They are fuck statue,' said Tommy. 'Very famous.'

'Genuine,' said the woman.

'I don't want that stuff,' I said. 'If I arrive in Australia with those they'll lock me up.'

Tommy, no longer smiling, collected half a dozen and handed them to the woman. 'This statue very, *very* popular in Australia,' he said. 'Lawyer buy, businessman, even . . . *famous jockey*.'

I chose a couple of plain pig carvings and didn't haggle over the price, the equivalent of a bottle of supermarket wine. Tommy counted his commission, handed over sullenly by the woman, and told me that Lombok pig statues were lucky. Back in the van he said his father, who hadn't spoken a word since we left the airport, now wanted to go home. I asked to be dropped in the middle of town. He stopped at the Selaparang Hotel in Cakranegara and, as we shook hands, his nervous laugh returned. Laughing, he indicated that I owed him money for petrol.

'How much?'

'Ten dollar.'

'Does that include the price of the van?' I asked.

He stopped laughing and peered at me. I gave him five dollars and went into the dimly lit little restaurant of the Selaparang where a vivacious Javanese girl named Tiwa made me a cup of nutty black Lombok coffee and sat chatting as I drank it. She told me about the Narmada festival when ducks are released on to a lake and boys plunge in and catch them, adding acidly that chasing ducks was all the Lombok men were good for. There was a long-standing tradition of elopement on the island but, all too often, the girl had to take matters in hand and carry off the boy. I asked her to elope with me and she grinned and playfully smacked my wrist.

'Only if you elope me to America,' she said. 'I have see picture . . . the big houses . . . the shops . . . California . . . the tennis and waterski . . . It is so *nice*.'

She had eyes the colour of ferns, a steady gaze and a seriousness of purpose which made me think that, one day, she would probably make it on her own.

Between the apron and the departure lounge at Salaparang airfield stood a white picket fence and a neat garden planted with crotons and flowering pink bushes. A small hand-painted sign had been placed among the flowers which, the man in the little snack bar said, was a prayer.

'It is holy,' he explained. 'It is for God blessing our aerodrome.'

He sold me a banana and I returned to my seat. By the garden were boxes, steeply roofed like miniature alpine chalets, containing the met. instruments. Stands of coconut palms grew beyond the runway while the mountain and its attendant hills were now a deep mauve and accumulating, around their tops, piles of towering, creamy cumulus. I thought of Jimmy Alger and Roger Mollard, the Imperial pilots who had flown the *City of Cairo* direct to Lombok from Surabaya, landing at Rambang where they were all obliged to turn to and manhandle heavy tins of unsuitable petrol. Captain Alger, recollecting the event, made no mention of heat, exhaustion or dirt. 'We found,' he said matter-of-factly, 'that the fuel was contained in 50-gallon drums, and that it had not only mostly evaporated away, but was contaminated by rust and sediment. However, by careful filtering, we obtained sufficient fuel from this stock and took off for Koepang.'

Now, all at once, the somnolent noonday silence was shattered by the ascending whine of an air raid siren. It had little effect on my dozen dozing companions but activated the snack bar man, who began throwing pots and pans around in a wild frenzy of activity. Announced by the siren, the Merpati Fokker came whistling in through the hilltop cumulus and, after its passengers had disembarked, he hurried aboard with four plates of meat and rice. Moments later he boarded again with vivid yellow custard and a bowl of snake fruit. When he bustled off, tray piled with dirty dishes, the passengers were summoned. The captain, wearing old-fashioned aviator Polaroids and chewing a toothpick, had his starboard engine fired up and running before we had even reached the plane. The two stewardesses wore tobacco-coloured uniforms with orange scarves about their necks. Dour, heavily built girls, they stood in their galley with folded arms and watched sullenly as a good-looking woman of indeterminate age walked up to the flight deck, opened the door and addressed the captain in a loud, hectoring voice.

She wore designer jeans and a silk blouse, her dark hair was cut modishly short and the self-confidence she exuded was as strong as her Dior perfume. The captain, a short, round-faced man with a massive neck, listened gloomily but did not respond. Instead, he got his other engine going and began to taxi. She continued her monologue until we reached the runway threshold, sat during take-off then, as we cruised out over the Lombok Strait, rose and resumed, her voice soon rising to a sustained shout. Eventually the captain handed over control to his co-pilot, left his seat and, face contorted, joined her in the doorway for a noisy, bitter bedroom quarrel to which those of us within earshot listened intently. It only ceased when we flew into black cloud and sudden, severe turbulence. He went back to work, slamming the door behind him, but she remained where she was, effortlessly riding the storm and watching us with a calm, mocking smile. Before sitting down she addressed the cowering stewardesses, saying something so deeply offensive that my neighbours tut-tutted and shook their heads.

The turbulence accompanied us all the way to Denpasar. The landing was a tempestuous affair, the aircraft seemingly attempting a sudden whip stall and double snap roll before the captain overruled it and brought it to earth with a comforting thump. We taxied into the terminal through streaming rain, passing a Garuda 747 all lit up as it headed for the runway with its wheels making waves in the flood. The Fokker parked and cut its engines. Nothing happened. While some of my companions dozed, lulled by the drumming of the downpour on the roof, I picked up a discarded copy of that day's *Jawa Pos (Java Post)* and glanced at the Flash Gordon comic strip. Flash and the Witch Queen, Azura, were standing before an antique spacecraft shaped like an iron boiler. 'It is an old ship, Flash, but reliable!' Azura said. 'Mine is a backward kingdom!' Then a Bahasia Indonesia speaker with wedge-shaped ears and horns growing out of his head burst in crying, 'Tele . . . tele. . . wah, kau tahu, bukan, Flash!' and someone opened the Fokker's door.

We sprinted through the rain to the Domestic Arrivals terminal where, mopping myself down with a handkerchief, I noted a crudely painted sign showing two rows of young European visitors. The tourists in the front row were unwashed, slouching and unkempt, those in the second row neat and smiling, with very good postures. The legend said, 'It Is A Must To Dress Correctly When Visiting Government Offices.' At that moment a couple came past who illustrated perfectly the idealized types the artist had attempted to capture, a personable, well-groomed pair walking hand in hand and looking at each other with affection. It was our captain and his querulous lady passenger, almost certainly man and wife.

I took a taxi to a hotel complex called the Pertamina Cottages, chosen because it was only a four-minute ride from the airport and because the tout at Ngurah Rai had promised a handsome discount. In the space of that brief period the driver offered to procure women, boys or smack, in that order, and sighed irritably when I turned him down. What had happened to the unworldly, shyly welcoming Balinese I had encountered more than a decade before? Mass tourism, that's what. An airborne invasion of Australians had since got under way, but I had come in the trough of the low season and there were few at the hotel. Instead, it was full of Japanese honeymoon couples who, when the rain ceased, joined me beside the pool. The women wore *haute couture* leisure outfits and everyone lay around in pairs, watching each other guardedly. Their charter, clearly, had just got in.

The barman brought me an iced Bintang. 'Get this down you,' he said. He told me he loved Australians and longed to visit Sydney. There was a sudden stirring among the Japanese. One of their number came plodding across the grass in full scuba-diving gear – black wet suit, mask, air tanks, flippers and a depth gauge; strapped to his thigh was the kind of sheath knife used for close-quarter combat with a giant squid. He was followed by his child bride, beaming with pride and looking fetching in pedal-pushers, a Lacoste T-shirt and plenty of chunky rhinestone jewellery. There was a low interested hum from their fellow-guests which turned into hisses of concern when the diver, doing a laboured goose step, fell over his flippers and crashed to the ground.

His bride looked mortified as, making low honking noises, he picked himself up and staggered on towards the pool. When he arrived at the shallow end he inserted his mouthpiece, switched on the air supply and jumped in. Then he raised a hand to us and plunged beneath the surface. The pool was three feet deep here and, for several minutes, he lay motionless on the bottom, sending up bubbles. I went and stood beside his wife who was gazing down at him with a frowning, troubled face. Could he have fallen asleep? Everyone was watching intently.

'Perhaps he's got the bends,' I said.

She gave me a scornful glance and turned away. I was considering the wisdom of reaching down and prodding him when, all at once, he kicked violently with his flippers, shooting forward like a torpedo coming out of its tube. He crashed into the side and got up with his mask hanging over his left ear, reeling and barking like a seal. He was standing there, going 'Kaark! Kaark! Kaark!' when, without any prior warning, the heavens opened up again. Everyone dashed for cover. A little green snake crawled to the end of a branch overhanging the pool and dropped in. As it swam past I asked, 'Have you got any poisonous snakes in Bali?'

'Small green ones,' said the barman, washing glasses.

'There's one in your pool.'

'The gardener can get it out again,' he assured me. 'We know that snake.'

The rain stirred the water into froth. He mentioned that Bali was lying in the path of a severe depression.

'Tropical Cyclone Ferdinand,' he said. 'They talk about it on Radio Australia this morning.'

A wind began to blow the rain around and swish through the trees. I thought of the flight to Timor in the morning and wondered whether I wanted to go after all. The barman had never been and said it was a good place to stay away from, very provincial, very primitive. The whole Timor exercise had begun to depress me, so I ordered another beer and asked if he knew any Balinese jokes. Yes, he said, had I heard about the man who went to the market to buy a fan? He insisted on the cheapest available, costing only 10 rupiah, but it soon disintegrated and angrily he returned and demanded his money back. The fan seller refused, because he had used it the wrong way. The trick with the 10-rupiah fan, he said, was to hold it motionless in front of the face while you shook your head from side to side.

As I left the barman was closing up. Tropical Cyclone Ferdinand had ensured he would be doing no more business that day. I showered and thought of going into town to see Soebawa Duarsa, who had been teaching English at the Denpasar University Faculty of Letters during my last visit. A charming, erudite man, he showed me over the School of English, a decaying single-storey structure set in a courtyard filled with weeds, clucking chickens and piles of rusting scrap metal. The library had shelves but few books. (The US Information Service, responding to his pleas, donated 14 copies of *The Story of Kit Carson*, five *Complete Pan Am Guides to the USA* and a volume of photographs taken by Jacqueline Onassis.) The reference section consisted of a single battered copy of *Webster's New World Dictionary*, shared by staff and students alike.

Later, over a drink, he told me of his students' passion for the novels of Thomas Hardy. The department possessed only one copy of each, so they took turns to painstakingly transcribe their own in longhand, turning *The Mayor of Casterbridge*, *Jude the Obscure* and *Tess of the D'Urbervilles* into six-inch-high piles of closely written exercise books. 'Hardy touches a chord in us,' he said. 'We think of him as very Balinese. It is his preoccupation with good and evil, I think, and his insights into the structure and complexity of village life.'

Soebawa Duarsa earned about four US dollars a month. A full professor earned six. All worked at other jobs to keep body and soul together. The Professor of Mathematics sold shirts at a roadside stall, the Professor of Physics (with degrees from London and Princeton) drove a three-wheel taxi. Later we went to dinner with a neighbour who was a consultant physician at the Denpasar hospital. A warm, ebullient man, he told me that the rate of cancer of the penis in Bali was the highest in the world.

It would have been nice to see my old friend again, but the light was failing and the wind bent the palms like longbows and made the dark waters of the bay foam and race. I tried to call him but the Faculty of Letters didn't answer and his home number wasn't listed. Perhaps he couldn't yet afford a telephone, perhaps he'd left the island. I poured myself a drink and switched on the television. They were showing Buck Rogers. I switched it off again, lay down on the bed and went to sleep.

Flight GA 612 to Timor was scheduled to depart at 0830. I woke before daybreak to hear wind and rain still rattling the window and large, lumpy waves falling heavily on the beach. The sky began to lighten without any visible help from the sun. A grey pigeon was blown out over the dark, choppy waters of the bay then blown back again. At Ngurah Rai two men sat on the steps of the Domestic Departures entrance cradling fighting cocks in their arms. The coppery plumage of the birds gleamed in the dull light, and their mad little eyes sparkled like chips of jet. The men said they lived near the airport and liked to bring their birds here in the mornings. The stream of people passing in and out kept them interested and stimulated. Mental alertness was an important factor when the cock came to fight.

Large, tough-looking characters began filtering through the entrance. They wore plain clothes but carried M16 rifles, and I knew they were going to Timor. The counter opened at 7.30 and the soldiers checked in their guns, the slings embroidered in gaudy colours, some brightly stitched with the Christian names of their owners. The clerk tied a Garuda destination label saying DIL to each and sent them down the conveyor belt, Bobby's gun following Eric's, which followed Donny's and Cedric's.

The clerk took my ticket, looked at it and held out his hand.

'Letter from Army,' he said.

I told him I had no letter from the Army. He shrugged and said I couldn't go to Kupang. It was a closed area under military control, and entry was not possible without written authorization from GHQ. This was news to me, and it made the memo scribbled by Mr

Suwardi of Air Transport seem a pretty poor hand to play. But it was all I had so, pessimistically, I passed it over. The clerk pondered it for a moment, said, 'You wait please,' and went away.

A pale, paunchy European in baggy shorts and a broad-brimmed straw hat approached and said, 'Pardon, but I could not help overhearing. This is most interesting. Timor! I have been trying to get in for seven years, but always the door is shut. Some very bad things are happening there. You are a technician, perhaps? An engineer like myself?' He spoke with a faint French accent.

'I'm a journalist,' I said.

'Oof!' he said, and laughed.

But when the clerk returned he was smiling. 'Okay,' he said. 'Mr Suwardi says you can go on the plane. But he does not know what will happen when you get to Kupang. Maybe the Army will make trouble.'

'I will bet my hat on it,' said the Frenchman.

'What kind of trouble?'

The clerk shrugged. 'I think they do not know you are coming. They are very strict about such things. Civil Aviation says you can go on the aeroplane because the aeroplane belongs to Civil Aviation. But in Kupang you must get off, and Kupang belongs to the Army. So you will see. Okay?'

'Okay.'

He gave me the boarding pass and waved aside my thanks; there were more soldiers waiting behind, growing restive. The Frenchman, catching a Garuda Airbus to Jakarta, suggested we take a coffee in the departure lounge. He wished to talk about Timor – not West Timor, my destination, but Timor Timor ('Timor' means 'east') where the Indonesians were engaged in a programme of genocide. Sipping his coffee, he said the Timorese victims were commonly shot, stabbed, injected with water, forcibly drowned in tanks, pushed off cliffs and thrown out of helicopters. If a relative made inquiries he was told the victim had been 'sent to Bali'. Many of those 'sent to Bali' remained unburied, their bodies tipped into ravines. Death came from starvation and malnutrition and disease was commonplace.

The Frenchman continued, 'There is much torture. In Jakarta last week a colleague told me that the District Military Commander in

Dili has even issued a manual to the torturers. It is a little book of do's and don't's. Failure to comply can mean loss of privilege for the torturers. This District Commander likes to run a tight ship.'

In West Timor there was no overt resistance to Jakarta and thus no trouble; what made the authorities there so twitchy was simply its proximity to the killing fields of the East. The two halves of the island, for centuries a source of prime sandalwood, had been split apart by treaty in 1913. The Dutch assumed control of Kupang and the West, the Portuguese of the East and, after the Dutch withdrawal in 1949, the West was ceded to Indonesia. The Portuguese, however, remained in the East, with a Governor installed at Dili, the capital. But their regime was oppressive and soon the native Timorese began calling for independence. The FRETILIN party won such a massive degree of popular support that the Portuguese Governor, his bishop and civil servants fled to an offshore island, leaving the FRETILIN leaders to form an administration.

'And, by all accounts,' said the Frenchman, 'it was a very good one. It behaved responsibly and with discretion, asking the Governor to return and supervise a five-year decolonization period. It invited international observers to come and witness its methods. It was honourable and above board.'

I pointed out that in 1974 Gough Whitlam, then Prime Minister of Australia, had such reservations about FRETILIN that he warned of the threat an independent East Timor would pose to the area.

The Frenchman shrugged. 'It was a disgraceful thing to say – and it gave the Indonesians the kind of international backing they needed. They wanted East Timor for themselves and, a few months later, began mounting illegal cross-border raids from Kupang. Then at the end of 1975 they sent in a full invasion force which, within three months, managed to kill 60,000 Timorese. To date they have killed an estimated 200,000 – a third of the pre-invasion population. Yet the major powers do nothing. At the UN Australia continues to vote with Indonesia when Third World nations protest about Timor. Others abstain. They do not wish to offend Indonesia. Indonesia has oil, Indonesia is anti-Communist and controls major seaways. So they continue to give Jakarta all its military hardware – some of which is used against the Timorese. The British supply warships, the West Germans submarines, the Australians maritime patrol aircraft, the French tanks. And the Americans, of course, give them *everything*. As a result their nuclear submarines are allowed to pass unhindered through the deepwater straits of Ombai-Wetar, just to the north of Timor Island.'

I had grown curious about my informant. Middle-aged civil engineers do not normally display such a precise and passionate knowledge of political affairs. He finished his coffee and explained.

'In Paris I knew a Timorese girl, very serene, very beautiful, a student. She had a room in my house. In 1977 she finished her studies and went home. We got one letter then there was silence. A year later we heard she had been murdered by men from HANSIP, the Indonesian Civilian Militia. More recently we got details. They had raped and tortured her first – lighted cigarettes, electricity and so on, and an interesting idea devised by the local HANSIP intellectuals, who made her stand with a table leg resting on each foot. More and more men then sat on the table. Neat, uh? That is the kind of technological innovation General Suharto likes to encourage – simple, smart, effective and cheap.'

Most of the passengers boarding the Garuda F-28 twin-jet were soldiers. Waiting for start-up I sat and watched the rain streaming over a wing painted with the registration PK-GKF and the warning 'Jangan Injak – No Step'. Moments later the plane climbed into Tropical Cyclone Ferdinand where, for a turbulent quarter of an hour, it sustained such a battering that even the soldiers cried out. One of them sat next to me, eyes closed, face taut, perspiring and deathly pale. Then we flew out of the storm into a warm porcelain sky. I peered back to take stock of Ferdinand and saw a towering citadel, its swirling black walls rising sheer from the sea to a point thousands of feet above us. It was following an easterly track and watching it recede, I wondered when our paths might cross again. The cabin attendants served a breakfast of rice and cold fishcakes. My neighbour gagged, jumped up and hurried back to the toilet, where he remained for a long time.

I took out my files. Imperial's *City of Cairo*, after refuelling on Lombok, ran into strong, persistent headwinds which forced it down to the calmer air only a few feet above the sea. The aircraft had been fitted with a luggage breast, a wind-driven generator and an enclosed cockpit, but these modifications simply served to slow it, cutting its speed to less than 100 m.p.h. The pilots, increasingly concerned about their fuel state, realized they wouldn't make it to Kupang, and determined to put down wherever they could. By the time Timor loomed over the horizon they were full of apprehension.

'It was even more alarming,' Captain Alger recalled, 'when I pulled up the nose of the aircraft to climb over the cliffs – the fuel practically disappeared from the boiler gauge type indicators and I realized that I must decide to land practically at once. I was very pleased indeed to see straight ahead of me what appeared to be a long stretch of grassland. The touchdown was perfectly normal in this grass, which turned out to be about five feet tall – I think they call it elephant grass – and we ran on for a few yards and I thought, well, that's that. But as we were slowing down the undercarriage hit quite a large rock which was hidden in the grass.'

My neighbour returned from the toilet, dropped into his seat and lay there, looking corpsed. We were overflying Sumba where, with luck, I would be calling the following day. It was a long, green, cloud-dappled island made up of rounded hills; here and there tin roofs flashed in the sun like mirrors. I returned to the *City of Cairo*, resting in a meadow with its undercarriage wrecked. Roger Mollard, the co-pilot, remembered that as they approached Timor with their fuel apparently spent – despite the extra 16 gallons in tins stowed in the cabin at Lombok and transmitted to the upper wing gravity tank with a Zwicky hand pump – they took a quick look at the terrain and decided to put down on a pony track. But, 'as we were making the approach Jimmy suddenly did a 90 degree turn to port and I thought, "Poor chap, the strain has been too much for him." Then, when we levelled off again, I saw a beautiful expanse of about 1,000 yards of green grass, and I thought, "Magnificent pilot I'm flying with." And it wasn't until we touched the top of the grass and he said "All off" and I switched off all three engines that we touched down and then ran for about fifty yards and hit one of those basalt rocks.'

The Imperial agent at Kupang, 'a Eurasian gentleman', brought porters to the scene and transferred the 290lbs of mail, 15,000 items in all, to the Kupang post office. There they were locked away by the

Dutch authorities until the ever-obliging Charles Kingsford Smith, summoned by telegram, arrived in the *Southern Cross* to fly them on to Darwin. As for the *City of Cairo*, she was dismantled and shipped to the Imperial base at Germiston outside Johannesburg where, down the years, engineers cannibalized her to provide replacement parts for the DH66s working the African route.

Now, in bright sunshine, we too made our landfall at Timor, approaching a low blue-green island set in a glittering sea. My neighbour opened his eyes and sat up. I asked him if he was getting off at Kupang. He shook his head. 'I go to Dili. Timor Timor.'

'Is there much shooting there?'

'Sure, mister. Plenty shooting.' He grinned and pointed his fingers. 'Bang bang bang.'

The Fokker banked sharply to the right and passed low over Kupang, a long, straggling collection of tin roofs strung along a blue bay. A fleet of giant outrigger canoes were moored offshore. We turned again and touched down on Runway O7, crossing the 1,500-yard grass veterans' strip which bisected it, more than half a century old and still operational. I was the only one disembarking here. The little terminal, hidden away behind trees, bore a notice saying 'STATION ELTARI-KUPANG'. There was no one in the Arrivals area though I could hear laughter and raised voices coming from the front of the building. A hen waddled past and headed out towards the parked Fokker where the the Dili-bound passengers stood gossiping in the shade of the wings. A door marked Mission Aviation Fellowship was locked and the little Bouraq counter near it deserted. Then a young man burst in and shouted 'Are you Mister Alexander?'

He seemed highly agitated, like someone bringing news of an impending tidal wave. When he managed to say that he was Poan, an air traffic controller delegated to look after me by Jakarta, I understood his distress: he had been ordered down from his tower to help me take on the Army. Mr Suwardi, who had called an hour earlier, was clearly going to give the military a run for their money and poor Poan had the baffled, hurt look of someone whose day had suddenly gone horribly wrong.

The Army launched its offensive immediately. A tall security man wearing a fancy gold scabbard appeared and spoke to me sharply in

Dutch. Mr Poan answered in Bahasia Indonesia. They began to argue. It became heated. Mr Poan fought his corner with surprising spirit and we were taken to the Guard Room where the soldier made a number of phone calls. Suddenly Mr Poan caught my eye and winked. I was not, as the soldier wished, to be held here in custody until the Fokker returned to Bali that afternoon. Instead I had to report directly to Army HQ in Kupang where the Colonel would decide what was to be done. As Mr Poan and I drove off in a Civil Aviation jeep his hands trembled on the wheel and there was a wild light in his eye. Facing down the soldier had made him exultant.

The road, rutted and empty, wound through grassy hills that went rolling down to the sea, good cattle country. I mentioned this and Mr Poan said, yes, there was a big ranch nearby with Australian cowboys. But I realized he didn't mean cowboys. He meant bloodstock experts. Could I go and see them? He said that would depend on the Colonel. We entered the outskirts of Kupang, a sprawling, tumbledown little port fashioned from pitchpine and tin and lacking any sense of past or future. What gave it authority was the great sweep of bright water lapping at its feet. It made Kupang shine. But the waterfront buildings were derelict and the air stank of fish. The Timorese, dark-skinned and sombre, had many of the racial characteristics of the Australian aborigines.

The Army HQ was a noisy, down-at-heel building like an impoverished provincial hospital. We had a long wait for the Colonel, a looming, gravel-voiced man in jungle-green fatigues who spoke no English. His holstered revolver sat in his in-tray, together with a pineapple and a packet of tea. We stood before his desk while he growled questions and opened a file on me. Into the file went my *Observer* accreditation, photocopies of every page in my passport, photocopies of a snapshot of my family, a used British Rail ticket from North Sheen to Waterloo and a newspaper cutting about a witch doctor turning up drunk to bless a new airliner in West Africa – all of which had been tucked into the back of the passport.

The Colonel made a number of phone calls then harangued Mr Poan for several minutes. I understood a compromise had been reached. Mr Poan nodded, cleared his throat and told me I was to go straight to the Immigration Department to fill out certain forms, copies of which would also be placed in my file. I must then proceed to the Flobamor Hotel in Jalan Kenanga Nomor and stay there till early the following morning when I would be put aboard the 0700 Merpati flight to Waingapu – on which I already held a booking.

It could have been worse. At least I had a foothold on Timor. The Colonel dismissed us.

In the jeep, on the way to Immigration, Mr Poan announced that I had formally been placed in the charge of Civil Aviation.

'If you run away there will be big trouble for me,' he said, anxiously.

I promised I wouldn't run away. We left the town and, out in the open grassland, ground up a hill with the gradient of a ski jump. Immigration, a large, isolated bungalow, stood in a shallow green valley on the other side. The staff, dressed like American admirals in baseball caps with gold-trimmed visors, greeted Mr Poan as an old friend. The Director scrutinized my completed forms, personally stamped my passport and warned me not to miss my flight.

'I will see to it!' said Mr Poan.

The Director laughed and clapped him on the back. 'Mr Poan the policeman!' he said.

On the way back to Kupang I asked whether we could call on the Australian cowboys.

'No,' said Mr Poan.

The Flobamor Hotel was a long, rambling, single-storeyed structure set back from a tree-lined road. The two Timorese clerks at the desk bickered and squabbled as I registered. We got a late lunch in the dining room, which had creaking ceiling fans and tables covered with worn oilcloth. I wanted to know my precise status on Timor. Was I, for example, free to take a stroll through the town this evening?

'No,' said Mr Poan.

'Well, can I pop down to the market and buy some mangoes?'

Mr Poan, tucking into his chicken satay, said, 'This is not mango season.'

'Coconuts, then.'

'You must stay here,' said Mr Poan.

'That means I'm under house arrest.'

He shrugged.

'I hope the Colonel's given me a guard,' I said.

He peered at the road. A crocodile of schoolchildren in blue uniforms went by, hand in hand. No guard was visible but later, after telling me he would return at 2000 hours, he sneaked out and spent a little time wandering around the environs of the Flobamor, looking surreptitiously behind the bushes and trees. I went to my room, filled with comfortable old Dutch furniture and a huge Dutch bed, and got out Cobham. He had flown in via the island of Bima, giving Lombok a miss. 'Owing to the general roughness of the sea in the open roads at Kupang we landed in a little bay a few miles to the south, at Tani, and here we found that the Dutch authorities had most courteously placed one of their government steamships at our disposal. As we approached we could see S.S. *Gemma* lying at anchor, and between the steamer and the shore was the red oil drum with a hook on top which was our mooring. After circling round the steamship, which appeared to be crammed full of ladies, we landed on the water and taxied up to our mooring, which Ward successfully hooked from the float-side.'

Here an uncharacteristically coy note crept into the account. Cobham was a star but, to date, had only had to deal with the adulation of other men – easy for a battle-hardened old ace like him. Now, confronted by a boatload of admiring Dutch women, he became as gruff as if recording a terrible landing. 'It was most embarrassing when, after climbing up the gangway and shaking hands with the captain, I found scores of feminine eyes centred unwaveringly upon me. After the little reception was over we were allowed to wash, change and make ourselves more or less respectable, and later in the afternoon . . . we steamed up to Kupang to drop our load of sightseers.'

Later I went and sat on the verandah outside the dining room. Dusk began drawing in. No military presence was visible out there under the lemon and apricot sky, but a couple of Indonesian civilians at a neighbouring table stared so intently that I wondered whether I had now become an assignment for the local HANSIP rozzers, a notion scary enough to make the hairs prickle briefly on the back of my neck. But then they resumed their conversation, soft-faced, clerky men with high complaining voices, probably bemoaning their postings to a remote dump like this. Bullfrogs began to boom in a marshy little pond beside the verandah. I suddenly felt isolated and vulnerable, and dark images swam into my head – gibbets, thumbscrews, people falling from helicopters, a HANSIP torture table. This train of thought was interrupted by the arrival of two middle-aged Englishmen who walked in, sat down and ordered beers. They looked at me curiously.

'Care to join us?' one said.

I joined them.

The other said, 'Thought you might have been Dutch.'

I told them I wasn't Dutch. They looked pleased. 'Jolly good.' They sipped their Bintangs. 'Ah, that's better,' they said, and told me they were business efficiency experts out from London to bring some order to Kupang's chaotic government offices. Then, as we sat chatting about Home Counties property prices and the plays of Tom Stoppard, our voices raised against the booming of the bullfrogs, another European loomed through the gloaming.

'Excuse me,' he said, diffidently, 'but they told me that people were speaking English up here. I'm English and it's been quite a time since . . .'

We all introduced ourselves. The young Englishman, Tim, a language teacher employed at the local university, said he knew my name. At home he was an *Observer* reader and now he spoke about various pieces I had written with a highly flattering degree of knowledge and warmth. 'Wait till I write and tell my friends I bumped into you in Timor!' he said. I reflected bemusedly that, though I had had to come to the ends of the earth to meet this perceptive, intelligent man, it had been worth the trip.

We went into dinner, Warren, Don, Tim and I. Everything was off except the chicken satay but we were in a party mood and told them to keep the satay coming. 'You can keep the beer coming too,' said Don to the puzzled waitress. 'We're starting as we mean to go on.'

As the banquet got under way I reflected that, once again, the silence of the warm, still Kupang night was being broken by the sounds of the British boisterously at table. Three times a week, when the plane came through, it must have been like this. Later, Mr Poan arrived with two sharp-faced young men wearing flared jeans and satin disco shirts, fellow air traffic controllers come to help explain the workings of Eltari. I opened my notebook and we got down to business, establishing that their old grass strip, used by some of the greatest names in aviation history, was still employed when a blustery crosswind swept the main runway, but it couldn't accommodate anything larger than a Dakota. Eltari averaged 20 aircraft movements a day, mostly Mission Aviation Fellowship Aztecs and Cessnas flown by a couple of Canadian missionary pilots. A charter company had operated services from Darwin until its licence was withdrawn some years earlier.

'Why?' I asked.

'Security problem,' said Mr Poan.

'That used to be a famous flight,' said Tim, who had overheard. 'Darwin to Kupang. It was as cheap as a country bus. For young Aussies in the sixties it was the classic start to the hippie trail.'

Mr Poan said that foreign aircraft rarely came now, though, from time to time, small ones were blown in by the weather. In 1979 Kupang was visited by Flight Lieutenant David Cyster of RAF Valley in Anglesey, flying a Tiger Moth in the footsteps of Bert Hinkler, the legendary Australian trailblazer. Setting out on his final leg, Cyster's speed was reduced to 30 knots by the notorious headwinds of the Timor Sea so he returned to Kupang and tried again, successfully, the following day. Hinkler was thus the only pioneer of whom Mr Poan and his colleagues had ever heard.

'In July and August,' he said, 'a big wind blows down the hill and makes downdraft on main runway. Landing is then at pilot's discretion. If there is a 27 knot plus crosswind component he must abort and go to alternative field.'

This statement was greeted with derision by two young men who had just thrown themselves down at a neighbouring table.

'Twenty-seven plus crosswind component never keep me out of anywhere!' cried one.

'That is absolutely no problem!' confirmed the other.

They were accompanied by a plump, giggling girl with her hair worn in bangs. Mr Poan examined them through narrowed eyes and muttered, 'That is Merpati crew who will take you to Waingapu tomorrow.'

I watched them with a flicker of unease. They began swallowing beer thirstily as Don and Warren mourned the decline of Welsh rugby and Tim talked nostalgically about the great railway line running over the Pennines from Settle to Carlisle. Other men drifted in and joined us. I asked if anyone here was my guard and three said yes. I bought them beers and toasted the Colonel's health.

The looming shadow of East Timor inevitably intruded on the evening. It was not discussed openly, but rather alluded to, small, persistent references dropped into the conversation and left there. Perhaps its proximity made comment dangerous, perhaps the business had been going on for so long, and had become such a familiar aspect of Timor life, that there wasn't much left to say. The people who told me things were Indonesians with a bit of drink inside them. I heard of soldiers trussing up the bodies of their victims on poles, like pigs, and dumping them in village squares for headcounts. I heard that FRETILIN prisoners were being held just down the road, in the Kupang goal; my informants whispered that it was a very bad place. The torturers were there, mild-mannered, self-effacing men who went around with the gravity of undertakers, known to everyone in town. One had joined the consortium of senior Army officers who now ran East Timor's coffee industry for their own personal gain. Their company traded under the name of P.T. Denok. All of them, including the torturer, had become fabulously rich.

(Eighteen months later, back in London, I read a report on East Timor prepared by Amnesty International, a bleak document that confirmed, among its list of charges, the existence of the torture manual of which the French engineer at Ngurah Rai had spoken. It even quoted from it. 'Avoid taking photographs showing torture, of someone being given electric shocks, stripped naked and so on. Remember that such photographs . . . should not be . . . obtained by irresponsible members of society.' It also announced the massacre, at Bobonaro just across the border during the month of my visit, of a hundred males. I remembered the soldiers who had boarded the plane, Bobby, Donny, Eric and Cedric, with their gaily embroidered rifle slings, then read that at Luro, in the same month, seven other Timorese were shot in a minor local operation. Amnesty published their names: Antonio Hornay, Jorge Pinto, Afonso dos Santos, Rui Manuel, Kote Lai, Victor and Americo Branco.)

The party broke up after midnight. Warren and Don went to their rooms, Tim set off down the dark road to his lodgings; Mr Poan and his associates had gone long before. Only the Merpati crew was left, the stewardess sleeping in her chair, the pilots sitting there heavy-eyed. They pulled up a chair for me and said they were sick of flying small planes to places like Kupang. They dreamed of joining the Garuda 747 fleet, of big planes, big money, big cities. The problem was that they had not shone at Curug, Indonesia's civil aviation school outside Jakarta.

'He fail Religion,' teased the co-pilot, nodding at his skipper.

'And *he* fail Management and Leadership,' said the skipper.

All Curug students, before graduating, are left in the jungle for several days without food or resources to test their ability to live off the land, eating monkeys and grubbing for roots. My friends, laughing and sending an exhausted waiter for more Bintang, said they had nearly starved.

'You ought to lay off the beer,' I said. 'You've got to start work again soon. Go to bed.'

The skipper yawned and looked at his watch. 'It's 0100. Early morning call at 0500, take off at 7. Six hours from bottle to throttle? Man, that's plenty.'

Mr Poan arrived at sunrise, looking rested and cheerful. 'Come and see this,' he said, leading me over the road to the Governor's Office. In the grounds was a pit containing two Komodo dragons, giant monitor lizards lying there like satiated crocodiles. Mr Poan said they had been brought from Komodo, a bleak little island 300 miles east of Bali, when they were babies. That clearly had been some time ago; one of these brutes was 10 feet long. 'The Governor give them a chicken each every two days. Do not go too near. Their spit is poison.'

I recalled that Cobham, at Bima, had been shown some captive dragons too – 'treacherous creatures which live chiefly on the wild hog, ponies and buck that abound on the island of Komodo . . . when they have dismembered their victims they swallow the portions whole' – and sent a dispatch home to London. Even stranger than the dragons was the way 'every newspaper made them grow day by day. In fact, one of the leading papers in Rangoon had a gigantic headline stretched across the whole sheet which told of land-lizards ninety yards long.'

The Merpati crew emerged from the hotel and tumbled sleepily into their van. Mr Poan, following it to the airport, seemed elated by the prospect of a quiet, trouble-free day ahead; he told me Mrs Poan sent her best regards. At Eltari a Mission Aviation Fellowship Aztec taxied past and he waved to the Canadian at the controls. Two Merpati aircraft stood on the apron, a Friendship and a Twin Otter. Moments later the crew emerged from the terminal, formed a conga line and went dancing away towards the Friendship, circled it and danced back to the Otter. Mr Poan was too astonished to speak. The skipper boarded the Otter backwards, hauling his co-pilot up by the armpits while the stewardess assisted with a series of heaves. 'Pull more,' she shouted. 'He heavy!' The plane rocked as they vanished through the door.

Mr Poan shook his head and went 'Tsk tsk tsk' but, suspecting this had been laid on for my benefit, I felt only moderately uneasy. Three other passengers were approaching. I thanked Mr Poan warmly, apologized for being such a nuisance and scrambled into the little Canadian-built 20-seat high-wing monoplane with its non-retractable landing gear. The stewardess sat at the front making up her eyes. I went and sat with her. The pilots turned and grinned at me. They were busy checking the alarm systems – fire and stall warnings blared and hooted briefly, startling the other passengers – and testing the radios, fuel pumps, battery temperature, navigation instruments, flying controls and master caution panel.

They were ready to start up. 'Where you want to go?' asked the skipper.

'Acapulco,' I said.

'Okay.'

The stewardess laughed and hunted in her handbag as the two small Pratt & Whitney turbo-props whined and the propellers began to spin. The Otter swung on to the runway and braked, the pilots running through their litany of pre-take-off checks, chanting autofeather on, speed governor okay, all circuit-breakers in, landing lights on, flaps set 10 degrees, flight controls full and free. Then the skipper reached up and pushed at the twin throttles above the windscreen. The engine note rose to a deafening howl and the aircraft vibrated wildly. As the stewardess, gazing into a pocket mirror, applied vivid orange lipstick the Otter rushed down the

runway and soared over the town and the little offshore island of
Semau. Then, on a westerly heading, it set out over the Sawu Sea
towards Sumba.

In terms of the Imperial route I was now going the wrong way.
Waingapu, on Sumba, had come before Kupang, but modern
schedules obliged me to do it in reverse. (To catch a Darwin flight I
would need to backtrack even further, all the way to Bali.) But in
1935 Kupang had been the traditional gateway to Australia, the
launching point for the most dangerous leg of the trip. Dr K.
Washington Gray, travelling on the Qantas DH 86 *Melbourne*
(commanded by Captain H. B. Hussey, who was assisted by Mr R.
A. Shepherd) had been preoccupied with the 500-mile ocean
crossing all the way from Singapore. Though meeting his pilots and
examining the aeroplane there had helped – 'Somehow the Timor
Sea crossing loomed less formidably ahead when I had seen the men
and the craft,' he reported in the *Gazette* – he was distinctly edgy as
they prepared to lift off from Kupang's grass runway. 'Here we are,
shivering on the brink, with the Timor Sea ahead. There's quite a
crowd to see us off, for it's Queen Wilhelmina's birthday and the
mail plane is still novelty enough to be welcome on a holiday. One
cheerful Dutch father and mother brought six children down and
left two at home ill.'

Now, with Timor fading behind, we droned over a flat green sea
marked with occasional drift lines of floating trees and coconuts.
The sky was cloudless and a misty pink line banded the horizon. I
was wondering whether Tropical Cyclone Ferdinand had changed
course or blown itself out when the stewardess tapped my shoulder
and pointed down. 'Whale!' she said. It was out on our port beam, a
small elliptical thing of shiny black glass with a lacy, frothing wake
behind it. Then it dived, leaving scarcely a ripple and, exhilarated by
the sighting, I called to a stooped wizened man seated across the
aisle and told him about it. He clutched a plastic shopping bag
decorated with a smudged likeness of Concorde and, frowning,
turned away and strengthened his grip on the bag.

Seventy minutes out of Kupang we made our landfall over
Sumba, approaching Waingapu across a succession of round,
chalk-topped hills and small, shadowy valleys filled with stands of
palms, bananas and sandalwood; some valleys were bright with

wild flowers, others had streams tumbling along their grassy floors. The bald hills and lush, mysterious little valleys went on and on, right across the island, the air coming off this uneven terrain making the Otter kick and sway. The Waingapu strip lay in a green hollow, like a formal garden into which we drifted, gently as a descending balloon. The pilots said the airport manager was Alfred Jacobus, a good man. Now they were going to Flores. They would spend the day island hopping east again and finish up tonight back in Kupang where, they promised, they would have a glass or two for me.

The terminal was set among trees, its empty control tower painted a cheery yellow. In the tiny, bare Arrivals Hall I asked for Mr Jacobus and was led through a shady courtyard to a room where half a dozen young men sat staring attentively at a blackboard on which a neat parallelogram had been chalked. They were being addressed by Mr Jacobus, who was trim and bespectacled and whose regulation blue shirt and trousers were so heavily starched that they seemed to hold him rigidly upright, like armour.

I introduced myself and asked when he would be free for a chat.

'I am teaching this people Procedures,' he said.

I said I could come back whenever it was convenient. He suggested 7 o'clock the following morning. Meanwhile, was there anything he could do? Perhaps I needed a lift into town; his driver and jeep were at my disposal. I asked the driver to take me to a bank. He was an eager youth in wraparound plastic sunglasses who, as we set off beside a slow brown river, told me he wanted to be a beelat.

'What's that?' I asked.

'Papa India Lima Oscar Tango, sir,' he said, honking his horn at a water buffalo.

Waingapu was hot and flat, its streets full of drifting white dust and a blinding white glare. From its ramshackle little port, where the driver stopped to buy fish for his mother, the hills of Flores loomed purple across the water. We called at the Merpati office to collect some cargo manifests; it was open to the road and managed by a fat, weary-looking woman who sat beneath a pair of faded company posters in magnificent carved sandalwood frames, listening to the crackling voices of her pilots on a giant crystal set. The town mosque was hung with large speakers, the town clock, standing in a dusty, wooded roundabout, had stopped at 10 to 3, and the bank with its vaulted, tiled roof looked like the villa of a millionaire Dutch planter.

Inside I told the clerk I wanted to cash a traveller's cheque for $100, the smallest denomination I had left. He peered at the cheque then gave it to the manager, who looked like a retired general and who, noisily sucking his teeth, examined my passport ('Ah, Bangkok! I have also been') and asked questions about my profession, place of domicile, marital status and reasons for visiting Indonesia. He wanted to know where I was staying in Waingapu. I said I had made no arrangements.

'You stay at Sandalwood.' This was an instruction; compliance, clearly, meant I was likely to get my money.

'Okay.'

'I will give you 9.237 roops for the dollar,' he said, trimming the rate a little and handing me his personal pen. I signed in the midst of a press of people, staff and customers alike, who had come over to watch, their demeanour solemn, as though witnessing the initialling of an important treaty. The manager and the clerk, bending low to ensure there was no forgery, blew warm breath on my hand. When it was done the manager nodded and the clerk, sighing, smiled at me.

Back in the jeep the driver warned that news of the transaction would spread quickly and I could expect to be visited by many people wanting to do business. Negotiating a deeply cratered track he said, 'Sell plenket.'

'Sell what?'

'Bravo Lima Alpha November Kilo Echo Tango, sir.'

We pulled up outside a dumpy two-storeyed building with a doormat outside saying 'Wellcome'. I registered in the restaurant, a small, airless room containing ten metal tables and an orange cat that kept hurling itself from end to end as though trying to bounce off the walls. The proprietor, a morose Chinese named Fung, directed me to a room containing two huge mahogany beds and a child's night light, a toy bear with miniature red bulbs screwed into its eye sockets. Mr Fung warned that the bear couldn't be turned off. In the bathroom there was a malodorous Asian toilet and a tank of stale water. Downstairs a burly blond European sat in a stony courtyard reading a James Clavell paperback. He was from Frankfurt and had come to Sumba to buy the fine *ikat* blankets for which, he said, the island was famous.

'They make blankets also on Timor and Flores but they do not have the quality of the Sumba *ikat*,' he said. 'Here the warp thread is dyed with natural local dyes, like indigo, and dried before it is woven with the weft. They do this many, many times to get the final design. Sometimes it will take many months to produce just one blanket. I go to the best villages, I learn about the best weaves, the best colourings, and then I buy the best blankets. Here I have bought three for a thousand dollars each. In Frankfurt I will sell them for a big profit; there is a vogue now for such naturalistic things. It is how I pay for my holiday. Next year I will go to Irian Jaya and buy the primitive Asmat artefacts, unique red, black and white carvings for which the Germans will pay a *fortune*.'

He showed me his three $1,000 blankets, dowdy fabrics decorated with human and animal figures worked in dull reds and blues, then stuffed them into a small jiffy bag and headed for the airport. He expected to be home in 30 hours, back at his office in 36. I watched his battered taxi bucking away up the rutted track and envied him a life that apparently contained no uncertainties, compromises or contradictions at all.

That evening the blanket sellers were waiting for me, a dozen figures squatting patiently in the courtyard, motionless as statues. Mr Fung's son, an energetic young businessman with a blanket shop in Bali, warned that they were selling rubbish: bad weaves, chemical dyes, poor designs. He was putting a cassette into the video machine, a Hong Kong kung fu film from which the government had removed all Chinese elements.

'So what's left?' I asked.

'Just fighting,' he said, sadly.

I got a Bintang and went into the courtyard. A breeze was coming off the sea, soothing and cool. The blanket sellers approached one by one, shadowy, soft-voiced men who accepted my refusals without rancour and drifted away again. Another guest joined me in the courtyard, the wizened man who had travelled on the Twin Otter from Kupang with the Concorde shopping bag. He had the bag with him now. I bought him a beer and asked what was in it.

He leant towards me and spoke in a low voice. 'Calibrations,' he said.

I looked at him. 'Calibrations?'

'Yes.' He sipped some beer. 'Tokyo good, Taiwan good, Wellington also good but Darwin best.'

'Best for what?'

He tapped his bag. 'For this.'

The kung fu video filled the courtyard with screams and the noises of combat. Many of the blanket sellers had stayed to watch, squatting in the darkness, peering through the windows. My companion said, 'Let us go to the town, mister, for eating.'

He rose, clutching his calibrations, and we set off along the track to a tiny, shadowy restaurant lit by a couple of kerosene lamps. The cook, clattering pans on a wood-burning stove, turned as we entered.

'*Hitler!*' he cried.

He and my companion shook hands warmly. Then we sat and ordered Special Chicken Goreng, a mess of charred bone served in a spicy peanut sauce.

'Are you really called Hitler?' I asked.

'Yes, mister.'

He ate with great appetite, crunching the bones between his teeth and slowly sucking his fingers. I wanted to know more about his name and his calibrations but he now chose to maintain a deep monastic silence. A cock walked in, crowed loudly then walked out again. The cook told me that the sale of spirits had recently been banned on Sumba, because strong drink made people drowsy and no work was done. I accompanied Hitler back to the hotel, ran a cordon of late blanket sellers and went to bed, the red eyes of the toy bear glittering fiercely in the darkness.

Alfred Jacobus offered me breakfast – sweet cakes and a choice of Jonny Cola or Sumba coffee, black as Guinness with a collar of grounds floating on top like chopped nuts. He occupied a well-appointed Ministerial-sized office with heavy curtains and deep pile carpets. The luxury of the premises seemed to embarrass him; he said his was a small airport with a single 1,500-metre strip and just one crash car. Until VHF radio had been installed a couple of years previously fires were lit to give incoming pilots the wind direction; a specialist fire team had burned green leaves and straw to make the maximum smoke.

The busiest days of Mr Jacobus's week were Sundays and Fridays, when he turned around a 748 and two Twin Otters. There was nothing on Mondays and Thursdays, but a 748 came through on Tuesdays and Wednesdays, and another, bound from Kupang to Denpasar and Surabaya, on Saturdays. I was due out on the Saturday 748 to Denpasar and said I hoped all was well with it since, early the following morning, I was scheduled to fly to Darwin.

He had news for me. 'You may have some problems because tomorrow is Quiet Day on Bali. Once a year the law says everyone must go to his home and stay there, making no noise. From midnight to midnight nobody may leave his house, drive a car or ride a bicycle. Even to walk is forbidden. On Quiet Day the roads must be empty and the island must be silent. People may not cook or sing. This applies also to the tourists. They have to stay in the hotel and eat only cold food.'

I wondered anxiously how the Quiet Day organizers felt about the racket of jet engines. Mr Jacobus offered a crumb of comfort.

'The Garuda DC9 to Darwin is the only international flight scheduled for tomorrow. If it depart early enough maybe they let it leave. But you perhaps will have to sleep at the airport. If you try to go on the road after midnight they will arrest you.'

I made an urgent mental note to see the Garuda people at Ngurah Rai that afternoon then asked Mr Jacobus whether he knew anything about the little Qantas biplanes that had called here half a century earlier.

He shook his head. 'There was an Australian pilot flying DC3s for Zamrud Aviation who always came here from Surabaya, Captain Jack Rife, Romeo India Foxtrot Echo, Rife, not Knife' – he beamed at me – 'but we haven't seen him for a few years. Everyone knew him, all the children loved him, people shouted "Hullo, Jack!" when he got out of the plane. He was a very big jolly fellow.' He ate a cake.

We went for a stroll and Mr Jacobus introduced me to some of his staff. There were 75 of them, all so young, eager and neatly turned out that it was like visiting a bustling little high school; everyone seethed with energy and commitment and yearned palpably for more aeroplanes to practise on. A girl from Cargo with a crisp white ribbon in her hair said the freight she dispatched consisted mostly of blankets.

'Sumba also once exported many slaves – before aviation age, of course,' added Mr Jacobus, his faint air of regret implying, perhaps, that he would not be averse to handling further consignments for the sake of some regular charter traffic.

The girl told me that women in Indonesian aviation enjoyed full equality of opportunity; why, one of the Bouraq 748 co-pilots, Mrs Cipplu, expected to get her command any day now. I said I hoped she would be taking me to Bali, and Mr Jacobus addressed the girl.

'Is Cipplu flying today? Find out, find out!'

The girl switched on her walkie-talkie. 'Is Cipplu on Bouraq to Bali at 1350?'

'Over, missy! Over!' muttered Mr Jacobus.

'Over!' sang the girl.

'Negative,' said a crackling voice. 'Today it is Natagawa, over.'

'Natagawa is half-Japanese,' Mr Jacobus explained. 'I think his daddy was a troop in the war.'

We walked out to the runway, a grass strip until 1978, and paused at the spot where, that same year, a Dakota out of Surabaya suffered undercarriage failure and came to grief with a broken wing and its tail stuck in the air. The wreckage had long since been removed, but the accident was still spoken of as the only untoward thing to have happened at Waingapu in recent memory. Here the air was noisy with birdsong, dew sparkled on the grass runway verges and the stately perimeter trees cast deep shadows. I thought it a peaceful, pretty place and wondered whether the travellers calling in for tea and biscuits en route to their nightstop at Kupang had remarked on it.

I said as much to Mr Jacobus who observed, probably accurately, that they may indeed have remarked on it but, in all probability, wouldn't have had the faintest idea where they actually were.

In the course of the next three hours Tropical Cyclone Ferdinand, approaching from the northwest, fell upon Sumba. The sky turned the colour of flint, rain began to clatter at the windows and the glass dropped as though suddenly vulnerable to gravity. The 748 from Kupang got in on time but the pilot, Captain Sumitro, wanted his nine joining passengers boarded as quickly as possible; he had no wish to hang around in this. As I began climbing the rickety steps Mr Jacobus suddenly thrust a parcel into my arms. 'Just Sumba blanket for souvenir,' he said shyly, then slipped away before I could thank him. The Cargo girl came out of the terminal and waved. Aboard the 748 there was a heated argument in progress between the pilots and their flight engineer, a round, balding man with his tie yanked halfway down his neck. The stewardess, basket of candies in hand, went and listened anxiously. For some time the engineer harangued them, gesturing at his control panel, but he failed to sway Captain Sumitro who abruptly fastened his harness and spoke sharply, silencing him. The Darts were started and running within the minute.

We climbed through squally showers into a lowering sky and levelled off for our two-hour run to Bali. It grew very dark. Captain Sumitro came aft for a brief word with the stewardess. He offered each of his passengers a clove cigarette then hastened back to his flight deck, stowing all loose objects and strapping himself in tight. The 748 began to pitch and roll. Rain sluicing across the windows produced the restricted visibility you get in a car wash. At the rear of the cabin a little girl in a pretty green dress began to cry. Captain Sumitro turned the flight deck lighting up to full. I thought I discerned the rattle of hail on the roof. The radios crackled with static and the motion of the 748 grew steadily more violent.

In the Imperial Airways *Pilot's Manual* turbulence was dealt with thus: 'Reports of bumpiness should be given according to the following scale of intensity:

> No bumps
> Bumpy
> Very bumpy
> Exceptionally bumpy.'

The section entitled 'Classification of Bumps' was brief, the manual's author – perhaps a pilot with limited bad weather experience – citing only two:

> 'Sharp bumps
> Slow sinking bumps.'

Neither accurately described the motion of the 748, which now resembled a manoeuvre combining elements of both the ski jump and the pole vault, the long downward rush followed by a violent vertical leap that took us, flexing and creaking, to the head of the next ramp. My suspicion that we were progressing through the core of a thunderstorm was reinforced when, out to the right, a giant flashgun started going off, filling the sky with wild eruptions of light. Then, for a moment or two, we flew into semi-clear air. The cloud deck below was the colour of granite. Line squalls marched into a black horizon veined by white lightning. Tossed from one storm cell to another we blundered on, nose up, nose down, in the approximate direction of Bali. Captain Sumitro was flying by hand. I watched his back for signs of spatial disorentation, tunnel vision, uncontrollable head-nodding or any of the other symptoms shown by pilots in extreme turbulence, but he just sat there, heading doggedly towards Ferdinand's outer perimeter. Sparks were not coming from his controls and they seemed not to be giving him electric shocks; nor were we wrapped in the ghostly radiance of St Elmo's fire. But the engine note changed constantly and, at one point, the speed brakes popped out and the 748 staggered as though it had flown into a wall.

Then, without warning, it ceased. We passed out of Ferdinand into a dim, calm sky. Captain Sumitro switched off the seat belt sign, loosened his harness and turned the controls over to Mr Natagawa. At the back the little girl stopped screaming. The stewardess rose shakily and made coffee for the crew. We were crossing the southern coast of Sumbawa, a prospect of deep bays, tall, surf-edged cliffs and amber beaches which gave off a curious glitter, like fool's gold. We tracked on over other green islands, wooded and beautiful, their graceful volcanic silhouettes set against a dark sea, then slid back into more cloud, woolly and benign now, and landed at Denpasar in heavy overcast.

The little girl vomited on the tarmac as she disembarked, weeping while her mother, a grave-faced, handsome woman, held her shoulders and comforted her. I hurried to the Garuda desk and asked the clerk whether the Quiet Day would affect the departure of the Darwin service. He said no, the authorities had given it clearance but, unless I was staying at a big hotel, I must be at the airport by midnight tonight, the hour when the Quiet Day started. The major hotels would each be allowed to send a minibus with its Darwin-bound guests provided it reached Ngurah Rai before 7 a.m.; Pertamina Cottages were among those granted the concession. But he warned that if I missed the minibus I missed the flight. The roads were closed to everyone, even those on foot.

There were soldiers patrolling the approaches to the Cottages and a crimson banner strung across the entrance saying 'Welcome to His Highness Prince Norodom Sihanouk'. I got my old room back, poured myself a beer and switched on the television. Flash Gordon was being pursued by a growling, yellow-clad demon which, though made of vegetable matter, was nevertheless the most powerful thing on the planet of Mongo. Flash evaded its slimy clutches, jumped aboard the Sky Train and made for a new galaxy, unaware that the monster was skulking in his cargo bay. It put a tentacle out of the window, reached forward, smashed the windscreen and seized Flash by the throat. Flash had been space-jacked! He advised everyone that he was losing power, and began turning a vivid, luminous green.

I switched it off and went in search of Prince Sihanouk. It had occurred to me that, like a real foreign correspondent, I ought to try and get an interview. He might even say something important enough to justify a collect call to the *Observer*'s copytakers in London. I finally ran him to ground in the lobby where he sat, talking quietly to two Balinese officials dressed stiffly in their Sunday best. When they withdrew I approached the man who, pulled out of high school at 18 by Cambodia's French colonial rulers and named king, had now forged an uneasy alliance with the mad Pol Pot in an attempt to oust the Vietnamese invaders from his country.

He greeted me amiably but said he did not wish to discuss politics just then; perhaps he would be making an announcement in a couple of days. So, with nothing much else to talk about, I asked him for the name of his favourite song. He smiled. 'Blue Moon,' he said and, as he walked out the door with his aides, he was humming it.

IV

The Garuda DC9, cruising at a height of 39,000 feet, took two hours and 20 minutes to reach Darwin. At Ngurah Rai the in-flight caterers, anticipating the needs of the 74 Australian passengers, had put aboard a lot of extra beer. People began demanding it the instant the seat belt sign was switched off and the stewards hastened up and down the aisle crying, '12 beer for 15 ABC, 14 beer for row 8, more beer for 20 D.' The men in seats 15 ABC had been drunk when they embarked. They were among those obliged to get to Ngurah Rai before midnight and, to keep them and their two or three dozen compatriots happy, the bar remained open. At 6.45, having driven down roads that were eerily silent and deserted, the feeling of having witnessed the aftermath of a nuclear attack was heightened when I found the terminal floor strewn with inert figures. Many boarded the aircraft whey-faced and groaning but take-off gave them a second wind and, waving away the proffered continental breakfasts, they called for more of the amber liquid. The hard drinkers, a minority of our complement, were viewed with marked distaste by everyone else, and responded by growing raucous and belligerently Ockerish.

I craned to look back, noting only an area of blackness low on the horizon where Bali had been. The sea was bruise-coloured and flecked with foam. Stately gunmetal-and-cream clouds crossed our path, trawling showers behind them, the rain cutting ragged patterns into the water. On the horizon plump pillars swirled upwards like bushfire smoke and hung, pall-like, several thousand feet above, obscuring the sun. We were flying through a sky filled with wind and weather and, as the jet slipped and staggered, the cabin attendants delivered the beer and breakfasts in a series of short rushes, getting a handhold on one seatback before venturing on to the next. We were approaching a shadowy wall of cumulo-nimbus, buttressed and domed like a cathedral. As we raced up to it I saw that all its constituent parts were moving independently of each other, governed by their own internal systems of pressures and temperature inversions.

The plane followed the route I had flown, in reverse, the previous day, tracking east, cutting south to Sumba, then on down to Timor, sighted 70 minutes into the flight. I chatted to a buxom, good-humoured Sydney girl who, looking down on Timor, said, 'We keep reading the most terrible things in the papers about what's happening there. You know the Timorese gave the Japs a real runaround during the war? They saved a hell of a lot of Australian lives, but what happened when they needed *us*? Bloody Gough Whitlam sold them down the river.'

At Timor we turned south off Airway White 43 – the designated track commercial aircraft operating this route must follow – on to Amber 464, which led all the way to Brisbane, and I reflected with real satisfaction that at long last I was setting out across the celebrated shark-infested Timor Sea just as the *ancien régime* had done all those years before. They, 'shivering on the brink' like Dr Washington Gray at Kupang, must have lifted off full of trepidation, anxiously contemplating the dangerous waters below while their pilots began a constant nervous monitoring of compass, speed and fuel gauge, senses alert for the sudden onset of the notorious headwinds. In the event, Washington Gray's reservations were soon replaced by a kind of euphoria. Waved on their way by the throng of Dutch sightseers, they were off and climbing 'up, up to 9,000, 10,000, 11,000, 12,000, 12,500. Yes, Darwin was right as usual, "45 miles an hour headwind on the ground, decreasing to nil at 11,000 feet; 10 miles an hour tail wind at 13,000 feet". Pretty good that, when you realize it had been projected from a point 500 miles away. Two hours out, three hours out; wonderful weather, all clouds left behind, clear as a bell from the floor to the stratosphere.'

Cobham, of course, had felt no qualms at all. 'Naturally we were quite confident about our engine and machine,' he wrote airily, 'and we knew that unless anything very unforeseen happened it was highly improbable that they would let us down. Really all we had to do was steer a good compass course and resign ourselves to a few monotonous hours of flying out of sight of land, relying on our compass to bring us eventually to our destination.'

But the Australians, who knew the moods of the Timor Sea better than he did, had taken certain precautions. The gunboat *Geranium* was standing by in Darwin Harbour with steam up and Cobham's proposed course, telegraphed ahead by the Dutch at Kupang, secure in her captain's pocket. Though grateful for these attentions, Cobham soared on secure in the knowledge that his was 'perhaps the finest aeroplane compass in the world. It is known as the Hughes Aperiodic and is the result of exhaustive mathematical research and experiment during the latter years of the war.' In the event, it proved to be of only marginal benefit. Soon the wind began to blow – 'we were flying right into the teeth of the southeast trades' – and he was obliged to drop to 50 feet and navigate by dead reckoning. The wind teased him mischievously. First it 'would be blowing head on to us, then it would veer a bit to our port, then again it would go over to our starboard and, as it veered, so I allowed a few points on the compass to rectify the drift.'

He had taken off at 7 a.m., Timor fading quickly behind him – 'the visibility was not very good that day' – and now, almost 60 years later, following his approximate path, the same conditions prevailed. Timor's long, low, sparsely wooded shoreline fell away as, aboard the DC9, the breakfast trays were collected and stowed, and the drinkers came under the direct authority of the sky marshal, a stooped, wiry security man who personally took their orders and delivered their beer with an air of quiet malevolence that frightened them. They asked, only half jokingly, if he carried a gun. He said yes, and he had been specially trained to shoot it in aeroplanes. They grew reflective, and most people settled down to sleep.

It was around here in 1942 that Captain A. Koch, carrying Army reinforcements from Darwin to Surabaya in the Qantas Empire boat *Corio*, was jumped by seven Japanese fighters. Though many of his passengers died and he sustained serious leg wounds, Captain Koch proceeded to give the enemy a master class in virtuoso evasive flying that is still talked about today. He took his lumbering flying boat down to sea level then raced it at high speed through the swell, snaking between the waves until the astonished Japanese, seeing his hull and floats almost clubbing the basking sharks, decided it would be foolhardy to try a second attack and withdrew. (But the *Corio*, mortally damaged with two engines on fire, could take little more. Captain Koch got the survivors out then swam five miles to Timor for help.)

Our two stewardesses had fallen asleep, curled in their seats like children. The skirt of one had ridden up her thigh, marked with the scars of tropical sores, and the sky marshal hurried along the aisle and pulled it down again. She jerked awake, slapping angrily at his hand and he explained himself, voice squeaky with embarrassment. I turned away to watch the weather coming in from the Arafura Sea, dark cumulu-nimbus skyscrapers bursting with rain and licked by flickering tongues of lightning. There was no break in the overcast ahead. We went bumping on through a thick, impenetrable mist of the kind which, before Imperial – leading the world – fitted its HP 42s with stabilizing instruments like the artificial gyro horizon, could cause such acute sensory deprivation in a pilot that he risked flying into the sea.

In 1933 the first of the company's aircraft to reach Australia ran into the winds and, once again, almost failed to make it. After the humiliating end of the *City of Cairo* in its grassy Timor meadow a year earlier, the company now urgently needed to prove it was capable of completing the marathon run that, perhaps rashly, it had promised to operate as a regular scheduled service. The new attempt was made by the largest and most modern machine in its fleet, the Armstrong Whitworth Atalanta *Astraea* – fitted with extra tankage at the insistence of its VIP passenger, Imperial's Air Superintendant Major H.C. Brackley, who had heard about the Timor Sea winds. Known to his pilots as 'Brackles', he was out to demonstrate not merely that the proposed service was technically feasible, but that a permanent air link between England and Australia made sound commercial sense. (In the event, he came home with the Qantas-Imperial joint venture compromise insisted upon by the Canberra government.)

Then, over the Timor Sea and way past the point-of-no-return, the pilots informed a horrified Brackles that he must don his Sidcot survival suit and prepare to ditch; the winds had been stronger than anticipated, the fuel was almost gone and there was still no sign of land. It wasn't just the seemingly imminent prospect of death by drowning that appalled him but, worse, the shame of having failed a second time. Brackles's bacon – and the company's good name – were saved moments later by a radio message from an enterprising Alsatian Franciscan named Father F. X. Gsell. Father Gsell, whose

Bathurst Island mission lay directly under the flight path to the mainland, had only a month earlier cleared a landing strip for aviators faced by precisely this kind of eventuality. The *Astraea* sputtered down in the nick of time. Brackles and his party were then obliged to spend 48 hours singing hymns with the Bathurst aborigines while the mission lugger *St Francis* sailed to Darwin to fetch petrol. (When the *Astraea* eventually took off on its last leg Father Gsell – later appointed Roman Catholic Bishop of Darwin – went along for the ride.)

Now, two hours and five minutes out of Denpasar, I thought I saw a faint, indeterminate smudge low on the southern horizon. The mist had thinned and I stared fixedly until I was certain this was no cloudy miasma or trick of the light. It began spreading along the skyline with an exhilarating substance and authority, and when I seemed to discern a yellow beach and a brief ripple of surf I rang elatedly for a steward and asked for champagne. He said they weren't carrying any so I ordered a cold beer instead, drinking to Australia as it continued its steady, stately advance, not much to remark on in terms of scenery, certainly, but for me a spectacle so moving that the blare of the Pratt & Whitneys sounded in my head like trumpets.

At this point Dr Washington Gray aboard the *Melbourne* inquired excitedly, 'Is it? Yes, there comes the faint darkening, away on the edge of the world – Australia!' while Cobham, so concerned by the effect of the winds on his fuel state that he had begun wondering whether he could get the plane down in such a heavy sea and even 'how long we could live on the rations that we had aboard', when 'a faint shade appeared on the horizon – a dim outline with a little kink in it which did not alter as we drew nearer – and I realized that it was land ahead and shouted through to Ward to tell him the glad news.' His dead reckoning had brought him to a point 100 miles from Darwin. He turned and coast-crawled until, at the conclusion of his formidable six-hour flight, 'the harbour of Darwin came into view and we discerned the yellow funnels of H.M.S. *Geranium* waiting there to receive us. As we alighted on the water a launch came out to meet us and we were taken on board and given a rousing welcome by the officials of Port Darwin.'

Now we flew along the coast too, running past a curving, indented shoreline of mud and mangrove, then beginning a steep descent over dark, pancake-flat islands and a long promontory. We overhauled a whizzing red speedboat containing a man and a topless brown girl who waved to us, banked over more mud flats and slid on to finals. The pilots, perhaps distracted by the sighting of the girl, made a kind of crash landing, the violence of the impact dislodging several of the cabin's sculptured wall panels. They clattered to the deck, making the sky marshal leap to his feet and glare fore and aft, looking very, very nervous.

Darwin, as we taxied in, was a scattering of highrise buildings glimpsed over a wooded green horizon. A fat, heavily bearded official in shorts signalled us to a halt with his batons. A dozen fat baggage handlers, truculent-looking men also wearing shorts, straggled towards the DC9's cargo hold. I had grown unaccustomed to the sight of Europeans doing menial work, and to manual workers with massive paunches hanging from their sagging belts. Recalling the thin, eager, fastidious ground personnel of South East Asia I watched as the door opened and yet another fat man entered and re-enacted the solemn ritual performed aboard every aircraft arriving in Australia, progressing slowly down the aisle with arms outstretched, the aerosol sprays in either hand intended to kill the plagues of foreign insects with which the DC9 was doubtless infested. He squirted the rear toilets then, like a portly archimandrite waving his censers, headed back to the nose, still spraying, gave the flight deck a lengthy burst and left without a word.

As we followed him down the steps I recalled that it was the Imperial Airways Experimental Production Section at Battersea that had first faced up to the problem of insects – specially the malaria-carrying anopheles mosquito – hitching rides in the equatorial regions. Under the personal direction of Colonel F.P. Mackie, the company's medical adviser, they 'perfected a system which they believe to be the most effective precaution which science has yet been able to devise against the menace of the mosquito'. The Phantomyst Vaporizer, fashioned from lightweight metal and installed in all Imperial aircraft operating on tropical routes, permeated the cabin 'with an insecticide distilled from a small wild flower called Pyrethrum that is specially cultivated for this purpose on the sunny slopes of Kenya and in the South of England'. Electrically powered, the Phantomyst discharged a fine, dry, almost odourless cloud which caused 'insects to succumb almost immediately'.

The Darwin immigration officers were an affable, courteous bunch who painstakingly tapped our names and passport numbers into their computers to ensure we were not required to assist with any ongoing police inquiries. Customs took a long time. Many of the DC9's passengers were unkempt, sunburned kids who had been travelling rough in the Third World. All their cases were opened and emptied, each sleeping bag unzipped and carefully examined, the contents of every bottle, tube and jar sniffed or tasted.

But the kids were clean. The one who got into trouble was me.

The inspector, a big, raw-boned, yellow-haired young man, peered into my bag and, perhaps noting that I was middle-aged and wearing a suit, began a fairly cursory examination of its contents.

Suddenly he froze. 'Christ!' he exclaimed.

'What's wrong?'

'Your bag's full of bloody *wood*!'

He dipped in his hands and brought them out heaped with Burmese chess pieces. 'Didn't you read your form?' he fumed. 'You got to *declare* this stuff. Failure to do so makes you liable to prosecution.' He beckoned urgently to a colleague. 'Wood can be a real bugger,' he continued, with a mixture of anger and earnestness. 'Burma, eh? I'll bet they've got some bloody horrible things running round up there. Some nasty little Burmese germ could be hiding in one of these pawns waiting to decimate the forests of Australia.'

I remembered my Lombok pigs and, chastened, handed them over, but the pigs were of only marginal interest. He and his colleague, grimly preoccupied with the gaily painted little cherry-wood chessmen, scrutinized each individually. Eventually the colleague said he reckoned they were clean and I was sent on my way with a warning and a flea in my ear.

At the door another official handed me a form entitled 'Malaria and You'. He said, 'You want to read that, mate,' so I read it in the taxi, noting that if I fell ill within six weeks I must, as a potential carrier, furnish my doctor with a list of the countries visited during the period abroad – 18 in my case – together with the form itself, which urged him to 'report immediately any suspected quarantinable disease – yellow fever, cholera, Lassa or any other viral haemorrhagic fevers, leprosy, plague, typhus and rabies – to the Commonwealth Director of Health in your State (addresses overleaf)'.

The taxi was taking me to the Cherry Blossom Motel, recommended at the airport because it was offering special off-season rates. I asked the driver, an overweight, unshaven civil servant who operated a cab on Sundays because he had cash flow problems, what the off-season was in Darwin.

'Aw, the Wet,' he said. 'You get a lot of rain, you get the odd cyclone.'

'Are there any around at the moment?'

'Yeah,' he said, turning down Daly Street and heading for the sea. 'There was one on the telly last night, quite a big joker, Cyclone Ferdinand, doing a bit of damage up round the Gulf.'

I laughed and told the driver that Ferdinand had been chasing me around Indonesia for the past two or three days.

'Go on?' he said.

At the Cherry Blossom on the Esplanade I got a shadowy little room reeking of beer. Somewhere along the dim corridor a couple were operatically having sex, the man a rumbling bass, his companion a soprano with a very loud upper register. Then somebody banged on the wall and shouted, 'Put a bucket over her head!' and the duet grew muffled.

I had been planning tonight's celebration dinner all the way from Jakarta, finally opting for a dozen native oysters followed by a prime flame-grilled sirloin steak the size of a Cadillac hub cap, slightly underdone. It would be served with a few new potatoes, some French beans and a crisp green salad in a vinaigrette dressing. The choice of wine would be made when I had seen a list and, perhaps, taken advice.

The man at the motel desk said the only restaurant open locally on a Sunday night was at the Travelodge, an easy half-mile stroll down the road, turning right at Doctor's Gully and the sign saying, 'Fish Feeding 400 Metres'.

The Travelodge was crowded, but a pretty Melbourne girl in a yellow smock got me a table then said I couldn't have a sirloin since Sunday was buffet night, a set price, set menu, self-service arrangement entitling you to eat everything you could hold. But Norm was doing really lovely roast beef in the Carvery, and he'd keep dishing it up till I dropped. I pondered the wines and chose a Hardy's Nottage Hill claret.

'Oh, beaut,' she said. 'That's one they serve on the airlines. You can do a whole bottle can you?'

I said I'd give it a try and went to look at the laden hors d'ouevres tables, joining one of the queues and chatting to a smiling, middle-aged woman who told me she was having her fourth crack at the starters. The Carvery could wait. 'Bit of traffic going down the little red lane tonight!' she remarked. I had a little lobster and some of Norm's beef which proved just as good as the waitress had promised. The claret tasted delicious, rich and full, with a hint of flowers in the bouquet.

But the evening was not a success. I found myself faintly nauseated by so much gluttony. Watching all these overweight people sweating as they attacked their mountains of grub, staggering slightly as they rose to get more, put me off my own. I left early and took my culture shock back to the Cherry Blossom.

Early next morning I would be flying to Katherine, the first of the overland stops made by the London service. Hunting through the Pink Pages for the flight reconfirmation number I found further evidence of Australia's conspicuous consumption, numerous ads placed by members of the car-wrecking trade, their size and prominence indicating that this was a very high-profile, high-yield area of business. Among them were Mercwreck ('Specialised Mercedes Wrecking'), Japanese Auto Wreckers ('Specialists in Wrecking All Types of Japanese Cars') and Jagdaim, who gave notice of their eagerness to reduce the cream of the British Leyland range to skiploads of scrap metal.

An editorial message, perhaps aimed at the wreckers, said, 'Speak Distinctly – your voice represents you and your company to the person at the end of the line. When speaking on the telephone be natural, relaxed and attentive. To make a good impression speak distinctly and directly into the telephone with your lips about 2 cm. from the transmitter. It is best to speak in a normal tone of voice –

neither too quickly nor too slowly.'

Following these instructions I reconfirmed my flight with Airlines of Northern Australia. Outside the wind was getting up and, once again, I heard the familiar flurry – audible even above the air conditioning's stentorian roar – of Ferdinand blowing buckets of rain at my window.

6
INTO THE WET

From Darwin to Brisbane

I

It was odd seeing white men on the flight deck again. The pilots of the Airlines of Northern Australia Fokker F-28 twin-jet *Horrie Miller* were greying, amply built and purposeful-looking, and they made heavy weather of the 30-minute flight to Katherine. The aeroplane went pitching through Ferdinand's squalls like a coaster, causing the earnest, beaky-nosed young man seated next to me to say he wished he hadn't had rabbit for breakfast.

He wore a broad-brimmed grazier's hat, tooled leather riding boots and a smart three-piece suit cut in vivid purple twill. His name was Clive, and he confided that he was going to Katherine for a job interview. 'I'm a licensed plumber and drainer,' he said, as the stewardess stooped to pour coffee. He peered down her blouse in an interested manner, as though her chest was an item of scenic interest to which the captain had drawn our attention on the tannoy. 'And my mate Kevin, sitting just across the aisle there, is in the same line of work.'

Kevin wore a boldly checked shirt and lay in his seat with his hands pressed to his temples. 'He suffers from a terrible fear of flying,' Clive explained. 'Actually, we're both going for a job teaching plumbing and draining to the abos, but I'm not even sure I want it. What I'm really after is a post office. My brother got a little one up in the country last year, the business and a three-room bungalow for $25,000. He'll never make a fortune, but you get a dollar every time someone makes a deposit or withdrawal from the Savings Bank.'

We began descending over grey-green gum forests and streaming red earth, banking across 'the Track', the 1,536-kilometre Stuart Highway running from Alice Springs to Darwin, linking Australia's dry centre with its Top End. The airfield was surrounded by dense stands of eucalyptus which, when we disembarked, filled the warm, wet air with their fragrance. I heard fluting birdcalls coming from the trees. The terminal was a shed with the name TINDAL on its tin roof in faded black letters. A small notice said 'Contact Refueller at Office – For After Hours Service PH 721613'. A steady drizzle fell as we hurried indoors. The roof leaked and there were deep puddles on the floor; one of the deepest had almost isolated an unattended Hertz desk standing in a corner. Only four of us disembarked. The Fokker started up its Speys and taxied away through the rain. An energetic bearded man, the local station manager, sold me a bus ticket into town and said, 'He's going to Tennant and Alice, then out to the Rock, sleeps in Alice, goes out to the Rock a couple of times in the morning then, in the arvo, comes scorching back up the Track again.'

The two plumbers and drainers told me aborigine elders would be present at their interview; the prospect seemed to make them edgy. Kevin said he had inherited his fear of flying from his Auntie Enid. 'The only time they ever got her on a plane she ran amok and tried to dismantle the bloody thing,' he confided. They were driven away in a government car while I boarded the station manager's van with the other passenger, a computer engineer summoned because one of the terminals at the bank needed attention.

'What's Katherine like?' I asked.

'Hard town to stay awake in,' he said.

The station manager, climbing behind the wheel, said, 'Aw, come on, it's a bonzer little place. I was in Brisbane for six years but I've never known anything like the social life in Katherine. It's non-stop parties and barbies every night and the friendliest people in the Top End.'

We pulled away past a couple of twin-engined Cessnas with the name Tillair inscribed on them. The station manager said one would probably be operating the afternoon service back to Darwin. Looking at the deserted little terminal standing forlornly in the rain I asked where they kept their control tower. Darwin, said the station manager; the blokes up there supervised all the local traffic. We drove along the Stuart Highway, running flat and ruler-straight through those silent, dripping gum forests. The town, neat and pretty, appeared suddenly through the trees, the Highway becoming a broad main street for a few hundred yards then, just as abruptly, sliding back into the forest again. I found a coffee shop in a covered arcade. At the next table three young aboriginal women sat with their babies, gossiping over cans of Coke. When one of the babies whimpered its mother lifted her T-shirt, which said 'Life is a Bed of Roses But Watch Out for the Pricks,' and suckled it.

I bought a coffee and got out Cobham. At Darwin he had exchanged the De Havilland 50's floats for wheels and set off 'due south over the bush to a place called Katherine, where we landed in a rather rough clearing to refuel. I am afraid the inhabitants were a little upset because we did not stay to lunch.' (He made amends on his return flight, though, spending the night 'at the local hotel, a rambling shanty built mainly of batons and sheets of corrugated iron. Our host, an Irishman, was well content with his lot, having a family of five or six charming daughters who, he boasted, did all the work and ran the place.')

When I complained about the rain to the proprietress of the coffee shop she said, 'Yeah, it's been a real bugger of a Wet,' and told me she had baked fresh meat pies for lunch. I asked her to keep one for me and walked to the bridge spanning the Katherine River, now running very high. The trees growing down on the drowned banks that contained the stream in the Dry were almost submerged, their tops bending before the swirl of the current. A couple of road trains thundered past, giant diesel prime movers with impact-absorbing armour on their bonnets, towing four double-decked trailers packed with cattle. The men in the street wore boots stained with the vivid red mud of the Top End. There were three airline offices serving Katherine's 4,000 population. I showed my old Imperial route map to the two men at Tillair. Between Katherine and Mount Isa the planes could, if the winds made it necessary, refuel at Daly Waters, Newcastle Waters, Anthony's Lagoon, Brunette Downs, Alexandria Station or Camooweal.

The men pondered the map. 'We do mail runs out to the Lagoon and Brunette,' said one, 'but the plane goes from Tennant.'

His colleague, who wore sky-blue shorts and had five pens stuck in his shirt pocket, said, 'No, we're not doing the Lagoon or Brunette any more. Brunette's got their own aircraft. They get the post themselves. So does Alexandria. But we can drop you at any of these strips for a $25 landing fee surcharge. We can do that right down the line. Would you want to stop off anywhere?'

'Not really.'

'Just booming in and out, are you?'

'That's about it.'

'Well, that's no problem. From Tennant we can take you out to Brunette and the Lagoon. Our bloke delivers in that area Thursdays. He could drop you in for a cup of tea.'

I told them, regretfully, that on Thursday I would be flying from Brisbane to Toowoomba and back, working to a very tight schedule that required me to be in London in eight days. Meanwhile, had they any idea where the old planes had landed hereabouts, half a century earlier?

'Tindal was RAAF, built during the war,' said the man with the pens. 'The veterans would have gone into the old dairy. Nothing to see now, though. They've put houses on it since.'

His colleague frowned. '*Fifty* years ago I reckon they'd have gone into the meatworks. In those days the town was on the other side of the river. It was just bush and grazing over here. The dairy land wouldn't have been cleared then.'

'Well, it would have been close. But they'd have gone into one or the other, your old fellers, meatworks or dairy, both had pastures you could land a plane on – once you'd shooed the bullocks off first.'

I thanked them and crossed the street for a drink. The pub was a shadowy, cavernous place where several dozen aborigines were getting drunk in an atmosphere of almost churchlike solemnity, sitting and swallowing their beer with the abstracted air of people trying to remember something important. A grizzled, whiskery old man in a battered felt hat, unable to focus his gaze, told me he had been with the Australian forces up in New Guinea during the war and, on reflection, reckoned he had been fighting the wrong side. 'You white men never done a bloody thing for us,' he said, without rancour. 'You the ones we should've turned the guns on.'

At the offices of *The Katherine Times* ('Your Town and Country Weekly') I bought a copy of the current issue and returned to the coffee shop where, over my meat pie, I read a front-page item headlined MISS SHOWGIRL QUEST ENTRANT.

'Sixteen year old Miss Lisa Meehan is the first entrant in the Katherine Miss Showgirl Quest. Lisa nominated because she wanted to have a go and do something different.

'She is currently working as an Apprentice Hairdresser at Barbara's Salon and has been there for nine months.

'Show Secretary Mrs Gail Trepka said she now has two entrants. The second entrant to nominate is Elizabeth Green who works in the Fruit and Veg shop.'

The 'Around Town' column reported that 'the usually immaculate Nola Sweetman' arrived at the Penguins' meeting in shorts and bare feet, having crossed a two-mile flooded creek to attend, while the 'Pine Creek News' column noted the sighting of a colony of 520 ghost bats. The pie was so good I had another. Then I walked back through the warm, steady rain to the Airlines of Northern Australia Office, passing smashed aborigines clustered around the door of the betting shop and swigging beer under the four-sided clock opposite the bakery, donated by the Katherine Rotary Club.

The bearded station manager, talking to a customer on his radio, gave me a wave. The customer, a woman named Mary, wanted an Apex flight to London in two weeks.

The station manager said, 'Look Mary, for an Apex you have to book a clear month before departure. To qualify? For the reduction? Over.'

Mary's voice emerged through a crackle of static. 'Can't I just give you a backdated cheque, over?'

'That's against the rules, over.'

'Oh, bugger the rules. I'll backdate the cheque and you backdate the ticket, over.'

'I dunno, I'd have to think about it. When could you get the cheque in, over?'

'When the creek goes down,' said Mary, 'unless you've got a carrier pigeon? The water's almost up to the house. It's like Noah's Ark out here, over.'

'Roger, Mary, listen, I'll see what I can arrange. I'll call again tomorrow, over and out.' The station manager put down the microphone with a sigh. 'Who'd want to work for an airline?' he inquired of the room at large. 'I'd rather do something easy – like shooting fish in a barrel.'

The next stop on the original route accessible by scheduled services was Mount Isa, the outback mining town. But it wasn't accessible from Katherine so I had to return to Darwin and catch a Trans Australia Airlines flight the following afternoon. The station manager drove me back to Tindal and unlocked his little terminal. Rain continued to drum on the roof and the puddles now lapped over much of the floor. The two plumbers and drainers emerged from the shelter of a dripping tree.

'Where's the Fokker?' asked Kevin.

'She doesn't come back up the Track till tomorrow arvo,' said the station manager. 'The Conquest's doing Darwin today. Tillair. Good little plane, Cessna turbo-prop, fully pressurized with a ceiling of 24,000. You'll get above all this weather.'

The Conquest, looking frail and small, was parked outside while two men holding crimson umbrellas stood peering into its port engine.

'I'm not going up in that thing,' said Kevin. 'That's a flaming Dinky Toy.'

I asked him how he had fared at the interview. He shrugged. 'They said they'd let us know.'

'Did any aborigines turn up?'

'Three,' said Kevin. 'Two elders and a boong.'

'The boong was married to the older elder,' Clive said. 'The younger elder was a welder.'

The men standing beside the Conquest called to the station manager who ran out, held a brief conversation with them then returned to report that the Conquest had packed up. 'You've got the 402,' he said.

When Kevin saw the 402, which seemed dwarfed even by the Conquest, he turned sharply on his heel and began walking back into the gum forest. Clive seized him and made him confront the tiny Cessna, now being examined by a lanky young man who walked round and round it under a crimson umbrella, his demeanour thoughtful, like a bomb disposal expert studying something unstable dug up on a building site. Then, abruptly, he scrambled aboard and started the engines. They made a tinny, yammering noise, like outboard motors at full throttle, and were still running flat out when the station manager, ignoring Kevin's shouted demands for directions to the bus stop, bundled us into the minivan-sized cabin, folded up the steps and slammed the rickety little door. I bagged the seat next to the pilot while the licensed plumbers and drainers scrambled into the ones behind, the aircraft dipping and swaying as we settled ourselves. The station manager banged on the roof and gave us a thumbs-up.

'Where are the parachutes, pilot?' Kevin demanded.

'Under the seats,' said the pilot, checking his flap settings and flight controls as we bumped out towards the runway on our Cleveland heavy-duty wheels.

Kevin reached into his bag and extracted a half bottle of Bundaberg rum. 'This is 100 per cent proof, Alex. Couple of swigs of this and they could fly me to the bloody moon and back.' He took a long swallow and sighed. 'What's your name, pilot?'

'Lucas,' said the pilot, turning on to the runway.

'Are you Jewish?'

'No,' said Mr Lucas. He murmured into the tiny microphone hanging from his ear like a bent twig, telling Darwin we were on our way then, with the windscreen wipers sloshing backwards and forwards, opened up his two continental flat-six turbocharged engines and took off through the rain. The Cessna went zooming over the trees and into a thick, wet mist, bumping about as it climbed.

'Are we doing any crop spraying today?' Kevin inquired.

'That costs extra,' said Mr Lucas.

Kevin passed the bottle to Clive, who swallowed the rum like milk. The air speed indicator showed 210 knots as, at 8,500 feet, we levelled off, a colonnade of frothy cu-nim pillars reaching up through the murk ahead. Mr Lucas, making constant small adjustments to his controls, guided us gently around them, taking the Cessna on a stately slalom through the dark and windy sky. He said you might get her up to 24,000, where the Conquest cruised comfortably, but she would be sluggish and unresponsive. She was happiest at this height.

The red and green country below streamed with water. At 8,500 feet the deluge was so sustained and heavy I reckoned we must be leaving a wake. Clive downed some more rum then suddenly cocked a finger at Mr Lucas's head and demanded to be taken to Cuba.

Kevin whinnied and began beating his knees with his fists while Mr Lucas, a serious-minded young man who had heard all the jokes before, merely pursed his lips and made an adjustment to the trim.

'We'll stop off in Sydney first, though, King's Cross,' said Clive, reminiscently. 'That's a very good spot. I once had a prozzie there with a butterfly tattooed on her bum. She charged me 50 dollars. Half a week's wages for a root! I must have been out of my mind. But I was heavily under the influence of the demon drink, and on the way back to Parramatta I ran into a verge and burst my front offside tyre. That was another 22 dollars. When I got home I fell over a bloody clothes horse my idiot grandma had left in the sleepout and broke my arm. Three weeks off work, 300 dollars down the tube.' He had another drink. 'What I broke was my humerus.'

We crossed flooded paddocks, the colour of pewter in the dull light. There were bird flocks, lorikeets, parrots and rock pigeons, flying sluggishly, as though their plumage was waterlogged.

Kevin said, 'Pilot, have you heard the one about the bear and the bunny having a gobble down in the woods one night? The bear shoves his paw . . .'

Mr Lucas, getting something on his headphones, glanced across and said, 'Darwin's closed. The airport's ringed by thunderstorms.'

The plumbers and drainers, past caring, urged him to forget about the airport and mount a kamikaze-style attack on the Town Hall instead. First, though, Clive thought he might go out for a little walk on the wing.

Mr Lucas said, 'The weather may have passed by the time we get there. If not we could fly a holding pattern till it clears, or head back to Katherine and try again later.'

He switched on his Bendix weather radar. The storms, suddenly reduced to blobs of soft green light, looked benign on the little screen, like strange bush flowers. The rain rattled on the roof and pinged off the nose. I counted four storms on the radar, but with corridors of clear air between. It was already apparent that Mr Lucas was planning to take us down the corridor separating storms two and three. Then the Cessna dropped several dozen feet and

shook as it struck solid air again, creaking like a new shoe. The storms on the radar momentarily flickered and paled, suffering the stresses of their own creation.

'It's the Luftwaffe!' yelled Kevin. 'Bandits at 3 o'clock, old bean!' He made the chattering noise of Browning machine guns then tapped me on the shoulder. 'Why aren't you drinking, Alex? As you see I'm drinking out of fear. I spend half my life in aeroplanes but you never get used to them. I used to work on the North Sea rigs and flew home millions of bloody times. The only thing that helped was grog. All the hosties knew me. I was the one who was always legless before we'd even crossed the bloody English Channel. I'll tell you something about those 747s, Alex. They don't like nasty weather. They're all over the fucking sky. The 747 behaves *very* badly in turbulence and that is a solemn fact. Ask any pilot. Ask *me*.'

He drained the bottle and handed it to Clive. 'You can throw that at the Germans,' he said. He turned back and continued, 'I was once in West Irian, Indonesian New Guinea, at a place called Fak Fak. We were building a road from sea level to a copper mine 11,000 feet up a mountain. I had two Balinese engineers working under me and they were the most cultivated men I ever knew. Jesus, they were clever little buggers, Alex. They could speak English, Dutch, French and Balinese, even the dialects of the local heathens who worked for us, jokers with bones through their noses who were always sloping off to eat someone or have a bit of a sing-song. Anyway, this mountain was a finger of pure copper sticking 14,000 feet up in the air and my Balinese told me a very interesting thing. At 12,000 feet there's a glacier, a real ice glacier only a couple of degrees south of the Equator, and do you know what they found there, sticking out of the glacier like a nail in a plank?' He lit a cigarette. 'They found a Dakota full of dead Australians. They'd been there 30 years, prisoners-of-war coming home from one of the Jap camps. Because of the cold the bodies were all perfectly preserved, all sitting there in their seats looking peaceful, as if they'd just fallen asleep.'

Mr Lucas reported that Darwin was open again. We could see the city and its coastline on the weather radar. The four storms were retreating but with the clear intention – according to Mr Lucas – of regrouping like cavalry and thundering back. We would slip in during the lull. Somewhere out to the left were Tumbling Waters and Rum Jungle; we began our descent near the township of Humpty Doo, humming through a huge dark sky suddenly suffused with a luminous purple light that touched our hands and faces and turned the flooded wetlands into wine, so tangible it seemed to give the Cessna extra buoyancy and lift. As we slid over the coast and made a wide, easy turn far out across the purple harbour Clive was moved to murmur, 'Isn't that nice? That's very nice indeed.'

I decided I was now making my true Darwin landfall and wondered whether the old timers had ever flown in through such calm, resplendent air, feeling a little like the angels. Mr Lucas, established on his glide slope, lowered his flaps and the little Cessna sank towards the glistening ribbon of runway, touching down with barely a tremor. As we taxied to the terminal there was a kind of euphoria in the cabin. We three passengers smiled at each other.

'Pilot!' cried Kevin. 'That was a bloody *joy* ride!'

II

The city's original airfield had been located at Fannie Bay, beyond the racecourse. Here the Smith brothers, Captain Ross and Lieutenant Keith (accompanied by two sergeants) landed their Vickers Vimy bomber on 10 December 1919, 28 days out of Hounslow. They were the first flyers to get from England to Australia and, for making their epic trip in under 30 days, won a £10,000 prize offered by the Australian Government. When Captain Smith had switched off his two huge Rolls-Royce Eagle engines he jumped down and, with characteristic Australian understatement, said, 'Well, we're here.' The brothers were knighted within the month and their sergeants, Wally Shiers and Jim Bennett, promoted to lieutenant and awarded the Air Force Medal. (Sir Ross Smith and Lieutenant Bennett perished together in 1922, while testing a Vickers Viking amphibian in which they planned to circumnavigate the globe; Sir Keith, ironically, became the Australian representative of Vickers and died, replete with honours, in 1955.)

Fannie Bay was where Ray Parer and John McIntosh, who left England intending to race the Smith brothers for the prize, arrived in their De Havilland 9 day bomber after an astonishing flight that lasted 237 days. They crashed repeatedly, almost got sucked into the crater of Vesuvius, were attacked by bedouin, disrupted numerous race meetings and polo matches with emergency landings, fitted their engine with an Indian car radiator in a largely fruitless attempt to stop it bursting into flames and finally, after being given up and presumed lost over the Timor Sea, zonked to earth at Fannie Bay with their tanks bone dry.

Another of the Australian immortals, the quietly spoken, disarmingly modest Bert Hinkler, landed his Avro Avian here in February 1928 at the end of the first solo flight from England to Australia. It was an achievement likened to the conquest of Everest – which would not be climbed for another 25 years – and it made Hinkler, who had navigated with pages torn from a school atlas, a towering international celebrity. (Five years later, attempting the record again, he vanished over the Alps; months afterwards a party of Italian charcoal burners found the wreckage of the Puss Moth containing his body – embalmed by the snows – high in the Pratango Mountains where a monument to him still stands.)

This was where Kingsford Smith landed in October 1930, having cut Hinkler's record by a full five days, and where, five months earlier, Amy Johnson, the first woman to make the solo trip, had arrived in her bottle-green De Havilland Gypsy Moth *Jason*, equipped with an Irving parachute and Pyrene fire extinguisher. A slim pretty girl from Hull, the 'Queen of the Air' and the 'Empire's Great Little Woman' returned home to a hysterical welcome and a *Daily Mail* banquet at the Savoy where among those tucking into the 'Oeufs poches Port Darwin' were Bert Hinkler, Louis Blériot, Malcolm Sargent, John Barbirolli, Evelyn Waugh, J. B. Priestley, Noël Coward, Ivor Novello, Cecil Beaton and Alfred Hitchcock.

Fannie Bay was also the original Australian point of entry for passengers on the London service. This was where the *Astraea* finally touched down from Bathurst Island at the conclusion of Imperial's proving flight, carrying Brackles and his Alsatian saviour Father Grell, and where Lady Edwina Mountbatten and a Major H. Philips, the first paying passengers to cross the Timor Sea, arrived

in April 1935. I decided it was time I saw Fannie Bay for myself and called John Haslett, leading light of the Northern Territory Aviation Historical Society, who said he'd be happy to show me around. He picked me up an hour later, an affable, quietly spoken man who drove me through watery sunshine to a tree-filled beachside suburb. We halted beside a long white building with a green roof.

'This was the old gaol,' said Mr Haslett, jumping out of the car, 'and the planes landed in its horse paddock. The gaoler's house was the first point of hospitality for the overseas flyers. They were always invited in for a wash and a leak. That was a tradition. Some *very* famous names have used the little dunny in there.'

He turned and gestured out to sea. 'For the incoming pilots and passengers the first sight of land would have been Bathurst and Melville, the islands up to the north. Then they came down across the Darwin Harbour Gap. Their first local landmark was the gaol and the old meatworks. The horse paddock was also the local golf course but play was suspended when an aircraft was expected. There was once a famous example of public disorder here, the day Parer and McIntosh were finally due, eight months after they'd set off from England. The bookies were out in force and a huge crowd had gathered, all laying bets. Most of the money said the pilots would drown in the Timor Sea; the plane was a flying junkyard and any disasters looking for a victim always homed in on those two like missiles. Only a few of the faithful backed them to make it and when the little De Havilland finally appeared over the Harbour Gap, several hours late, the winning punters had to be rushed into clink and locked up for their own protection.'

I wondered what the Imperial passengers had made of this place, travelling from a grassy field yellow with summer buttercups beside Purley Way, to a tussocky horse paddock where brawny golfers, constantly alert for snakes, played under the gaze of convicted criminals. The paddock has since been absorbed by the town. Part, a stretch of dual carriage highway named Ross Smith Avenue, took us to other streets with evocative names: Vimy Lane, Amy Johnson Drive, Hinkler Crescent. I told Mr Haslett that Croydon had a Hinkler Close (it has a Cobham Close and an Imperial Way as well).

'Better than calling them after politicians,' he said. 'At least these are names we can look up to.'

Beneath a flowering poinciana in a Giles Street garden stood a plaque marking the spot where the Smiths' Vimy touched down on Australian soil, lovingly polished like a regiment's battle honours. Mr Haslett and I walked quietly from garden to garden, coming upon a plaque commemorating the flight of Amy Johnson in another. These silent green acres seemed suffused with a curious presence. Once they had rung to the thunder of old engines and the sounds of cheering crowds. Here my pioneering passengers disembarked, cramped, stiff, deafened by the racket of their six-cylinder Gipsies but light-headed because the Timor Sea was now safely behind them – and here too the stars had come down from their firmaments to claim new records. News of their achievements went out along the submarine cable that ran from Darwin to Kupang – and back up the route to London – earning them a worldwide celebrity scarcely credible today. They were fêted wherever they went, and lionized like royalty.

Beyond the garden stood the original Qantas hangar, erected in 1934, now used for storage by the Department of Civil Aviation. On its roof was the mast and metal bracket that once held the windsock, while the old radio shack looked as good as new.

'They knew how to build in those days,' Mr Haslett remarked. 'When Cyclone Tracy blew away a lot of Darwin that hangar only lost a couple of sheets of roofing iron.'

We looked at the old Parap Hotel, at which passengers carrying on to Brisbane were put up for the night. It was a typical Northern Territory neighbourhood pub but there was no time to try the beer since I had a plane to catch and first, at Mr Haslett's insistence, was to meet Ossie Osgood, a veteran bush pilot who would speak to me with the authentic voice of an older, better breed of man; from him, it was promised, I would learn a thing or two.

We drove through Parap to the airport, pulling up at the offices of Arnhem Air Charter, a low, nondescript building adjoining a hangar. Three drunken aborigines slept on benches by the door. Inside, at a desk heaped with correspondence, sat a stocky, balding man suffused with energy and a restless, simmering impatience. He wore spectacles in the manner of someone unaccustomed to them

and, as we walked in, snatched them off self-consciously, crying, 'Paper! Paper! I'm bloody drowning in it!'

He jumped up and shook hands. Mr Haslett asked him how he was keeping.

'The Department's running me *ragged*,' said Ossie Osgood, explaining, for my benefit, that the mastery of Australia's skies was now firmly in the hands of civil servants fired by a consuming passion for forms. 'They sit in their offices,' said Ossie, 'dreaming up new ones that all have to be returned on or before a certain date, filled out in triplicate and countersigned in 17 places. Half of them wouldn't know an aeroplane if it flew through the window and looped the loop in their flaming *bedrooms*. They probably wouldn't even wave to the pilot.'

Mr Haslett, leaving for another appointment, said, 'Don't get too carried away, Ossie. Remember this bloke's got to get the TAA to Isa at 1435.'

Ossie said, 'There'll be a delay. The airport's closed. Some cowboy down on exercises from the Singapore Air Force skidded his Skyhawk and blocked the runway. They'll have that poor bugger sitting there doing paperwork till he's old and grey.'

He saw Mr Haslett to the door then ordered some coffee and said, 'My favourite film was *Those Magnificent Men In Their Flying Machines*. I liked the old aircraft, the stunts, the actors, the story and the tune. They were all excellent. But do you know what I liked best?'

I shook my head.

'*No bloody Department*!'

Ossie left school at 14, was given two spanners and the task of dismantling half a dozen discarded Avro Ansons right down to the last nut and bolt. A spell in the Australian National Airways engine overhaul shop in Melbourne earned him money for flying lessons, but never enough. He was still learning when he joined the RAAF as a trainee mechanic at Wagga Wagga where his weekly expenditure left him with 6/6 to pay for lessons costing 28/- an hour. His course was thus a protracted affair and, when he couldn't afford to fly, he went to the public library and read all the aviation books, specially the memoirs of the pioneers and the war aces. Their deeds and personalities were only of secondary interest. What preoccupied

him most was *how they got out of trouble.* Ossie began absorbing
the theory of emergency procedures from the experiences of pilots
making split-second decisions in combat or crisis, seated at a table
in the Wagga Wagga Public Library. He says what he learned there
stuck. And it's what he's still telling the youngsters today – go away
and read the old books.

He finally won his licence in 1952 and went crop spraying in
Western Australia. As a novice without influence among his elders
he always got the worst assignments – awkward, undulating terrain
with trees (or cliffs) at the perimeter. But during that period he was
the only registered Western Australian crop sprayer not to crash
and, leaving the great and good nursing their fractures and sprains,
he signed up with the flying doctor at Port Hedland.

'It was terrific and it was lousy,' he said. 'I once had to help a
father pull his two dead sons out of a burned house. Another time
a couple of kids died on me in the plane. I've carried plenty of
bodies in my time but kids always hit you the hardest; that day
I could hardly see because of the tears. But then I've had babies
born on board, just the mum and me, and coming in with them
both doing well was the greatest feeling in the world. You flew day
and night, in all conditions. Once we had a night call to pick up
an abo who'd been in a fight and came aboard with an axe in his
head. We got off the strip after mixing it with the wallabies as
usual, then ran into the most tremendous storm. The patient was
haemorrhaging – you've never seen anyone bleed like that – and we
were all over the sky. But we got him to hospital all right and the
doc fixed him up. It was a valuable lesson for me because I was
forced beyond my known limits. I managed things in that storm I
never knew I could do. And that's what flying's all about – or used
to be.'

Ossie, footloose and restless, moved north to look for uranium,
contour flying at 20 feet with onboard instruments to measure the
readings, learning to work with an eye peeled for sticky beaks
paying too much attention to his course and heading. 'If people saw
you getting interested in a particular hill they'd nip out and peg it
before you'd even landed. So you had to fool them, always mixing
up the hills, going low and slow over the bad ones, quick and casual
over the good. A bloke called Joe Fisher was the boss pilot and

he taught me a lot. He was a very clever man, a real master of deception.'

Eventually, ready to go it alone, Ossie started Arnhem Air Charter and accepted any work that came his way. He flew the offshore islands for uranium, the mainland beaches for minerals and various inland tracts for timber. Then, using an Italian high-wing twin, he undertook the first coastal surveillance work in Australia, ten-hour patrols every day for 23 months. 'You went low and never exceeded 140 m.p.h. because at that height your vision suffers from distortion and, since this was security work, you couldn't afford to miss a trick. Couldn't do it any more, though. My sight's going now; for that kind of thing I'd have to depend on the youngsters.'

He employs eight young pilots who, periodically, drive him crazy. 'They're all IFR, instrument-rated, which means they never look out of the windows and are ignorant of the terrain they're flying over. A while ago I called my lads together and asked them to name all the rivers between the Adelaide and the Alligator – which they're crossing every day. They didn't know a single one so I told them to go away and learn the names and, a month later, I asked the question again and got precisely the same result. They hadn't a flaming clue.'

The youngsters' instrument-induced isolation from the world below is not just a bee in Ossie's bonnet. It has also cost him revenue. In the face of stiff competition he won a contract to take aerial pictures for a scientific project studying the interaction between wild geese, buffalo herds, a marsupial rat and a certain strain of grass. Did the rats depend on the buffalo, the buffalo on the grass, the geese on the rats or vice versa? To make a record of the correlation between the species Ossie had to fly a careful pattern between a series of white drums, taking pictures at specified points between the markers. It was a visual job, requiring a high degree of concentration. He did it himself for a while then, needed back in Darwin, turned it over to one of the young men, carefully briefing him beforehand. But his replacement chose not to look out of the window. Instead, he flew a compass course between the drums, curved far off course, took meaningless pictures and lost Ossie the contract.

Ossie, not given to compromise, was still angry. The man's attitude, not the lost business, upset him most. He said the trouble with these blokes was that they didn't like getting their feet wet and hadn't read the old books. What they wanted were jobs with the airlines. There was no glamour in the work up here and, to prove it, he cited a couple of examples of the things local bush pilots were routinely expected to do. Once, carting buffalo meat, he picked up a man whose leg had nearly been severed by a chain saw. 'I threw half the meat off the plane, put him on top of the other half and flew him to hospital. I lost that contract as well. The meat I offloaded was ruined because of the blow flies and the rest was ruined by human blood. But I wouldn't have done any different and I told them so.'

Then, recently, he was asked to take a policeman to an outlying homestead and help get a body out of a creek. 'It had been there for eight days. For the flight back we had to put the body in a bag. When I got home I wouldn't let the wife touch me. I stood under the shower for an hour, scrubbing myself, then I disinfected and washed every item of clothing I had on me.' He glanced at his battered watch and asked whether I wanted a sandwich.

I said that sounded like a very good idea.

'We'll nip home,' he said. 'It's only five minutes away.'

He jumped up then, looking oddly furtive, said, 'Come into the hangar a moment. There's something I want to show you.'

What he showed me was a tiny biplane with an open cockpit, its wings and fuselage painted in the livery of an RAF Spitfire. 'My pride and joy,' he said, laying an affectionate hand on it. 'A Pitts Special, strictly for aerobatics. I take her up once or twice a week. The only problem is that I'm too old to push high negatives Gs any more. She's American but I've tried to camouflage the fact with the livery. I belong to the generation that believes anything with a pair of British wings is best. I'd give ten years of my life to fly a Spitfire. I nearly *bought* one once. A bloke in Brisbane had a Spit for sale – well, enough of one to rebuild it and turn it back into a serviceable aeroplane. I talked to him on the phone then flew straight down to meet him. He never turned up.'

We walked to the car. A group of his young pilots stood outside watching the activity on the runway. The Singapore Skyhawk,

tipped forward on its nose, was being towed away, followed by a procession of fire engines.

'What's the word from the tower?' Ossie asked.

The men looked at him blankly. 'The tower, Ossie?'

'It might be a good idea if someone asked them when the airport's opening for business.' He nodded at the aborigines slumbering on the benches. 'We've got passengers waiting.'

'Good-oh,' said one of the pilots, going indoors.

'Don't be deceived by those abos,' Ossie said. 'Some of them are very, very rich men, sitting on mineral reserves you couldn't even imagine. It's only when the white Australians realize just *how* rich that we'll get race war in this country.'

His house, in a quiet street, sat in a pretty tropical garden. The ground floor contained an office piled with Departmental directives and a workshop where Ossie and his teenage son made model aeroplanes which they flew together in a paddock well away from the airport flight path. Ossie said taking the models out on a fine clear morning was a very nice way of relaxing.

'Don't you ever get sick of flying?' I asked.

He looked astonished. 'I'll get plenty of time off when I'm dead.'

'What if they make you an angel?'

He beamed at me. 'Now you're talking!'

Upstairs there were more model planes in the living room. 'Non-operational, these,' he said. 'Just decorative.' Mrs Osgood, alerted by telephone, had made sandwiches and coffee. She was a slim, good-looking woman with intelligent eyes and a quick, amused smile.

'Alex is off to Isa when they open the runway,' Ossie said.

'That'll be a treat for you, Alex,' she said.

'What's Isa like?' I asked.

'It will make even Darwin seem like Paris in the spring,' she said.

Ossie picked up an orange glass jug. 'Remember Cyclone Tracy, the hurricane that struck Darwin on Christmas Day 1974? It blew most of this house away. The roof went and that wall over there. We were open to the elements but this jug, sitting unprotected on a table, came through without a scratch.'

He replaced the jug and we sat down to our sandwiches. 'I lost one of my engineers that night. His house fell in on him. When they

found him he was holding his dead baby in his arms.' He ate for a while in silence. 'Things were pretty bad at the airport, too. All my aircraft were wrecked. One finished up on top of a Friendship, another screwed its tail through the hangar wall. After the storm the looters came. You wouldn't credit what they stole. I walked around with a pistol in my pocket and moved a camp bed into the office, where I slept with an M-16 beside me. Gough Whitlam declared us a national emergency and ordered that all available resources be poured into Darwin. The only thing he hadn't reckoned on was the civil servants. I went and told them we'd lost our roof and asked for some tarpaulins. But they didn't give me tarpaulins. What they gave me was forms. *Forms*! It was their finest hour. Then, one sunny day long after we'd got the roof back on and Tracy was just a bad memory, a truck pulled up outside. The driver said, 'Mr Osgood, I've got the tarpaulins you indented for. You got to acknowledge receipt by signing the delivery dockets here, here and here.'

'What did you say to him?' I asked.

Ossie drew breath, ready to tell me, but Mrs Osgood, coming back into the room, interrupted quickly and skilfully. She clearly had no wish to hear again the profane, blood-curdling monologue declaimed that day by her husband to the tarpaulin man, and said, 'Dear, the office just phoned to say the runway's open and Alex's plane will be going in 35 minutes.'

In July 1938 Darwin's bureaucrats even made international news. The Imperial Empire flying boats *Challenger* and *Capella* landed on the harbour at the end of the company's first flying boat service from England and, among the passengers celebrating the inaugural, were seven eminent British journalists. While the Darwin Health, Customs and Immigration people attended solemnly to their copious paperwork, everyone had to remain on board – despite the fact that a heavy sea was running. Many of the passengers, journalists included, became ill. Darwin got such a scathing press as a consequence that, when the next Imperial boat arrived, everyone was ashore and bound for their hotel a mere nine minutes after splashdown.

The 727 operating the service to Brisbane, via Mount Isa, was called the *Bert Hinkler*, which pleased me. We flew at 31,000 feet

through the detritus of Ferdinand, now finally retired to the western
Pacific to blow itself out, bumping across a landscape where the
lush, vivid wet season colours grew steadily more restrained. Only
the banks of the creeks retained their greenness, the intricate twists
and turns leading to their many confluences looking, from this
height, like the pattern of a huge primal brain.

Twenty minutes from landing the country assumed a reddish
tinge. Pale spinifex grass appeared, then gums and mulga trees, all
throwing long shadows in the evening light. There were red rocks
and low red hills with bare, wind-scoured tops. We descended over
a lake with white ghost gums protruding from the water. Other
lakes were visible away to the left, interlocking, of a stunning
Mediterranean blue. A cab driven by a sad-faced woman took me to
the Dalpura Motel. She said Isa was a man's town really. I was given
a mess of stringy chicken and over-ripe avocado in the Dalpura's
empty dining room. 'It's that newvel kewzeen,' said the waitress, a
thin, bony girl with a streaming cold. 'Bloody awful, eh?' She
removed the plate unbidden. On the loudspeaker a fiddler and
accordionist played droning Irish laments until, mercifully, the tape
broke. I crossed a dusty lot filled with parked lorries to my chalet.
The air conditioning had conked out and I lay there, sweating and
dreaming of Brisbane on the morrow.

III

The Dalpura's breakfast menu included rump steak and eggs, and
spaghetti on toast. The long-distance lorry driver in the next chalet
had both, all piled on to a single plate and brought to him by a big,
unsmiling aborigine woman whose legs were as heavily muscled as
a man's. I walked into town, crossing the small bridge spanning
the Leichhardt River, a swampy brown creek with rushes and
yellow flowers like bush primroses growing along its banks. The
mine – copper, lead, silver and zinc; its soaring industrial chim-
ney the tallest in the southern hemisphere – was constant and

inescapable. The broad, hot streets were flanked by covered sidewalks. Many of the single-storeyed buildings seemed to be drive-in bottle shops. People moved lethargically. The air, shimmering above the roof tops, was faintly tainted with the smells of sulphur and stale beer. I went into a bookstore and asked what they had on Isa.

The assistant's eyes flickered vaguely across the shelves. 'We're mostly mystery and suspense,' she said. 'But you could try the library. It's up at the Civic Centre? Beside the courthouse? There might be a book there.'

The library was modern, spacious and well-stocked. No books on the town existed, but they let me see some archive material, old cellophane-wrapped documents and photographs set aside for schoolchildren doing projects. There was nothing about the airfield or the original Qantas service, and the lady at the counter knew of no one who might be able to help.

'Isa's mostly just the mine,' she said. 'Usually when people retire they get out as fast as they can. All I can tell you is that the first flying doctor flight in history was up to Isa from Cloncurry in 1927 for a chap with a broken pelvis.' She smiled. 'Some of those early flying doctors were real cowboys. I heard of one round Katherine way who beat up an open-air cinema one night, going in so low he was all lit up by the projector and threw this huge shadow on the screen. Afterwards the Civil Aviation Department wanted the cinema manager to sue him, but the manager just made him pay one and six – the cost of a seat in the front stalls.'

I was reminded of the librarian's story as another lady cabby took me back to the airport past the drive-in movie place, now being killed off by the videos, and the local flying doctor's office where a little De Havilland Drover sat on a plinth by the gate. She told me it had been rebuilt from the wrecks of a couple of Drovers found at nearby stations. Apprentices from the mining company worked on the fuselage, two teams of citizens on the wings. 'There was terrific rivalry to get the first wing finished,' she said. 'Bets were made and it just about split the town, half the population cheering on one wing, half the other. In a place like this you can get a bit obsessive about such things.'

We turned up the airport approach road beside a huge sign saying

'Winners Rent Hertz' and drew up at the airy little terminal surrounded by bougainvillaea and flame-of-the-forest trees. In the garden of a nearby bungalow a woman was washing down a single-engined Cessna with a hose. At the Ansett Airlines desk the clerk said my bag would have to go into the hold. I told him it was an approved cabin-sized bag that had travelled under my seat virtually all the way from England.

'Approved by who?' he asked.

'The airlines.'

'Not this airline, mate,' he said, amiably, allowing me to retrieve my notebooks before fastening a label saying BNE to the handle and hauling it over the counter. Clutching them like an urn containing the ashes of a loved one I went to the bar to get some coffee. There were display cases nearby containing samples of the materials produced at the mine, dross, sinter, lead slag and anode slimes, cross-sections of copper cake and shot firing wire.

There was more copper in the little airport shop – egg cups, spoons, napkin rings and anti-rheumatism bracelets. A Lear Jet landed and three high-spirited young men in shirtsleeves disembarked and walked through the terminal, talking and laughing boisterously. A few minutes later two of them returned, sombre as pall bearers, climbed into the Lear and took off again. Passengers for AN 39, the Boeing 727 service to Cairns, Townsville and Brisbane, began filtering in. I chatted to a girl who had been visiting friends near Gunpowder Creek. She had green eyes and a faintly perplexed look, and told me it was so hot there that she had seen a parakeet faint and fall out of a tree.

At the bar a man said that Mount Isa had once been the world's largest city, bigger even than France. In a brash gambit calculated to squeeze more urban development funds out of central Government the local authorities declared that all the land from the Tropic of Capricorn up past Dismal Creek towards Bang Bang lay within Isa's new city limits, hundreds of thousands of square miles of it. The government had taken no notice but the boundaries remained. 'You can walk through the place in a few minutes,' he said, 'but technically it takes a couple of hours in a jet to get from one side of town to the other.'

The Ansett 727 touched down on time from Alice. A dozen of us

were boarded within minutes and, as it began taxiing, a stewardess switched on the public address system and welcomed joining passengers to this flight bound for Cairns and southern ports. Those nursing infants were asked to share their oxygen with them if spare masks were unavailable during emergencies.

I was seated next to a good-looking, vivacious Chinese girl named Angela who owned Cantonese restaurants in Cairns and Mount Isa. She said there had been a strike at the mine the previous week. 'It lasted five days. The atmosphere was very tense. I live in Cairns, and it was one of the reasons I came down here. The other was staff. That is always a big problem. There is no local Chinese community at Isa to recruit from so I must use Australians. But they don't stay. They drift in, then they drift on again. No one stays too long in Isa. The people there always seem to be in transit.'

Our route would take us past Quamby, Granada, Savannah Downs and Crooked Creek, then across the Gregory Range and Atherton Tableland to Cairns and the Pacific coast. The 727 cruised high, affording only brief glimpses of the earth through gauzy cloud and heat haze. The cattle stations, homesteads and tiny communities scattered along our path remained obscured. The only signs of habitation were occasional tracks like random lines scrawled in the dust with a twig. The huge dry hinterlands of Australia were just a succession of merging colour zones – the ochre zone, the mustard zone, the slate zone, the granite zone, then the mossy zone turning ever greener as we neared the forests and fern banks of the Atherton Tableland. We were heading northeast, way off the old Qantas beat. From Isa that had gone southeast, towards Winton, Longreach, Blackall and Charleville, making for Brisbane.

Angela, born in Hong Kong, had brought her family with her to Australia. Her mother and brother helped run the Cairns restaurant, her fiancé managed the one in Isa. Business was good. She wore large diamonds on her fingers and more slipped discreetly down the front of her dress. Fished out for my inspection was a platinum plaque bearing the words LOVE OF LIFE worked in chickpea-sized stones and designed by a friend for her 25th birthday. Her passion for Australia was such that she had vowed not to take an overseas holiday until she had explored it properly. The problem was time. She was too busy even to get married.

The Pacific loomed ahead, blue grey in the smoky afternoon light. Cairns airport was ringed by wooded green hills, one of which dropped sheer to the back of the terminal. We parked beside a pair of blue, white and yellow DC3s of Air Queensland and walked past a solitary coconut tree into the departure lounge. There were rows of brightly coloured seats and a little coffee bar tucked away at the end. I looked up the number of an old friend who lived in Cairns, a girl I had not seen for a dozen years, and put through a call.

'Can I speak to Liz?' I said to the man who answered.

'Liz isn't here,' he said.

'Do you know where I can find her?'

'Belgium,' he said.

'*Belgium*?'

'Yeah. She married a bloke who works in Brussels.'

'Okay,' I said, and went to the coffee bar for a Coke. Then, summoned back to the plane, I followed a hugely fat man up the stairs. His wheezing, snail-like ascent caused the trim young executive behind me to click his tongue and mutter that they should be putting the poor bugger aboard with a fork-lift truck.

The fat man subsided into his seat like a collapsed soufflé then fumbled helplessly with the two ends of the belt, which reached no further than his braces.

'You're going to need an extension for that,' said a stewardess, fetching him an extra couple of feet of buckled webbing. Watching him clip it on reminded me of a flight I had once made from Sydney to Melbourne in the company of the late and much-missed James Cameron, the finest British journalist of his generation. As the jet climbed steeply away from Sydney the chair of the obese giant sitting in front of him tore loose from its mountings and tipped its 20-stone occupant, crimson-faced and open-mouthed, into James's lap. Cameron, thin and frail, was having his legs crushed but, until the flight attendants arrived to haul the seat upright again, he conducted a courteous conversation with the man and, characteristically, managed to learn a thing or two about him.

The Townsville sector would take only 30 minutes. The 727 lifted off down a valley. Hills streamed past our right wingtip before we turned out to sea and set a southerly course along the coast. The sun had come out and the tide was rising on the Great Barrier Reef,

a series of foaming aquamarine crescents, curves and horseshoes that extended for 1,250 miles, battlements and canyons of coral almost as brilliantly coloured as some of the creatures it fed and sheltered – the Sweetlip Emperor, the Harlequin Tusk Fish, the Red Fire Fish, Blue Spotted Stingray and Lined Butterfly Fish.

We crossed Rockingham Bay and a chain of islands: Dunk, Hinchinbrook, Pelorus, Orpheus and Great Palm then, tracking into Townsville, closed on the coast again, passing the towns of Bambaroo, Mutarnee and Rollingstone. The 727 rocked wildly in some rogue sea wind as it descended past Magnetic Island, hilly, wooded, deeply indented, and turned on to finals, whizzing low over a cemetery and coming down on a flat green plain. We were directed to our stand by a plump, white-haired woman wielding her batons as crisply as a dispatcher on an aircraft carrier. The stewardesses, handsome, ebullient girls, told us that transit passengers could remain aboard. One of the men getting off said he had turned down his inflight sandwich because he thought he would get a meal on this sector. The girls laughed. 'We couldn't do dinner in half an hour,' they said but, as he left the aircraft, pressed a sandwich on him anyway. He said 'Ta very much' and ate it as he trotted away down the steps.

A few minutes later we climbed away over marshy, puddled fields, shining in the evening light, across a flotilla of yachts in Bowling Green Bay, their patterned sails glowing like exotic silks, and on past a wilderness of mudflats and mangroves. We were following a long, gently curving brown beach fringed with heavy surf when they came round with the drinks trolley. I had a whisky and so did my neighbour, an elderly man with close-cropped grey hair and a clipped grey moustache. He was a retired engineer returning from a visit to his daughter in Townsville, but London-born and London-trained.

When I told him about my trip, he smiled and said, 'As a student I once had to do a paper on the history of Imperial's wing de-icing devices. Three types were considered, and I can still remember the damned things.' Warmed by the whisky he recited them: 'One, the Goodrich pulsating boot; two, the Dunlop porous leather sleeve with an Ethylene glycol-Ethyl alcohol solution; and three, Kilfrost grease, a compound developed by the railways to stop points

freezing in cold weather. That's the one they went for, the grease, possibly because the company had a close relationship with the railways. The old Southern Railway was a major shareholder in Imperial, and the flying boat base at Southampton was built on land leased from Southern. De-icing was introduced in 1937, along with seat belts, fire extinguishers and various aids for the pilot – artificial horizons, directional gyroscopes and so on – after a big flap about safety. One of their boats, the *Cavalier*, had crashed in the Atlantic and caused a tremendous fuss in Parliament.'

Dinner was roast lamb, carrots, broccoli and potatoes, served with a quarter bottle of classy Aussie claret. In the fading light we went steaming down the long, shadowy beaches. The moonless Pacific turned from pearl grey to black, the sky to the west over Australia from an exuberant swirl of orange and plum to a faint luminous smudge, like the glow from live embers. In first class the voices, fuelled by free liquor, grew more boisterous, the laughter less restrained, until it sounded as though an impromptu party was being thrown in the forward cabin.

I sat immediately behind the partition dividing the classes and could see, reflected in the dark window, a first-class meal being demolished by a sinewy brown arm with its sleeve rolled up and a gold Rolex Oyster on the wrist. It worked its way through a giant chunk of pâté encased in pastry and a pound or two of beef. Periodically the small hand of a stewardess stole into the window to refill his wine glass. He and his neighbour were conversing noisily about the State Mangroves Board, and the butt of their jokes was an official referred to as the Commissioner of Mangroves. Could this be true? If so, these two held the Commissioner in very low esteem.

We had swung inland. Occasional lights passed below. The captain, whose name was Gary, told us we were now 77 miles out of Brisbane. 'Trust all you good people enjoyed the ride,' he said. My neighbour, noting that the bar was about to close, offered me a brandy to celebrate the end of my trip. I demurred, pointing out that I still had a couple of day excursions to make back into the Queensland hinterlands. 'Better give him a double,' he said to the stewardess. He told me he had once known a pilot who worked for a brand new airline named British Airways, formed in the autumn of 1935 to operate European services. 'This chap flew the night

mail to Berlin,' he said. 'It went whatever the state of the weather and was the only scheduled British service where the crew wore parachutes.'

The lights of Brisbane began lapping over the horizon and rising up my window. I drank the brandy and reflected that this glittering city would have seemed wholly alien to the London passengers. Then it had been a sleepy tropical port, acres of tin roofs sprawling around a town hall. Now it was a place aggressively on the make, sleek, full of money and optimism. As we banked and slid down towards Eagle Farm airport I felt no particular elation. There was a sense of relief at having finally got here, but otherwise just the need for a shower and bed.

I entered the baggage hall, still clutching my notebooks, to claim the bag confiscated by the clerk at Mount Isa. My neighbour retrieved his case, shook hands and departed. Eventually everyone else left as well, and I was left alone with a solitary bag sitting, unattended, on the carousel. It looked like my bag, but it wasn't. What a way to get to Brisbane, I thought, without even a toothbrush or a change of socks. Reflecting that losing your luggage was probably the most appropriate way to end an airline safari I asked an official if everything had come ashore from AN 39. He said yes, and directed me to an office where I would have to fill out the appropriate Baggage Irregularity forms.

But some instinct made me check the taxi rank first. A man in a gaberdine raincoat was placing my luggage in the back of a cab and preparing to climb after it. I grabbed him before he was even through the door. He was middle-aged and overweight, and he thought he was going to be mugged.

'I think you've got my bag,' I said.

He stared at me, then hauled the bag out again and looked at it. 'Oh, my God,' he said. He was American.

His wife sat inside. She got out again. I explained that a very similar bag stood in the hall and he went to fetch it. She said agitatedly, 'Jerry gets so foxed at airports,' and lit a cigarette.

When Jerry returned the cab driver asked me where I was going. I said the Crest Hotel.

'These people are just about next door,' he said. 'You want to share? There's a discount.'

I looked at the Americans. 'Do you mind?'

Jerry clapped me on the back. 'Hell, *no*. After what I just did to you I guess we're almost kissin' cousins.'

IV

The last sectors of the old route were being done in reverse order, a compromise between current schedules and the few days left to me. Though I toyed with the idea of spending them by the hotel pool my journey had gradually acquired an obsessive, slightly feverish momentum of its own. Those bits still missing, the original stops between Mount Isa and Brisbane, needed to be filled in or else the enterprise – which now seemed to be assuming a curious kind of structural integrity – would be incomplete, like an unfinished jigsaw or a wing without flaps.

So next morning I set off for Toowoomba on the Darling Downs, once the penultimate halt of the London service. First I spent a few minutes at Eagle Farm pondering the *Southern Cross*, Sir Charles Kingsford Smith's 'old bus' which, though Dutch-built and powered by American engines, had been turned into an Australian national shrine. Now standing entombed in a glass-fronted display unit near the terminal, the venerable Fokker monoplane, bought secondhand from Sir Hubert Wilkins (who employed it on Arctic surveys) and fitted with three big Wright Whirlwind radials, was the flimsy conveyance in which Kingsford Smith and his Australian co-pilot, Charles Ulm, having trained themselves to stay awake for 40 hours at a stretch, travelled from Oakland, California, to Brisbane – the first ever trans-Pacific flight. Their longest leg, 3,130 miles from a Hawaiian beach to a rugby ground in Suva, Fiji, took 31 hours. Three days later they lifted off from Suva for Eagle Farm where, after negotiating storms that knocked out their radios and earth indicator compass, they were welcomed by a wing-wagging escort of local aircraft and 15,000 wildly excited Queenslanders.

Later Kingsford Smith used the *Southern Cross* to make the first crossing of the Tasman to New Zealand. This time he was

accompanied by Gordon Taylor who, when an engine conked out, calmly climbed up on to the high wing to attend to it. He did this a number of times in the course of the flight, clinging on in the 80-knot air flow 3,000 feet above a choppy sea while he tinkered with his spanners, crawling back and forth across the smooth, fabric-covered surface, painstakingly taking oil from one engine and pouring it into the next. Taylor got the Empire Gallantry Medal (now called the George Cross) for that and later, after he had completed some memorable flights of his own, they knighted him too.

I took a last look at the old plane, remembering photographs of it at Croydon and Darwin after breaking records to both places, then went into the terminal to get my boarding pass for Toowoomba. The flight was called and five of us scrambled aboard the Sunstate Airlines Embraer Bandeirante, a robust little 21-seater built in Sao José dos Campos, Brazil. My neighbour, a balding, voluble man with a giant 'Australia for Jesus' sticker on his briefcase, told me that Qantas had started up in Longreach but soon moved here to Eagle Farm, where they built the airfield's first private hangar and established their headquarters. 'That's why those old London flights finished in Brisbane, and not down south. They were just about the only important thing those greedy business folk in Sydney and Melbourne couldn't get their thieving hands on.'

We rose through a bright, sunny morning and went buzzing along over woods and orchards, racing the traffic on the Warrego Highway. Sue, the stewardess, who was blonde, extrovert and short (height restrictions were imposed on cabin staff by the Bandeirante's hollow log-sized fuselage), pointed out a market garden where you could get the most amazing carrots. Then she took me up front to admire the view and meet the boys. Toowoomba lay dead ahead, high on the Darling Downs.

'Oh, it's a pretty spot, green as Sussex, you'll like it,' said the captain, John Sherriff, who had a movie star's looks and a moustache finely twirled at the ends. 'I'll do a circuit so you can see for yourself.'

We crossed the grassy lip of the Downs and made a wide, lazy circle over Toowoomba, a city bursting with trees and gardens. 'Sometimes I reckon you can even smell the roses up here,' John

remarked, turning on to finals and landing gently on a runway with a steep uphill gradient. In the tiny, deserted terminal, hung with gaudy orange lanterns, he warned me to be back in 90 minutes to catch the return flight. A taxi took me into town past stands of jacarandas, camphor laurels and liquid ambers. The centre bustled with shoppers. The streets were broad and freshly swept. I drank a coffee and read the paper then set off to find a museum, enjoying the slight chill that altitude lends to the Darling Downs. But a barrister sunning himself outside the Law Courts said he reckoned the town had no museum so I caught a taxi back to the airport and told the driver, a large, solemn man with the manner of an archbishop, that I had been looking for someone who know about the early days of aviation in Toowoomba.

'If you'd come a year ago,' he said, 'you could have talked to my late uncle. He was one of the first employees of Qantas, on the accounts side, and very close to the founder, old Hudson Fysh of Blessed Memory, who would do anything to turn an extra penny. It was a dashed funny show in those days by all accounts. My uncle particularly relished the time they took a press photographer out over Moreton Bay to get pictures of a new Matson liner. The aircraft was a flimsy biplane with open cockpits, and in the photographer's cockpit, sir, a snake suddenly appeared. The snake and the photographer then embarked on a pitched battle high above the bay and, in the process of kicking the snake to death, the photographer – albeit unwittingly – began to demolish the aeroplane. He accomplished this with such speed and efficiency that by the time the pilot got the remnants of his little De Havilland back to Eagle Farm he was, by all accounts, almost as hysterical as his passenger.'

He laughed. 'But Toowoomba has played its part in the aviation history of this country. Sir Hudson's daily flight up from Brisbane was the first regular airline service in Australia, launched despite our notorious fogs. The local fog can be a real pea-souper, what you would call a London Particular, and it closes that little airport down tighter than a bottle of rum on a Methodist Sunday. Well, I *say* fog, sir, but really it's cloud. We're 2,200 feet above sea level here, and in the mornings the cloudbase can settle on the Downs and sometimes, like an old gentleman in a comfortable armchair, stay there all day.'

Twenty minutes later the Bandeirante laboured up the alpine runway and climbed over a barnyard containing the wingless fueslage of a Canberra bomber in which, Sue said, the farmer kept chooks. My neighbour, a local horse breeder, asked whether I knew of any Saudi princes who might be in the market for a promising colt, and Sue told me she liked flying over sugar cane best. 'Up around Bundaberg they've got miles and miles of it, the colour of jade, and in the middle of the cane there are hidden gardens tucked away, only visible from the air and full of fruit and flowers, just gorgeous.'

We could see Brisbane, sprawling ahead, hazy on the edge of a green plain and, when we were down, I thanked the crew for a very jolly outing.

John grinned and said, 'It's been a pleasure, mate. Ta ta for now.'

Trans Australia flight 262, the twice-weekly Fokker Friendship service to Longreach via Blackall, left on time next morning at 0730. This was to be my last day flying along the old route and it promised to be a long one; six and a half hours in the air, sufficient time to cross the Atlantic in a jet. The Fokker, carrying a couple of dozen passengers, whined out to the threshold as we learned from the public address system that our cabin attendants, Di and Anne, would serve a light breakfast during the sector to Blackall, estimated to take two hours 35 minutes.

Half an hour into the flight we were cruising over heavily wooded hills with grassy valleys running between them, some containing meandering, tree-lined rivers. We crossed a small town, orderly as a planner's blueprint, which Di thought was Chinchilla. 'But don't take that as gospel,' she warned, a big, brown-skinned, healthy-looking girl with beautiful green eyes. Its cricket ground was shaped like a champagne cork, with a dusty fast-bowlers' wicket sitting in the centre. Our route would take us near the homesteads of Pony Hills, Hutton and Womblebank, and on past Baffle Creek, Tambo and Mount Iniskillen into Blackall, by the Barcoo River. The grasslands gradually slipped away behind, growing ever paler, like clover turning to straw, until we were back over the dry red centre. The sky was cloudless and hazy with heat. Most of the passengers dozed.

Di dropped into the seat beside me and talked about the Book of Revelations. 'What's really weird is the way all the prophecies are coming true,' she said. 'The founding of the state of Israel?' She held up a finger. 'One. The Arabs getting all that wealth and power? From their oil? Two. Islam and the Ayatollah and the way it's spreading all over the place? Even Malaysian girls have started to wear those, you know, yashmaks. Three. The nuclear holocaust? Those old men in Revelations foretold the destruction of the world by nations fighting with the atom bomb; they even reckoned it would start in the Middle East, which is what a lot of people think today because some idiot like Gaddafi could go and let one off.' She paused, fingers in the air. 'What's that?'

'Four.'

But at that moment her sombre Old Testament mood was broken by the voice of the co-pilot coming over the PA. 'This is First Officer Don Hill speaking. We should have you over the top of Blackall in 15 minutes and on the ground in 20.'

Di jumped up to help Anne tidy the plane as its shadow descended over a flat plain baking in the sun like gingerbread. We went bumping past the town, a spread of corrugated iron roofs with a cricket ground at one end and a race track at the other, and suddenly the cabin buzzed with flies. People slapped at them with folded newspapers while we landed and came to a halt beside a breezeblock shack where two teenagers, a boy and a girl, sat and considered us. Heat boiled off the ground and out of the sky with the promise of greater heat to come. Though the London service did not call here, Blackall had still made its mark; nailed to the wall of the tiny terminal was a plaque announcing that this was the first aerodrome in Australia taken over by a local authority under the local ownership scheme. The kids pondered me gravely.

'How are you doing?' I asked.

'Okeydoke, thanks,' said the girl.

'Fair to middling,' said her friend.

The local agent, who wore a broad-brimmed straw hat, hauled a laden trolley away from the Fokker. 'See you later, eh?' he said to Di and Anne, who were leaning in the doorway. To the rest of us he shouted, 'All aboard!' and, within minutes, we were heading northwest on the 30-minute hop across the Alice River to

Longreach – more galvanized iron roofs and limp peppercorn trees, another racecourse. But the airfield here was a grander affair – empty of traffic but boasting an elegant little terminal, bright gardens and a small hangar with the legend Q.A.N.T.A.S. painted on the front in faded brown letters.

This was the Qantas heartland – and thus a primary stop on the old route – because it was here, in 1921, that the Queensland and Northern Territory Air Services first began trading. The infant company's aim had been to link the main centres of western Queensland but its horizons broadened quickly. Only 12 years after carrying its first passenger (an 81-year-old grazier named Alexander Kennedy) it began operating the international service from Singapore, the final link in the Imperial chain. In 1938, 16 years after carrying Mr Kennedy, the company boasted a London office and British landing rights, and its Empire class flying boat *Cooee*, under the command of Captain P. W. Lynch-Blosse, operated the first Qantas service all the way to Southampton.

I chatted to a portly, freckled old man wearing a white cricket hat and sunglasses who was waiting to see a friend off. He said he had been born and bred in Longreach, and remembered Hudson Fysh, Ginty McGinness and Arthur Baird, the mechanic who had given up his little garage business to join the firm.

'Fysh was a tall, skinny feller, very quiet. Never said much but, by God, he knew what he wanted. I was just a nipper but we all got caught up in the excitement of what they were doing. The first plane he brought in here was an old British Avro triplane they called "the tripe" with Sunbeam Dyak engines, I think, or maybe Gnome rotaries. Sometimes I took ice up to his house for the Coolgardie safe – it dripped through hessian to keep the food cool – and he'd give me a threepenny bit. When a plane was overdue there'd be real anxiety in the town because, in them days, accidents weren't too uncommon. Fysh only crashed once, up at Jericho, but the others all went down several times. Fysh even fired a pilot for persistent crashing. He was a bloke called Scott, who wrote poems and played classical piano, and whose old man had been Master of the King's Music back in London. On Saturday nights the hands from the stations would come into town for a few beers, hear about this musical poet and pick fights with him.' The old man chuckled.

'What they didn't know was that he'd been heavyweight boxing champion of the Royal Air Force. Scott might have been good at Beethoven but he could also knock over an 18-stone shearer without even putting his glass down. He was an outstanding flyer, too.'

'A C.W.A. Scott won the England to Australia air race in 1934,' I said.

He nodded. 'Same bloke. Beat the Dutch into second place. Those pilots were big shots in Longreach, and us kids all wanted to be like them. Hudson Fysh sensed the mood and even started a flying school here, but it didn't work out. Too much turbulence. It's this heat, you see, it can make the air very violent and it scared us youngsters off; it takes a special kind of character to deal with that. Longreach should have been the cradle of aviation in Australia, but now, apart from the old hangar, there's nothing left to show that one of the world's great airlines actually started life here.'

He excused himself and went to join his friend, an even older man who was checking in at the little desk beside the hangar, facing the garden and open to the elements. The TAA agent behind the desk wore a hat turned up round the brim. Perspiration dripped from under his spectacles and ran down his plump pink cheeks. As he took my ticket and ran his pencil down the passenger list Don Hill, our youthful first officer, stood at his shoulder and examined the list too.

'Thirteen,' he said, gloomily. 'It's going to be one of those days.'

A harassed-looking woman in a blue dress stood nearby. She had come with us from Brisbane and said she was supposed to be going on to Winton, a 45-minute flight away, but now the pilot of her elderly little two-seater had his head and arms buried in the engine.

'Is that a Wackett?' I asked.

She smiled tiredly. 'I really wouldn't know. But I wish it would get a move on. I'm expected home for lunch. The family's meeting me. When we get going we'll follow the Landsborough Highway; if something goes wrong you just land on the road and hitch a lift.'

There had been flies at Blackall, but they were nothing compared with the flies here, which came racing across the field in a series of massed low-level attacks, trying to flatten anyone who stood in their way. They went crashing into the Fokker and even flew into

walls. Today the Longreach flies, perhaps inspired by the Michael Caine movie down at the drive-in, were pretending to be killer bees.

The TAA agent hauled a baggage trolley out to the plane as the skipper, who had red hair and a red beard, jumped down and strolled ashore.

'Guess what,' said Don Hill, standing at the check-in desk. 'We've got thirteen.'

'Thirteen's always been lucky for me,' said the skipper, glancing at his watch then looking towards the Fokker which was being refuelled by a youth with a small, chugging mechanical pump. Its blue exhaust fumes merged with the heat waves eddying from the tarmac, lending them colour and definition. The agent had vanished into the hold. Banging noises indicated that he was busy stowing baggage and freight. Then he emerged, and the youth disconnected the pump and towed it away behind a yammering little tractor.

'Let's go,' said the skipper.

'All aboard for Blackall, Charleville and Brisbane!' cried the agent.

Di and Anne awaited us in the doorway. 'Welcome back to the Ritz of the skies,' said Di. 'You're a real glutton for punishment, I must say.'

We went whining out to the threshold of the runway from which Hudson Fysh, Ginty McGinness, Arthur Baird, Lester Brain, young Scott and the rest first launched their audacious enterprise upon the world. As the Fokker, vibrating wildly, began to roll, I wondered whether they ever realized that news of their early achievements had reached all the way to London, even permeating the airless corridors of Whitehall. When Sir Samuel Hoare was trying to convince a sceptical Cabinet and hostile Treasury that civil aviation had a future, it was Qantas that he held up to them as an example.

He wrote the Government a succession of memos. One – characteristic of the others – said, 'In spite of primitive machines, no radio, no night flying and no weather forecasts except for an occasional telephone message from a garage proprietor in Charleville, the flights had been sufficiently dependable for the company to obtain a contract for carrying the mail.'

When we were airborne I chatted to a wiry, eager-looking man seated across the aisle who told me I should have seen Longreach

during the Korean War. 'Wool was selling for £1 a pound and all the daughters at the homesteads were packed off to finishing schools in Europe. There were burned-out Mercs in the paddocks just like Arabia today – a bloke'd wreck his car and, if he walked away from it, go and buy another one. Nobody makes that kind of money any more, but it's still a good place to live. The races are a big occasion here. What we do is drink. A couple of years ago, at Ladies Day, a bloke got so plastered he fell into the fire. They hauled him clear, blazing like a torch, and put him out with beer. He was okay, just went grogging on, but that night he dropped out of the tree he was sleeping in and broke his leg.'

We bounced stormily back into Blackall. He disembarked while the rest of us scrambled out to stretch our legs, but the agent only gave us a minute. 'Everyone back in the Fokker, ladies and gents!' he cried, and soon afterwards we were clambering unsteadily into a hot, hazy sky towards Charleville – the penultimate stop of my trip.

Cobham had come this way sixty years earlier. At Longreach 'were the headquarters of the Q.U.A.N.T.A.S. [sic] Air-route and, what was more, a small air-craft works where they were building our own type of aeroplane under licence from the De Havilland Company.' Then he crossed a great forest to Charleville, landing at dusk before 'an enthusiastic crowd, many of whom had motored over bush tracks for anything from a hundred to two hundred miles to see our machine.'

The shack in which the sweating passengers from the London service were given hot tea and bully beef sandwiches as big as bibles had been replaced by a small, airless terminal containing a plaque commemorating the occasion when Hudson Fysh took old Alexander Kennedy from Charleville to Cloncurry in 1922. Here Di and Anne left us, wandering away lugging their suitcases, pausing briefly to speak to their replacements, older, worldlier women who seemed to have been seconded from the interstate jet fleet. The passengers waited outside in the shade of a bauhinia tree. A lean, rangy man in his sixties said, 'It gets lovely flowers, a kind of mauvy white, but she's looking a bit scraggy now. Old age, I reckon. It catches up with all of us in the end.'

I sat under the bauhinia too, and looked at the Imperial *Gazette* which, in February 1937, boasted that 'nine Captains of Qantas

Empire Airways, the company which, in association with Imperial Airways, operates the Singapore-Brisbane section of the England-Australia route, have among them now flown approximately 5,000,000 miles, or a distance equivalant to two hundred times round the world, at the equator.' It added, 'Some indication of the wide appeal of the Singapore-Brisbane air service is supplied by the fact that representatives of 22 nations, drawn from 71 different professions, occupations and callings, have entered and left Australia by air liners of Qantas Empire Airways since passenger carrying was inaugurated on 7 April 1935.' These, we were told, included judges, barristers, rubber planters, aviators, graziers, geologists, opticians, circus managers and artistes, cinematographers, radio engineers and traffic experts.

Cobham, after spending the night here, remarked that aircraft took off from Charleville 'amid a terrific cloud of red dust, for the aerodrome is on bare red soil without any turf whatever'. Now the Fokker, making a less flamboyant exit, climbed away over a comfortable tree-lined town on a course that would take us across the Maranoa River to Brisbane and, finally, the end of the Imperial Eastbound Route. My neighbour, a small, trim, dark-haired woman with clear green eyes, was wearing a charm bracelet and, among the dozen assorted items dangling from it, I spied a tiny gold flying boat. She smiled when I asked about it, confessing she had been a flying boat fan since childhood, when she travelled from Rose Bay in Sydney up to Brisbane aboard the venerable Qantas stalwart *Coriolanus*. I said I had first got airborne in the very same plane, for heaven's sake, and we began talking with the spontaneity of old friends. Listening to the pleasure with which she recalled her trip I understood why the thirty 20-ton Empires built by Short Bros. at Rochester managed to secure such a hold on their passengers' affections – and why, when BOAC withdrew them in 1947, there was mourning all down the routes.

The years, in retrospect, have turned the Empires into the China tea clippers of their day, craft of such consummate grace and elegance that they are able to evoke nostalgia even among those too young to have known them. Now they have become synonymous with Imperial; mention the airline and all people want to talk about are the boats.

Part of their charm, of course, was that they were equally at home in two elements. Many of their fittings were maritime. They had twin decks, cabins, retractable bollards and forward mooring compartments equipped with drogue cases, boat hooks and tackle; there were bilge pumps under the decking, even a mast with a masthead light. And they were built by shipwrights who launched them, with all the traditional ceremony attendant upon these occasions, down tallow-smeared slipways into the Medway. The Empire could handle rough water like a coaster but then, miraculously, was able to leave it behind, the four supercharged 740 h.p. Bristol Pegasus engines taking it up at 950 feet a minute (with the airscrews in coarse pitch) and giving it a cruising speed of 200 m.p.h.

The old boats were celebrated too for their sumptuous fixtures and fittings. The *Coriolanus*, when we travelled in her, was still configured for wartime operations; the famous beds had been removed and the accommodation, we recalled, was fairly spartan. The pre-war machines were a very different matter. Neither of us had ever seen one but we knew about them all right and, like historians resurrecting aspects of life in some forgotten civilization, mused over the fact that Australia-bound passengers travelled from Waterloo Station to Southampton in a Pullman Special with rose-pink table lamps and a sign on the roof saying 'Imperial Airways Empire Services'; a fleet of fast pinnaces then ferried them out to their aircraft moored on the Solent. The Empire's upper deck was off-limits to passengers. Reached by a metal ladder leading from the bow mooring compartment, it housed the cockpit, the Radio Officer's cabin and, aft of that, a roomy office with a desk for the Ship's Clerk.

The boats slept 16, accommodating them downstairs in the Forward Smoking Cabin, the Midship Cabin (situated behind the kitchen where the Steward, wearing a chef's *toque*, prepared meals), the Aft Cabin and the legendary Promenade Deck Cabin where, during the day, people could stroll, mingle, admire the view and make jokes about being aboard a tiny airborne Cunarder. In the morning mattresses and bed linen were stored in ceiling hatches. The Ship's Clerk, whose own personal ladder led down to the pantry, was expected to descend after dinner and lend a hand with bedmaking duties.

I told Anthea – my neighbour – that my sister and I had done the washing-up for the steward on *Coriolanus*. She said she helped wash the breakfast dishes *and* prepare morning coffee, served with chocolate cake and bowls of ice cream. We talked about the exhilaration of take-off and recalled that, when the throttles were opened and the bow wave covered the windows with foaming green water, it was like sitting in a submarine which surged up from the depths, then miraculously – and very slowly – took to the air, the droplets raining down from its hull making the surface below look as if it was being swept by a passing shower.

Her captain had smoked a foul-smelling pipe carved like a bison's head and sought investment tips from her father; mine used salty language and got gloomily drunk in New Caledonia. They were unusual men who, like their craft, needed to be comfortable with both elements, air and water. The Imperial flying boat pilots did their amphibious conversion courses at Hamble on Southampton Water where, according to the London *Times*, the trainee was 'required to learn how to manage his craft among the dhows, tramps, tankers and liners which he may find at his alighting place'. The duties of a land-based pilot, who needed only to turn into the wind and take off, were elementary by comparison. The flying boat commander 'must first slip his moorings or pick up his anchor, he must taxi around (sometimes across a wind in one direction and a current in another) until his engines are warm, and if the weather is rough he may have to steady his boat with a drogue on every turn.'

At Hamble the pilots had to cope with sailing dinghies and fast motor launches before graduating to a little Cutty Sark amphibian and, finally, a three-engined Rangoon, learning to handle it on the water with the flair and precision of tugboat skippers. They also attended lectures ashore on knot tying, towage, salvage and the use of Admiralty charts.

Anthea recalled that, to amuse the younger passengers, her steward unfurled a roll of toilet paper from the galley window which, fluttering along the portholes of the three rear cabins, caused the drunker grown-ups to gape and clutch their foreheads. I said all I had seen going out the galley window were potato peelings and empty tins; our steward sent all his garbage tumbling thousands of feet into the sea.

Items were also dropped from the legendary Boeing-built Clippers belonging to Imperial's rivals, Pan American. In 1937 a passenger travelling from New York to Bermuda reported that, 'From time to time the navigator would open a porthole and throw out a shining bulb filled with aluminium powder. When it struck the water it broke and the powder trailed brightly through the waves, giving the navigator the wind drift, which he carefully recorded on his instruments. From time to time, too, we were all asked to remain quiet, while the navigator took the sun's bearings on the sextant.

'The door to the crew's compartment was open all the way, and we could see the bronzed, white-clad men bending over their charts in a room not unlike the chart room of a dirigible. Dinner was served presently – a real chicken course dinner, with fine linen and silver on the tables. The captain came in and ate at his own table nearby.'

The author returned to New York aboard Imperial's Empire boat *Cavalier*, noting that 'there were many novelties on this English ship, and we found it even roomier than the clipper. Its upper deck is reserved for the crew's quarters so that, unlike the clipper, the passengers cannot see the operation of the ship. There is a promenade deck on the *Cavalier too*, if you please.'

He failed to mention what they gave him to eat, but a random dinner menu from her sister ship *Corsair* included pâté de foie gras or grapefruit, roast chicken, ox tongue, York ham, Russian salad, green salad, peaches and sauce Melba, golden figs, three kinds of cheese, 'toast Imperial', biscuits, desserts, crystallized fruits and coffee. Each boat carried a small but impressively stocked wine cellar, located aft of the Smoking Cabin.

Soon after the anonymous American correspondent made his trip the *Cavalier* crashed into the North Atlantic, killing three; the survivors spent ten hours in the water before being rescued by a passing tanker. Anthea and I remembered the sense of security our boat had given us, the feeling that, though plated and riveted like an ice-breaker, it seemed so light in the sky it might have been fashioned from feathers. The notion of anything going amiss was inconceivable, yet the *Cavalier* had not been the only Empire boat to go down. The *Capricornus* crashed in France (on Imperial's maiden flying boat service to Australia), the *Calpurnia* at Habbiniyah

in Iraq, the *Courtier* at Athens, the *Capella* at Jakarta, the *Challenger* at Mozambique, the *Cygnus* at Brindisi and the *Centurion* at Calcutta; the *Coorong* foundered and the *Connemara* burned and sank when a lighter from which she was refuelling blew up.

On the Fokker they gave us coffee and cake. Anthea dozed. I looked at my watch – 35 minutes to Brisbane. I sat there, half asleep myself, brooding on the Imperial phenomenon, the ghost I had been chasing across the world. When it merged with British Airways on 1 April 1940, to become BOAC, the new company's assets included a staff of 3,600, 109 overseas stations and 77 aircraft. (There would have been more, but two of the great Handley Page 42s were wrecked by March gales while parked at a country flying club near Bristol; Captain Tweedie's old favourite, *Hanno* collapsed like a house of cards while the *Heracles* was blown through a barbed wire fence and came to rest, shredded, in a field of silver beet.) Imperial, in its day, had been one of Britain's most celebrated and formidable international concerns, yet there was a strange ambivalence about it – inevitable, perhaps, when an enterprise dedicated to exploiting the most advanced technology of the twentieth century found itself administered by a management born and rooted in the nineteenth, men still half in love with the steam train and horse. A shaken Lord Reith was introduced to their private, Edwardian world when he left the BBC in 1938 to become Imperial's managing director and, on his first morning at work, walked into premises shabbier than those of an East End tailor.

'I was brought to the door of an old furniture depository behind Victoria Station. It was Imperial Airways; a plate on the wall said so. Inside were some counters, luggage on the floor, a few people standing about – a booking office, evidently. I inquired of a young man behind one of the counters where the head office was. He pointed to a dark and narrow staircase; up there, he said. The managing-director's office? Second floor, he thought. Having ascended thither I went along a passage also dark and narrow, between wooden partitions, peering at the doors and wondering which to try first. Here it was – a bit of paper with 'Managing-Director' written thereon. From Broadcasting House to this.

'And the first decision demanded of me was an indication of what

had happened to me otherwise. Would I approve the expenditure of
£238 on passengers' lavatories at Croydon?'

We dropped into Eagle Farm through high, hazy cloud. The sun
glinted on the river and made the calm, windless Pacific beyond
gleam like cloth-of-gold. Now my mood was celebratory and I
wanted champagne. Anthea lived in Sydney and her flight went in
an hour – time to share a bottle with me at the airport bar. We drank
to the conclusion of my trip, and to flying boat bores the world over.
She invited me to stay when I passed through. Her husband, a
lawyer and amateur pilot, liked flying boats too. I explained that I
had to hurry home to attend my son's confirmation at St Paul's. If
the 747 arrived on schedule I would have five hours to get to the
cathedral. She warned that five hours, in the context of a flight all
the way from Brisbane, was a pretty slim margin; weather,
headwinds, mechanical problems, they could all eat into it. I said
that possibility was very much on my mind.

Then it was time for her to go. We finished the bottle and, before
heading for the departure lounge, she gave me a kiss. 'That's for our
yesterdays,' she said.

Well, they were behind me now, just words in my notebooks,
voices in my head, a magpie's trawl of ephemera reaching back half
a century or more. Driving away from Eagle Farm I looked over for
a last glimpse of the *Southern Cross* but, due to some trick of sun
and shade, Kingsford Smith's 'old bus' began to dematerialize until,
with an incandescent flash of reflected light, it was no longer there.

EPILOGUE

After several weeks spent scrambling in and out of small aeroplanes the British Airways Boeing 747 *City of Aberdeen* seemed as cavernous as a dance hall. The four giant Rolls-Royce RB 211 turbojets whined thunderously as it lifted off from Eagle Farm on a warm, humid afternoon and turned south towards Sydney. Its route home would be an abbreviated version of my route out, with stops at Singapore, Kuala Lumpur and Muscat. I looked at my watch. It said a few minutes after 3; we were bang on schedule. So far so good, I thought, and relaxed a little.

A cheery, brown-eyed girl from Somerset gave us tea, sandwiches and slices of Black Forest gateau. As she cleared away the things we began our descent, passing the great coathanger bridge and the little Opera House set beside it like a beautiful surrealist ark blown in from the sea. At Kingsford Smith Airport there was a crew change and a delay while ground engineers replaced one of the three onboard inertial navigation units. I recalled that when Cobham arrived in Sydney he was welcomed by 'a record crowd of sixty thousand people' and a gang of brawling press photographers who set about each other with such abandon that 'one could hear the cracking of tripods as they were broken in the scrum'. (He stayed with the Governor of New South Wales, Sir Dudley de Chair, then flew on to Melbourne where he and Ward 'were amazed to find a crowd of at least a hundred and fifty thousand' rioting as they landed.)

We were summoned back aboard. A steward said, 'Ladies and gentlemen, the new equipment has been installed and switched on, but we have a further 20-minute wait while it warms up.'

The engines were started half an hour later, at sunset. We took off over the Pacific, climbing into a smoky red sky and ambling down the coast for a few minutes before turning inland over a network of tidal creeks spanned by little Meccano bridges.

After dinner – prawn cocktail, pan-fried fillet steak or loin of lamb with savoury mushroom stuffing – they doused the cabin lights and showed a Dudley Moore movie, but I lost the thread within minutes and listened to some vintage rock 'n' roll, then Verdi's *Te Deum*, instead. Outside it began to grow stormy. The captain stopped the music to warn that we were approaching an area of turbulence. 'They're having a bit of weather up here,' he said as we bumped through heavy cloud and rain. He kept flashing his landing lights, checking conditions ahead like a motorist using full beam to pick up distant landmarks. A steward brought me a cup of coffee and said we were passing through the outer perimeter of Tropical Cyclone Joe.

Ferdinand had a clone! I learned that, appropriately, as we sailed out over the Timor Sea towards Bali (which slipped by unseen in the darkness) and Surabaya (passed too far to seaward for a sighting). On the stroke of midnight, Sydney time, an Air India 747 shot past in the murk a couple of thousand feet below, lit up like a Christmas tree, whizzing back the way we had come. As we descended towards Changi Airport with lightning playing along the misty green hills of Sumatra I calculated that we were now running an hour and 40 minutes late. The 747 nosed up to that huge terminal like a tug berthing a glass-hulled ocean liner, and the Cabin Services Officer said, 'Please don't wander too far from your departure gate, which is Bravo 21. The aircraft stops in Singapore for only 45 minutes.'

Due to extra consignments of baggage and freight, however, it stopped for 65 minutes. The brief leg to Kuala Lumpur was made with the storm flashing and crackling merrily away to port. We arrived in heavy rain, two hours behind schedule, and the captain warned there would be a further delay while ground staff replaced the cracked cover of a landing light.

Half an hour later he said, 'Sorry about the hold-up. We're missing one of the components, a metal attachment to hold the new glass in position. They're having to improvise one specially for us.'

I imagined sweating Malaysian blacksmiths frantically hammering tin ingots into a shape appropriate to our needs. When we finally took off we were running three hours behind which, if nothing went wrong at Muscat and there were no traffic jams on the M4 motorway

into London, would still leave a couple of hours to get from Heathrow to St Paul's.

Supper was smoked salmon cornets with veal medallions or breast of chicken in a paprika cream sauce, but I couldn't face more food and looked at the route map instead. The six-and-a-half-hour leg would take us across the Bay of Bengal, past the Nicobar Islands to Madras, then up to Bombay and over the Arabian Sea to Muscat. Much later I opened my window blind and discovered we were flying through a magnificent Indian night filled with constellations of frozen fireworks, some so close the 747 seemed to be weaving its way through them. Dying stars went arcing through the fixed ones like tracer bullets; there was more shooting star traffic up there than planes stacked over Heathrow in a rush hour fog.

At dawn we approached the rocky grey coast of Oman. The cleaners at Seeb International came through like locusts, forcing passengers stretching their legs to jump on to seats until they had passed. One of the cleaners beamed at me. 'Good night!' he said. A Gulf Air Tristar beside us started up and went whining away from the blocks. We followed moments later, got breakfast high over Dubai – fresh grapefruit segments and a creamed kingfish pancake with cheese sauce – then settled down for the last and longest leg of the trip, eight hours and ten minutes.

The heat below soon gave way to cloud which cleared, only briefly, above the Balkans. Before it closed in and locked up the landscape for good, I saw three tanks moving along the floor of an icy white valley. All at once the tanks became airborne and flew out of the valley in formation. Thirty-four hours without sleep and my eyes were playing tricks. The sky was suddenly filled with darting specks, all keeping station outside, so I closed the blind and asked for a very strong Bloody Mary.

We broke out of the eight-eighths cover smack over the top of Richmond, my home town, on a grey, wintry day, still running three hours late. My wife, looking terrific and bubbling with news, drove me home for a change of clothes at a speed which significantly exceeded the legal limit. In the garden the daffodils were out. We took a taxi to St Paul's, arriving just five minutes before the start of the service. My son had come straight from his school, associated with Wren's great cathedral for centuries and the reason why,

traditionally, its students were confirmed there by the Lord Bishop of London.

We hurried downstairs to the crypt, filled with parents, friends and teachers. There was no sign of the boys, who were being kept under wraps backstage. The Bishop processed up the aisle in full canonical fig accompanied by an honour guard of chaplains in their silks. The High Master read from Ezekiel, 'Then will I sprinkle clean water upon you, and ye shall be clean,' but omitted the rest of the verse — 'From all your filthiness, and from all your idols, will I cleanse you' — which would have got a loud, unseemly laugh from the 14-year-old candidates. The School Chaplain read from St Luke, the boys were confirmed by the Bishop and, after the Offertory Hymn, the Eucharistic Prayer, the Sanctus and the Benedictus, parents were invited to join the children for their first Communion. We went forward and I saw my son. He grinned.

'Hullo, Dog Brain,' he said. 'You made it.'

We knelt as the Bishop of London, reputedly one of Mrs Thatcher's favourite churchmen, came around with the wine. His eye, when it met mine, was cold, his look baleful. I responded by turning my own terrible bloodshot gaze upon him and was punished by having the chalice instantly withdrawn. He passed on quickly but his chaplain, smiling and round-faced, carried a chalice too and I drank my wine from that.

A quarter of an hour later, as the organist played Gigout's exhilarating Toccata, we left the cathedral. The sun broke through and flooded London with a lovely pale champagne-coloured light that washed away the last vestiges of my tiredness. I suddenly felt as fit and happy as I had ever felt in my life. My wife promised us a special celebration dinner, the details of which were to remain secret. I hailed a taxi. A pretty little British Aerospace 146 airliner, powered by four hushed Avco Lycoming turbofans no louder than the noise you hear in seashells, passed over St Paul's and headed up the river towards Westminster. I gave it only the briefest of glances before following the others into the cab and asking the driver to take us home.